Next Generation Excel

Modeling in Excel for Analysts and MBAs

Next Generation Excel

Modeling in Excel
for Analysts and MBAs

ISAAC GOTTLIEB

WILEY

John Wiley & Sons (Asia) Pte. Ltd.

Other Wiley Editorial Offices

John Wiley & Sons, 111 River Street, Hoboken, NJ 07030, USA

John Wiley & Sons, The Atrium, Southern Gate, Chichester, West Sussex, PO19 8SQ, United Kingdom

John Wiley & Sons (Canada) Ltd., 5353 Dundas Street West, Suite 400, Toronto, Ontario, M9B 6HB, Canada

John Wiley & Sons Australia Ltd., 42 McDougall Street, Milton, Queensland 4064, Australia

Wiley-VCH, Boschstrasse 12, D-69469 Weinheim, Germany

Library of Congress Cataloging-in-Publication Data

ISBN 978-0-470-82473-3

Typeset in 10.5/13pt Sabon-Roman by Thomson Digital

Printed in Singapore by Toppan Security Printing Pte. Ltd.

10 9 8 7 6 5 4 3 2 1

To Gilda

Let a wise person hear and that person will gain insight,
thus, one who understands will attain leadership.

Bible, *Proverbs* (Chapter I, Verse 5)

Contents

A Word from the Author

I have taught people how to utilize Excel for business since 1997. My focus has always been on the applications needed in a business environment.

As a result of years of teaching the application's extensive possibilities, I have found that step-by-step and hands-on approaches are the most effective.

When you get to the heart of the matter, you will find that the author is "speaking" to the reader, as I am doing now. This book was voluntarily written in a very informal tone, to keep the learning process as dynamic as it can be in a classroom or workshop setting.

I wanted to create a book that appeals to students, as well as practitioners and instructors. All the techniques in this book have been developed first with the professors and students attending my classes and workshops. What is in this book is the distillation of the feedback of many years' teaching. I have learned what people really want to know about Excel. One thing is certain: they don't want to read long, complicated explanations. They want a simple answer with visual figures or pictures; therefore, this book is filled with short explanations and "screen shots." It is organized in a way to help you "hit the ground running," and quickly at that!

I have verified the application of this book's subject matter outside of the classroom—in putting together projects, generating business plans, and other decision-making instances. I have applied the various techniques time after time in a variety of consulting projects. All the examples in this book are the direct result of real-life, hands-on experience.

Most people who use Excel want and need fast answers to their problems. The special features of the Excel software are covered in a manner inviting the user to apply the knowledge immediately.

While the book is written with Excel 2007 in mind, most chapters have an appendix for Excel 2003 or earlier versions, when the latest version implied different manipulations of the software. Every chapter has a few review questions at the end (with the answers!) to ensure that you really understand what you have read, by applying the knowledge to different problems to be solved than the ones covered in the chapter. I cannot encourage you enough to do these exercises.

WHO SHOULD READ THE BOOK?

You will find this book useful if you . . .

- spend more than 10 hours a week using Excel—you will save hundreds of hours a year applying this knowledge;
- are a decision maker at any level—you will improve your decision-making ability;

- are an analyst in the areas of accounting, finance, marketing & sales, HR, or strategy—you will learn to handle your analysis in a more efficient and creative way;
- have to make quantitative or graphical presentations;
- are an executive and have to train your staff in time-saving process applications;
- are an executive assistant—you can better support management with your improved skills;
- are an entrepreneur and need to create business plans;
- are dealing with accounting, marketing/sales, HR, finance, or other business disciplines;
- are a student or plan to become one;
- will be in a position to have to train people to use Excel.

Acknowledgments

Special thanks to Ms. Marianne Tan of our Executive MBA offices in Singapore. This book was actually her idea—she took the notes I give to students and handed them (to my great pleasure!) to Ms. CJ Hwu, Senior Publishing Editor at John Wiley & Sons (Asia). I am grateful to both for their support in this endeavor. I am grateful also to Ms. Lucie Alary for the countless hours spent proofreading the chapters' drafts, before they took the shape of a book. In her meticulous manner, she read the text, made suggestions, and pointed out many details which have improved the book a great deal.

Also thanks to my friends Avi Miller and Manny Zachodin. They acted as my sounding board as I developed the material for my Excel workshops and through the process of writing this book. They have been teaching MBA and other workshops with me for the last 10 years using the material in this book. Their wisdom, experience and feedback enabled me to improve the quality of many of the topics covered. I am grateful for their time, effort and of course their friendship.

The usual disclaimer is in order: Any mistakes in the work are my own.

Introduction and Overview

This book has eight parts. Read it in order or feel free to jump directly to any of the parts.

Part I explains how to use Excel efficiently. It covers the AutoFill, efficient selection, and highlighting functions in Excel. You will also learn how to use keyboard selection shortcuts. The second topic covered shows how to insert formulas or functions and the use of absolute versus relative addressing. The last two chapters describe the naming of cells and ranges and how one creates charts.

Part II covers two commonly needed skills: the use of the IF functions, which make Excel an invaluable tool for decision-making purposes, and the Text manipulation functions.

Part III introduces Statistical Tools. Statistics in Excel provide the user with a set of tools helpful in sorting out and solving a variety of problems. This part covers descriptive statistics and simple regressions.

Part IV is called "What-if Analysis." What-if analysis enables the user to find out what will be the impact of change. This part of the book shows you how to take advantage of the What-if tools in the decision-making process. It demonstrates features such as naming cells for modeling, the goal seek, one- and two-way data tables, and the effective use of scroll bars.

Part V covers two chapters, Multi-Page Systems and Lookups. Most Excel users either keep their entire model or information on one worksheet or—when they use a number of sheets—do not take advantage of structuring the workbook/system so that they can use Excel more effectively. Studying the Multi-Page chapter will remedy this shortcoming.

The second portion of Part V discusses lookup functions. It demonstrates how to perform an exact lookup and how to perform range lookups. After you understand the lookup function described, you will be able to perform any of the other lookup functions.

Part VI loosks at the Data menu and ribbon. This part of the book deals with the Data menu features of Excel. It covers all the following topics: Sorting data, Filters, Creating and Using Data Forms, Grouping Data, Subtotals, and Pivot Tables.

Part VII deals with the variety of Financial Tools Excel comes equipped with. What are the most frequently used financial formulas available, including those in the Analysis ToolPak, and how do we apply them using Excel efficiently?

Part VIII explains how to use the Solver Add-in. Solver is an Excel Add-in, which, in very simple terms, is a software tool for "solving" mathematical systems of equations for optimizations. This part of the book does not attempt to teach the mathematical aspect of using the Solver but it will demonstrate how to put it to good use for three different applications. The first application explains how to use the Goal Seek when you want to have more than one changing cell or decision variable. The second application demonstrates efficient use of the Solver for a linear optimization problem. The last case explains its use in a non-linear optimization problem.

The CD files include:

- Excel files for Excel 2007;
- Excel Files for Excel 2003 and earlier versions.

PowerPoint presentations for all the figures in the book are also included in the CD should you want to use the material for training.

Using Excel Efficiently

Part I describes how Excel, the widely-used spreadsheet software, can be used efficiently to help build your spreadsheet for a variety of purposes. As an MBA student, an analyst, or an executive, you will develop enough expertise to perform the same tasks you were performing before—using other means—much faster and in a more efficient way. This part of the book demonstrates tools, shortcuts, and techniques for carrying out some common tasks quickly and efficiently.

Carrying out different tasks—this part will not turn you into an Excel expert in a short time, but by the end you should improve the tasks you can do—the types of tasks that make Excel into such an incredibly powerful and flexible tool for modeling, finance statistics, and data manipulation.

In Part I: Using Excel Efficiently we will cover the AutoFill, efficient selecting, and highlighting in Excel. You will also learn how to use keyboard selection shortcuts. The next topic covered is how to insert formulas, activate functions, and use absolute and relative addressing. The last two parts are the naming of cells and ranges, and creating simple charts.

CHAPTER 1

AutoFill

The AutoFill feature in Microsoft Excel can automatically fill in cells with commonly used series (numbers, months, and days of the week) or with custom lists you can create. This chapter will demonstrate how to use the drag handle and other ways to fill in information. These operations work in all directions; top down, down up, left to right, and right to left. Figure 1.1 demonstrates this feature.

Select two adjacent cells and release the mouse. When you hover again over the lower right corner, your mouse pointer should change shape to a crosshair (+) called a drag handle. You can click and drag down the column and Excel will continue the initial two-cell series for you.

You can AutoFill several types of data including, but not limited to, numbers, dates, days, and annual quarters by selecting cells and dragging the handle as shown in Figure 1.1.

By default, a number of AutoFill lists are pre-installed in the program. For a list of the available AutoFill series, go to the Widows icon, click on Excel Options, and click on the Edit Custom Lists button. See Figure 1.2.

You may add your own lists as needed to Custom Lists. This will be explained at the end of the chapter.

Try to use the following example for using the Custom Lists shown in Figure 1.3. We filled in the information in the sheet. You may want to open the *AutoFill* sheet in the Excel file for Chapter 1 on the accompanying CD. The example illustrates the use of the AutoFill feature in Excel.

Select the first two values in column B (B2 and B3), click on the lower right drag handle of cell B3, and pull the drag handle down toward cell B10.

Dragging down the information created the desired AutoFill effect of continuing with the same series of numbers: 6, 9, 12, 15, . . . , 30. Try to drag down the information shown in columns C and D. You will create the information shown in Figure 1.4.

After you experiment with a couple of columns, try a more efficient way: select two vertical adjacent cells E2:E4. Release the mouse for a moment. Go to the drag handle. This time—do not drag—just **double-click.** Excel will drag it for you. See Figure 1.5. It will complete filling for you to the end of the adjacent column on the left. You may try double-clicking with more than one column selected at a time. Double-click works only in one direction: down.

You may want to try it yourself. As shown in Figure 1.6, all of the columns selected are highlighted and the crosshair handle appears at the lower right corner of the final column. In Figure 1.7, you can see the results after using the AutoFill double-click.

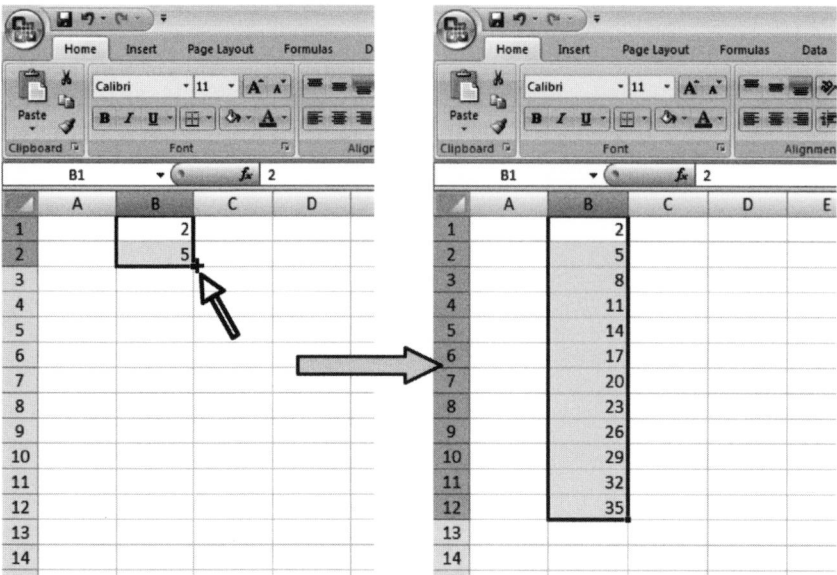

Figure 1.1   Using the drag handle

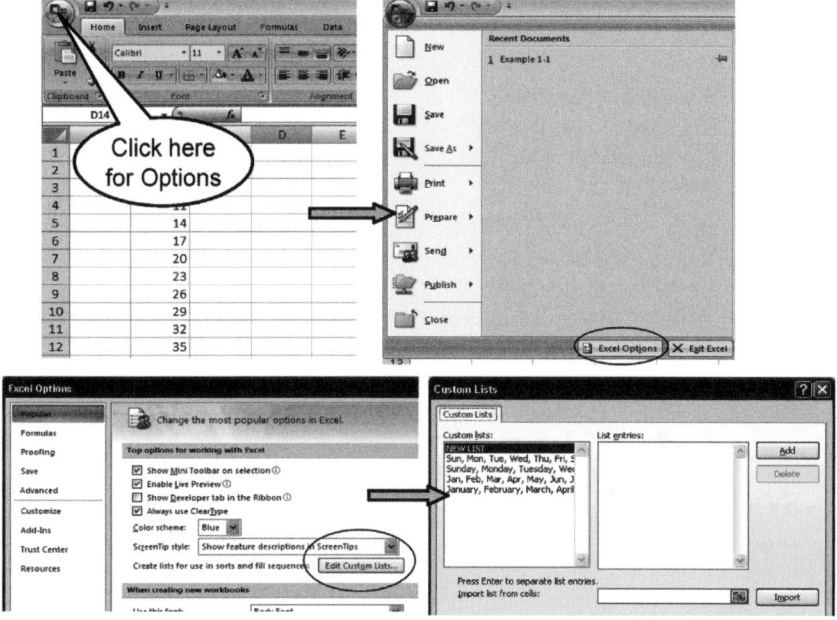

Figure 1.2   Custom Lists

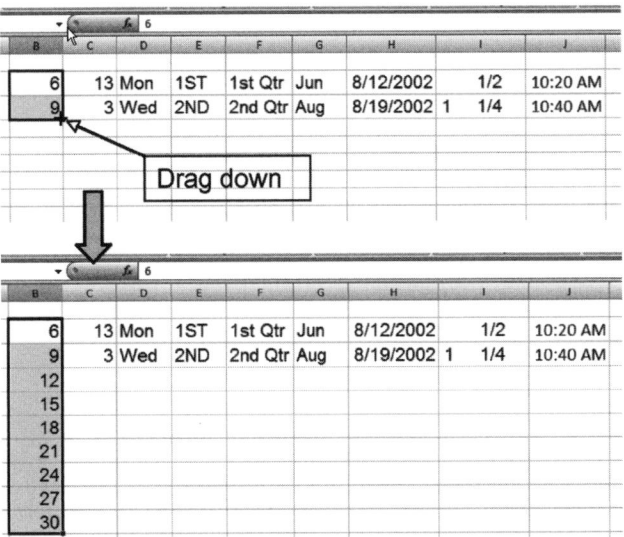

Figure 1.3 Drag handle and AutoFill

More features of the AutoFill function will be discussed in the context of regressions in Chapter 3. I will also explain the concept of Time in Excel in Chapter 3.

Creating Custom Lists in Excel enables you to use these lists as demonstrated with the AutoFill function. Custom Lists let you use them when you sort in Excel. In addition to sorting in numerical or alphanumeric order, you can also sort with these Custom Lists or with the ones you create. You can use the list created here later to sort a database.

B	C	D	E
6	13	Mon	1ST
9	3	Wed	2ND
12	-7	Fri	
15	-17	Sun	
18	-27	Tue	
21	-37	Thu	
24	-47	Sat	
27	-57	Mon	
30	-67	Wed	

Figure 1.4 "Dragging" down the information

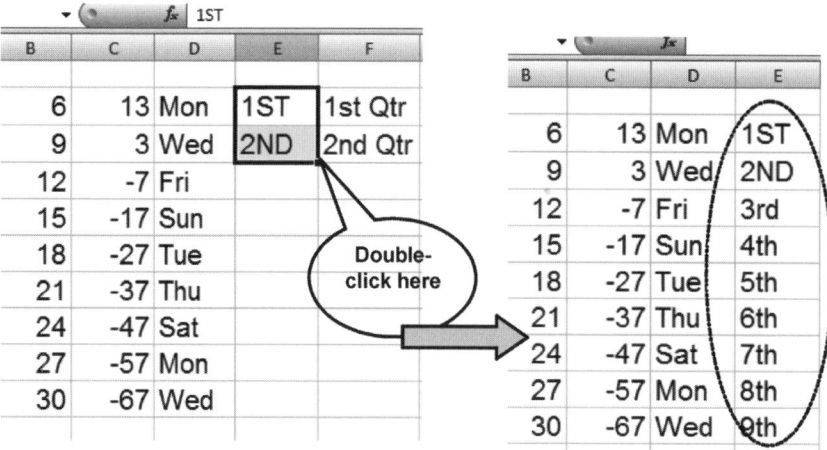

Figure 1.5 Double-click the drag handle

B	C	D	E	F	G	H	I	J	K
6	13	Mon	1ST	1st Qtr	Jun	8/12/2002		1/2	10:20 AM	
9	3	Wed	2ND	2nd Qtr	Aug	8/19/2002	1	1/4	10:40 AM	
12	-7	Fri	3rd							
15	-17	Sun	4th							
18	-27	Tue	5th							
21	-37	Thu	6th							
24	-47	Sat	7th							
27	-57	Mon	8th							
30	-67	Wed	9th							

Figure 1.6 Highlighting more than one column

B	C	D	E	F	G	H	I	J	K
6	13	Mon	1ST	1st Qtr	Jun	8/12/2002		1/2	10:20 AM	
9	3	Wed	2ND	2nd Qtr	Aug	8/19/2002	1	1/4	10:40 AM	
12	-7	Fri	3rd	3rd Qtr	Oct	8/26/2002	2		11:00 AM	
15	-17	Sun	4th	4th Qtr	Dec	9/2/2002	2	3/4	11:20 AM	
18	-27	Tue	5th	1st Qtr	Feb	9/9/2002	3	1/2	11:40 AM	
21	-37	Thu	6th	2nd Qtr	Apr	9/16/2002	4	1/4	12:00 PM	
24	-47	Sat	7th	3rd Qtr	Jun	9/23/2002	5		12:20 PM	
27	-57	Mon	8th	4th Qtr	Aug	9/30/2002	5	3/4	12:40 PM	
30	-67	Wed	9th	1st Qtr	Oct	10/7/2002	6	1/2	1:00 PM	

Figure 1.7 AutoFill result

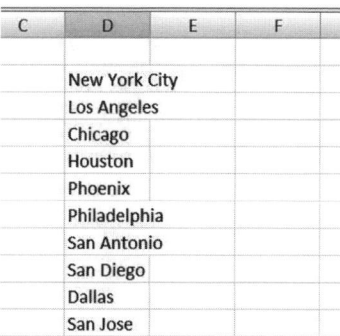

Figure 1.8 Custom List example

To create a Custom List in Excel, you need to type the list in a range on a sheet as shown in Figure 1.8. I used a list of the 10 largest cities in the USA where your company may be doing business as an example.

Refer to Figure 1.2 for how to access the Custom Lists menu. Go to the Office icon, click on Excel Options, and click on the Edit Custom Lists button. The result is shown in Figure 1.9.

Now all you have to do to make the list of the ten largest cities in the US, sorted by population size, part of your Excel Custom List, is click on the empty cell on the menu to the left of the Import button and select the cells on the sheet. Click on the Import button and the list is now part of your Custom Lists. See Figure 1.10.

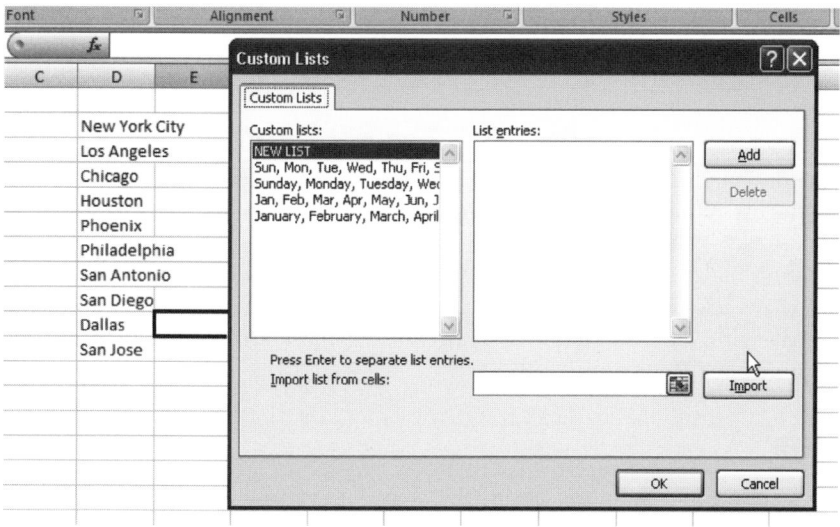

Figure 1.9 Create a Custom List

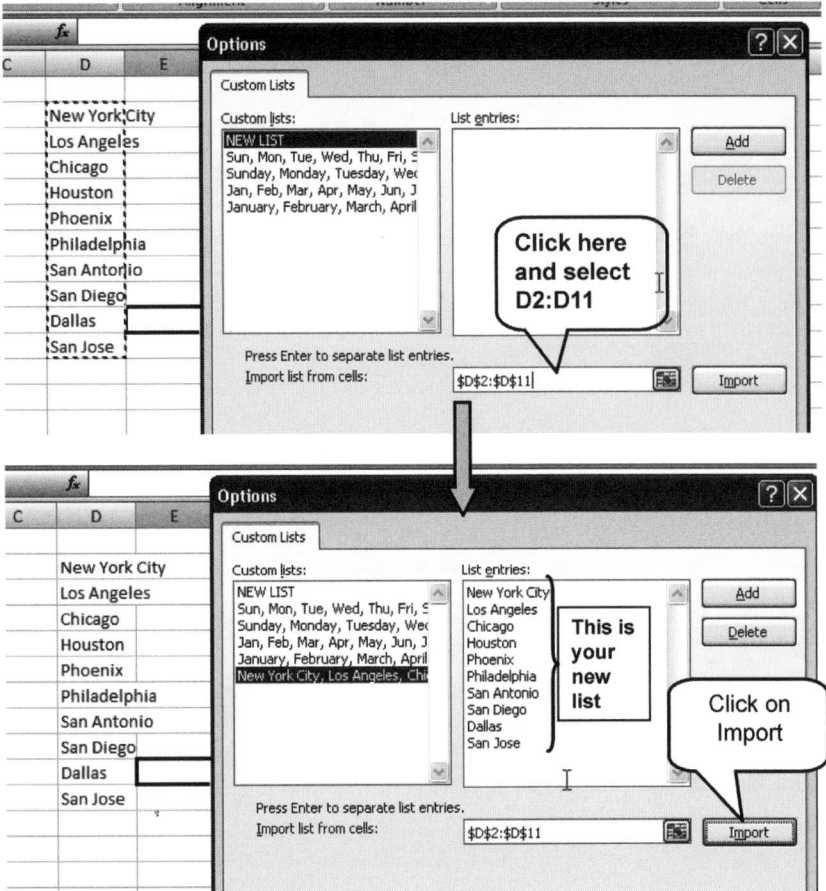

Figure 1.10   Custom List result

AutoFill Options

When you complete dragging any of the AutoFill lists, you will see a small Options icon at the bottom right of the list. When you click on the icon, it will allow you to choose one of the options. See Figure 1.11.

The AutoFill option recognizes days and dates. When you click on the menu with a list of dates or days of the week, Excel provides you with the additional options of choosing days, weekdays only—without weekends—or even spacing the list out, incrementing the dates by months or years. See Figure 1.12.

Right-Drag AutoFill

When you right-click and drag a numeric series, the menu offers you additional features as shown in Figure 1.13. The additional feature that could help us more than the others on the list is the Growth Trend feature. We can think of many other applications once we

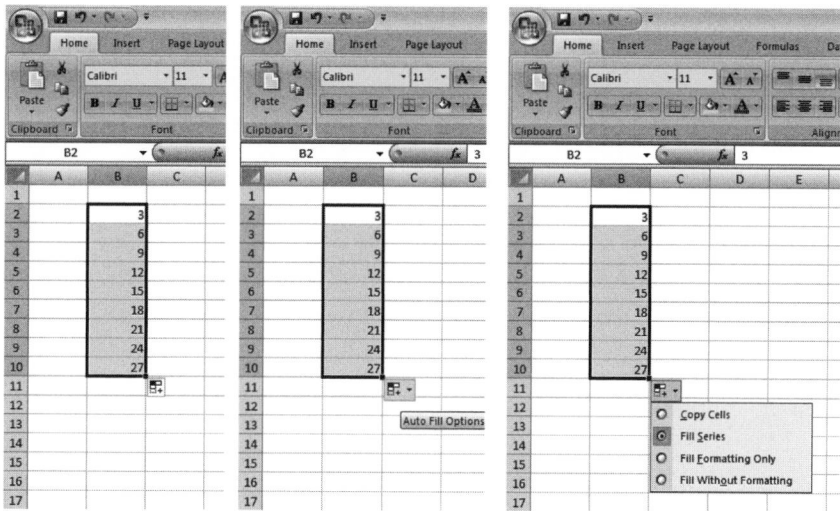

Figure 1.11 AutoFill options

understand what it can do. The following are two examples that can illustrate the power of this element in Excel.

If you need to create an exponential list of 2^2, all you to do is type the first two terms in the series (2 and 4) and the Growth Trend feature in the list will create the series as show in Figure 1.14. It will result in 2, 4, 8, 16, and so on. Using this idea, we can create a

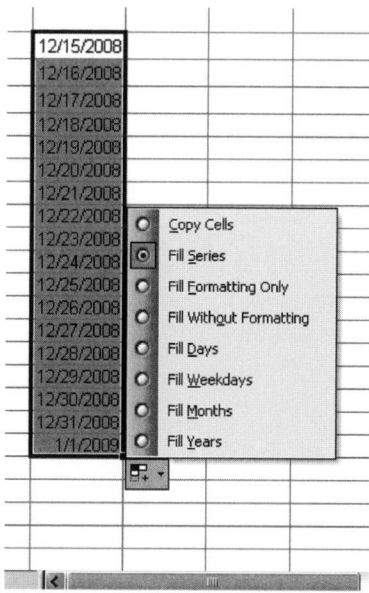

Figure 1.12 AutoFill menu

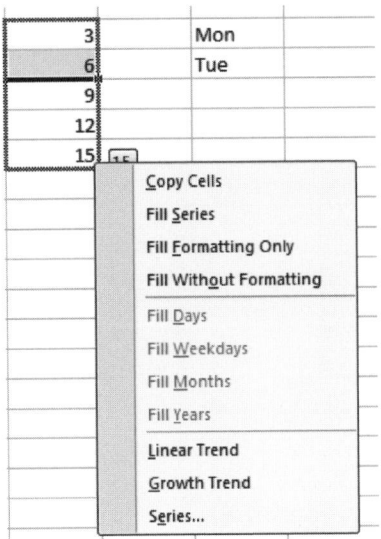

Figure 1.13   Choosing AutoFill options

2	3	1	100%
4	9	1.1	110%
8	27	1.21	121%
16	81	1.331	133%
32	243	1.4641	146%
64	729	1.61051	161%
128	2187	1.771561	177%
256	6561	1.948717	195%
512	19683	2.143589	214%

Figure 1.14   Exponential trend results

compounded interest series. If you want a growth factor of 10 percent a year, you can type 1.0 and 1.1 or 100 percent and 110 percent and the Growth Trend feature will do the rest as illustrated in Figure 1.14.

APPENDIX—DOING IT IN EXCEL 2003

Custom Lists Menu: There are two examples shown in this chapter that are slightly different in Excel 2007 than in Excel 2003. Both examples deal with the procedure to access the Custom Lists menu in Excel 2003. In the 2007, version we used the Office icon to get to the Excel Options menu and the Custom Lists menu.

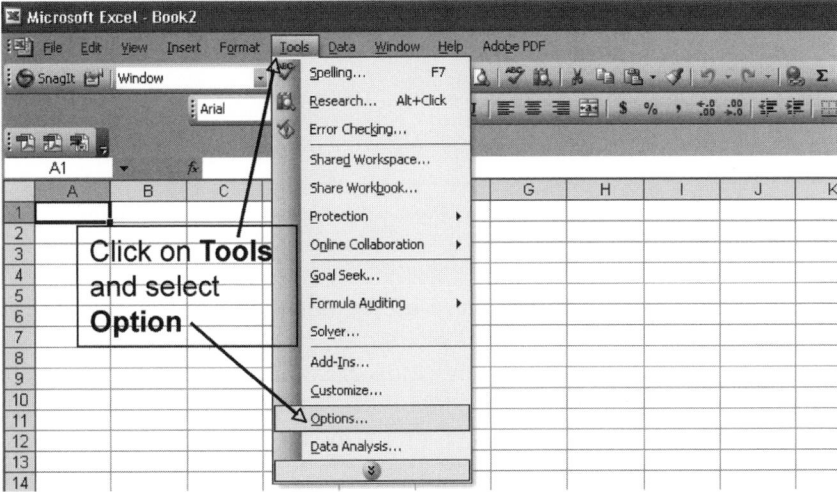

Figure 1.15 Options menu in Excel 2003

In Excel 2003, you click on the Tools menu and then select Options. See Figure 1.15

The Options screen appears and you can select the Custom Lists tab. See Figure 1.16. All the other features of importing custom lists are the same as in Excel 2007—as described above.

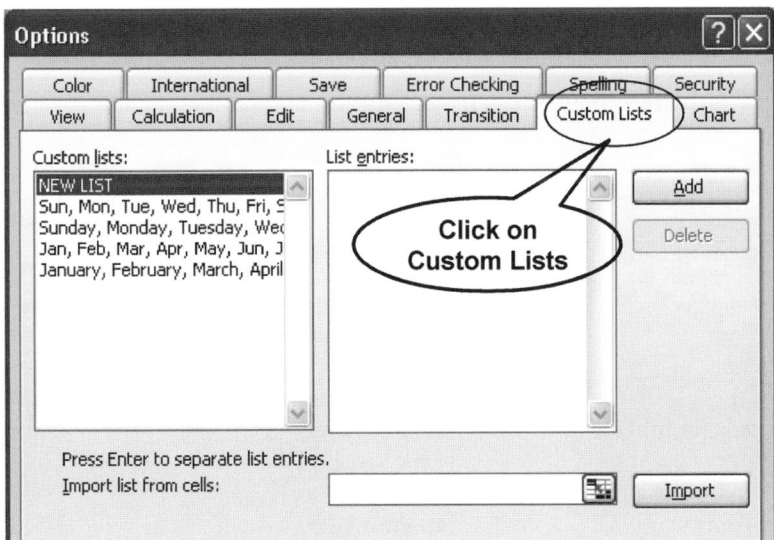

Figure 1.16 Custom Lists menu in Excel 2003

REVIEW QUESTIONS

You will find these examples in the Excel Chapter 1 file:

1. The chapter problems sheet of Chapter 1 has the following data:

5	22	Tue	12/12/2009	4 1/2	November	6:30 AM
6	17	Thu	12/17/2009	7 1/4	January	7:30 AM

Use the AutoFill feature to extend the first column with the values 5 and 6 creating the list through 10 as shown here:

5	22	Tue	12/12/2009	4 1/2	November	6:30 AM
6	17	Thu	12/17/2009	7 1/4	January	7:30 AM
7						
8						
9						
10						

2. Use the double-click AutoFill feature to fill up the rest of the table resulting in a complete table.

5	22	Tue	12/12/2009	4 1/2	November	6:30 AM
6	17	Thu	12/17/2009	7 1/4	January	7:30 AM
7	12	Sat	12/22/2009	10	March	8:30 AM
8	7	Mon	12/27/2009	12 3/4	May	9:30 AM
9	2	Wed	1/1/2010	15 1/2	July	10:30 AM
10	-3	Fri	1/6/2010	18 1/4	September	11:30 AM

3. Use your Excel Options menu to create a custom list of the 10 largest suspension bridges in the world:

Bridge	City/Region	Country
Akashi Kaikyo Bridge	Kobe- Awaji Route	Japan
Xihoumen Bridge	Zhoushan Archipelago	China
Great Belt Bridge	Halsskov Sprogo	Denmark
Runyang Bridge	Yangtze River	China
Humber Bridge	Barton-upon-Humber	United Kingdom
Jiangyin Suspension Bridge	Yangtze River	China
Tsing Ma Bridge	Tsing Yi-Ma Wan	Hong Kong
Verrazano Narrows Bridge	New York City	USA
Golden Gate Bridge	San Francisco	USA
Yangluo Bridge	Yangtze River	China

ANSWERS

1. Select the two first figures 5 and 6. Click on the grab handle and drag down until you see the value 10.
2. **a.** Select the rest of the table as you see in the figure.
   b. Double-click on the grab handle.

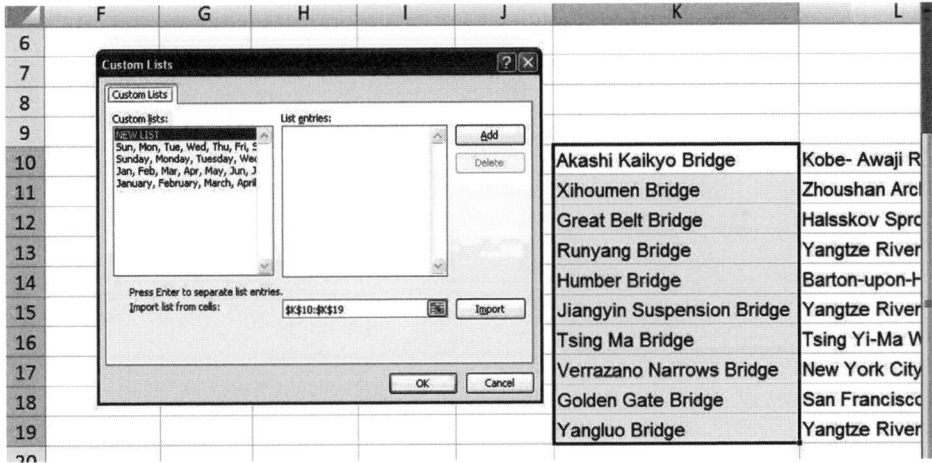

3. Click on the Office icon. Select Excel Options at the bottom of the menu. Click on Edit Custom Lists in the middle of the menu. (In Excel 2003, use Tools ⇒ Options ⇒ Custom Lists.) On the resulting menu, select the range K10:K19 and click on Import.

CHAPTER 2

Selecting Efficiently In Excel

Dragging the mouse is probably not the most efficient way of selecting a range in Excel. If you select a small range, it may be more effective to hold the Shift key down and use the arrow keys to select the range. In many instances, you have to select large ranges of data. This chapter will describe a number of techniques to select this data in a more efficient way.

Selecting an Entire Sheet To select an entire sheet, either click on an empty cell and use CTRL+A, or click on the small cell between column A and row 1. See Figure 2.1.

Selecting a Section To select any continuous data or section, click on the first cell of the section, then press Shift and click on the last cell of the section. You can also reverse the process, click on the last cell, then press Shift and click on the first cell of this section to select, keeping the Shift key pressed down. See Figure 2.2.

Selection Shortcuts To select the current region in Excel, click on any cell in the region and use CTRL+Shift+* (star). See Figure 2.3.

You can select an area from a currently highlighted cell or cells to the end of the data in that region's column. Select the cell or cells and press CTRL+Shift+↓ (down arrow). See Figure 2.4.

Using the same concept, you can select an area from a starting cell (or cells) to the end of the data on that region's row. You select the cell(s) and click CTRL+Shift+→ (right arrow). See Figure 2.5.

Any part of the region can be highlighted (selected) by first selecting a cell, a row, or a column in a region and then by using CTRL+Shift+←, CTRL+Shift+↑, or as shown above

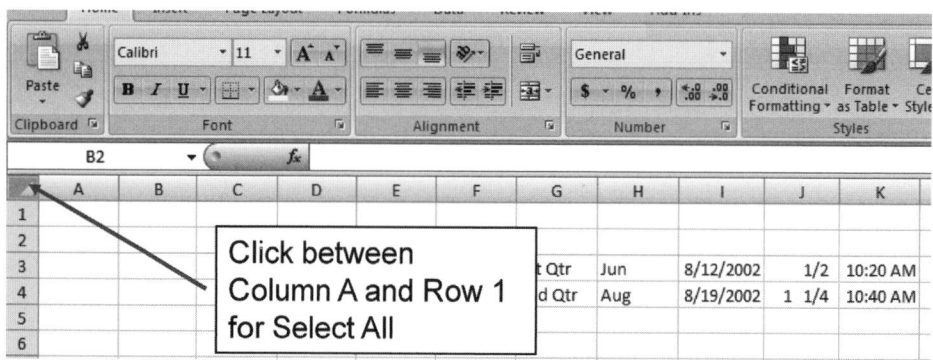

Figure 2.1 The Select All button

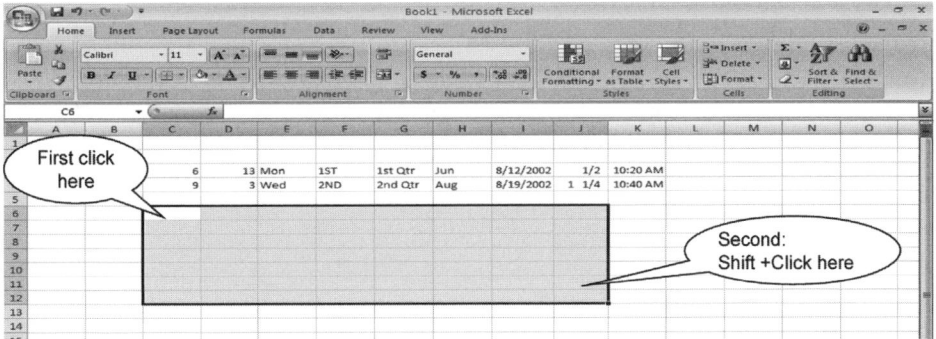

Figure 2.2   Selecting a region without dragging

CTRL+Shift+→, and CTRL+Shift+↓, to extend the selection to the end of that region in the direction we wish. CTRL+Shift+ any arrow key (↓↑→←) will enable selection from the starting cell(s) until the end of the data range in the direction of the arrow.

   With larger spreadsheets you may want to go back to the beginning of the sheet or to the end of the data on the sheet. To go back to cell A1, press CTRL+Home; to reach the last cell of the sheet use CTRL+End.

   Also try CTRL+Shift+End to select the data from the current cell to the last active cell on the sheet. To go to the first cell of a row, press the Home key.

   Extend and Add mode: After you select a starting cell, you can press F8 to enable the Extend mode (indicated on the right of the status bar by the letters EXT in Excel 2003 or Extend Selection in Excel 2007). Now you can use the arrows and select from that point on by repeatedly pressing on the arrow keys in the direction you want to select. See Figure 2.6.

C	D	E	F	G	H	I	J	K
Click on any cell in the region and use CTRL + Shift + *								
6	13	Mon	1ST	1st Qtr	Jun	8/12/2002	1/2	10:20 AM
9	3	Wed	2ND	2nd Qtr	Aug	8/19/2002	1 1/4	10:40 AM
12	-7	Fri	3rd	3rd Qtr	Oct	8/26/2002	1/3	11:00 AM
15	-17	Sun	4th	4th Qtr	Dec	9/2/2002	2 1/4	11:20 AM

C	D	E	F		H	I	J	K
6	13	Mon	1ST	1st Qtr	Jun	8/12/2002	1/2	10:20 AM
9	3	Wed	2ND	2nd Qtr	Aug	8/19/2002	1 1/4	10:40 AM
12	-7	Fri	3rd	3rd Qtr	Oct	8/26/2002	1/3	11:00 AM
15	-17	Sun	4th	4th Qtr	Dec	9/2/2002	2 1/4	11:20 AM

Figure 2.3   Use CTRL+Shift+* for selecting a region

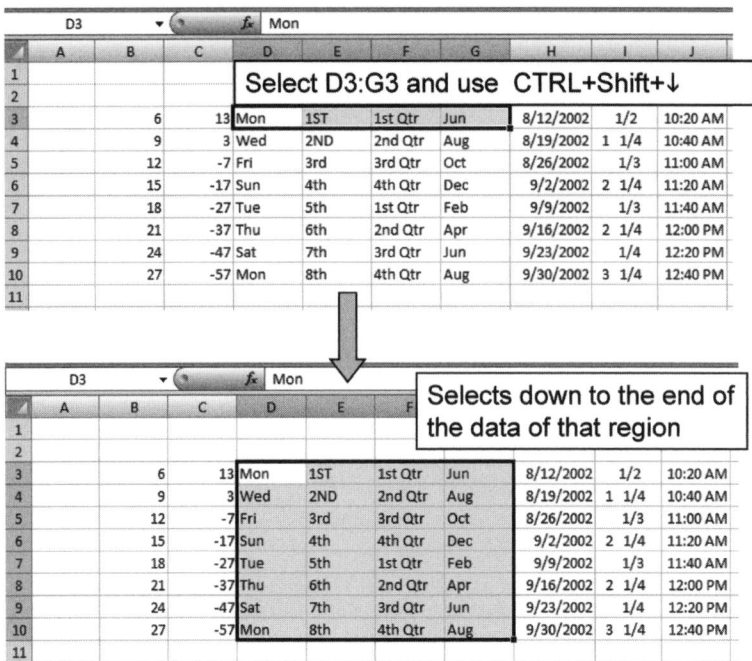

Figure 2.4   CTRL+Shift+↓ to select down

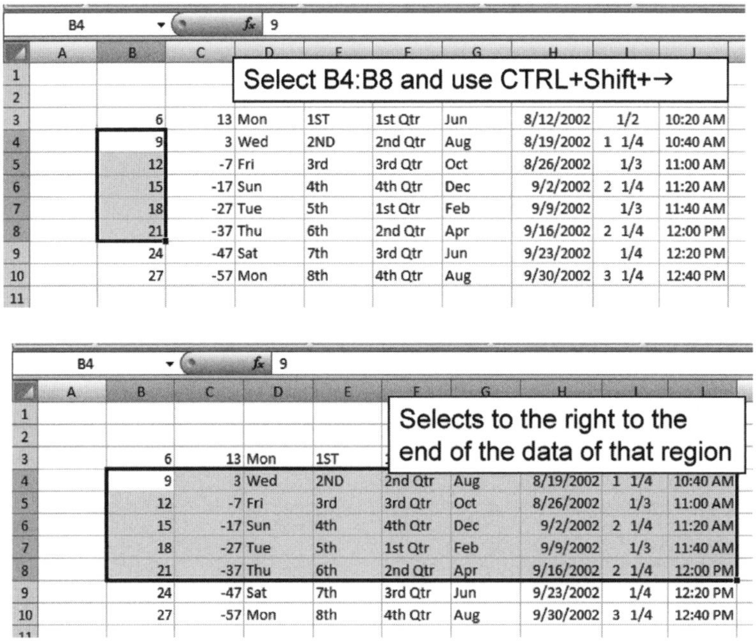

Figure 2.5   CTRL+Shift+→ to select to the right

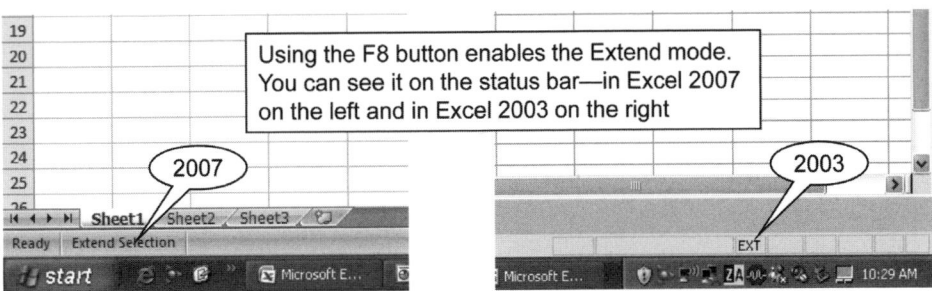

Figure 2.6 Extend mode

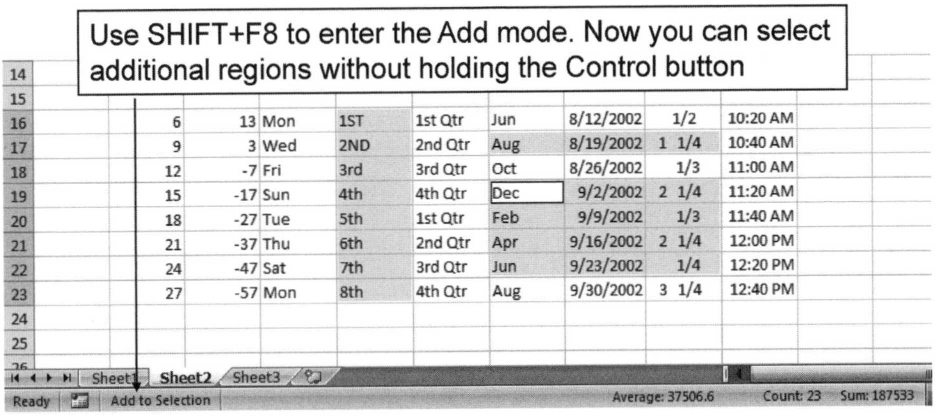

Use SHIFT+F8 to enter the Add mode. Now you can select additional regions without holding the Control button

16	6	13	Mon	1ST	1st Qtr	Jun	8/12/2002	1/2	10:20 AM
17	9	3	Wed	2ND	2nd Qtr	Aug	8/19/2002	1 1/4	10:40 AM
18	12	-7	Fri	3rd	3rd Qtr	Oct	8/26/2002	1/3	11:00 AM
19	15	-17	Sun	4th	4th Qtr	Dec	9/2/2002	2 1/4	11:20 AM
20	18	-27	Tue	5th	1st Qtr	Feb	9/9/2002	1/3	11:40 AM
21	21	-37	Thu	6th	2nd Qtr	Apr	9/16/2002	2 1/4	12:00 PM
22	24	-47	Sat	7th	3rd Qtr	Jun	9/23/2002	1/4	12:20 PM
23	27	-57	Mon	8th	4th Qtr	Aug	9/30/2002	3 1/4	12:40 PM

Ready · Add to Selection · Average: 37506.6 · Count: 23 · Sum: 187533

Figure 2.7 Add mode reads "Add to Selection"

If you wish to select non-continuous regions, using the Add mode is much more efficient than holding the CTRL key while dragging the mouse. The Add mode allows selecting desired blocks of ranges without holding down the CTRL key. If you press SHIFT+F8 simultaneously, the status bar will indicate ADD. You can then use the mouse and select additional regions. See Figure 2.7. The Add mode in Excel 2003 or previous versions of Excel is indicated on the right side of the bottom of the screen.

REVIEW QUESTIONS

You will find these examples in the Excel Chapter 2 file:

1. On *Sheet 3* of the workbook Chapter 2, select the entire database using a shortcut:

	A	B	C	D	E	F	G	H	I
1									
2		Employee	Employee No.	Gender	Dep	Job		Seniority	Age
3		Alfano, Vincenzo	1101	M	4	Electrician		7	48
4		Bai, Ye	1102	M	3	Machinist		5	32
5		Barile, Brad	1103	M	2	Electrician		12	36
6		Bedard, Greg	1104	M	1	Carpenter		15	35
7		Campbell, Jaime	1105	F	3	Carpenter		13	32
8		Cao, Lei	1106	F	1	Electrician		4	23
9		Capra, Ivana	1107	F	2	Electrician		23	45
10		Chen, Wei-Ta	1108	M	3	Machinist		7	25
11		Chen, Jie	1109	M	1	Carpenter		0	48
12		Cohen, Sari	1110	F	2	Electrician		0	22
13		Dharam, Nimisha	1111	F	3	Carpenter		15	35
14		Fidler, Megan	1112	F	1	Electrician		6	45
15		Ghanooni, Michael	1113	M	2	Electrician		3	34
16		Hobbie, Kelly	1114	F	3	Machinist		2	28
17		Huang, Xiuhua	1115	M	1	Carpenter		8	41
18		Inozemtseva, Irina	1116	F	4	Electrician		11	45
19		IP, Andrew	1117	M	4	Carpenter		3	33
20		Jiang, Nan	1118	M	1	Carpenter		0	38
21									

2. On the same sheet select C2:D2. Use a shortcut to select the two columns:

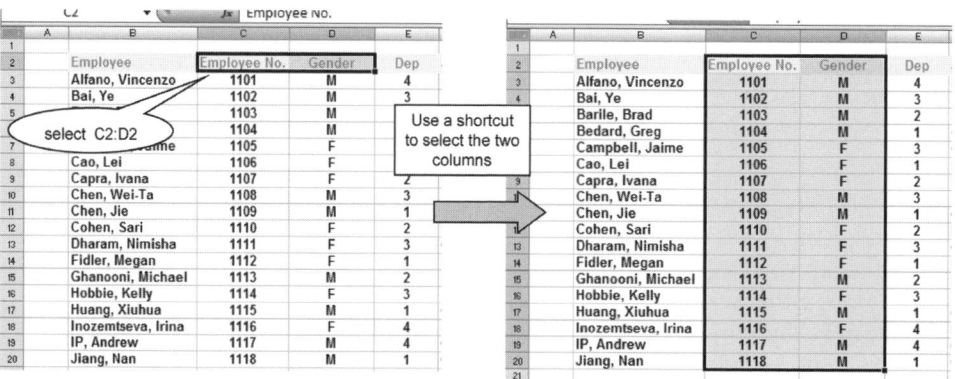

3. Start in cell G16. Use a shortcut to select the region C10:G16.

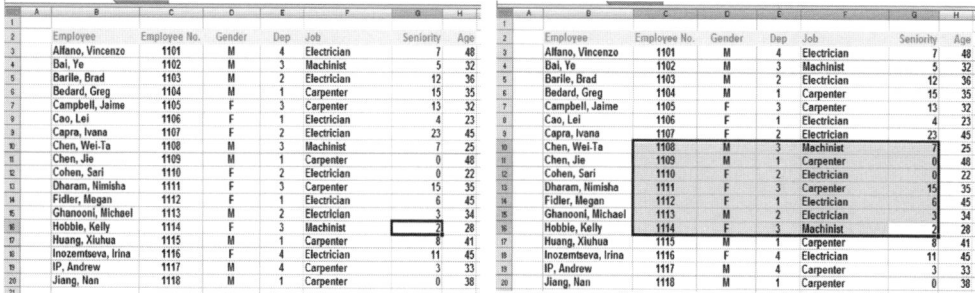

ANSWERS

1. Click anywhere in the region and use CTRL+Shift+* or CTRL+Shift+F8.
2. Select C2:D2. Use CTRL+Shift+↓.
3. Use Shift+click on C10.

Formulas, Functions, and Relative and Absolute Addressing

This chapter explains formulas, functions, and the addressing features or issues in Excel. I will show simple and advanced ways to create formulas and functions more efficiently. The focus is on speed, accuracy, and the ability to duplicate and repeat the functions and the formulas—saving valuable time and effort.

In Figure 3.1, you can see a simple payroll example that you can find in the Excel workbook Chapter 3. The sheet is named *Simple Payroll Before*. To calculate the salary, Hours worked x Rate in cell E3: Type the = (equal) sign first; then click on cell C3, type *, and click on cell D3. When you press the Enter key, the formula will calculate the result. Note how the cursor will skip down to cell E4. Once you are in cell E4 and you want to duplicate the result for all other employees, you have to select E3 again. This is an extra step. In order to save this additional step you can do one of two things: after entering the formula, rather than pressing the Enter key, either you click on the green check sign √ (to the left of the formula bar) or use CTRL+Enter. The cursor will remain in the selected cell. See Figure 3.1.

When the operation is completed in cell E2, we are ready to copy/drag down the formula to the rest of the cells in column E—all the way to E8—the last cell that has data/information in the adjacent column D. We do not copy and paste, and though you can drag down, it is not the most efficient way. (Imagine if you had 2000 employees!) Point to the drag handle, on the lower right corner of the cell, and when the mouse pointer takes the shape of a crosshair (+), double-click and the formula will be transferred/copied to the rest on the cells in column E. Figure 3.2 shows the results.

Relative and Absolute Addressing

You will notice that copying or dragging a formula does not copy the values down. You copied the formula only. Figure 3.3 shows all the formulas on the sheet. To reveal the formulas on a sheet choose CTRL+` (CTRL+accent mark) or CTRL+~ (tilde). Notice that the formula reads =C3*D3 in row 3, =C4*D4 in row 4, =C5*D5 in row 5, and so on for all the other rows. This is called "**Relative Addressing.**" The address is relative to the position of the row and the column.

You may now choose again CTRL+` or CTRL+~ to turn back to the initial view, showing the values, not the formulas. CTRL+` or CTRL+~ acts as a toggle—you can go from one view to the other.

If you use the Enter button when you complete the operation in cell E3, Excel takes you down to cell E4

	Weekly Salary Calculations			
Last Name	First Name	Rate	Hours	Salary
Alfano	Vincenzo	17.63	38.00	=C3*D3
Bai	Ye	12.73	40.00	
Barile	Brad	11.05	39.00	
Bedard	Greg	11.90	38.00	
Campbell	Jaime	12.14	40.00	
Cao	Lei	11.19	39.00	
Capra	Ivana	13.18	32.00	
Chen	Wei-Ta	10.77	40.00	

	Weekly Salary Calculations			
Last Name	First Name	Rate	Hours	Salary
Alfano	Vincenzo	17.63	38.00	669.94
Bai	Ye	12.73	40.00	
Barile	Brad	11.05	39.00	
Bedard	Greg	11.90	38.00	
Campbell	Jaime	12.14	40.00	
Cao	Lei	11.19	39.00	
Capra	Ivana	13.18	32.00	
Chen	Wei-Ta	10.77	40.00	

If you wish to stay in cell E3, use the check sign √ or use CTRL + Enter

	Weekly Salary Calculations			
Last Name	First Name	Rate	Hours	Salary
Alfano	Vincenzo	17.63	38.00	=C3*D3
Bai	Ye	12.73	40.00	
Barile	Brad	11.05	39.00	
Bedard	Greg	11.90	38.00	
Campbell	Jaime	12.14	40.00	
Cao	Lei	11.19	39.00	
Capra	Ivana	13.18	32.00	
Chen	Wei-Ta	10.77	40.00	

	Weekly Salary Calculations			
Last Name	First Name	Rate	Hours	Salary
Alfano	Vincenzo	17.63	38.00	669.94
Bai	Ye	12.73	40.00	
Barile	Brad	11.05	39.00	
Bedard	Greg	11.90	38.00	
Campbell	Jaime	12.14	40.00	
Cao	Lei	11.19	39.00	
Capra	Ivana	13.18	32.00	
Chen	Wei-Ta	10.77	40.00	

Figure 3.1   Use CTRL+Enter to save a step

The next step on the simple payroll spreadsheet is to calculate the tax for all the rows. We want to multiply the salaries in column E by the Tax Rate in cell G1 as shown in Figure 3.4.

This time it is different. If we use the same procedure described above, we could calculate the tax in cell F3, namely multiply E3 by G1 and transfer/drag the formula to the rest of the cells in the column—column F. If you use the same procedure, you will run into a problem. Since Excel is using the "**relative addressing**" concept, it will multiply F3 by G2, F4 by G3, and so on. G1 is the only cell that contains the tax rate information. The cells G2, G3, and the following cells are empty. See the results and the problem in Figures 3.4 and 3.5.

	Weekly Salary Calculations				
ame	First Name	Rate	Hours	Salary	Tax
	Vincenzo	17.63	38.00	669.94	
	Ye	12.73	40.00		
	Brad	11.05	39.00		
	Greg	11.90	38.00		
ell	Jaime	12.14	40.00		
	Lei	11.19	39.00		
	Ivana	13.18	32.00		
	Wei-Ta	10.77	40.00		

Double-click here

	Weekly Salary Calculations				
ame	First Name	Rate	Hours	Salary	Tax
	Vincenzo	17.63	38.00	669.94	
	Ye	12.73	40.00	509.20	
	Brad	11.05	39.00	430.95	
	Greg	11.90	38.00	452.20	
ell	Jaime	12.14	40.00	485.60	
	Lei	11.19	39.00	436.41	
	Ivana	13.18	32.00	421.76	
	Wei-Ta	10.77	40.00	430.80	

Figure 3.2   Double-click to copy down all the results

	E16	▾	fx		
	A	B	C	D	E
1			Weekly Salary Calculations		
2	Last Name	First Name	Rate	Hours	Salary
3	Alfano	Vincenzo	17.63	38	=C3*D3
4	Bai	Ye	12.73	40	=C4*D4
5	Barile	Brad	11.05	39	=C5*D5
6	Bedard	Greg	11.9	38	=C6*D6
7	Campbell	Jaime	12.14	40	=C7*D7
8	Cao	Lei	11.19	39	=C8*D8
9	Capra	Ivana	13.18	32	=C9*D9
10	Chen	Wei-Ta	10.77	40	=C10*D10

Figure 3.3   Relative Addressing

Other than the correct result in cell F3, all the others result in a zero (0). Revealing the formulas in Figure 3.5 shows that using G1 in the formula with relative addressing causes the rest of the cells in column F to use G2, G3, G4, and so on in the formulas. The other cells are all empty and they cause the problem encountered in Figure 3.5.

To overcome this relative addressing problem, we have to be able to refer to cell G1 in all the formulas in the cells in column F. This concept, using a specific cell and not a range, is called **Absolute Addressing**; we want all formulas in the series to refer to one specific cell only. To do so, we have to change G1 in these cells' formulas to read $G$1. When you see the $ signs in G1, it means that G1's status in the following formulas in the column has been changed from **Relative Addressing** to **Absolute Addressing**.

As shown in Figures 3.5 and 3.6, you want to use absolute addressing for G1 in cell F3. Select cell F3, type =, click on E3 and type *, and click on G1. Before doing anything else, press the F4 key on the keyboard. The F4 key changes G1 to read $G$1. This is referred to as "**Absolute Addressing.**" When you use Enter (or as explained before, click the green check sign √ to the left of the formula bar or CTRL+Enter) you can double-click the lower left corner of F3, and it will transfer the formula to the rest of the cells in the column (or you may drag the formula down). If you check, all the cells in column F contain the absolutely addressed $G$1. See Figures 3.6 and 3.7.

	A	B	C	D	E	F	G	H
	SUM		▾	X ✓ fx	=E3*G1			
1		Weekly Salary Calculations					10%	Rate
2	Last Name	First Name	Rate	Hours	Salary	Tax		
3	Alfano	Vincenzo	17.63	38.00	669.94	=E3*G1		
4	Bai	Ye	12.73	40.00	509.20			
5	Barile	Brad	11.05	39.00	430.95			
6	Bedard	Greg	11.90	38.00	452.20			
7	Campbell	Jaime	12.14	40.00	485.60			
8	Cao	Lei	11.19	39.00	436.41			
9	Capra	Ivana	13.18	32.00	421.76			
10	Chen	Wei-Ta	10.77	40.00	430.80			

Figure 3.4   Cell G1 has to have absolute addressing

	Workbook Views		Show/Hide			Zoom	
F3	▼	f_x	=E3*G1				
	A	B	C	D	E	F	G	H

	A	B	C	D	E	F	G	H
1			Weekly Salary Calculations				10%	Rate
2	**Last Name**	**First Name**	**Rate**	**Hours**	**Salary**	**Tax**		
3	Alfano	Vincenzo	17.63	38.00	669.94	66.99		
4	Bai	Ye	12.73	40.00	509.20	-		
5	Barile	Brad	11.05	39.00	430.95	-		
6	Bedard	Greg	11.90	38.00	452.20	-		
7	Campbell	Jaime	12.14	40.00	485.60	-		
8	Cao	Lei	11.19	39.00	436.41	-		
9	Capra	Ivana	13.18	32.00	421.76	-		
10	Chen	Wei-Ta	10.77	40.00	430.80	-		

The reason the cells in column F resulted in 0 (-) is because the formulas refer to empty cells

			G	H
1	lations		0.1	Rate
2	**Hours**	**Salary**	**Tax**	
3	38	=C3*D3	=E3*G1	
4	40	=C4*D4	=E4*G2	
5	39	=C5*D5	=E5*G3	
6	38	=C6*D6	=E6*G4	
7	40	=C7*D7	=E7*G5	
8	39	=C8*D8	=E8*G6	
9	32	=C9*D9	=E9*G7	
10	40	=C10*D10	=E10*G8	

Figure 3.5   Cells F4 to F10 resulted in zero

When you reveal all the formulas—you can see that all the formulas are calculated with G1 as the absolutely addressed cell.

Other Functions

In addition to using formulas, Excel has a variety of different useful functions. I will demonstrate here the use of a few of them.

A commonly used function in Excel is the AutoSum function. In addition to all the conventional ways to insert functions, AutoSum has a special icon, the Greek capital Sigma Σ. If you like, you could sum the Hours, Salary, and Taxes columns on the same simple payroll function sheet. Start in cell D11 summing the Hours column D3:D10. When you select the D11 cell—all you have to do is click on the Insert Sum icon Σ and see that Excel will attempt to calculate the sum of that column as shown in Figure 3.8.

To complete the operation, you can press Enter or click the check sign √. A much more efficient way is to just double-click the AutoSum icon. Try it. The result can be seen in Figure 3.9.

To use all other functions in Excel, you can insert the function by using the Function icon f_x next to the formula bar or by using the shortcut Shift+F3. To insert the Average function

	Workbook views			Show/Hide			Zoom		
	SUM	▼	X ✓ *fx*	=E3*$G$1					

	A	B	C	D	E	F	G	H
1			Weekly Salary Calculations				10%	Rate
2	**Last Name**	**First Name**	**Rate**	**Hours**	**Salary**	**Tax**		
3	Alfano	Vincenzo	17.63	38.00	669.94	=E3*$G$1		
4	Bai	Ye	12.73	40.00	509.20			
5	Barile	Brad	11.05	39.00	430.95			
6	Bedard	Greg	11.90	38.00	452.20			
7	Campbell	Jaime	12.14	40.00	485.60			
8	Cao	Lei	11.19	39.00	436.41			
9	Capra	Ivana	13.18	32.00	421.76			
10	Chen	Wei-Ta	10.77	40.00	430.80			

When we use F4 G1 becomes absolutely addressed as $G$1; and the results are shown below.

	F3	▼	*fx*	=E3*$G$1				

	A	B	C	D	E	F	G	H
1			Weekly Salary Calculations				10%	Rate
2	**Last Name**	**First Name**	**Rate**	**Hours**	**Salary**	**Tax**		
3	Alfano	Vincenzo	17.63	38.00	669.94	66.99		
4	Bai	Ye	12.73	40.00	509.20	50.92		
5	Barile	Brad	11.05	39.00	430.95	43.10		
6	Bedard	Greg	11.90	38.00	452.20	45.22		
7	Campbell	Jaime	12.14	40.00	485.60	48.56		
8	Cao	Lei	11.19	39.00	436.41	43.64		
9	Capra	Ivana	13.18	32.00	421.76	42.18		
10	Chen	Wei-Ta	10.77	40.00	430.80	43.08		

Figure 3.6 Use absolute addressing for cell G1

in cell D12, click the Function icon or use Shift+F3. The Function menu will appear on the screen. Click on the drop-down menu and choose Statistical. See Figure 3.10.

On the menu, select Average and click OK. In the first cell of the Average menu cell, select D3:D10 and click OK. It will result in the average. See Figure 3.11.

Once you have the two functions as shown in Figure 3.11, you can select the two results in D11:D12 and place your mouse pointer at the drag handle as shown in Figure 3.12.

	E	F	G	
			0.1	R
	Salary	**Tax**		
	=C3*D3	=E3*$G$1		
	=C4*D4	=E4*$G$1		
	=C5*D5	=E5*$G$1		
	=C6*D6	=E6*$G$1		
	=C7*D7	=E7*$G$1		
	=C8*D8	=E8*$G$1		
	=C9*D9	=E9*$G$1		
	=C10*D10	=E10*$G$1		

Figure 3.7 G1 is absolutely addressed

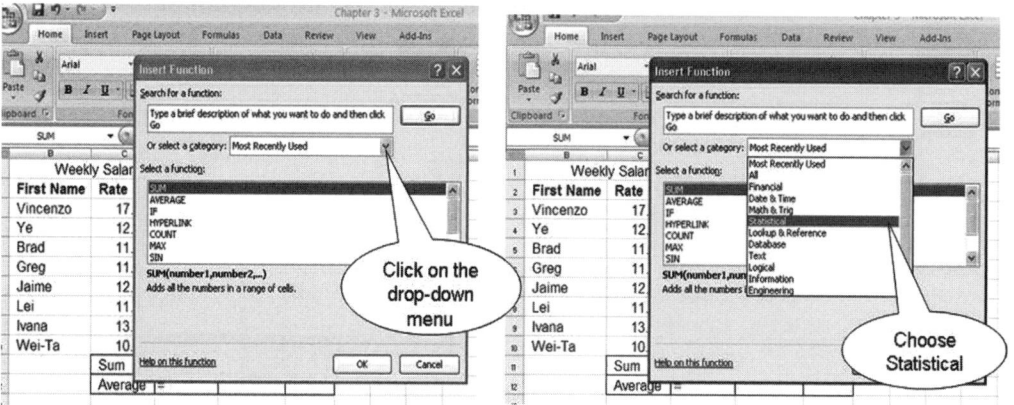

Figure 3.8 AutoSum

Figure 3.9 AutoSum result

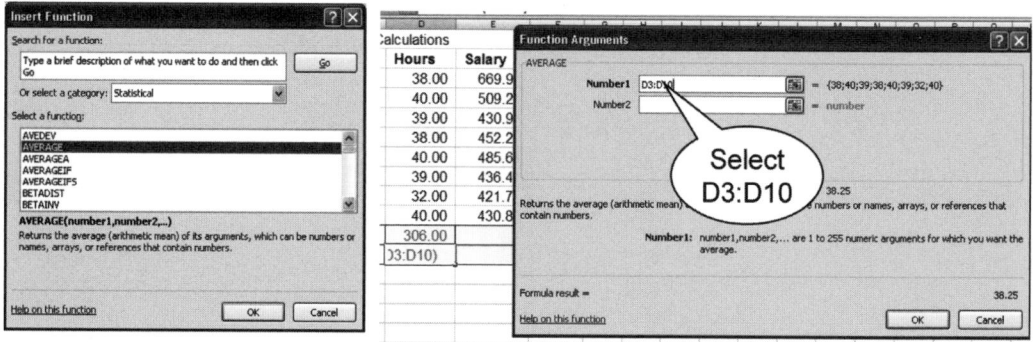

Figure 3.10 Excel function menus

Now drag it to the right through column F, taking advantage of the relative addressing in the sum and average of all three columns. The results and formulas are shown in Figure 3.13.

This chapter introduced formulas, functions, and the addressing issues in Excel. We showed how to use these formulas in a simple way. We also demonstrated how to take advantage of the shortcuts and the dragging to duplicate the results for entire columns and rows. The focus is on speed, accuracy, efficiency, and the ability to duplicate the functions and formulas. We will use these techniques again throughout the rest of the book.

Figure 3.11 Select the data in the menu

D11	▼		f_x	=SUM(D3:D10)					
	B	C	D	E	F	G	H	I
1	Weekly Salary Calculations					10%	Rate	
2	First Name	Rate	Hours	Salary	Tax			
3	Vincenzo	17.63	38.00	669.94	66.99			
4	Ye	12.73	40.00	509.20	50.92			
5	Brad	11.05	39.00	430.95	43.10			
6	Greg	11.90	38.00	452.20	45.22			
7	Jaime	12.14	40.00	485.60	48.56			
8	Lei	11.19	39.00	436.41	43.64			
9	Ivana	13.18	32.00	421.76	42.18			
10	Wei-Ta	10.77	40.00	430.80	43.08			
11		Sum	306.00					
12		Average	38.25					
13								

Figure 3.12   Drag the results to the right

	B	C	D	E	F	G
1	Weekly Salary Calculations					10%
2	First Name	Rate	Hours	Salary	Tax	
3	Vincenzo	17.63	38.00	669.94	66.99	
4	Ye	12.73	40.00	509.20	50.92	
5	Brad	11.05	39.00	430.95	43.10	
6	Greg	11.90	38.00	452.20	45.22	
7	Jaime	12.14	40.00	485.60	48.56	
8	Lei	11.19	39.00	436.41	43.64	
9	Ivana	13.18	32.00	421.76	42.18	
10	Wei-Ta	10.77	40.00	430.80	43.08	
11		Sum	306.00	3,836.86	383.69	
12		Average	38.25	479.61	47.96	

	C	D	E	F
1	Weekly Salary Calculations			
2	Rate	Hours	Salary	Tax
3	17.63	38	=C3*D3	=E3*$G$1
4	12.73	40	=C4*D4	=E4*$G$1
5	11.05	39	=C5*D5	=E5*$G$1
6	11.9	38	=C6*D6	=E6*$G$1
7	12.14	40	=C7*D7	=E7*$G$1
8	11.19	39	=C8*D8	=E8*$G$1
9	13.18	32	=C9*D9	=E9*$G$1
10	10.77	40	=C10*D10	=E10*$G$1
11	Sum	=SUM(D3:D10)	=SUM(E3:E10)	=SUM(F3:F10)
12	Average	=AVERAGE(D3:D10)	=AVERAGE(E3:E10)	=AVERAGE(F3:F10)

Figure 3.13   The Average and the Sum for the three columns

REVIEW QUESTIONS

You will find these examples in the Excel Chapter 3 file:

You will find the sheet *Review Questions* in the Excel File Chapter 3 as shown in the figure here:

	A	B	C	D	E	F	G	H	I	J
1	Part Number	Units Sold	Price	Total Sales	Sales Tax			Sale Tax Rate	8.25%	
2	D4T11	12435	62.95							
3	B1112	3466	45.99							
4	H4TT	12102	80.6							
5	FR90	14391	91.35							
6	SS34	3910	70.23							
7	NK34	6219	20.65							
8	Z1167	23213	4.2							
9	THSS	12109	13							
10	Z3411	36145	8.25							
11	Totals									
12	Lowest									
13	Highest									
14	Average									
15										

1. Calculate the Total Sales in cell D2.
2. Double-click on the drag handle in D2 to calculate the rest of the values in column D.
3. Calculate the Sales Tax in column E, using I1 as an absolute address.
4. Calculate the lowest, highest, and average for each of the columns.

ANSWERS

See the results and the formulas:

	Part Number	Units Sold	Price	Total Sales	Sales Tax
1					
2	D4T11	12435	62.95	782,783.25	64,579.62
3	B1112	3466	45.99	159,401.34	13,150.61
4	H4TT	12102	80.6	975,421.20	80,472.25
5	FR90	14391	91.35	1,314,617.85	108,455.97
6	SS34	3910	70.23	274,599.30	22,654.44
7	NK34	5219	20.65	107,772.35	8,891.22
8	Z1167	23213	4.2	97,494.60	8,043.30
9	THSS	12109	13	157,417.00	12,986.90
10	Z3411	36145	8.25	298196.25	24601.19063
11	*Totals*				
12	Lowest	3,466.00	4.20	97,494.60	8,043.30
13	Highest	36,145.00	91.35	1,314,617.85	108,455.97
14	Average	13,665.56	44.14	463,078.13	38,203.95

	Part Number	Units Sold	Price	Total Sales	Sales Tax
1					
2	D4T11	12435	62.95	=C2*B2	=D2*$I$1
3	B1112	3466	45.99	=C3*B3	=D3*$I$1
4	H4TT	12102	80.6	=C4*B4	=D4*$I$1
5	FR90	14391	91.35	=C5*B5	=D5*$I$1
6	SS34	3910	70.23	=C6*B6	=D6*$I$1
7	NK34	5219	20.65	=C7*B7	=D7*$I$1
8	Z1167	23213	4.2	=C8*B8	=D8*$I$1
9	THSS	12109	13	=C9*B9	=D9*$I$1
10	Z3411	36145	8.25	=C10*B10	=D10*$I$1
11	*Totals*				
12	Lowest	=MIN(B2:B10)	=MIN(C2:C10)	=MIN(D2:D10)	=MIN(E2:E10)
13	Highest	=MAX(B2:B10)	=MAX(C2:C10)	=MAX(D2:D10)	=MAX(E2:E10)
14	Average	=AVERAGE(B2:B10)	=AVERAGE(C2:C10)	=AVERAGE(D2:D10)	=AVERAGE(E2:E10)

CHAPTER 4

Naming Cells and Ranges

When you use names in Excel to address or represent a cell, a range of cells, or constants, you can make your functions and formulas much more meaningful and so much easier to handle. It is much easier to use Average(Sales) than Average(B738:B897). Another example is when using names in a meaningful way in a formula: Use Cost_January+Cost_February instead of A2+A3. I prefer to use **names** in Excel when I calculate statistics on a large range of numbers.

Excel allows you to define a name or names in a variety of ways. Once you adopt the practice of using names in your workbooks, you can easily update, audit, and manage these names. I will show you that naming cells or a range of cells can save you precious time and effort when you use them for calculations, statistics, and decision-making applications. I will also demonstrate that names are helpful in presenting your calculations to an audience or when you copy your formulas to other applications such as Word and PowerPoint.

All the cells in Excel are automatically given a specific name that places them in a specific column and row position—the address. In many situations, you may want to rename a cell or a range of cells to make it easier to refer to the data, which those cells or ranges contain. The following demonstrates the concept with a simple example.

Naming a Single Cell

In the example in the workbook Chapter 4, in the sheet called *Names Concept* I would like to use a tax rate of 15 percent. Instead of using absolute addressing, I would like to name the cell corresponding to that 15 percent tax and call it "Tax." The value 15 percent was entered in cell G1. See Figure 4.1.

To name cell G1 "Tax," select the Name box, above column A and to the left of the Formula bar. Type the word Tax and click Enter. This will name cell G1 Tax, in addition to its original name/address G1. See Figure 4.2.

From now on, you may use this new name anywhere in this workbook. For example, if you type a formula in any cell: =200*Tax, it will result in the value 30. Using the Name box is only one way to name or rename cells or ranges. There are a number of other ways.

To illustrate again how to use the name in the above example, try calculating the tax for all the entries in column F. Type = in cell F3, click on E3, type *, and click on cell G1. It will show up as =E3*Tax, as you can see in Figure 4.3.

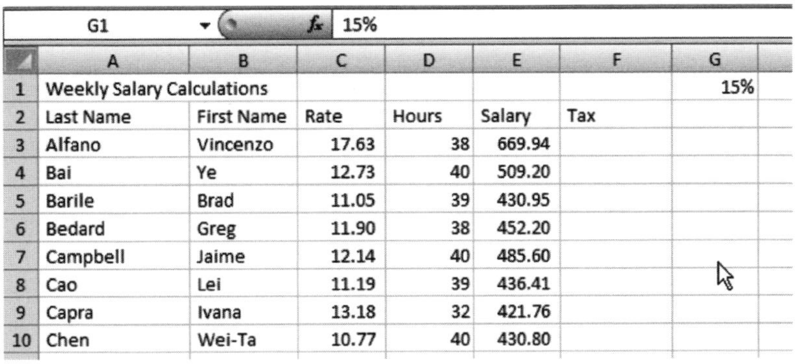

Figure 4.1   Use a name for cell G1

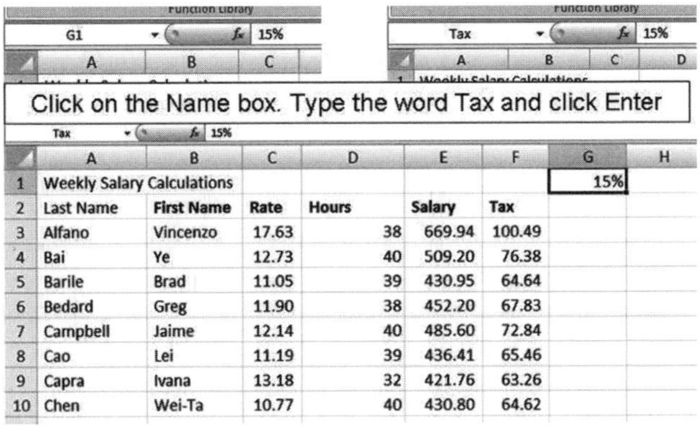

Figure 4.2   Naming a cell in Excel

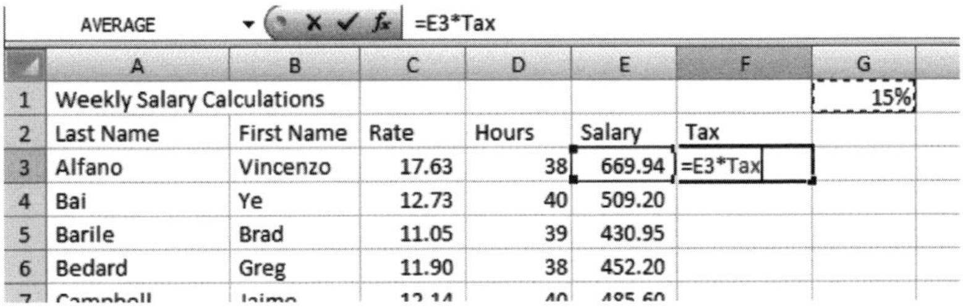

Figure 4.3   Use the name "tax" in the formula

Now you can complete the operation (Enter) and either drag the result down or double-click the lower right corner of cell F3 resulting in the tax calculation for all cells in column F. See Figure 4.4.

One additional advantage of using the name concept is eliminating the use of the absolute addressing concept. Another advantage is the fact that you don't have to search for the cell containing the tax rate of 15 percent. You can just type Tax (it is not case-sensitive—so

	C	D	E	F	G
					15%
ie	Rate	Hours	Salary	Tax	
	17.63	38	669.94	100.49	
	12.73	40	509.20	76.38	
	11.05	39	430.95	64.64	
	11.90	38	452.20	67.83	
	12.14	40	485.60	72.84	
	11.19	39	436.41	65.46	
	13.18	32	421.76	63.26	
	10.77	40	430.80	64.62	

	C	D	E	F	G
					0.15
	Rate	Hours	Salary	Tax	
	17.63	38	669.94	=E3*Tax	
	12.73	40	509.2	=E4*Tax	
	11.05	39	430.95	=E5*Tax	
	11.9	38	452.2	=E6*Tax	
	12.14	40	485.6	=E7*Tax	
	11.19	39	436.41	=E8*Tax	
	13.18	32	421.76	=E9*Tax	
	10.77	40	430.8	=E10*Tax	

Figure 4.4 Using the name tax

you can type tax) in the formula and it will result in the 15 percent—even if the Tax cell was on a different sheet in the Excel workbook.

The above example illustrates the simplest way of creating a name for a single cell. I will show a number of other examples and techniques to name a range of cells and to use more efficient ways to create names.

Naming a Range of Cells

If you have, for example, a set of 20,000 numbers in a range and you want to obtain different calculations for the range, you may not want to select the range or type the range address in the function more than once. In the second example, on the sheet called "*Statistics,*" I entered the values in the range B1:E5000. I would like to calculate for the range the average, sum, standard deviation, and the median.

I clicked on a single cell in the range and selected the range by using the shortcut CTRL+Shift+*. I clicked on the Name box, typed the word Data, and clicked Enter. I changed the name of the range and the range B1:E5000 is now called Data. See Figure 4.5.

	Data	▾	fx	885	
	A	B	C	D	E
1		885	817	890	1765
2		1644	1491	1723	1072
3		1323	1455	910	942

4997		1512	1332	1344	878
4998		800	1561	1106	1770
4999		1612	1189	1373	1224
5000		1602	859	1484	1554
5001					

Average: 1300.13755   Count: 20000   Sum: 26002751

Figure 4.5 The range B1:E5000 now has the name "Data"

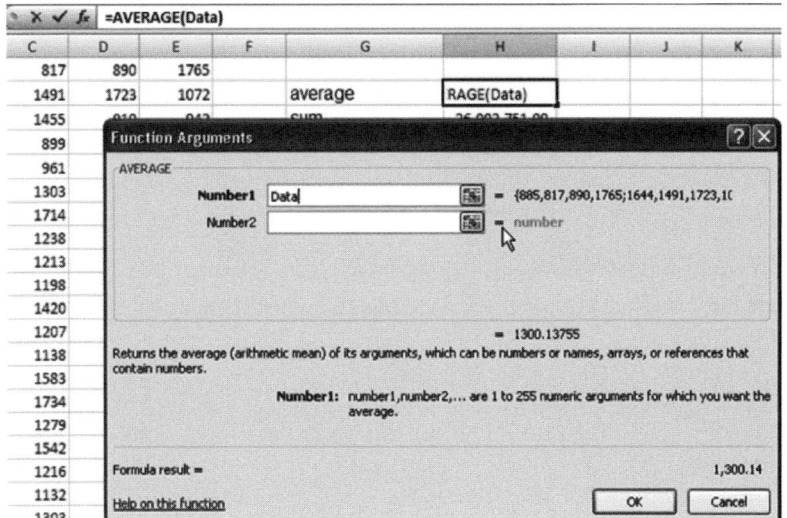

Figure 4.6 Use the name "Data" instead of B1:E5000

Afterward, it is possible to use the name for the range to obtain the calculations mentioned above. See Figure 4.6. I did not have to select B1:E5000 or type B1:E5000. I just typed in the word Data.

I used the function f_x icon to calculate all the other functions. (You may also use Shift+F3 to get to the Function menu.) See the result in Figure 4.7.

As I explained earlier, it is much easier to handle and understand functions when they read =SUM(QuarterOneSales) than =SUM(B7:B18). It is more meaningful when you calculate a formula to read =Jan09 Sales-Dec08 Sales than =C7-C6.

Using the Name Menu to Create Names

In the following example, I will use the Excel menu to create names. In the sheet *Name Menus* of Chapter 4's workbook, I would like to create names for the different ranges. See Figure 4.8. In this example, I will call the range C3:C8 Sales, D3:D8 Cost, and the range E3:E8 Profit.

The other ranges will also be named. C3:E3 will be named Jan, C4:E4 will be named Feb, C5:C6 will be named Mar, and so on.

	F	G	H
1			
2		average	1,300.14
3		sum	26,002,751.00
4		standard deviation	287.61
5		median	1,299.00
6			

	G	H
	average	=AVERAGE(Data)
	sum	=SUM(Data)
	standard deviation	=STDEVP(Data)
	median	=MEDIAN(Data)

Figure 4.7 Using the range name "Data" in formulas

	A	B	C	D	E	F
1						
2			Sales	Cost	Profit	
3		Jan	34	27	7	
4		Feb	36	26	10	
5		Mar	38	25	13	
6		Apr	40	24	16	
7		May	42	23	19	
8		Jun	44	22	22	
9						
10						

Figure 4.8 Naming the ranges by the headers and the left column

The header in row 2 and the information in column B will be used to create the range names. As you select the range B2:E8, go to the Formulas ribbon and click on Create from Selection. See Figure 4.9.

When you click on the **Create Names from Selection** the menu shown in Figure 4.10 allows you to create the names shown on the top row and the names in the left column of the selected range.

Now that you have created these names, you can utilize them in formulas and functions on the same sheet or other sheets in this workbook.

To locate the different named ranges you have created, go to the drop-down menu next to the Name box and select any name; the range that it represents will be highlighted on the data range itself. See Figure 4.11.

Now you can take advantage of these names and ranges. For example, you can calculate the sum of Sales. Without the name, you would have had to use the formula =SUM(C2:C8). Now you can simply use the formula =SUM(Sales) resulting in the sum seen in Figure 4.12.

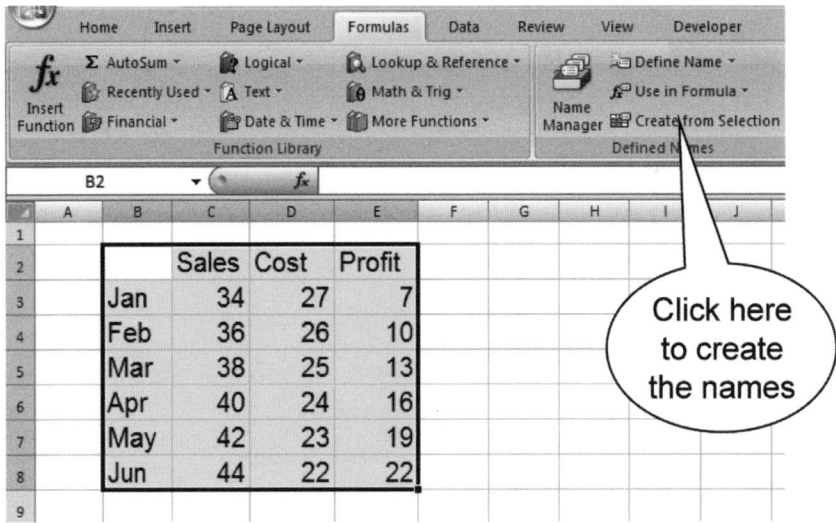

Figure 4.9 Create Name from Selection

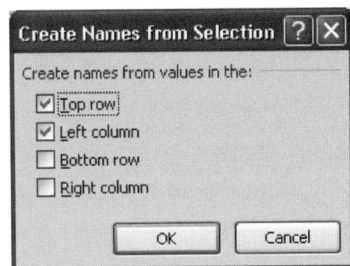

Figure 4.10   The Name menu

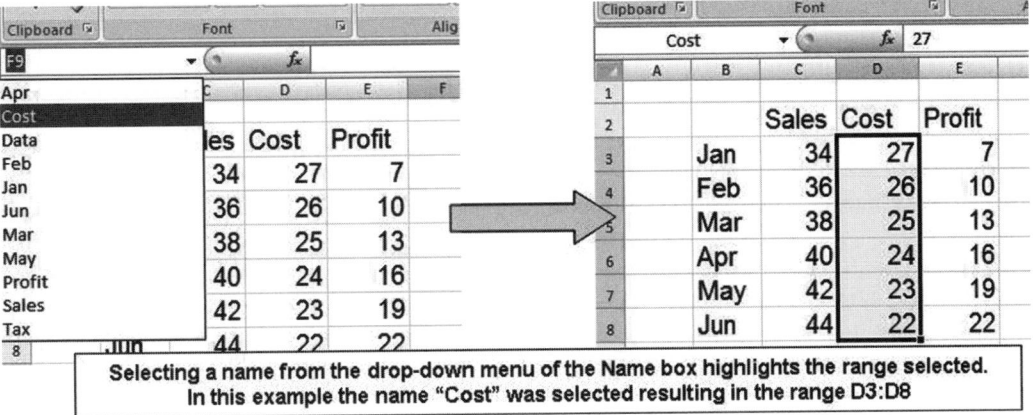

Figure 4.11   Selecting a range using the Name box

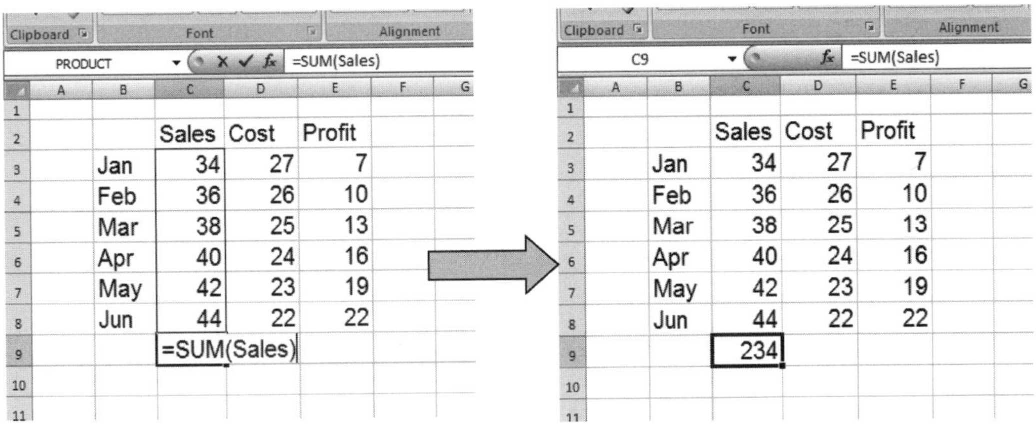

Figure 4.12   Using the Formula=SUM(Sales)

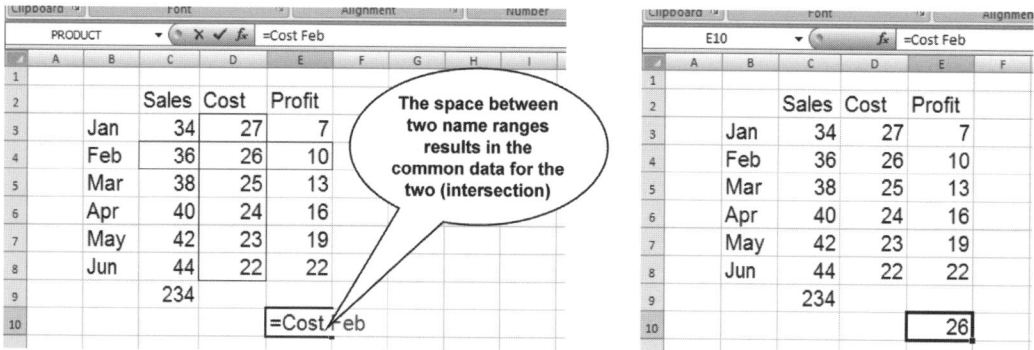

Figure 4.13   Selecting an intersection of two named ranges

Try other combinations with the created names. Try =SUM(Cost). Experiment with =SUM(Cost,Profit). Try something else: =Cost Feb (=Cost+space+Feb.) This will result in the in the intersection of the Cost and Feb: 26. See Figure 4.13 for the intersection.

More About Names   You can use the **Name Manager** menu to delete or modify existing names. Just click on the **Name Manager** and experiment with this menu. See figure 4.14 for the Name menu. With the Name Manager, you can either click on the Edit button or edit the name or delete any of the names you want to delete.

To paste the list of names, simply press the F3 key and choose Paste List. It will list all the names on your spreadsheet. See Figure 4.15.

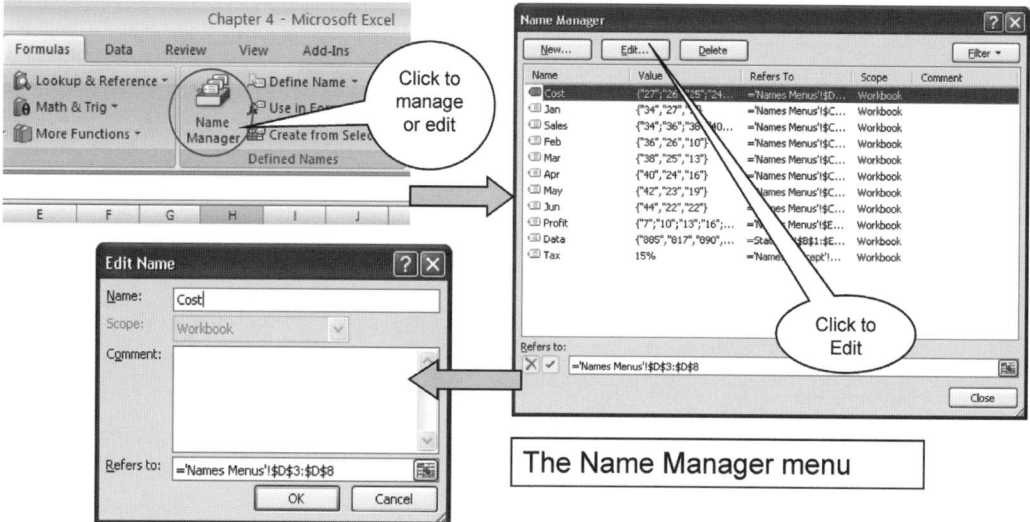

Figure 4.14   Managing names

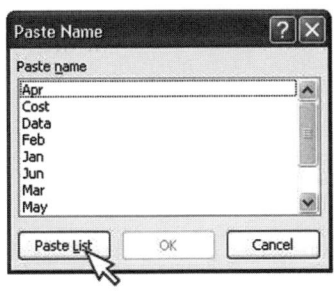

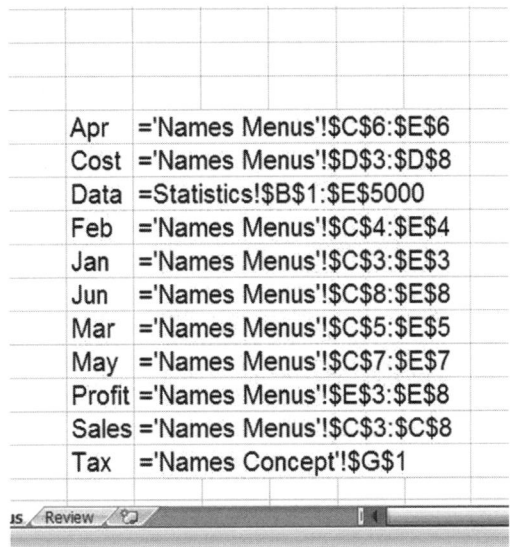

Apr	='Names Menus'!$C$6:$E$6
Cost	='Names Menus'!$D$3:$D$8
Data	=Statistics!$B$1:$E$5000
Feb	='Names Menus'!$C$4:$E$4
Jan	='Names Menus'!$C$3:$E$3
Jun	='Names Menus'!$C$8:$E$8
Mar	='Names Menus'!$C$5:$E$5
May	='Names Menus'!$C$7:$E$7
Profit	='Names Menus'!$E$3:$E$8
Sales	='Names Menus'!$C$3:$C$8
Tax	='Names Concept'!$G$1

To paste the list of names simply click on the F3 key and choose Paste List

Figure 4.15   Paste Name List menu

I will be able to demonstrate the advantage of this naming feature later in this book with other applications and examples. This is a very powerful feature of Excel that many people fail to take advantage of.

APPENDIX—USING THE NAMES MENU IN EXCEL 2003

In Excel 2003, or previous versions, the Names feature appears under the Insert menu. In the following example, I will use the Excel menu to create names. In the sheet *Ranges* of the Excel 2003 Chapter 4 workbook, I would like to create names for the different ranges. See Figure 4.16. In this example, I would like to call the range C3:C8 Sales, D3:D8 Cost, and the range E3:E8 Profit. The other ranges will also be named. C3:E3 will be named Jan, C4:E4 will be named Feb, C5:E5 will be named Mar, and so on.

The header in row 2 and the information in column B will be used to create the range names. As you select the range B2:E8 use: Insert ⇒ Name ⇒ Create. See Figure 4.17.

When you click on Insert ⇒ Name ⇒ Create, the menu shown in Figure 4.18 allows you to create the names shown on the top row and the names in the left column of the selected range.

Now that you have created these names, you can utilize them in formulas and functions on the same sheet or other sheets in this workbook.

To change, edit, delete, or modify the names in Excel 2003 or a previous version, Insert ⇒ Name ⇒ Define. The Define Name menu will allow you to add, edit, or delete any of the names as shown in Figure 4.19.

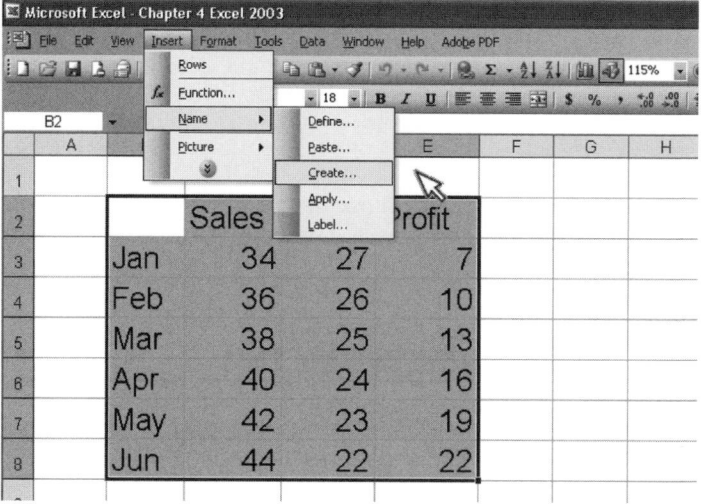

Figure 4.16   The range for names to be created

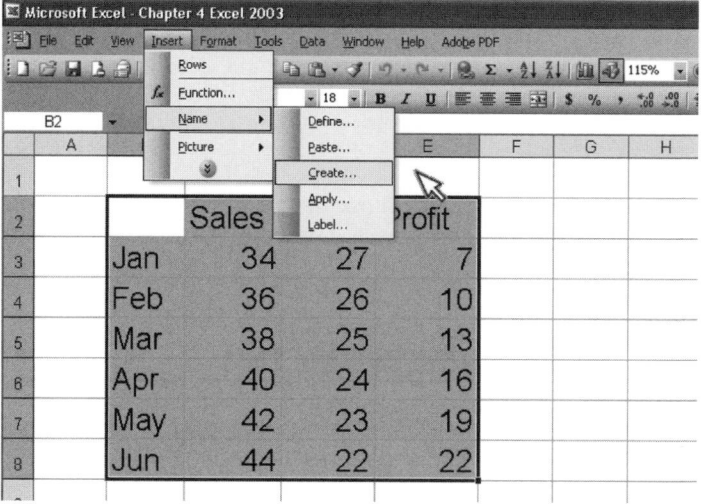

Figure 4.17   Use: Insert ⇒ Name ⇒ Create from the menu

Figure 4.18   The Create Names menu

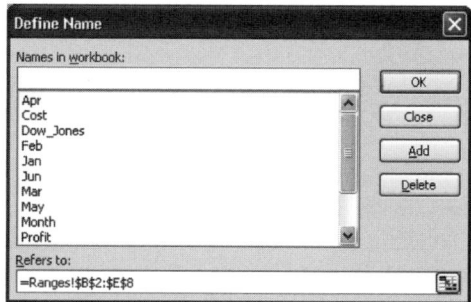

Figure 4.19   The Define Name menu in Excel 2003

REVIEW QUESTIONS

You will find these examples in the Excel Chapter 4 file:

1. On the sheet *Review* of Chapter 4, name the region H4:J11 Statistics.

2. Using the Names menu name C4:C7 Quantity, D4:D7 Price, E4:E7 Revenue, C4:E4 Qrt_1, C5:E5 Qrt_2, C6:E6 Qrt_3, and C7:E7 Qrt_4.
3. Use the names you just created in review problems 1 and 2 to:
   a. Calculate the sum of the region H4:J11.
   b. Calculate the sum of all the Quantities C4:C7. Add the Revenues for the second and third quarters using the intersection feature of the name.

ANSWERS

1. Select the region H4:J11. Type the word "numbers" in the name box and click Enter. See figure.

2. Select B3:E7 and use the Create from Selection menu shown in the figure to create names.
3. Once you created the names, you can use the names in the formulas.
   a. = SUM(Numbers) – for the region named in answer 1.
   b. = SUM(Quantity). =SUM(Revenue) – for the names created in answer 2.

CHAPTER 5

Excel Charts

Charts convey much more information than just reading spreadsheet data. Charts make it easier to see what is hiding behind the numbers. In this chapter, you are going to find out how to generate and format Excel charts. I will demonstrate how to use some of the different types of charts and the common techniques to deal with all Excel charts.

Quick/Instant Chart

To get a quick/instant chart from data in Excel, select any cell in the data range as shown in Figure 5.1 (alternatively select the entire range B3:E8) and press the F11 key. When you use the F11 key, it generates a clustered column chart (the default chart) on a new sheet. You will find it on the sheet *Simple Chart* in the Excel file Chapter 5.

If you wish to change the default chart type after Excel created it, right-click on an empty space inside the chart, and then select Change Chart Type in the local menu. A window with chart options will pop-up and allow you to select a different chart type. See Figure 5.2.

An alternate way to select a different chart type:

When you create a chart, Chart Tools appear on the ribbon. This Chart Tools ribbon shows Design, Layout, and Format tabs. Click on the Design tab under Chart Tools, in the Type group click Change Chart Type, and select another chart type.

Creating a Chart Using the Menu

Using the Insert ribbon to insert charts will allow the creation of a variety of charts in a controlled approach. This can be explained with a simple example.

The easiest way to create a chart is by arranging the reference data in the way that Excel expects it; namely, position the data or names you want on the X-axis (the horizontal axis) in the first column.

This is done by entering the data you want to appear on the X-axis on the left-most column of the reference data. You may arrange it in different ways—but doing so, you may have to go through additional steps to create the desired chart. The example I chose, which you can see in Figure 5.1, lists months' names on the left column of the data set because I want them to be positioned on the bottom or the X-axis of the chart.

Using the same data as for the first example, I can create a column chart, the very first chart on the menu. I chose to create a chart using only the first and second columns of the data. Select the first two columns in the data range B2:C8 and click on Columns in the Insert ribbon, as shown in Figure 5.3. Excel will generate the chart shown in Figure 5.4.

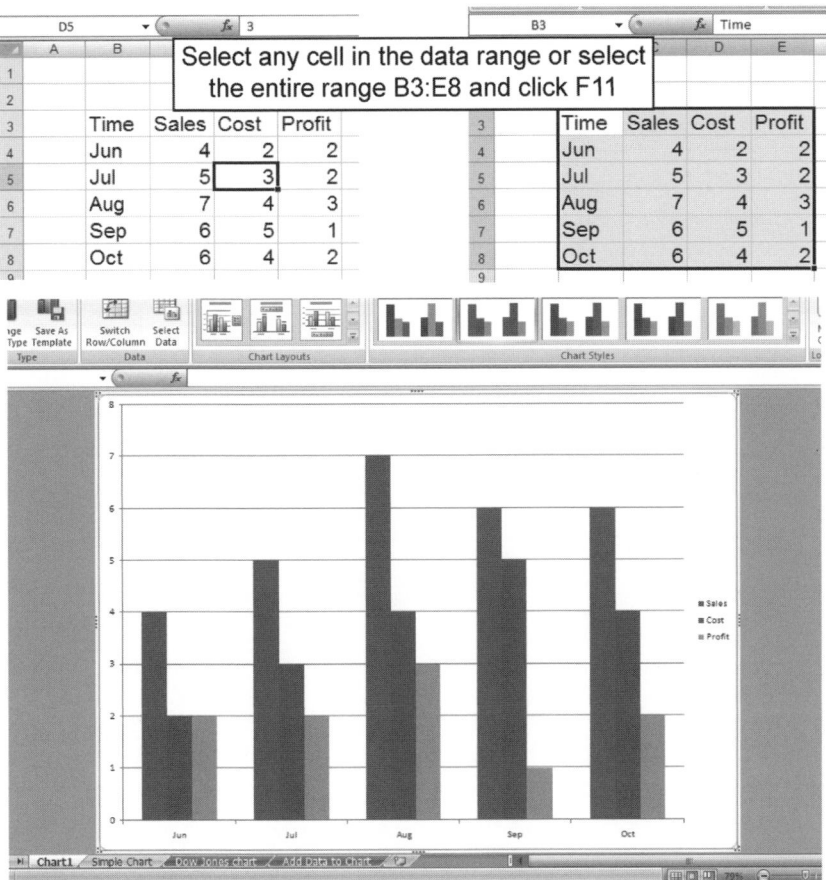

Select any cell in the data range or select the entire range B3:E8 and click F11

Figure 5.1   The F11 key creates an instant chart

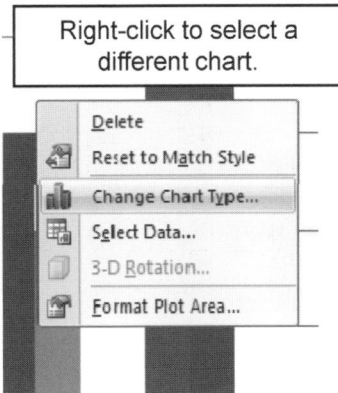

Right-click to select a different chart.

Figure 5.2   Right-click to change chart type

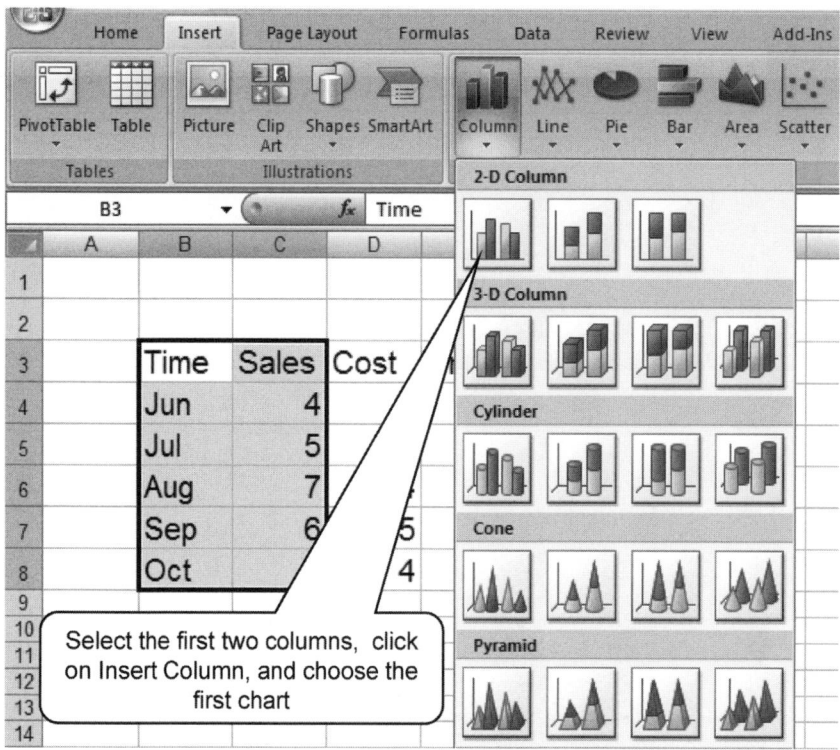

Figure 5.3 Insert a chart

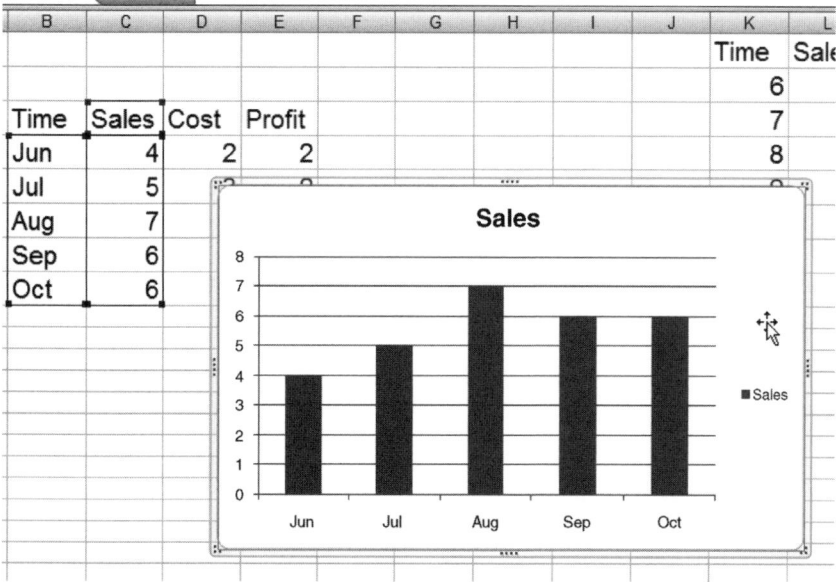

Figure 5.4 Two-dimensional column chart

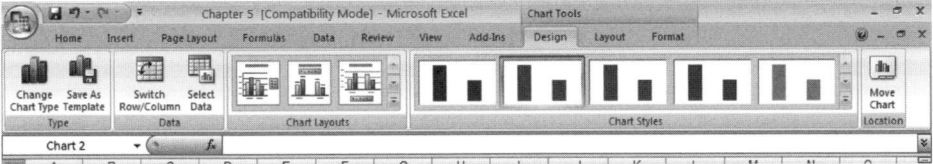

Figure 5.5 Chart Tools ribbon

When you create a chart, Excel displays the Chart Tools ribbon. You can also access the Chart Tools ribbon at any time when you select a chart. See Figure 5.5.

Try some of the features on the ribbon, for example the design part. Click on the drop-down menu at the far right for more options and choose a different look/format for your chart. The detailed procedure is illustrated in Figure 5.6. The redesigned chart is shown in Figure 5.7.

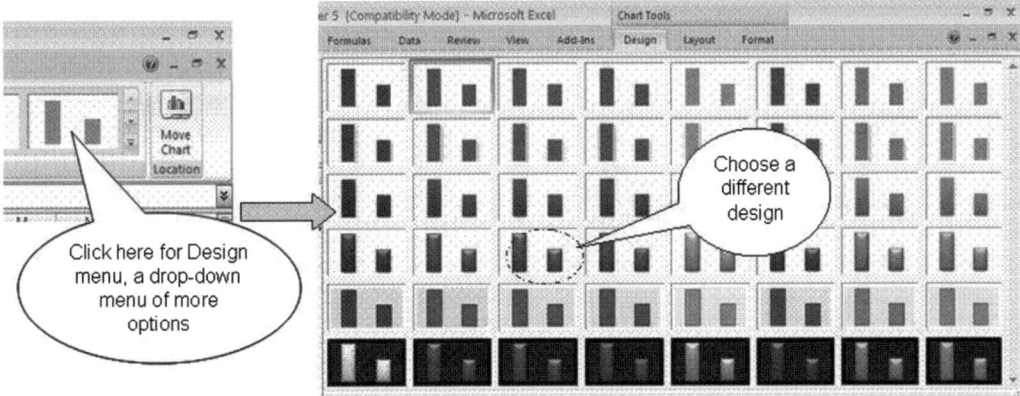

Figure 5.6 Redesign the chart

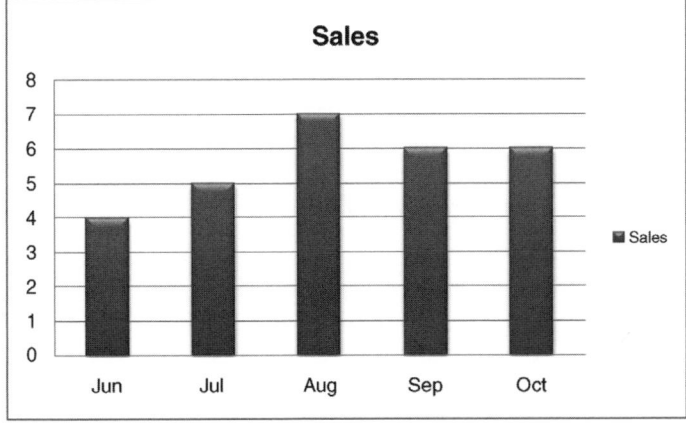

Figure 5.7 New design

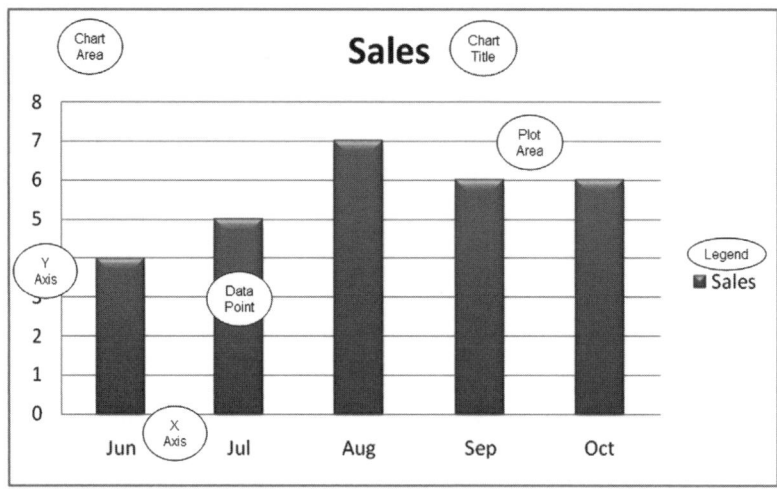

Figure 5.8   Chart parts

You should experiment with the other features of the Chart Tools ribbon to explore the various possibilities. The ribbon can assist you in changing the design, layout, and chart type; selecting different data; or moving the chart to a different location.

It is also important to understand the chart elements. When you need to create or modify charts, identifying these elements enables you to create, amend, or design a specific part of the chart. Figure 5.8 identifies these elements.

After a chart is created, any of its elements can be individually modified. You may want to change the way that axes are displayed, amend the chart title, move the legend, or display other chart elements:

For the axes: You can specify the scale and adjust the interval between the values or categories. You can also add tick marks to make it easier to look at the chart and its scale.

For the titles: You may add titles and data labels to a chart. This displays the information in your chart. You can add titles to the chart, axis, and the data labels.

For the legend or data table: You may show or hide a legend, change its location, or even change the legend entries. You can display a data table (the data used to build the chart). The legend keys can be formatted to have the appearance of your chart elements.

I will discuss these and other chart options when charts will be used in upcoming chapters. I will discuss them in the context of trend lines, formatting, and other situations.

Adding More Data to an Existing Chart

Look again at the previous example. For reference, it is illustrated once more in Figure 5.9. The chart was created from the two first columns of the data. The Months in the first column are used to show the time progression on the X-axis. The Sales information is in the second data column. It was used for the Y values of the chart.

Once you have created a desired chart, you may want to **add** part or all of the spreadsheet data to the existing chart. In this example, you will want to add the Cost and Profit columns.

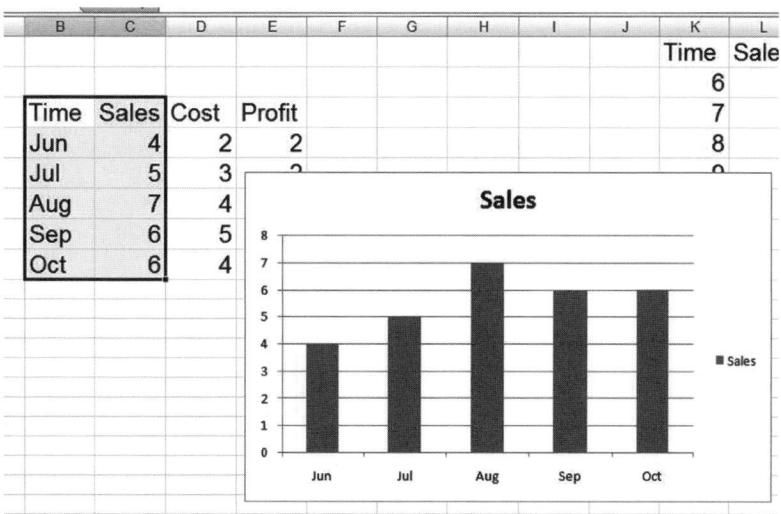

Figure 5.9 The initial chart before adding more data

Proceed using the following steps: Select the data D3:E8, click the Copy icon (or CTRL+C), click anywhere on the chart, and then click the Paste icon (or CTRL+V). Alternatively, it is possible (after data selection) to use the mouse right-click, copy, select a chart area, then paste using the local menu after another right-click. The data will be added to the chart. See Figure 5.10.

Very Important Facts About All Excel Charts: Selecting a Series All Excel charts have some common characteristics. All data series (in our example, the sets of columns in the charts) can be selected the same way. If you click on a single column once, all of the columns of that particular series will be marked. (For example, all of the sales columns will be marked if you click on a single column of the sales series.) If you click on the same column a second time, it marks the individual column only.

Use the rule: First click marks all of the points (columns) in a series—the second click marks the individual point (or a single column). See Figure 5.11. Marking a series this way (first click for all the points and second click for the individual point) works in all charts in Excel.

The advantage of being able to mark individual columns rather than the entire series is the possibility of formatting the individual column versus the entire series.

If you wish to format the individual column (say Sales for Jun), you may do so after selecting that column by itself (the second click). If you right-click after the individual selection, it is possible to format that column by itself. Figure 5.12 demonstrates the procedure.

This is simple. When an individual column is marked (second click), you can format the individual column by itself. On the local menu, use Format Data Point.

To format the entire series, click only once to select the series and repeat the procedure explained in Figure 5.12. The complete series will be formatted as shown in Figure 5.13.

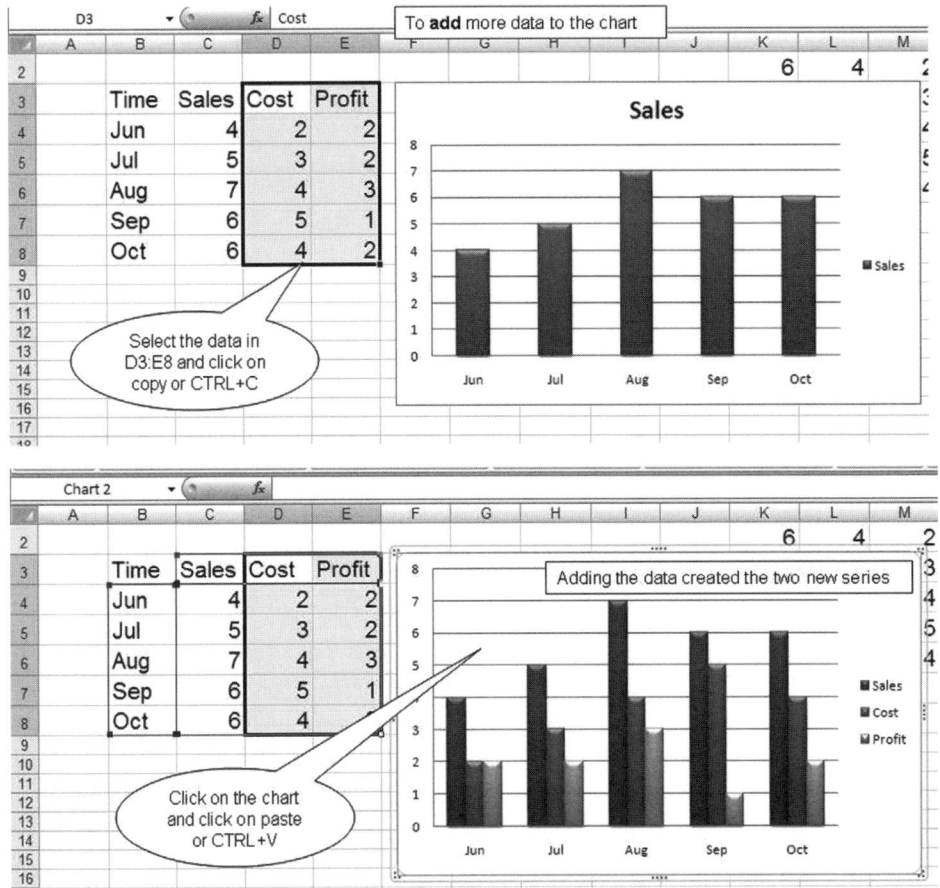

Figure 5.10   Adding data to a chart

More about Charts

Chart creation in Excel is a powerful tool with many possibilities. I chose to demonstrate only a few charts that are frequently used in the business world. I will discuss the difference between a line chart and a scatter chart. I will also demonstrate the use of three-dimensional charts.

Scatter Charts and Line Charts   Scatter charts and line charts are very similar especially when you create a scatter chart with lines connecting the points—these charts look and feel like a line chart. However, there is a fundamental difference between them.

Scatter charts are used to display and compare numeric values, such as statistical data. These charts are helpful to show the relationships among the numeric values of several data series. You can plot two groups of numbers as one series of XY coordinates.

Line charts are used to display continuous data over time against a common scale. They are good for showing trends in data at equal intervals. In line charts categorical data is

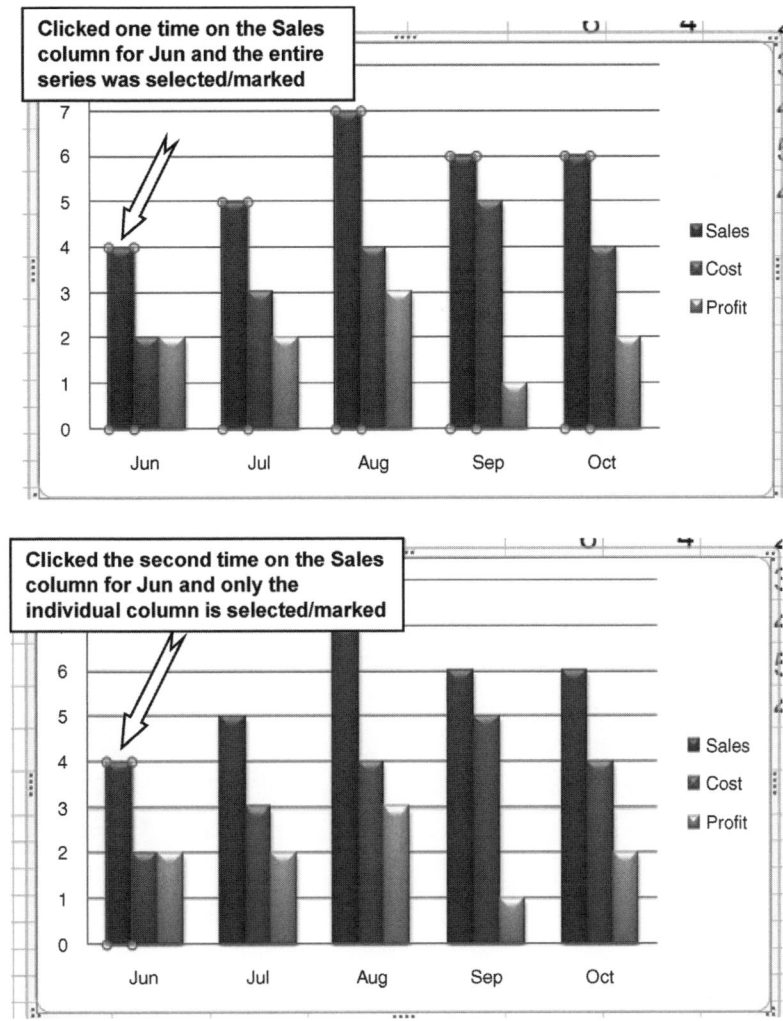

Figure 5.11 Select a series or a single data point

distributed evenly along the horizontal X-axis, and values are distributed evenly along the Y axis.

Choose between the two options using this rule: use line charts if the data has non-numeric X values—and use scatter charts for numeric X values. The following example will clarify the fundamental difference.

On the sheet named *Line vs. Scatter* of the Excel Chapter 5 file, I selected sales data from 1990 to 2008. I created a line chart and a scatter chart for the same data. The line chart in Figure 5.14 distorts the data since the years, on the X-axis, are not displayed proportionally. Look at the X-axis values: the years' labels are spaced evenly, even though the data (the difference between the periods) is unequal. They are not spaced proportionately.

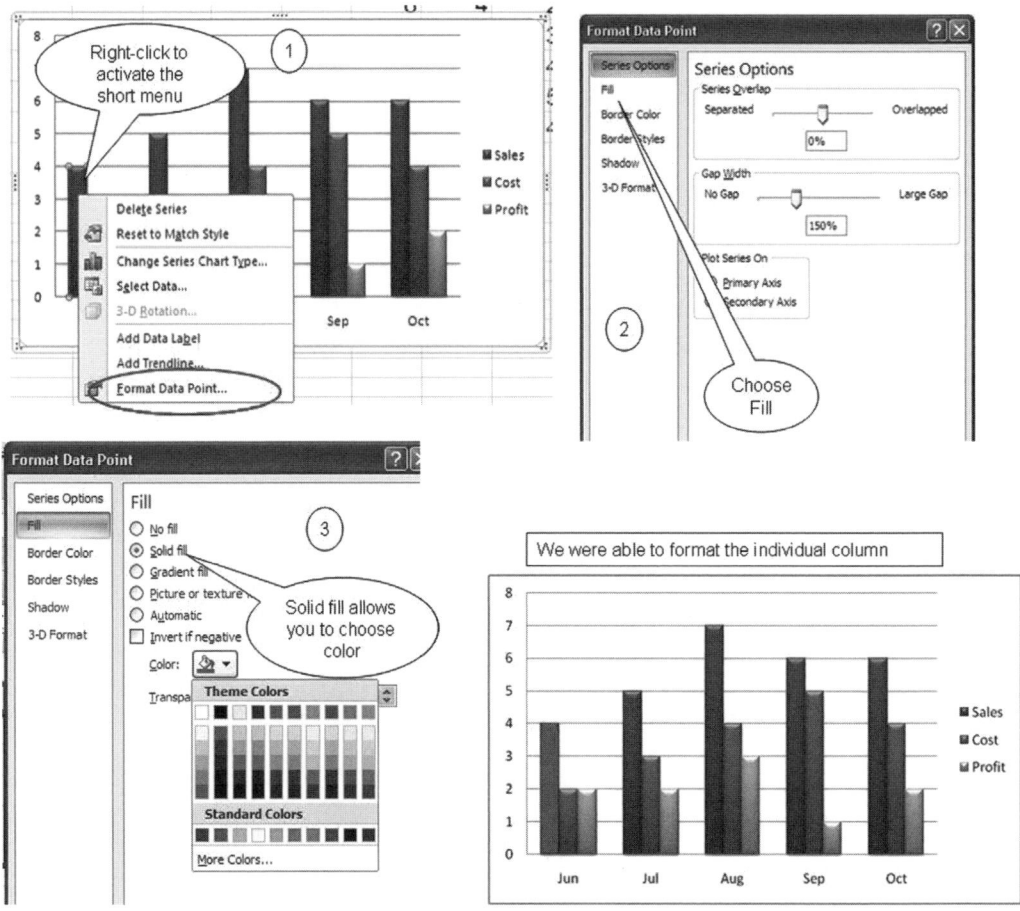

Figure 5.12   Format chart menus

The scatter chart, shown in Figure 5.15, tells a different (in this case, more accurate) story. You can see the real picture—underscoring the difference between the line chart and the scatter chart. The latter displays the data as it should, since the X-axis data is not continuous in our example.

Three-Dimensional Charts—Column and Pie

Returning to the data used to create the first chart on the sheet *Simple Chart,* I will create a three-dimensional column chart, as well as a pie chart. The first example, a 3-D column chart, is shown in Figure 5.16. The figure shows the steps to create and move the chart to a new sheet.

Excel labels this chart as "Clustered column with a 3-D visual effect."

Once you have created the column 3-D chart, you may format it for your presentation. Right-click on an empty area in the chart and choose the 3-D Rotation. The menu enables you to rotate and change the way the chart looks. See Figure 5.17.

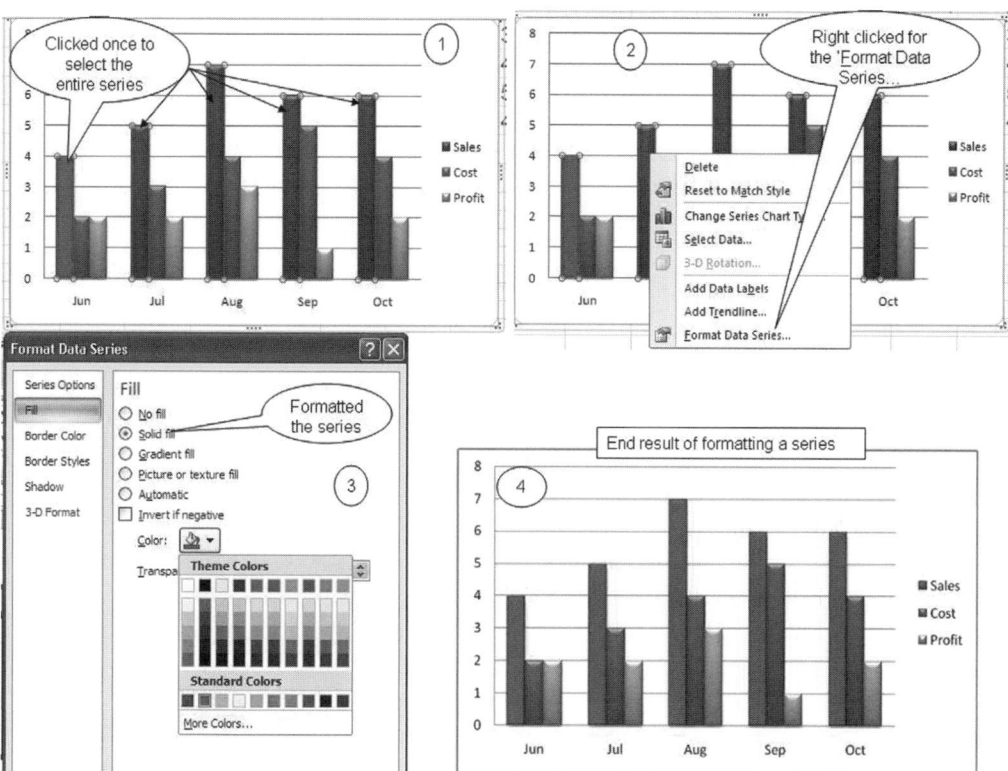

Figure 5.13 Formatting a series

Figure 5.14 Using a line chart distorts the results if the data is not continuous on the X-axis

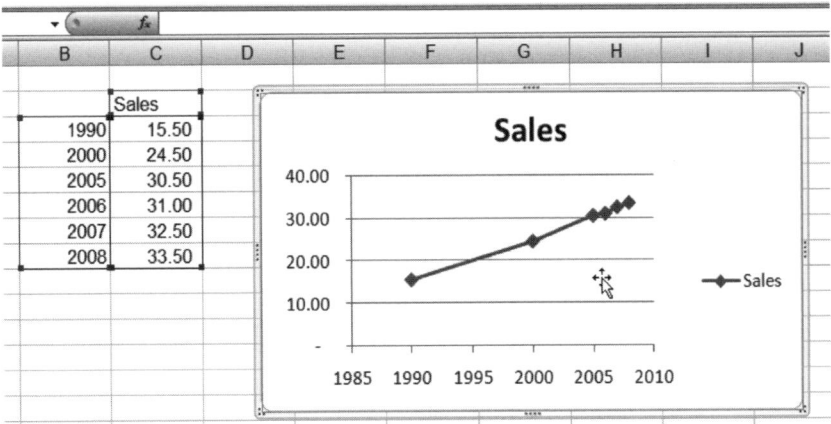

Figure 5.15   The scatter chart is more accurate for this data

The chart can be formatted to send a clearer message to your audience. There are many different formatting possibilities and options. Here is one example where I want to compare apples and bananas. I will use the same type of chart just created, however, you can apply this formatting technique to any chart type. We can copy and paste the pictures in a

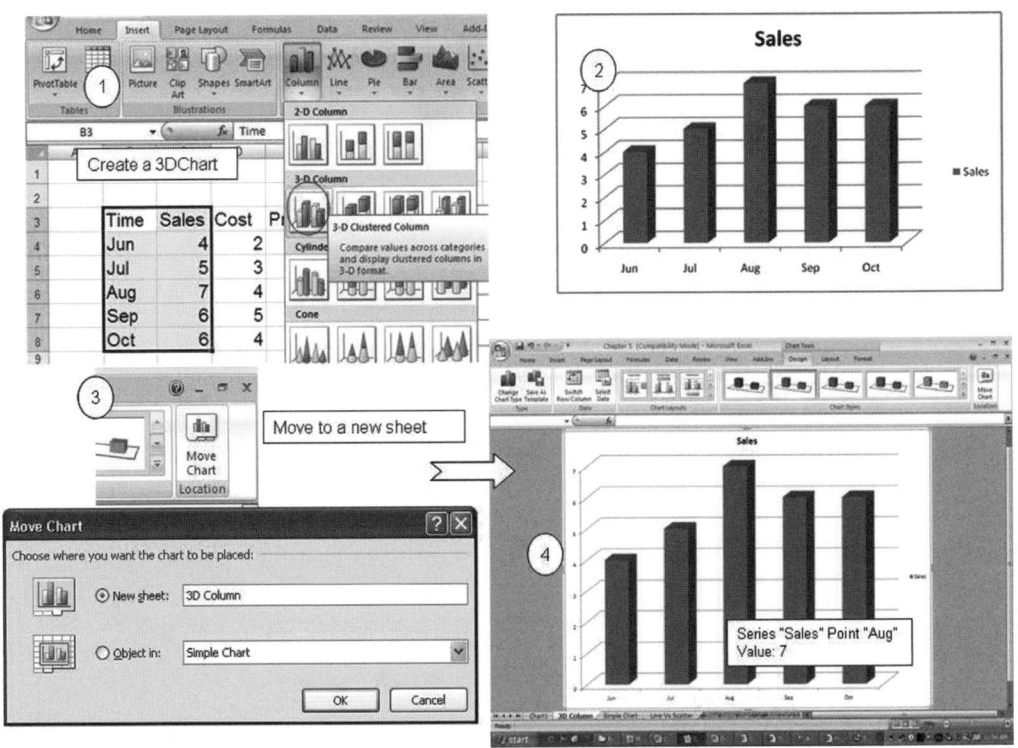

Figure 5.16   Create and move a chart to a new sheet

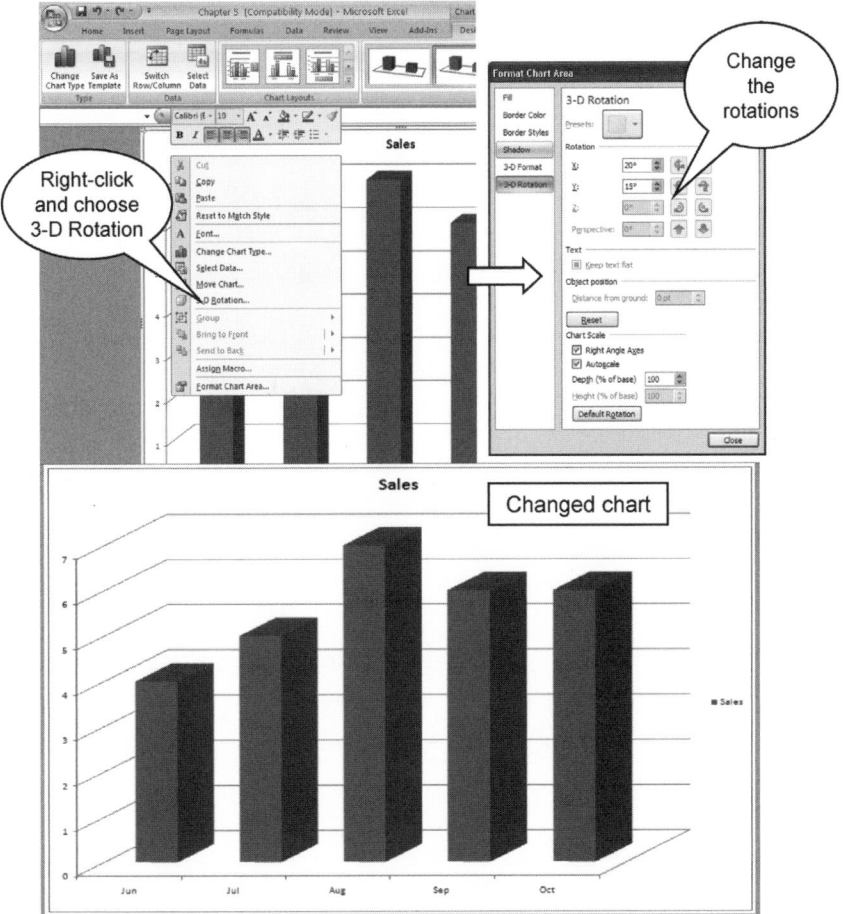

Figure 5.17 The 3-D View menu

spreadsheet in order to use them in the chart. See the spreadsheet with the data and pictures in Figure 5.18. I will create a 3-D clustered column chart, and will use the pictures selected to obtain a stronger visual effect for this chart.

The chart in Figure 5.19 was created with the sales data on the sheet *Apples and Bananas*.

We will use the pictures in Figure 5.18 to "dress" this chart.

To enter the apple picture as the Apples data point, I had to select the individual column in the chart. I clicked the first time to select the series and then clicked again on the Apples column to select the individual column. I reverted to the sheet with the pictures, and selected and copied the picture of the apple.

After the apple image was copied, I went back to the sheet with my chart, clicked on the Apples column and clicked on the paste icon. The result is in Figure 5.20.

I wanted the picture stacked to scale. To do so, I right-clicked on the column and chose the Format Data Point to create the desired effect.

Figure 5.18   Pictures to be used in charts

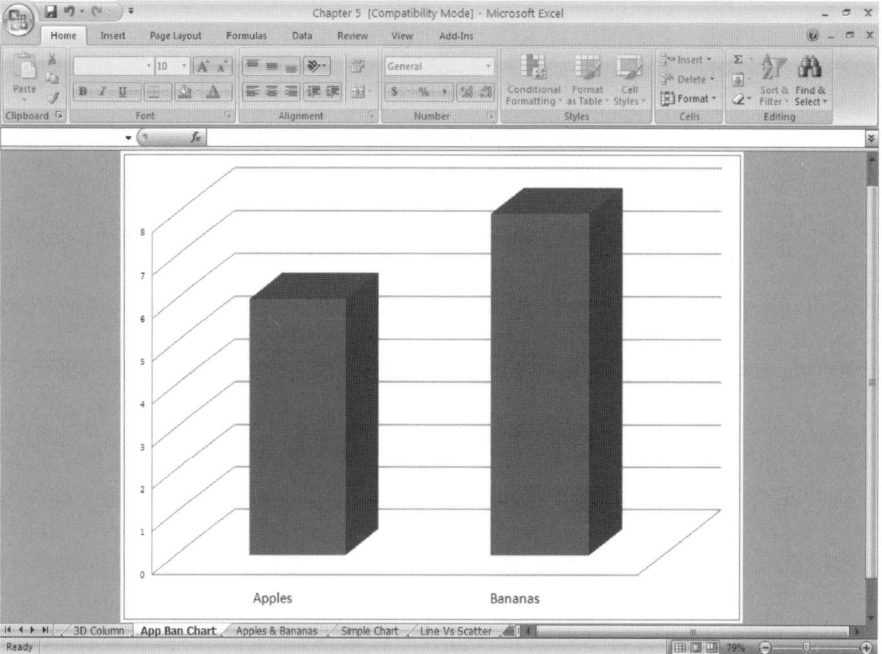

Figure 5.19   3-D column chart for sales results

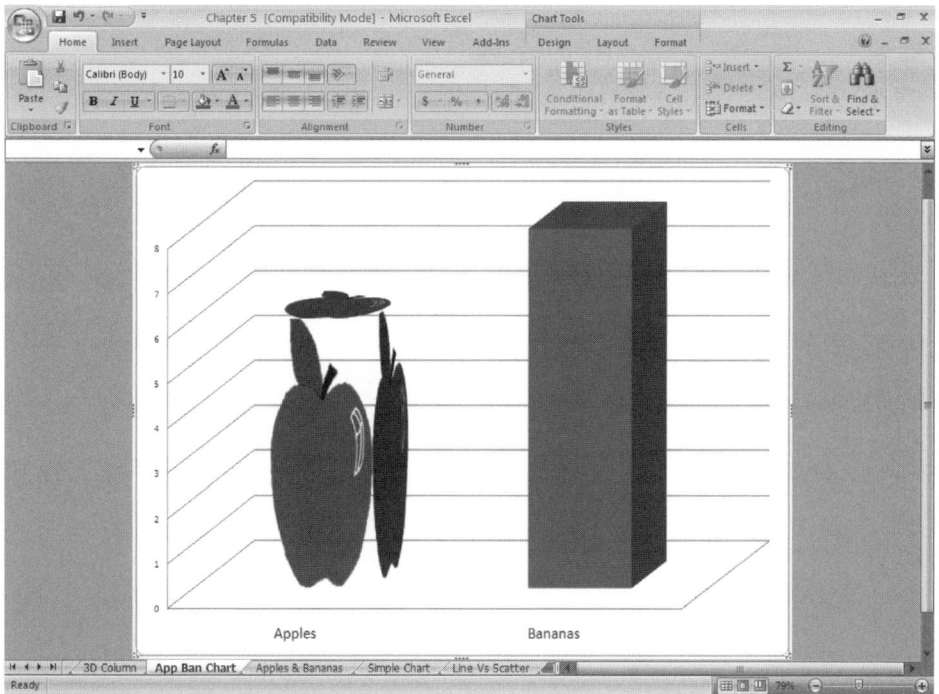

Figure 5.20 Paste the picture on the column

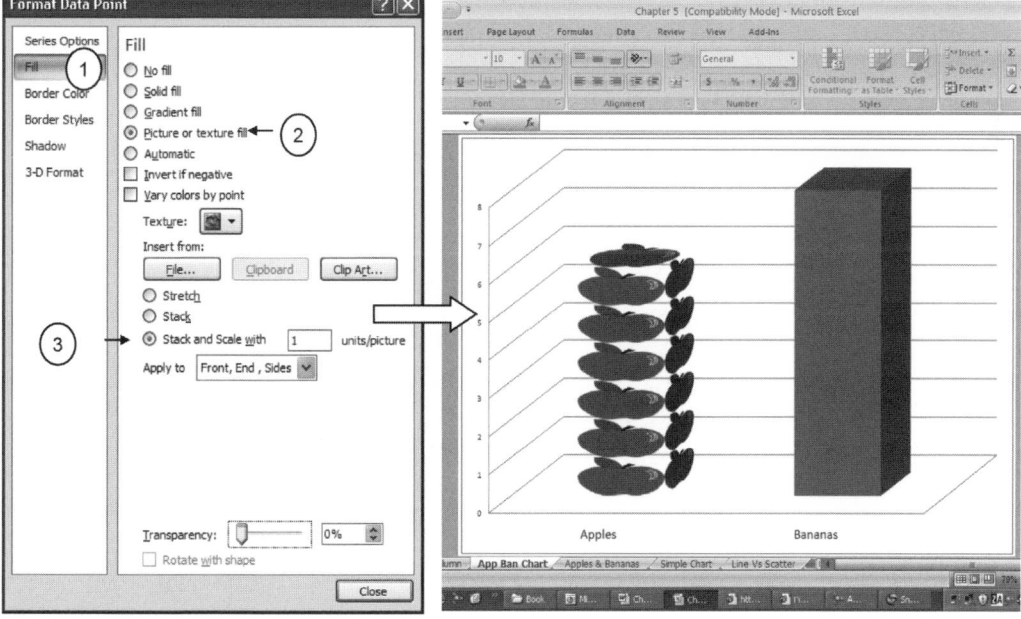

Figure 5.21 Stacking the picture

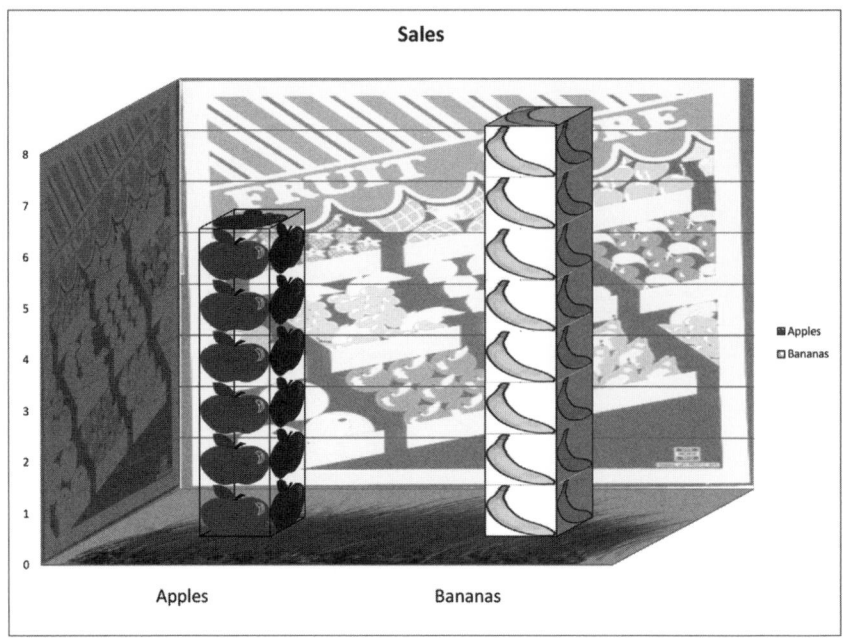

Figure 5.22 Complete chart

The Format Data Point menu allowed me to choose stacking the picture as shown in Figure 5.21 (Fill: Picture or texture fill, Stack and Scale).

What is left now is to copy and paste the picture of the banana to the second column (format it to be stacked to scale), copy the fruit store picture and paste it on the wall using the Paste icon, and copy the grass picture and paste it on the floor using the Paste icon. See the result in Figure 5.22.

Figure 5.23 Creating a 3-D pie chart

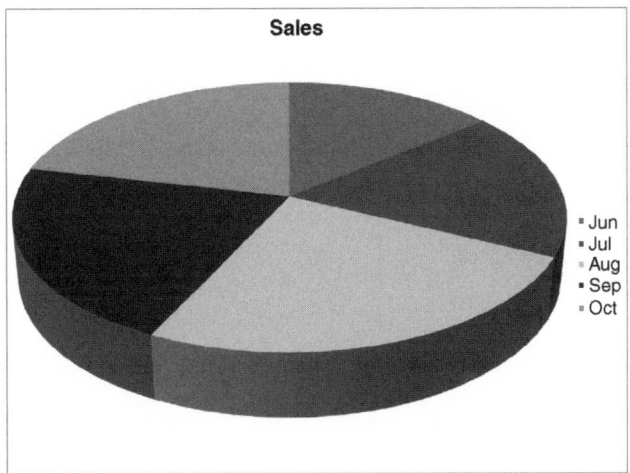

Figure 5.24   3-D pie chart

Pie Charts

To create a simple pie chart, select the data and proceed with the steps of the Chart Wizard as shown in Figure 5.23.

I right-clicked on the chart and moved it to a new sheet. The resulting chart is in Figure 5.24.

The pie chart—as all the other Excel charts created from a series—can be selected using the same rule we used before: **the first click selects the entire series—second click, the individual data point.** In the example of Figure 5.24, I clicked the first time on the blue data point representing June sales. I clicked on it a second time—so as to select the individual data point. I was then able to drag it out to put more emphasis on the June sales for my presentation. See Figure 5.25.

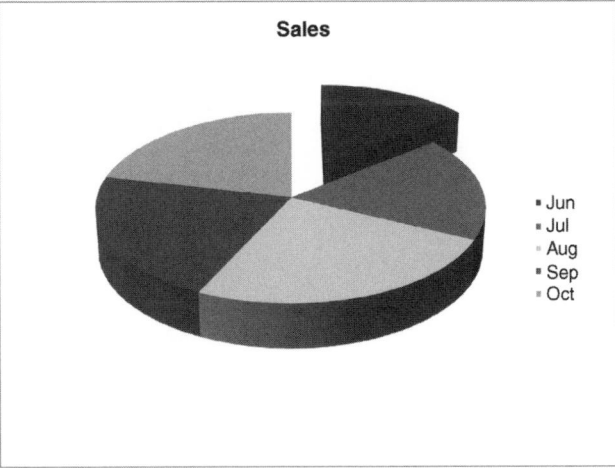

Figure 5.25   Moving out one part of the chart

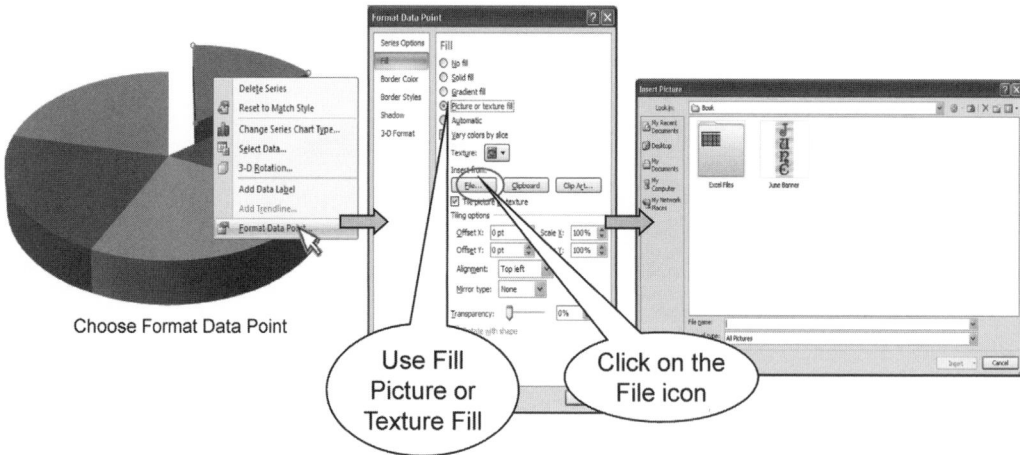

Choose Format Data Point

Use Fill Picture or Texture Fill

Click on the File icon

Figure 5.26   Formatting a pie chart

Try again the other options Excel provides for charts. Right-click and use the 3-D rotations.

To enter pictures into a pie wedge, right-click on the data point (June in our example). Choose Format Data Point and use Fill ⇒ Picture or Texture Fill. Click on the File icon and select a picture. See Figure 5.26.

The resulting chart is shown in Figure 5.27. With the pie chart, you cannot copy and paste pictures as you did with the other charts. With pie charts, you have to "insert" pictures.

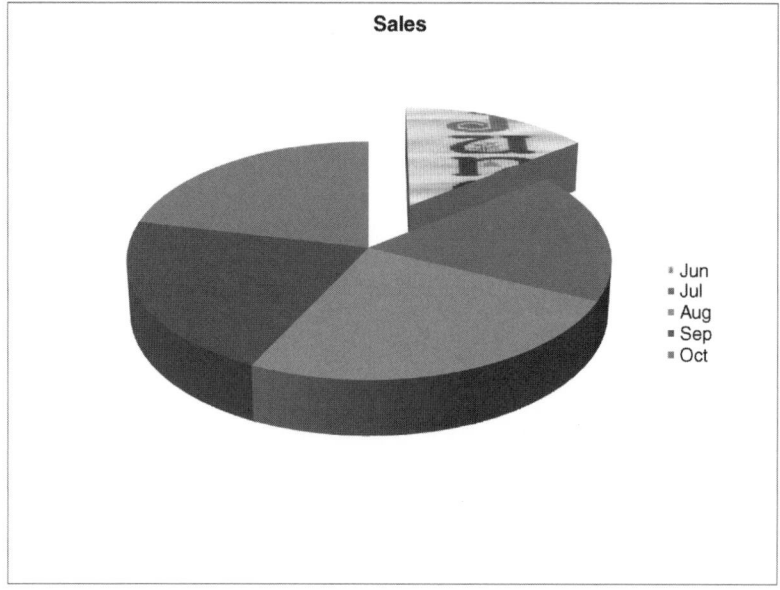

Figure 5.27   Pie chart with a picture

APPENDIX—GENERATING CHARTS IN EXCEL 2003

Creating a Chart Using the Wizard

Using the Chart Wizard (or alternatively the Insert menu ⇒ Chart) you may create a variety of charts. We will start with simple charts.

The easiest way to create a chart is by arranging your data in the way that Excel expects it; namely, try to position the data or names you want on the X-axis (the horizontal axis) on the leftmost column of the chart reference data. You may arrange it in different ways—but you will have to go through additional steps to create the chart you desire.

Using the same data from the previous example (Figure 5.23), create a column chart using the first and second columns data only. Select the first two columns and click on the Chart Wizard. See Figure 5.28. The data is on the *Simple Chart* sheet of the Excel file Chapter 5.

Select the very first chart type that pops up and proceed by clicking the Next button on the menu. On the left part of Figure 5.29 appears the menu that lets you change the data on the chart.

When you click the Next button in the chart window, you get to specify many of the features of the chart. If you ignore or forget any of the steps, you will still be able to access these formatting options when the chart is already completed.

The window under the Titles tab allows you to enter the labels for the chart header as well as the names for the X and Y axes. See Figure 5.30. The Axes and Gridlines menus allow you to specify their attributes.

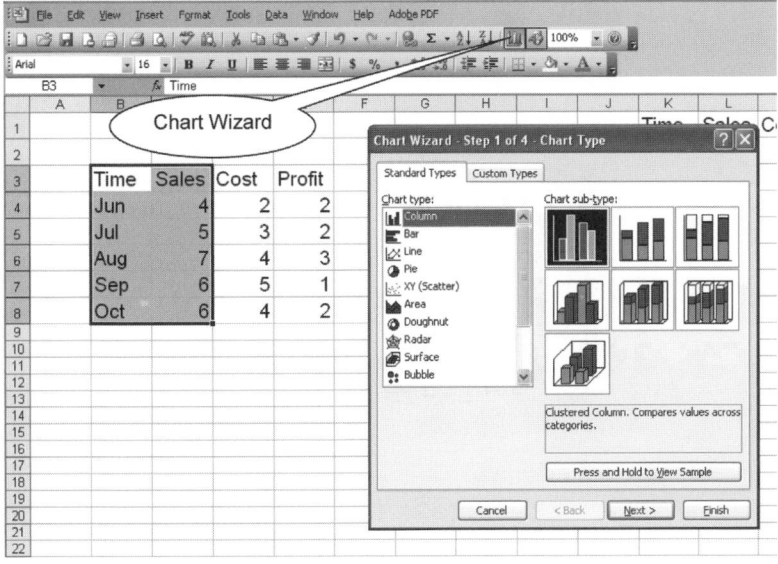

Figure 5.28   Chart Wizard

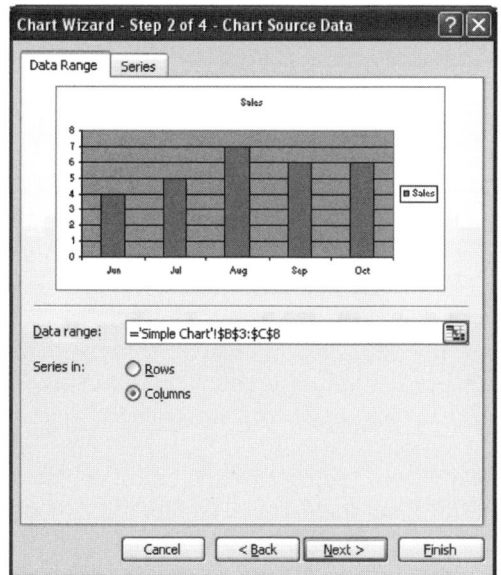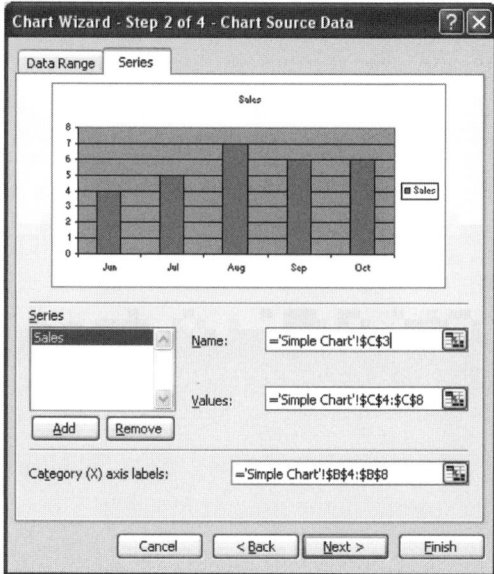

Figure 5.29   The Chart menus

In Figure 5.31 you see the other options available from the Chart Wizard tabs. The legend tab allows you to specify whether you want a legend and if so, where you would like to position it on the chart. The default position is on the right.

The Data Labels menu allows showing the values, the series, and/or category names on the chart. With the Data Table checked you will have the complete data of this chart shown under the chart itself.

The last step in creating the chart is to specify the location of the chart. I chose here "As object in" in the same sheet; you also have the option to place the chart "As new sheet" in the active workbook. See Figure 5.32.

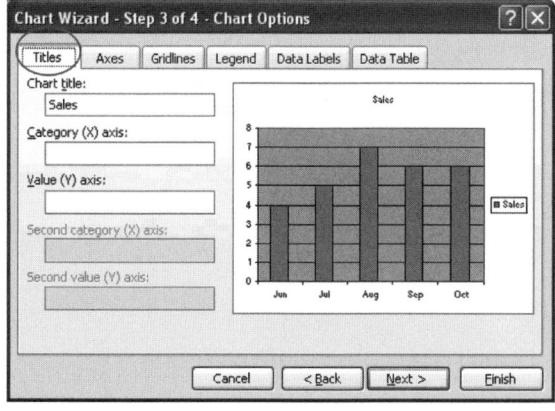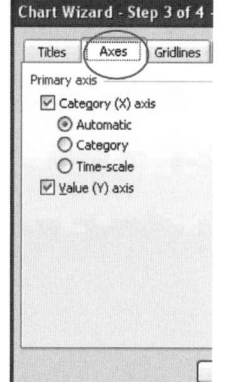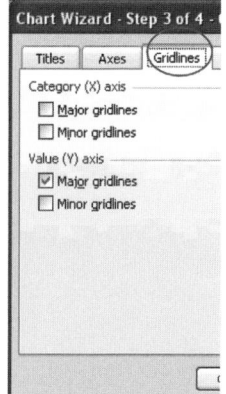

Figure 5.30   Chart features

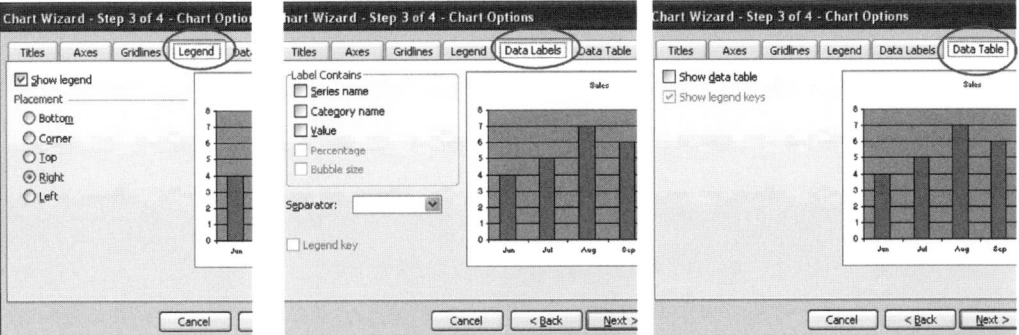

Figure 5.31   Chart options

The end result is illustrated in Figure 5.33.

If at some time in the future, you wish to change any of the chart features or change the chart's location, you may do so by right-clicking on an empty space on the chart. See Figure 5.34. A local menu allows you to choose your preferences. You may change the chart type, add or delete data within the source Data, or bring back the Chart Options for the different attributes shown in the previous figures.

For this chart, we used the months in the first column for the time on the X-axis and the sales information of the second data column for the Y values of the chart. If you wish to **add** the rest of the data to the chart, the cost and profit columns, proceed using the following steps:

1. Select the data D3:E9, click the Copy icon (or CTRL+C).
2. Click anywhere on the chart and then click the Paste icon (or CTRL+V).

The data will be added to the chart. See Figure 5.35.

Alternatively, it is possible (after data selection) to use the mouse and drag the data into the chart. The data will be added to the chart.

All charts in Excel have some common characteristics. All data series (in our example, the sets of columns) can be marked the same way. If you click on a column once, all the columns in the series will be marked. For example, all of the sales will be marked if you click one of the sales columns. If you click on the same column a second time, it only marks that individual column.

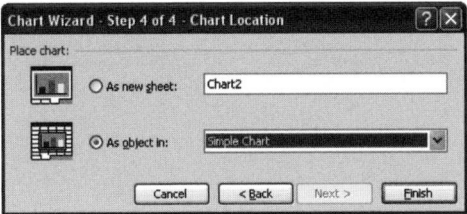

Figure 5.32   Chart Location options

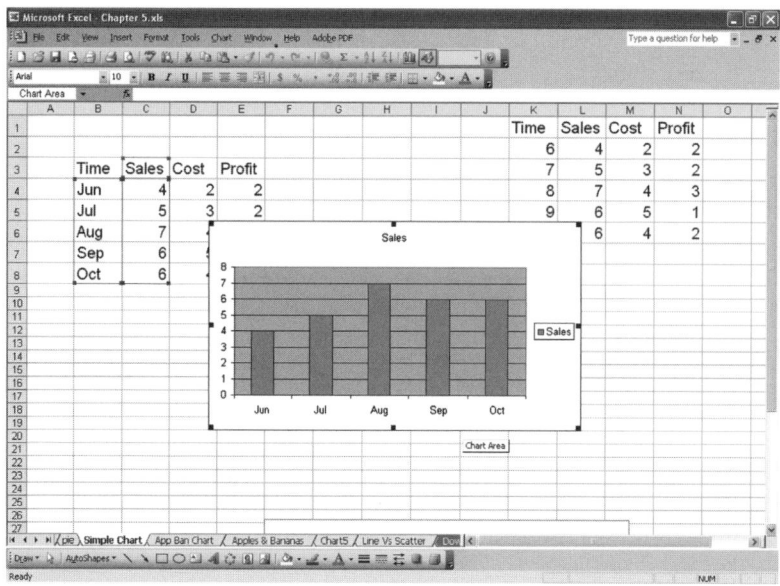

Figure 5.33 Finished chart

Use the rule: First click marks all of the points (columns) in a series—the second click marks the individual point (or a single column).

See Figure 5.36. Marking a series this way (first click for all the points and second click for the individual column) works in all charts in Excel.

If you right-click after all of the points are marked, you can format the entire series (in the local menu use Format Data Series). If an individual column is marked (second click) you

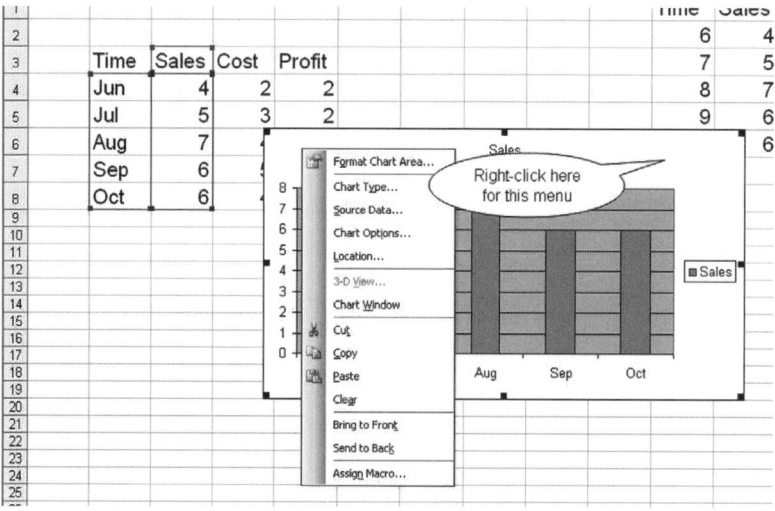

Figure 5.34 The Chart menu

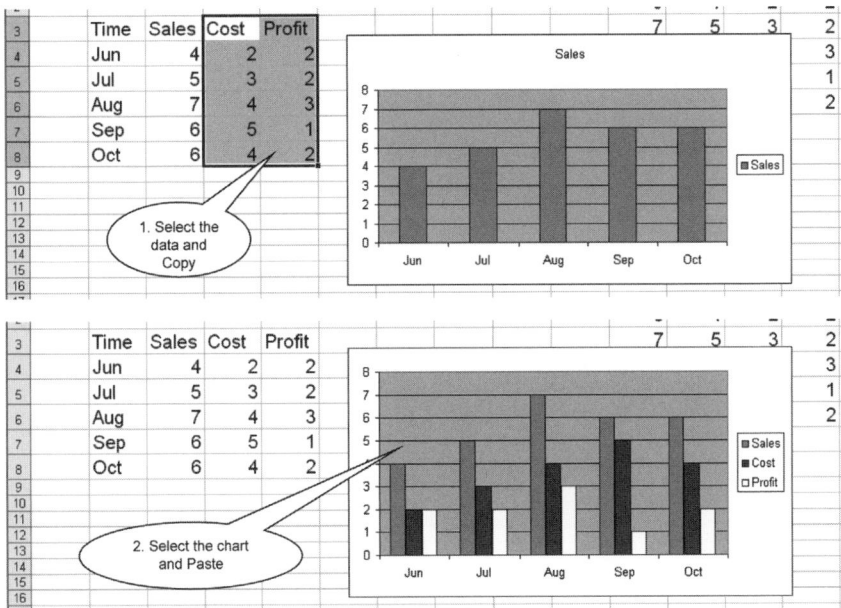

Figure 5.35 Adding data to a chart

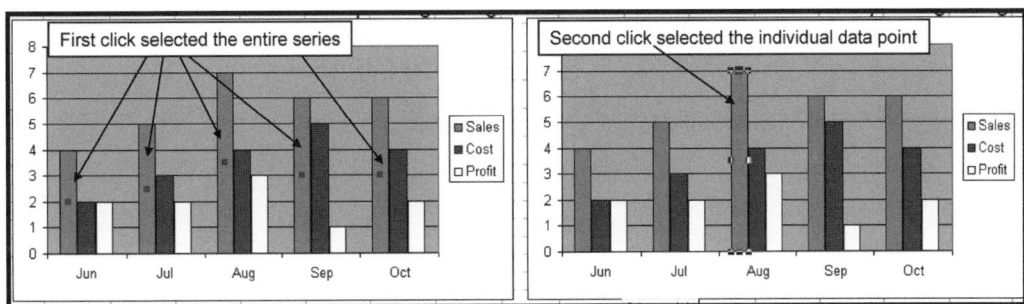

Figure 5.36 Selecting a series or a data point

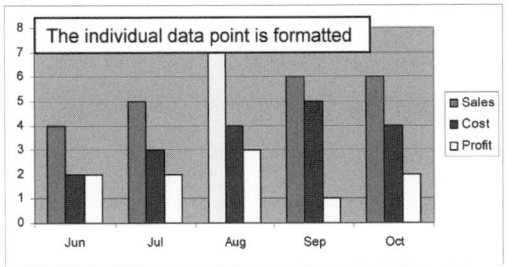

Figure 5.37 Data series vs. data point formatting

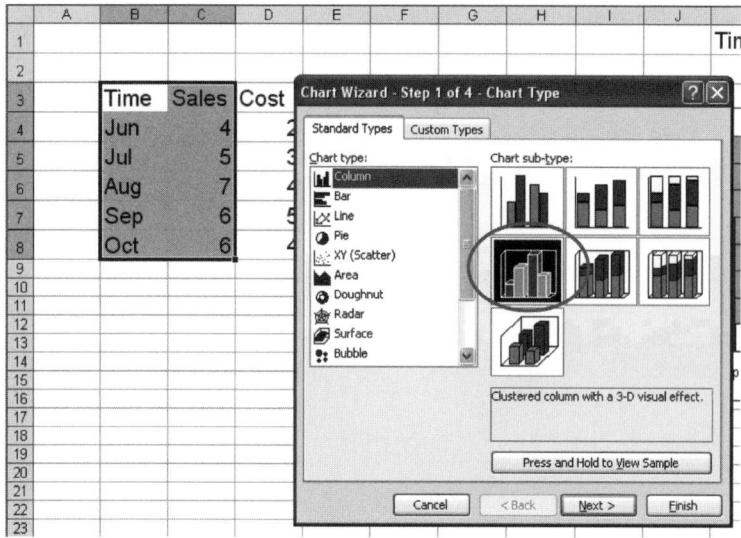

Figure 5.38 3-D column chart

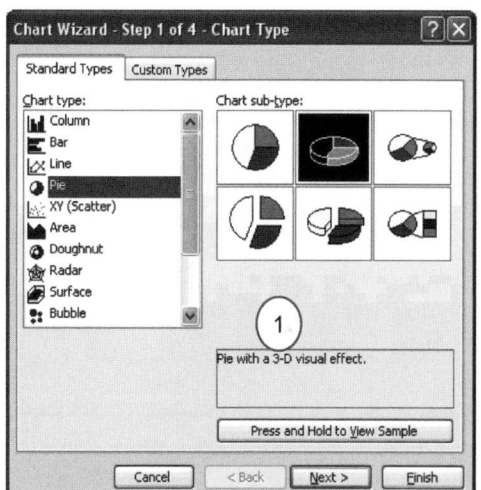

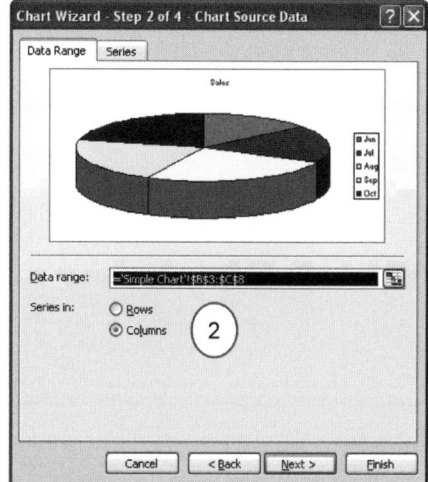

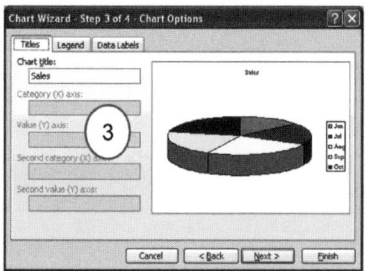

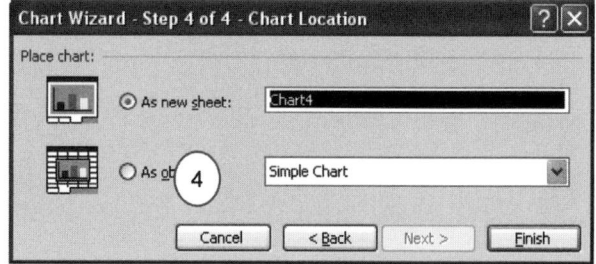

Figure 5.39 Pie Chart Wizard. Steps to create a chart

can format the individual column by itself (in the local menu use Format Data Point). See Figure 5.37.

More about the Chart Wizard

The Chart Wizard can be used for a variety of charts. This section illustrates a few of these options.

Three-Dimensional Charts—Column and Pie   Using the same data, we will create a three-dimensional column chart and a pie chart. A 3-D column chart is shown in Figure 5.38.

This chart is called "Clustered column with a 3-D visual effect." You may go back to the text in this chapter to find out how to paste pictures into the chart.

Pie Charts   To create a simple pie chart, select the data and proceed with the Chart Wizard steps as shown in Figure 5.39.

Given that you followed my steps—this chapter does not need review questions.

IF Functions and Text Manipulations

Part II covers two commonly needed skills: the use of the IF functions, which makes Excel a better tool for decision-making purposes, and the Text manipulation functions.

The IF function can be used when the information you want in a cell is conditional— IF you need to specify two (or more) different answers for a cell based on conditions you determine. For example, if the hourly rates are different for regular and overtime. Or if the commission rates are lower for less than $10,000, are higher for over $10,000, and are much higher for sales over $30,000. The IF function is similar to the statements you may see with software programming. It is similar to the steps you would take when using a computer programming language without coding.

Text manipulation in Excel has some powerful tools. The first section in that part will demonstrate how to separate data confined in a single column—spreading it into a number of columns. Data acquired from different sources may come as a text file—or may be separated with spaces, commas, or other delimiters. You will learn how to separate the data into columns.

CHAPTER 6

IF Functions

SIMPLE IF FUNCTIONS

The IF function is a frequently used function. When decision makers and analysts are looking for an optimal solution to a given problem, they often need to take into account complex models. The IF function allows the decision makers to consider more than one alternative.

The simplest IF function in Excel answers first the question: "Is a condition true or false?" and then the software proceeds to take action based on the answer. The IF function has three parts/arguments:

- Logical test—what are we asking? Or what is the question?
- Value if true—what do we want displayed if the answer to our question is "true?"
- Value if false—what do we want displayed if the answer is "false?"

The syntax or the structure of the IF function is as follows: =IF(logical test, value if true, value if false). Within the parentheses, you create the three parts/arguments separated by a comma (,).

Or in simpler terms:

=IF (condition, action or value if condition true, action or value if condition false).

Consider a simple example:

In Figure 6.1, I have two groups of numbers (1 and 2) and I want to point out the numbers in group 1 that are larger than the ones in group 2 in the same rows. I want to type "yes" when they are larger and "no" when they are not. I use the IF function to do so.

I inserted the IF function in cell C2:

=IF(A2>B2, "yes","no")

The IF function in cell C2 has three parts: The logical test is A2>B2. The value if it is true is "yes." The value if it is false is "no." See Figure 6.2.

For cell C2, the result should be "yes." See Figure 6.3.

For cell C3, the result should be "no"—since the value in A3 is equal to the value in B2—not greater. The rest of the results are shown in Figure 6.4. The left side of Figure 6.4 reveals all the formulas, using CTRL+ˋ (left apostrophe or accent mark earlier) or CTRL+~ (tilde). The right side shows the results.

In the next example in Figure 6.5, I show how to use the IF function to calculate regular time and overtime in a weekly payroll. The overtime rate is different than the regular working hours' rate. Employees' salaries are calculated the following way: IF an employee worked

C2 *fx*

	A	B	C
1	Group 1	Group 2	Test: Group 1 > Group2
2	6	5	
3	4	4	
4	3	6	
5	6	2	
6	5	5	
7	4	1	
8	3	2	

Figure 6.1 Using the IF functions for comparisons

MEDIAN *fx* =IF(A2>B2,"yes","no")

	A	B	C	D
1	Group 1	Group 2	Test: Group 1 > Group2	
2	6	5	=IF(A2>B2,"yes","no")	
3	4	4	IF(logical_test, [value_if_true], [value_if_false])	
4	3	6		
5	6	2		
6	5	5		
7	4	1		
8	3	2		

Figure 6.2 The IF function

C2 *fx* =IF(A2>B2,"yes","no")

	A	B	C
1	Group 1	Group 2	Test: Group 1 > Group2
2	6	5	yes
3	4	4	
4	3	6	
5	6	2	
6	5	5	
7	4	1	
8	3	2	

Figure 6.3 The group 1 number is larger than the group 2 number

	A	B	C
1	Group 1	Group 2	Test: Group 1 > Group2
2	6	5	=IF(A2>B2,"yes","no")
3	4	4	=IF(A3>B3,"yes","no")
4	3	6	=IF(A4>B4,"yes","no")
5	6	2	=IF(A5>B5,"yes","no")
6	5	5	=IF(A6>B6,"yes","no")
7	4	1	=IF(A7>B7,"yes","no")
8	3	2	=IF(A8>B8,"yes","no")

	A	B	C
1	Group 1	Group 2	Test: Group 1 > Group2
2	6	5	yes
3	4	4	no
4	3	6	no
5	6	2	yes
6	5	5	no
7	4	1	yes
8	3	2	yes

Figure 6.4 The IF functions and the results

Figure 6.5 Using the IF function to calculate overtime

up to 40 hours a week, the salary = **Rate** × **Hours worked**, otherwise I calculate his salary for the first 40 hours to be **Rate** × **40,** plus one and half times the rate (Rate × 1.5) for the hours worked over 40 (Hours worked > 40).

In cell E3 I have the following function:
=**IF(D3<=40,C3*D3,40*C3+(D3-40)*1.5*C3)**

The IF function in cell E3 has three parts:
- The logical test is **D3<=40**: Regular time only?
- The value if true: **C3*D3**: Regular time only. Rate × Hours worked.
- The value if false: **40*C3+(D3-40)*1.5*C3**. 40 × Rate + Overtime × 1.5 × Rate.

See Figure 6.6.

To activate a function, you can use the Excel Functions menu, the fx icon, or the Shift+F3 shortcut. Select the functions menu (click fx or Shift+F3). Select Logical and choose IF. See Figure 6.7.

Figure 6.8 shows the result on the left. When you double-click the drag handle, the function is automatically dragged down (copied) all the way to the end of the adjacent column, as shown on the right side of Figure 6.8.

Figure 6.9 reveals all the formulas, using CTRL+` or CTRL+~.

Figure 6.6 The IF function for overtime

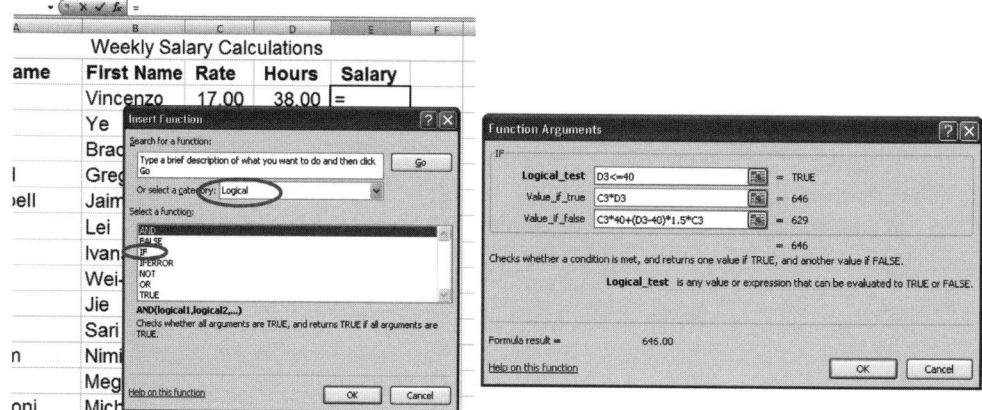

Figure 6.7   The IF Function menu

	Last Name	First Name	Rate	Hours	Salary
2	**Last Name**	**First Name**	**Rate**	**Hours**	**Salary**
3	Alfano	Vincenzo	17.00	38.00	646.00
4	Bai	Ye	12.00	45.00	
5	Barile	Brad	11.00	49.00	
6	Bedard	Greg	11.		
7	Campbell	Jaime	12		
8	Cao	Lei	11.00		
9	Capra	Ivana	13.00	32.00	
10	Chen	Wei-Ta	10.00	64.00	
11	Chen	Jie	18.00	33.00	
12	Cohen	Sari	15.00	31.00	
13	Dharam	Nimisha	17.00	30.00	
14	Fidler	Megan	16.00	32.00	
15	Ghanooni	Michael	12.00	38.00	

E3   fx =IF(D3<=40,C3*D3,C3*40+(D3-40)*1.5*C3)

Double-click here

	Last Name	First Name	Rate	Hours	Salary
1		Weekly Salary Calculations			
2	**Last Name**	**First Name**	**Rate**	**Hours**	**Salary**
3	Alfano	Vincenzo	17.00	38.00	646.00
4	Bai	Ye	12.00	45.00	570.00
5	Barile	Brad	11.00	49.00	588.50
6	Bedard	Greg	11.00	62.00	803.00
7	Campbell	Jaime	12.00	41.00	498.00
8	Cao	Lei	11.00	39.00	429.00
9	Capra	Ivana	13.00	32.00	416.00
10	Chen	Wei-Ta	10.00	64.00	760.00
11	Chen	Jie	18.00	33.00	594.00
12	Cohen	Sari	15.00	31.00	465.00
13	Dharam	Nimisha	17.00	30.00	510.00
14	Fidler	Megan	16.00	32.00	512.00
15	Ghanooni	Michael	12.00	38.00	456.00

G14

Figure 6.8   Double-click to duplicate results

	Last Name	First Name	Rate	Hours	Salary
1					Weekly Salary Calculations
2	**Last Name**	**First Name**	**Rate**	**Hours**	**Salary**
3	Alfano	Vincenzo	17	38	=IF(D3<=40,C3*D3,C3*40+(D3-40)*1.5*C3)
4	Bai	Ye	12	45	=IF(D4<=40,C4*D4,C4*40+(D4-40)*1.5*C4)
5	Barile	Brad	11	49	=IF(D5<=40,C5*D5,C5*40+(D5-40)*1.5*C5)
6	Bedard	Greg	11	62	=IF(D6<=40,C6*D6,C6*40+(D6-40)*1.5*C6)
7	Campbell	Jaime	12	41	=IF(D7<=40,C7*D7,C7*40+(D7-40)*1.5*C7)
8	Cao	Lei	11	39	=IF(D8<=40,C8*D8,C8*40+(D8-40)*1.5*C8)
9	Capra	Ivana	13	32	=IF(D9<=40,C9*D9,C9*40+(D9-40)*1.5*C9)
10	Chen	Wei-Ta	10	64	=IF(D10<=40,C10*D10,C10*40+(D10-40)*1.5*C10)
11	Chen	Jie	18	33	=IF(D11<=40,C11*D11,C11*40+(D11-40)*1.5*C11)
12	Cohen	Sari	15	31	=IF(D12<=40,C12*D12,C12*40+(D12-40)*1.5*C12)
13	Dharam	Nimisha	17	30	=IF(D13<=40,C13*D13,C13*40+(D13-40)*1.5*C13)
14	Fidler	Megan	16	32	=IF(D14<=40,C14*D14,C14*40+(D14-40)*1.5*C14)
15	Ghanooni	Michael	12	38	=IF(D15<=40,C15*D15,C15*40+(D15-40)*1.5*C15)

Figure 6.9   The actual IF functions' formulas revealed

Nested IF Functions

In many cases, you will need to have more than the two choices offered with the simple IF function. For example, if you want to enter letter grades for students depending on their achievement on a test: A for 90 and up, B for 80 and up, C for 70 and up, and D for 60 and up. Otherwise, they fail and receive an F. See Figure 6.10.

	A	B	C	D	E	F	G	H
1	Last Name	First Name	Final	Letter Grade				
2	Alfano	Vincenzo	84			<	60	F
3	Bai	Ye	66			≥	60	D
4	Barile	Brad	81			≥	70	C
5	Bedard	Greg	68			≥	80	B
6	Campbell	Jaime	87			≥	90	A

Figure 6.10   The need for nested IF functions—more than one decision

Here are the details of that request:

- IF C2 contains a value of 90 or more, then you want to have an A in D2.
- IF C2 is between 80 and 89, then you want a B in D2.
- IF C2 is between 70 and 79, then you want a C in D2.
- IF C2 is between 60 and 69, then you want a D in D2.
- IF C2 is less than C, then put an F in D2.

To do so, you have to enter the following formula in cell B1:
=IF(C2>=90,"A",IF(C2>=80,"B",IF(C2>=70,"C",IF(C2>=60,"D","F"))))
Figure 6.11 and Figure 6.12 show the results.

Nested IF—Payroll Example

Using the same payroll example, I can extend it to have a nested IF function as follows: IF an employee worked up to 40 hours, I will pay him the regular rate, IF he worked over 40 but less than 60, I will pay him 1 times for the overtime, IF he worked over 60 hours, I should

IF		=IF(C2>=90,"A",IF(C2>=80,"B",IF(C2>=70,"C",IF(C2>=60,"D","F"))))										
	A	B	C	D	E	F	G	H	I	J	K	L	M
1	Last Name	First Name	Final	Letter Grade								
2	Alfano	Vincenzo	84	=IF(C2>=90,"A",IF(C2>=80,"B",IF(C2>=70,"C",IF(C2>=60,"D","F"))))								
3	Bai	Ye	66									
4	Barile	Brad	81									

D2		=IF(C2>=90,"A",IF(C2>=80,"B",IF(C2>=70,"C",IF(C2>=60,"D","F"))))										
	A	B	C	D	E	F	G	H	I	J	K	L	M
1	Last Name	First Name	Final	Letter Grade								
2	Alfano	Vincenzo	84	B								
3	Bai	Ye	66									
4	Barile	Brad	81									

Figure 6.11   The nested IF formula

	A	B	C	D	E	F	G	H
1	**Last Name**	**First Name**	**Final**	**Letter Grade**				
2	Alfano	Vincenzo	84	B				
3	Bai	Ye	66	D				
4	Barile	Brad	81	B				
5	Bedard	Greg	68	D				
6	Campbell	Jaime	87	B				
7	Cao	Lei	70	C				
8	Capra	Ivana	86	B				
9	Chen	Wei-Ta	82	B		<	60	F
10	Chen	Jie	75	C		≥	60	D
11	Cohen	Sari	80	B		≥	70	C
12	Dharam	Nimisha	79	C		≥	80	B
13	Fidler	Megan	69	D		≥	90	A
14	Ghanooni	Michael	77	C				
15	Hobbie	Kelly	55	F				
16	Huang	Xiuhua	67	D				
		Irina	57	F				

Figure 6.12   Nest IF results

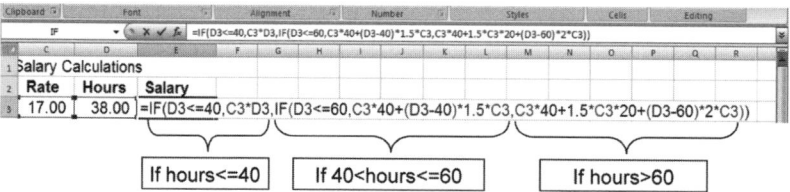

=IF(D3<=40,C3*D3,IF(D3<=60,C3*40+(D3-40)*1.5*C3,C3*40+1.5*C3*20+(D3-60)*2*C3))

	C	D	E	F	G	H	I	J	K	L	M	N	O	P	Q	R
1	Salary Calculations															
2	**Rate**	**Hours**	**Salary**													
3	17.00	38.00	=IF(D3<=40,C3*D3,IF(D3<=60,C3*40+(D3-40)*1.5*C3,C3*40+1.5*C3*20+(D3-60)*2*C3))												

If hours<=40	If 40<hours<=60	If hours>60

Figure 6.13   Nest IF with two decisions

pay him 1 times for the overtime for the hours between 40 and 60, BUT I will pay him 2 times the rate for the hour he worked over 60.

Figure 6.13 and 6.14 illustrate the above example. This example has two IF conditions:

	A	B	C	D	E
1		Weekly Salary Calculations			
2	**Last Name**	**First Name**	**Rate**	**Hours**	**Salary**
3	Alfano	Vincenzo	17.00	38.00	646.00
4	Bai	Ye	12.00	45.00	570.00
5	Barile	Brad	11.00	49.00	588.50
6	Bedard	Greg	11.00	62.00	814.00
7	Campbell	Jaime	12.00	41.00	498.00
8	Cao	Lei	11.00	39.00	429.00
9	Capra	Ivana	13.00	32.00	416.00
10	Chen	Wei-Ta	10.00	64.00	780.00
11	Chen	Jie	18.00	33.00	594.00
12	Cohen	Sari	15.00	31.00	465.00
13	Dharam	Nimisha	17.00	30.00	510.00
14	Fidler	Megan	16.00	32.00	512.00
15	Ghanooni	Michael	12.00	38.00	456.00

Figure 6.14   Nested IF results

REVIEW QUESTIONS

You will find these examples in the Excel Chapter 6 file:

1. On the sheet *Practice IF*, I have a table of salespeople's annual sales. Use an IF statement to calculate commissions for annual total sales with the following rates: $10,000 or less, commission is 5 percent and for anything over $10,000, commission is 7 percent.
2. On the same sheet and example, calculate using nested IF:

Sales	Commission
Below 5000	2.0 percent
Between 5000-15000	3.0 percent
Between 15000-25000	3.5 percent
Above 25000	4.0 percent

ANSWERS

1.

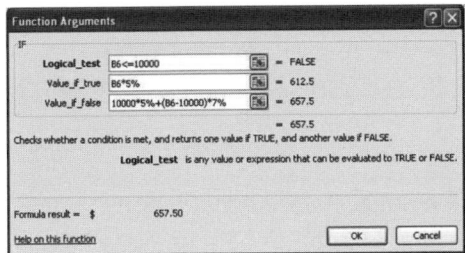

2. This is a nested IF:
      =IF(B6<=5000,B6*2%,IF(B6<=15000,5000*2%+(B6-5000)*3%,IF
   (B6<=25000,5000*2%+10000*3%+(B6-15000)*3.5%,5000*2%+10000*3%+
   10000*3.5%+(B6-25000)4%)))

CHAPTER 7

Text Manipulation

TEXT TO COLUMNS

When processing data from other sources, you may either get information where all the data is in one column or receive text files, which have the same problem. Upon opening the file, all the data is condensed in a single column. Excel has a feature that enables you to separate the data into individual columns. Look at the data on the sheet shown in Figure 7.1. The cells in column one contain all the information that should be spread out over a number of cells.

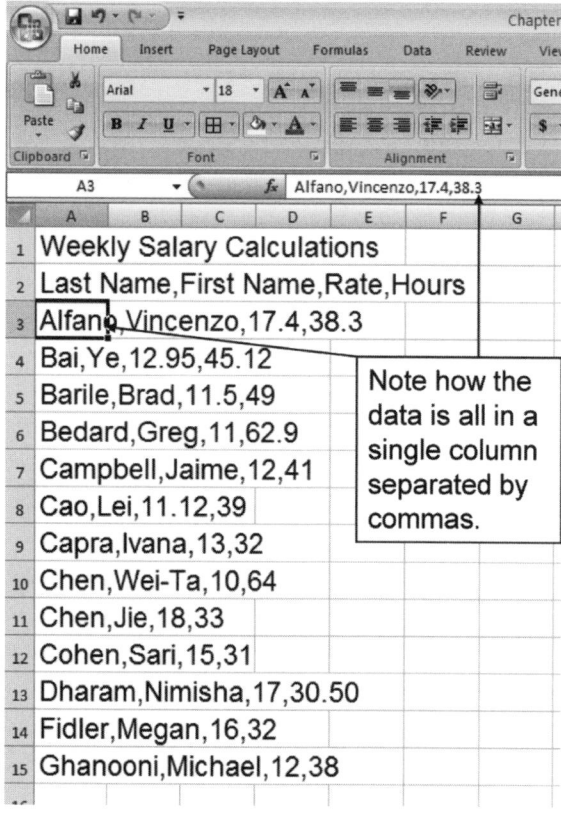

Figure 7.1   All the text is in one column

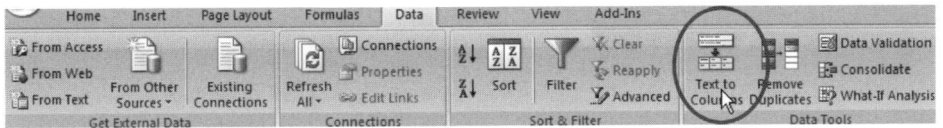

Figure 7.2 The Text to Column menu location on the Data ribbon

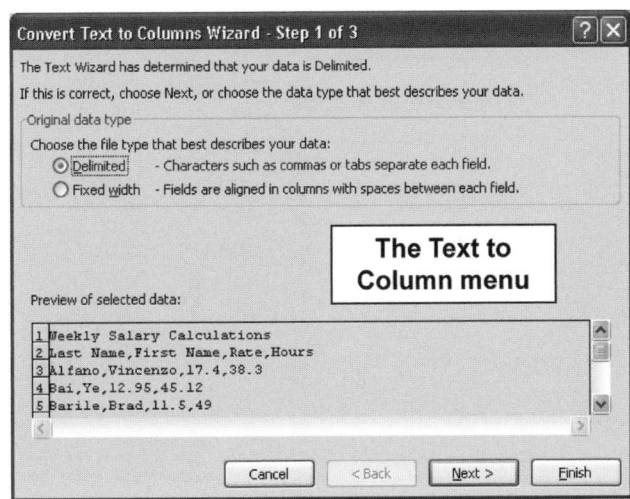

Figure 7.3 The Text to Column menu

You can see in the formula bar that all the information is the in cell A3: Alfano, Vincenzo,17.4,38.3. To correct this problem, you could use the command in the Data menu called Text to Column to reformat your data. Use the **Text to Column** feature to separate the data into individual columns. See Figure 7.2.

Note that the data, in the cell, is separated by commas. (Excel refers to data with a separator such as a comma as "delimited" data.) Separating the data into individual

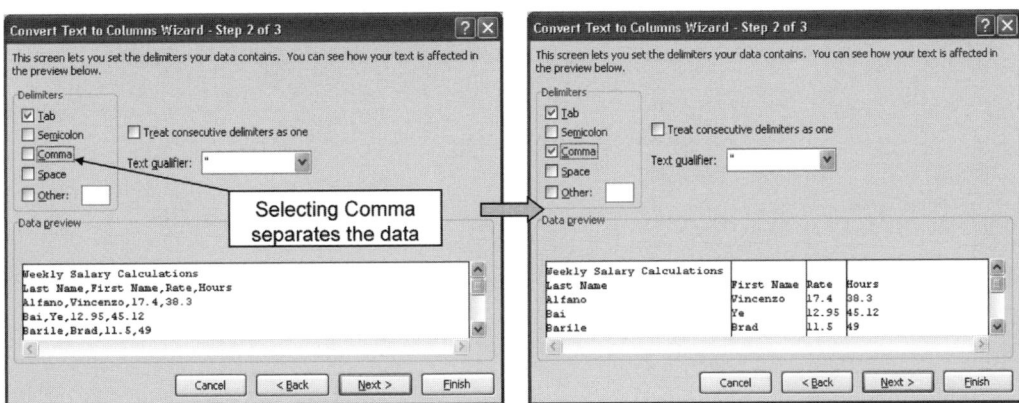

Figure 7.4 Use the Delimited option

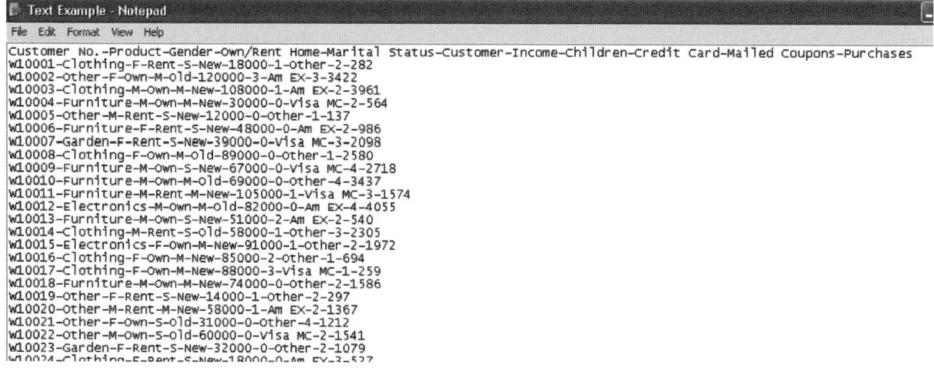

Figure 7.5 The data before and after

columns is done through the **Text to Column** menu. Select column A and activate the menu. See Figure 7.3.

The menu has two options, Delimited or Fixed width. Since this data is of assorted sizes and it is separated by commas, apply the Delimited option. See Figure 7.4.

Figure 7.5 shows the data before and after it was separated.

```
Text Example - Notepad
File  Edit  Format  View  Help
Customer No.-Product-Gender-Own/Rent Home-Marital status-Customer-Income-Children-Credit Card-Mailed Coupons-Purchases
W10001-Clothing-F-Rent-S-New-18000-1-Other-2-282
W10002-Other-F-Own-M-Old-120000-3-Am EX-3-3422
W10003-Clothing-M-Own-M-New-108000-1-Am EX-2-3961
W10004-Furniture-M-Own-M-New-30000-0-Visa MC-2-564
W10005-Other-M-Rent-M-New-12000-0-Other-1-137
W10006-Furniture-F-Rent-S-New-48000-0-Am EX-2-986
W10007-Garden-F-Rent-S-New-39000-0-Visa MC-3-2098
W10008-Clothing-F-Own-M-Old-89000-0-Other-1-2580
W10009-Furniture-M-Own-S-New-67000-0-Visa MC-4-2718
W10010-Furniture-M-Own-M-Old-69000-0-Other-4-3437
W10011-Furniture-M-Rent-M-New-105000-1-Visa MC-1-1574
W10012-Electronics-M-Own-M-Old-82000-0-Am EX-4-4055
W10013-Furniture-M-Own-S-New-51000-2-Am EX-2-540
W10014-Clothing-M-Rent-S-Old-58000-1-Other-3-2305
W10015-Electronics-F-Own-M-New-91000-1-Other-2-1972
W10016-Clothing-M-Own-M-New-85000-2-Other-1-694
W10017-Clothing-F-Own-M-New-88000-3-Visa MC-1-259
W10018-Furniture-M-Own-M-New-74000-0-Other-2-1586
W10019-Other-F-Rent-S-New-14000-1-Other-2-297
W10020-Other-M-Rent-M-New-58000-1-Am EX-2-1367
W10021-Other-F-Own-S-Old-31000-0-Other-4-1212
W10022-Other-M-Own-S-Old-60000-0-Visa MC-2-1541
W10023-Garden-F-Rent-S-New-32000-0-Other-2-1079
W10024-Clothing-F-Rent-S-New-18000-0-Am EX-3-577
```

Figure 7.6 A text file with data

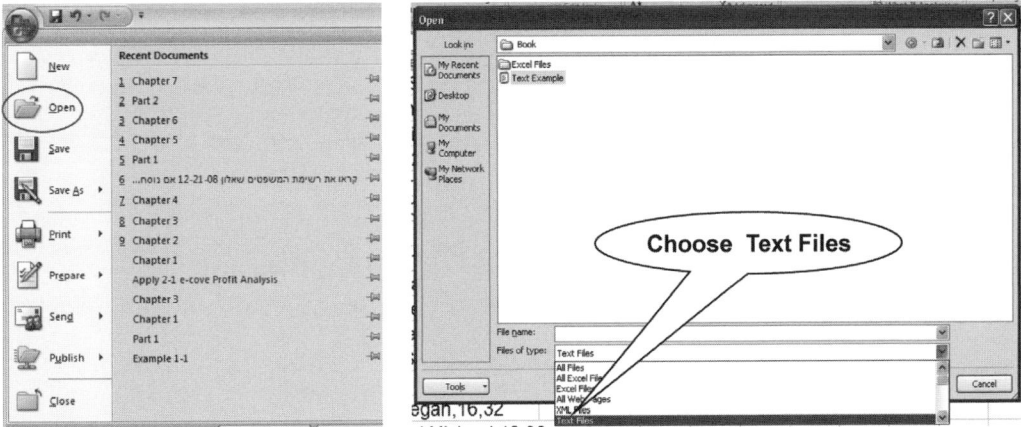

Figure 7.7 Opening a text file in Excel

Opening Text Files

From time to time, you may have to process data in a text file. You can use the same manipulation through the File Open menu to separate the data as you did in the previous example. The data shown in Figure 7.6 is part of a text file with 1,000 lines of data. The text file on the accompanying CD is called *Text Example*.

Note that the data is separated with a dash "-." Use the Open file as shown in Figure 7.7. Choose Text Files for Files of type in the drop-down menu.

The Text Import Wizard pops up. It is identical to the Text to Column menu and the procedure is the same. See Figure 7.8.

The end result is shown in Figure 7.9.

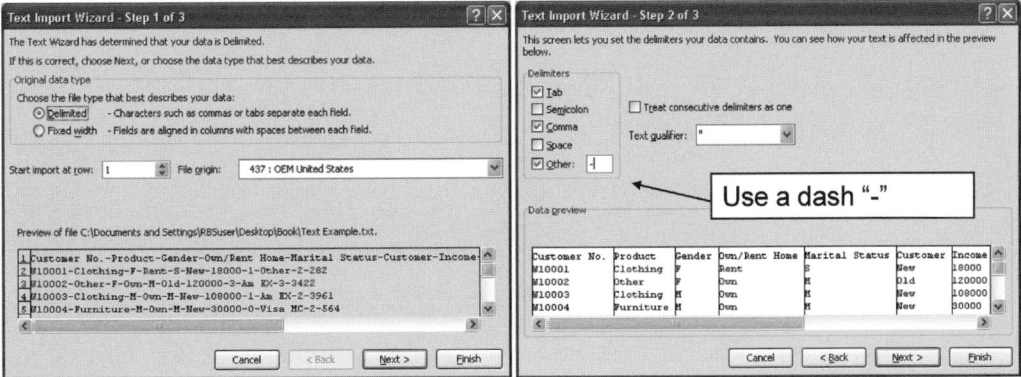

Figure 7.8 Using the Text to Column menu

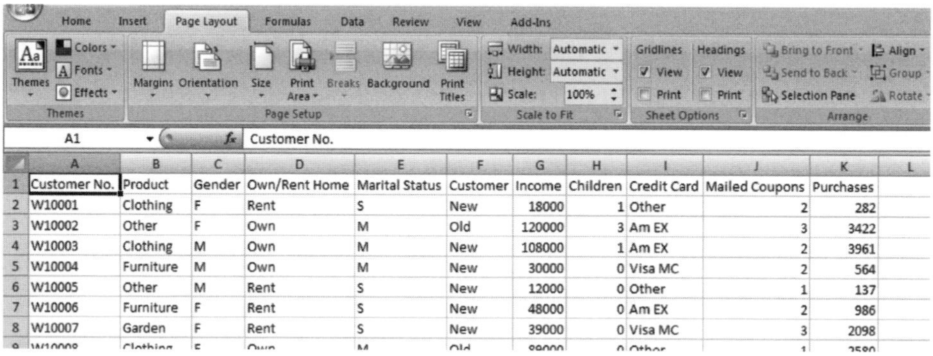

Figure 7.9   Separated data

One More Example   On the sheet called *Data* on the Excel file called Chapter 7, I have information downloaded from http://forecasts.org/data/index.htm. This is the Dow Jones Industrial Average from January 1945 through January 2006. The data, as you may find on many sites, is in a text file format, see Figure 7.10. The goal is to separate the data into individual columns. Because of the way the text is formatted, you will want to do it in two stages. Start with the "space" separating the date and average first (see Figure 7.11) and only later separate the date with the "period." If you start with the period, you will have a problem with the averages ending up in two columns.

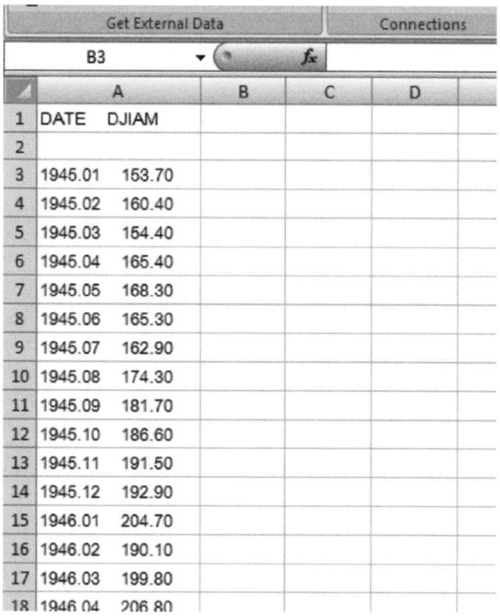

Figure 7.10   Dow Jones Industrial Averages

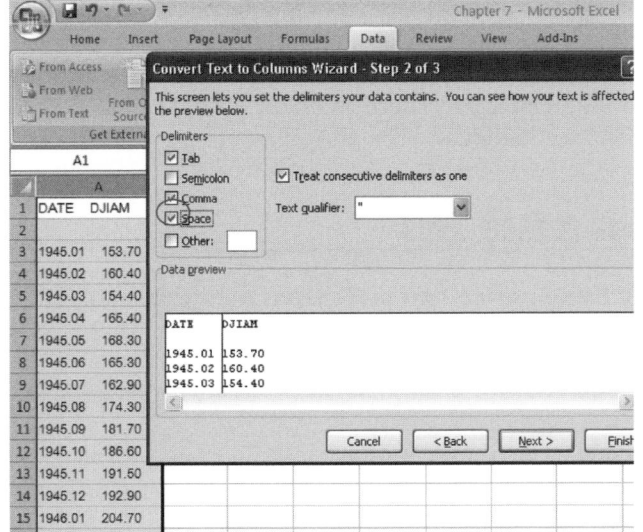

Figure 7.11 Using the Text to Column menu

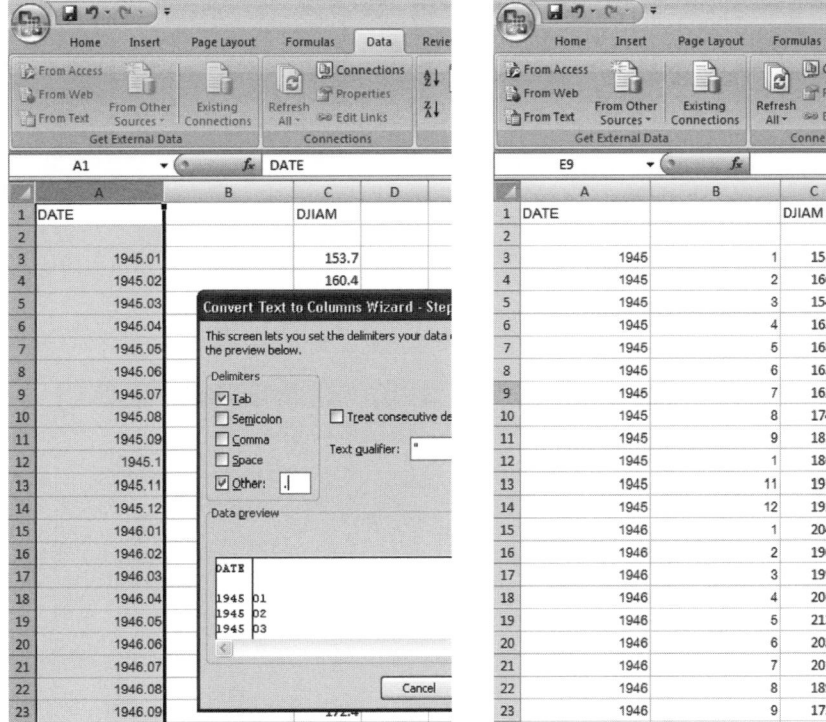

Figure 7.12 Separated data

In Figure 7.12, you can see how we first inserted an extra column and then separated column A.

This chapter demonstrated how "parsing" (to analyze or separate into more easily processed components) in Excel can be a very simple procedure. Without the use of the Text to Column feature in Excel, this could be a very tedious and lengthy operation.

APPENDIX—USING TEXT TO COLUMN IN EXCEL 2003

In Excel 2003 or previous versions of Excel: use the **Text to Columns** feature under the **Data** menu to separate the data into individual columns. See Figure 7.13. The rest of the process is identical to the Excel 2007 process. Select column A. Use Data ⇒ Text to Columns.

On the menu choose Delimited, which means separated. On the following menu, select Comma. See Figure 7.14.

When you select Finish, the data will be separated. See Figure 7.15.

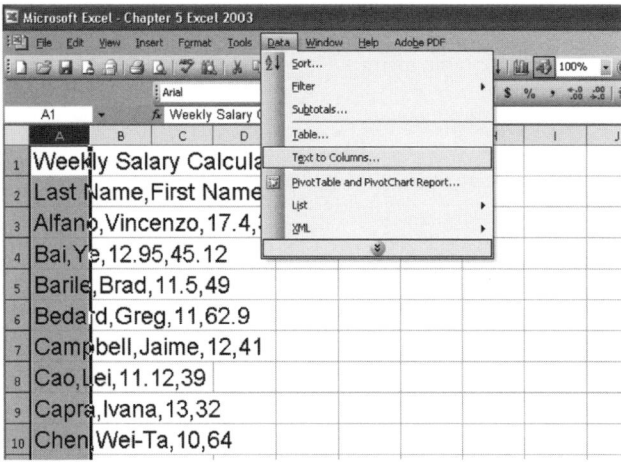

Figure 7.13   Text to Column in Excel 2003

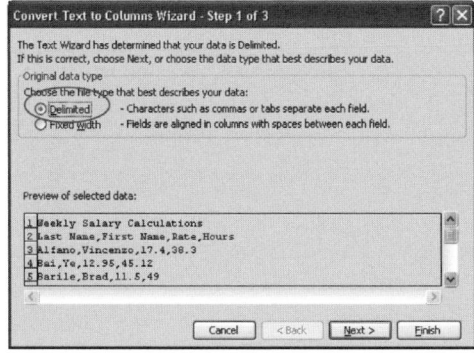

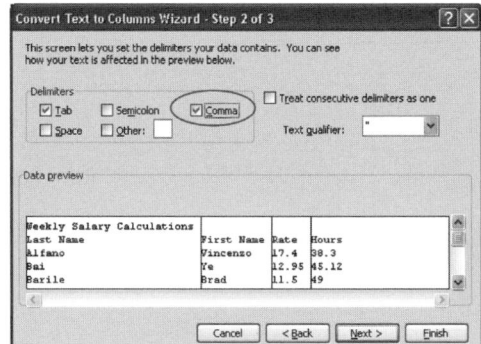

Figure 7.14   Text to Column in Excel 2003

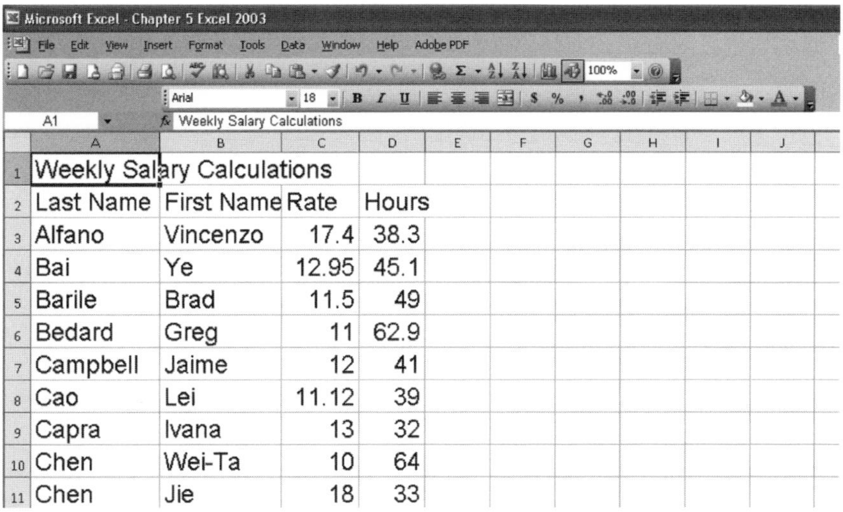

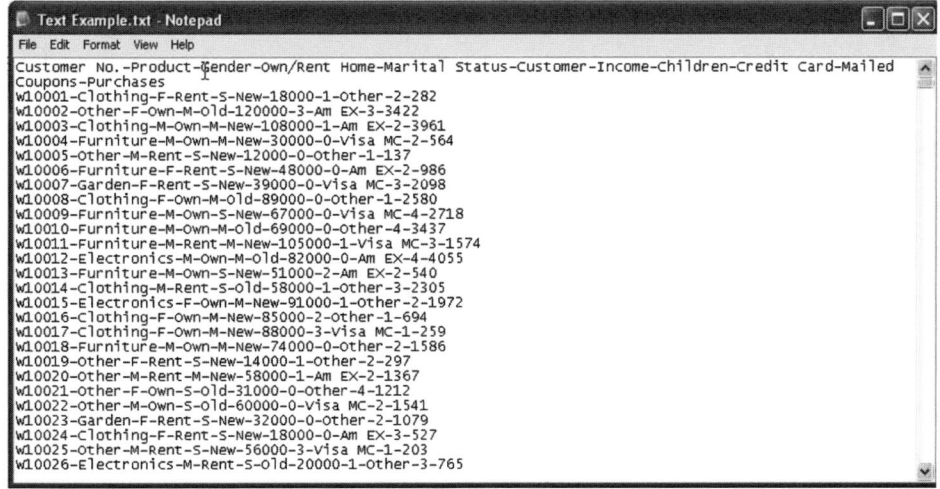

Figure 7.15   Separated data

Opening Text Files in Excel 2003

From time to time, you may get data sent to you as a text file and you can use the same menu through the File Open menu to separate the data as was done in the previous example. The data shown in Figure 7.16 is part of a text file with 1,000 lines of data. The text file is called *Text Example* on the accompanying CD.

Figure 7.16   Text file with data

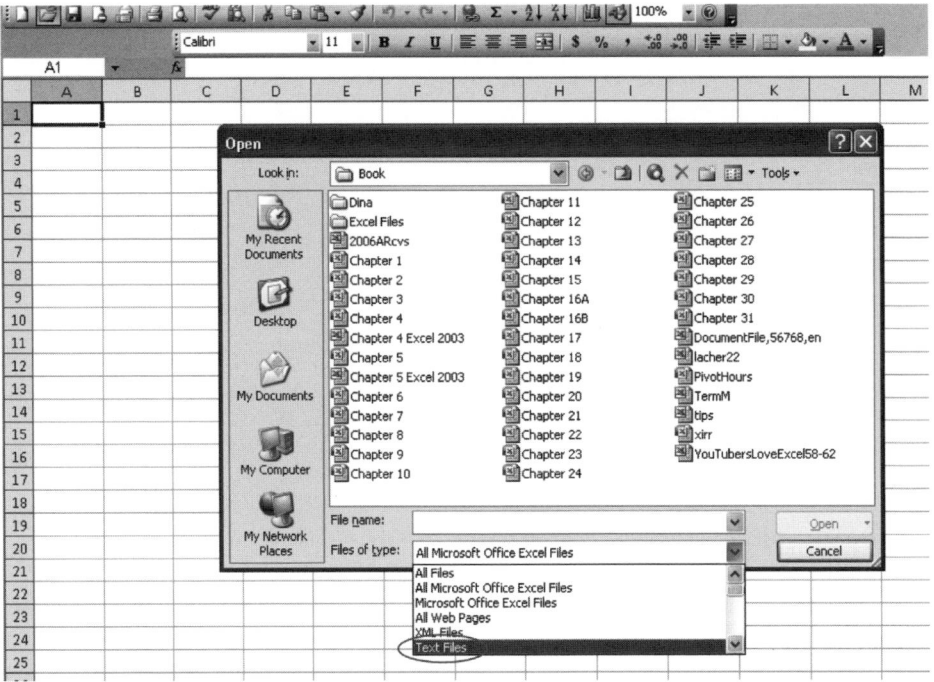

Figure 7.17   Opening a text file with Excel 2003

Note that the data is separated with a dash "-." Use the Open file as shown in Figure 7.17. Choose Text Files for Files of type on the menu.

The Text Import Wizard pops up. It is identical to the Text to Columns menu and the procedure is the same. See Figure 7.18.

The end result is shown in Figure 7.19.

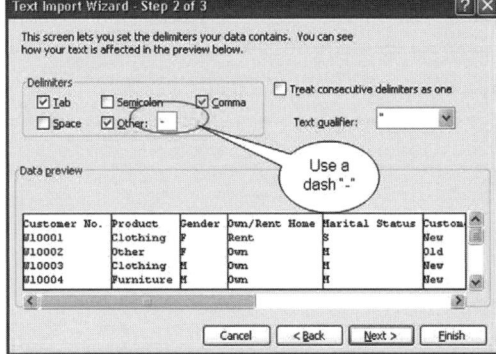

Figure 7.18   Text to Column menu

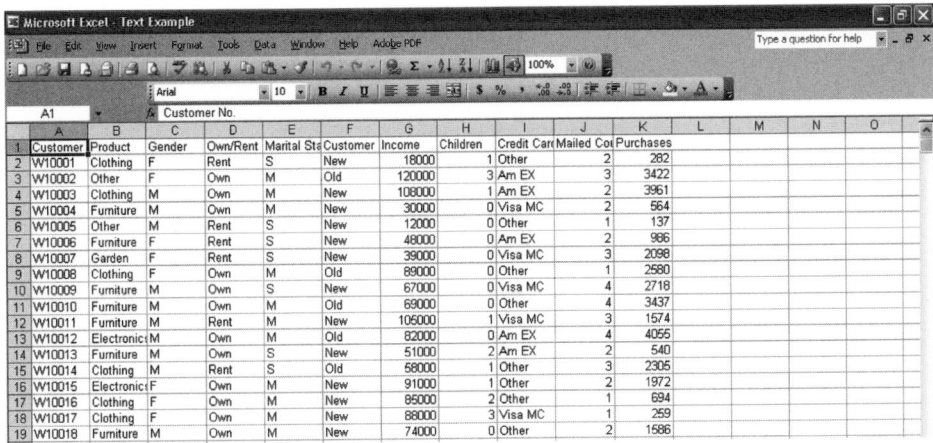

Figure 7.19   The data separated into individual columns

REVIEW QUESTIONS

You will find these examples in the Excel Chapter 7 file and the text file called *Text*:

1. In the *Review* sheet of Chapter 7, **parse the data in the last column.**

Name	Address	City, State and Zip
Vincenzo Alfano	167 Magnolia	Baltimore, MD 21200
Ye Bai	24 Golf Lane	Snow, OK 74567
Brad Barile	1017 Spring Ave	Wilbraham, MA 01095
Greg Bedard	6 Timber Road	Pittsford, NY 14534
Jaime Campbell	312 Maple Ave	Elwin, IL 62532

2. This time open the text file named *Text* on the CD or data files. Using Excel, separate the data into individual columns.

ANSWERS

1.

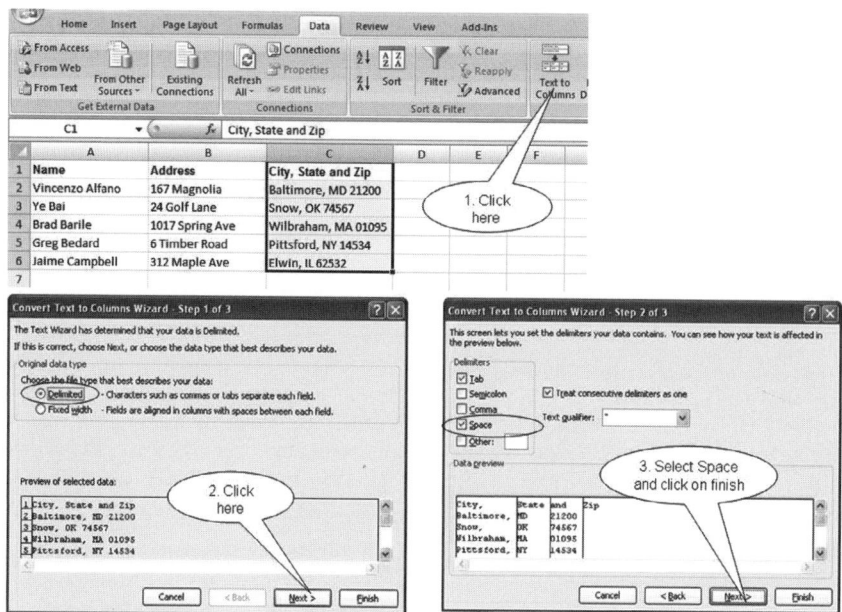

2. Open the text file named *Text* using Excel as shown on the figure below. Make sure to select Text on the menu "Files of type:". Follow the procedure of the answer to problem one. This time the text is delimited (separated) with a / (slash).

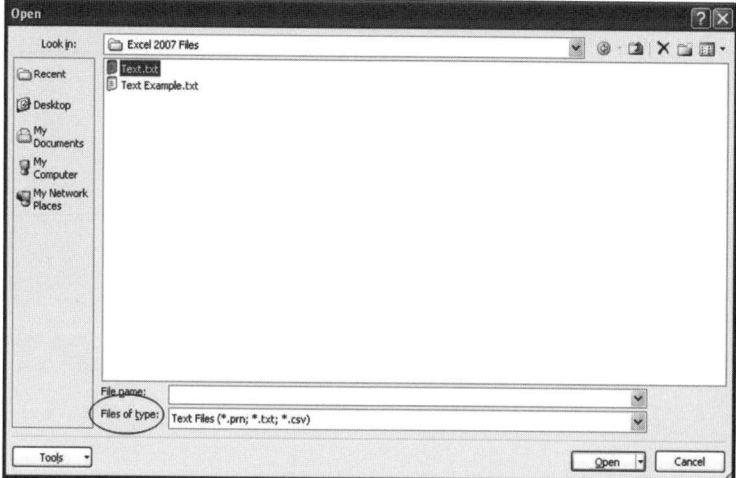

Statistical Tools

Statistics are needed to make better and informed decisions, quantify markets, identify important trends, answer questions for strategic planning, and support key business proposals with hard data. What statistics in Excel provide you with, is a set of tools that enables you to solve and sort out a variety of problems. In this part, I will cover descriptive statistics and simple regressions.

Two approaches can be taken in solving the problems of descriptive statistics using Excel. The first one is to use the built-in functions. The second one is to use the Excel add-in called the Analysis ToolPak. Both methods will be covered here.

I will also show two different methods for regressions: The built-in functions as well as the Analysis ToolPak Excel add-in.

How can statistics help you with your business decisions?

- By providing a user-friendly summary of data/information (that is, charts).
- Allowing the test of a hypothesis: for example, verification that an increase in advertisement will affect sales levels. Conclusive decisions can be reached from the data interpretation.
- Comparing information from different sources.
- Predicting how likely an outcome is for a particular event.
- Knowing when to employ a statistician and being able to communicate with him.

Where could you use statistics in business?

- In conducting research;
- In the interpretation of press articles;
- In developing your critical and analytical thinking skills;
- In becoming a better-informed consumer.

Descriptive Statistics

In this chapter, I will start with statistical analysis of the data on the sheet called *Statistics* in the Excel workbook Chapter 8 shown in Figure 8.1.

The data in column A contains a list of 500 students' IQs. I selected the range A1:A500 and named the range "DATA." I used the procedure described in chapter 3. If you expand the name box above A1 by clicking the drop-down arrow/menu to the right of the field and then select the name DATA, it will highlight the range of named cells A1:A500.

DESCRIPTIVE STATISTICS

In this section I am going to calculate several frequently used statistics functions. I will start with the mean, the highest value, the lowest value, the standard deviation, the median, and the mode.

Let me begin with the average. I select the cell D3 where I would like the answer to be located, and then select f$_x$ (Insert function) or use Shift+F3. Choose the category Statistical, then the function Average. See Figure 8.2.

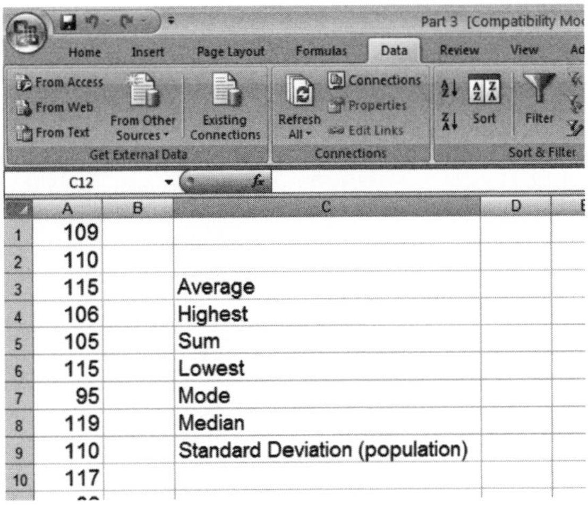

Figure 8.1 Data is on the sheet *Statistics*

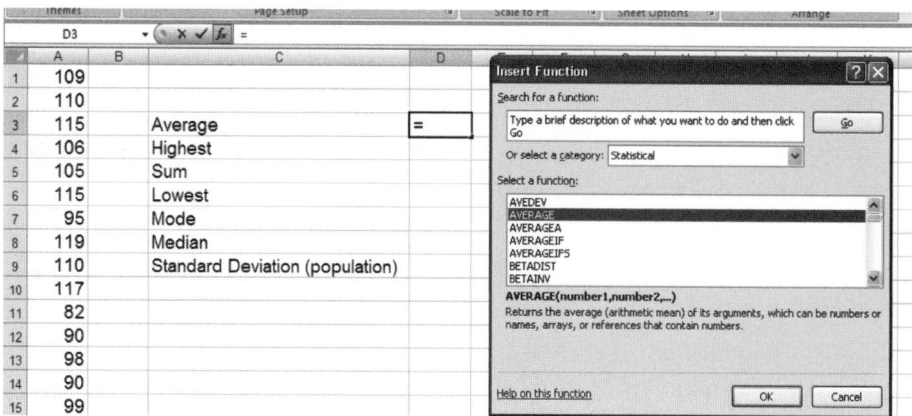

Figure 8.2   Insert function, the average

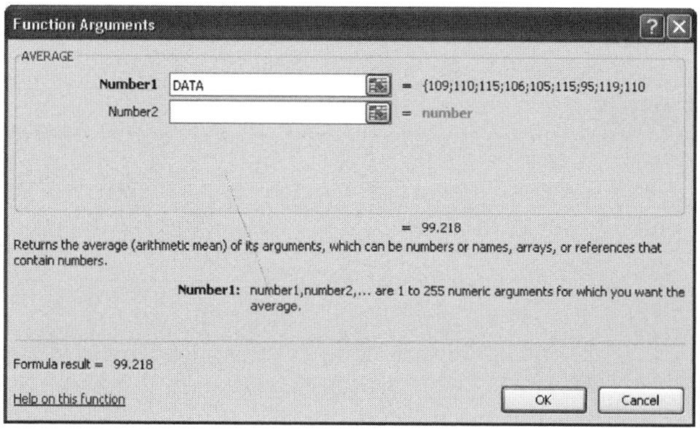

Figure 8.3   The Average menu

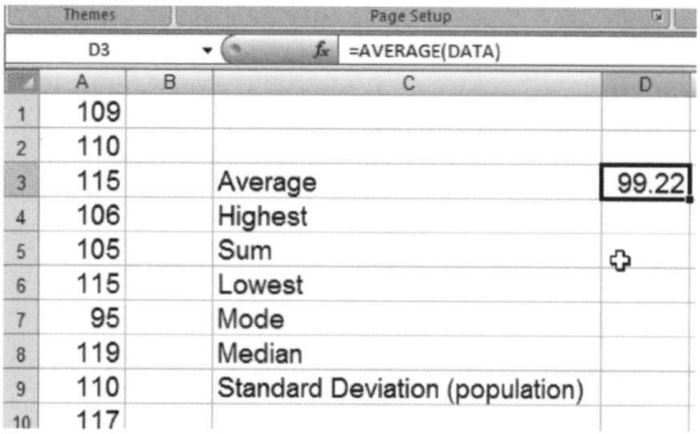

Figure 8.4   The average of the data

Average	99.22
Highest	129
Sum	49609
Lowest	61
Mode	102
Median	100
Standard Deviation (population)	9.93

Average	=AVERAGE(DATA)
Highest	=MAX(DATA)
Sum	=SUM(DATA)
Lowest	=MIN(DATA)
Mode	=MODE(DATA)
Median	=MEDIAN(DATA)
Standard Deviation (population)	=STDEVP(DATA)

Figure 8.5 The calculated values and the formulas—the results are shown on the left and the formulas are shown on the right

A menu to insert the function arguments will appear—since the goal is to compute the average of our data set, I could select the range A1:A500, but as the range was previously named DATA, I can simply type in the word DATA and click OK to obtain the average. See Figure 8.3.

The result is shown in Figure 8.4.

I repeated the process on the same sheet using the Function icon, f$_x$—this time I used the functions for the highest value in the range (Excel function MAX), the lowest value (MIN), the MEDIAN, the MODE, and the standard deviation (STDEVP). It is preferable to use STDEVP for the standard deviation as the calculation applies to a large population. In this example, there are 500 values. If it was a small sample (<30) I would have used STDEV. The results are shown in Figure 8.5, which contains the results on the left and reveals the formulas on the right. I can use either CTRL+` or CTRL+~ to reveal all the formulas.

Try it one more time—this time using shortcuts to calculate the statistics. I chose to go over it again with shortcuts, since it may save you valuable time when you use Excel and functions. I am going to demonstrate it with the highest value—MAX—and the SUM. For the MAX value I used Shift+F3 to activate the Functions menu. When the menu appeared I used F3 for the Names menu. I chose DATA and pressed Enter and I had the answer—as you can see in Figure 8.6. Try it—it saves time.

For the SUM, I saved time by typing the shortcut ALT+= in the cell where the result should appear. After SUM appears in the cell, use F3 to call up the name list. Select DATA and hit Enter. It is demonstrated it Figure 8.7.

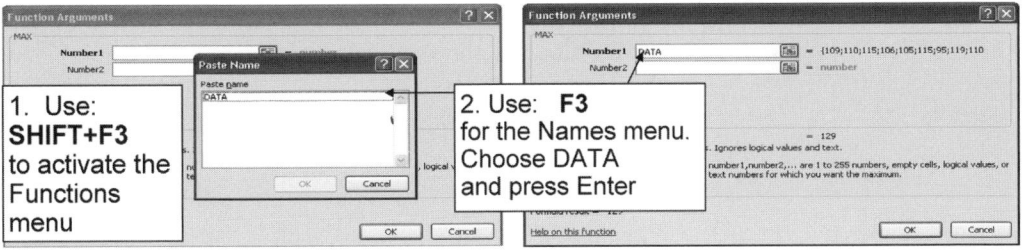

Figure 8.6 Using F3 for named data

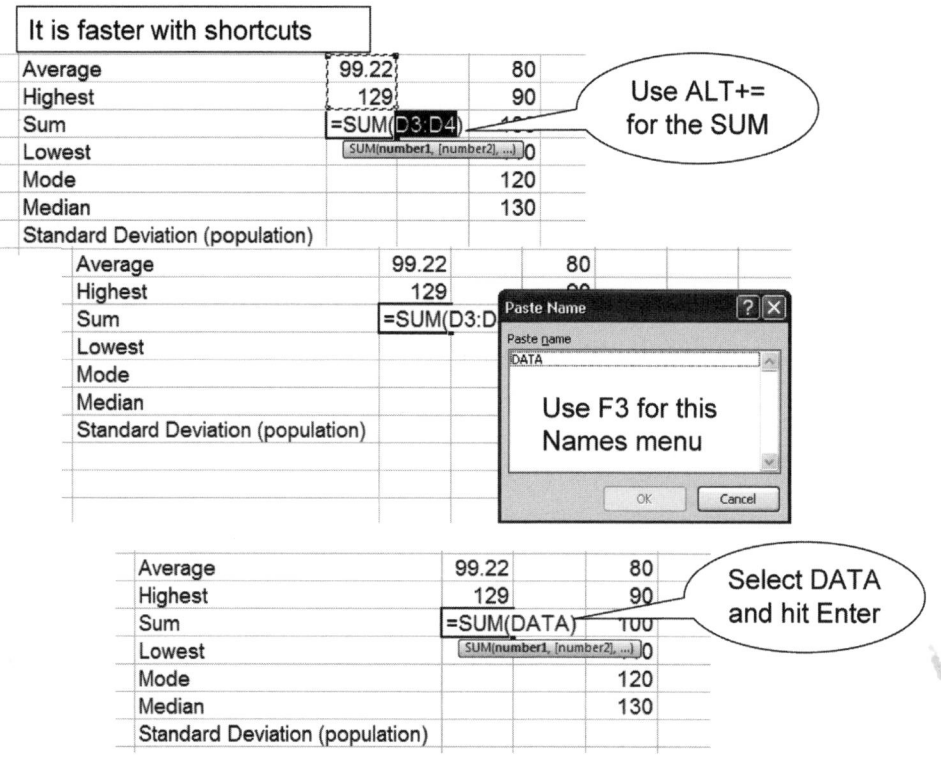

Figure 8.7 Getting the SUM, using ALT+=

REVIEW QUESTIONS

You will find the data on the *Review* sheet in the Excel file Chapter 8:

1. The data on the sheet *Review* of Excel file Chapter 8 has 20,000 values in A1:D5000. Name the data in A1:D5000 with a meaningful name like Numbers.
2. Use the Excel statistical functions' menu to calculate the following: the average, the highest and lowest values, the standard deviation, the mode, and the median.
3. Use Excel shortcuts to calculate the sum and the average of the data.

ANSWERS

1. Select the range A1:D5000. Type the word "Numbers" in the Name Box and click Enter. See figure below.

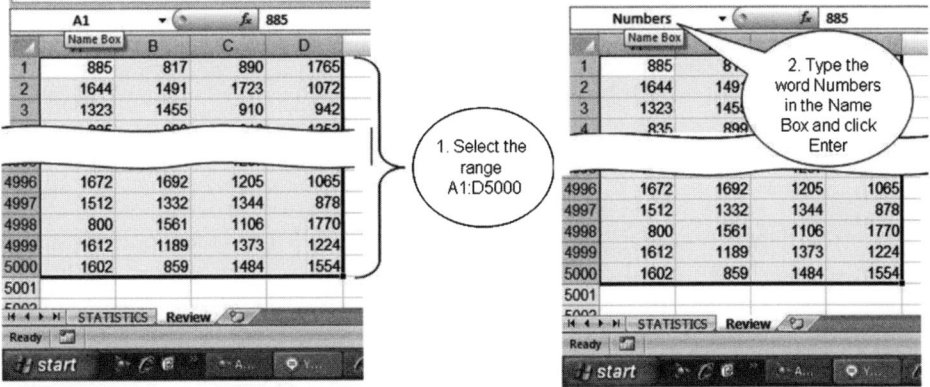

2. Average 1,300.18, highest 1,799, lowest 800, standard deviation 287.61, mode 1,559, and median 1,299.
3. Sum: 26,002,751, Average: 1,300.18.

Frequency Distributions

In this chapter you will find out how to generate frequency distributions and frequency distribution charts from a data set. Frequency distributions enable you to better understand the data and the way it is arranged rather than just looking at the data or the statistics. Frequency distribution allows you to see if the data is symmetric, skewed, or flat and detect other information that the statistics could provide.

I will use the same data used in chapter 8. You can find the data on the Excel file called *Chapter 9*. I calculated various statistics in chapter 8 for that same data. Two important values were found that will help in determining the frequency distribution range: the lowest and the highest values. The lowest value is 61 and 129 is the highest. See Figure 9.1.

The first step is to create a list of bins in column F, which will be used to establish the boundaries for the groups I wish to form for the frequency. In other words, each one of these bins represents the **upper limit** of the group's frequency occurrence. Since I established that the lowest number, or MIN, is 61 and the highest number is 129, I created bins that will encompass this range. I used 70 as the first bin in order to count all of the numbers/values below 70 (and above 61 the lowest number). I used 130 as the upper limit of the highest group/bin since the largest number found was 129. The rule of thumb, for frequency distributions, is to find the range of values (MIN & MAX values) and to create anywhere from five to 15 bins. I chose to use seven bins/groups in this example.

I typed the word Frequency in cell G1. This word will be visible later for my chart. The results of my frequency calculations are going to be in the range G2:G8. See Figure 9.1.

	G4			f_x				
	A	B	C		D	E	F	G
1	109						BINS	Frequency
2	110						70	
3	115		Average		99.22		80	
4	106		Highest		129		90	
5	105		Sum		49609		100	
6	115		Lowest		61		110	
7	95		Mode		102		120	
8	119		Median		100		130	
9	110		Standard Deviation (population)		9.93			
10	117							

Figure 9.1 Frequency bins are in F2:F8

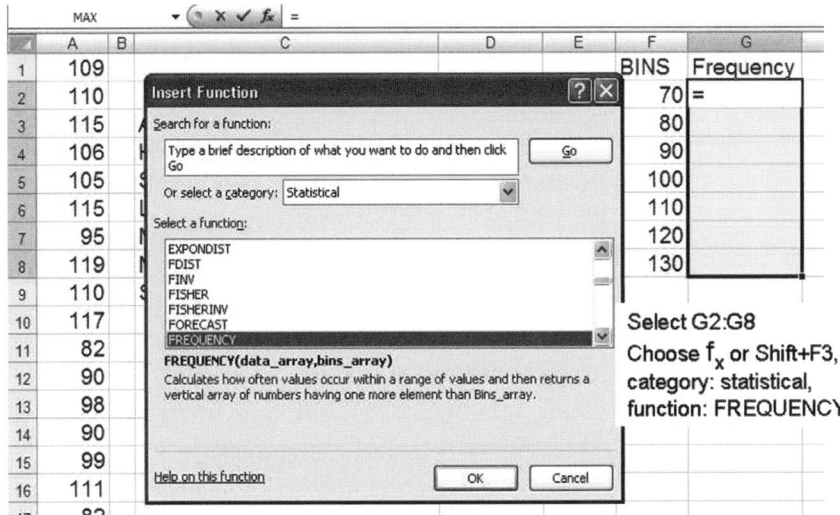

Figure 9.2 Select G2:G8 for the frequency

The results of the frequency distribution will be entered using Excel in the range G2:G8. Since frequency is an array function, it is very important to select all the cells that the answer is going to be calculated in. Select G2:G8. Choose the insert a function, f_x or Shift+F3, category: Statistical, function: FREQUENCY. This navigation is shown in Figure 9.2.

The Function Arguments window will pop up. In the Data_array cell type: DATA (or if you did not name the range DATA, select the cells on the sheet or type A1:A500). In the Bins_array cell, select the bins F2:F8. See figure 9.3.

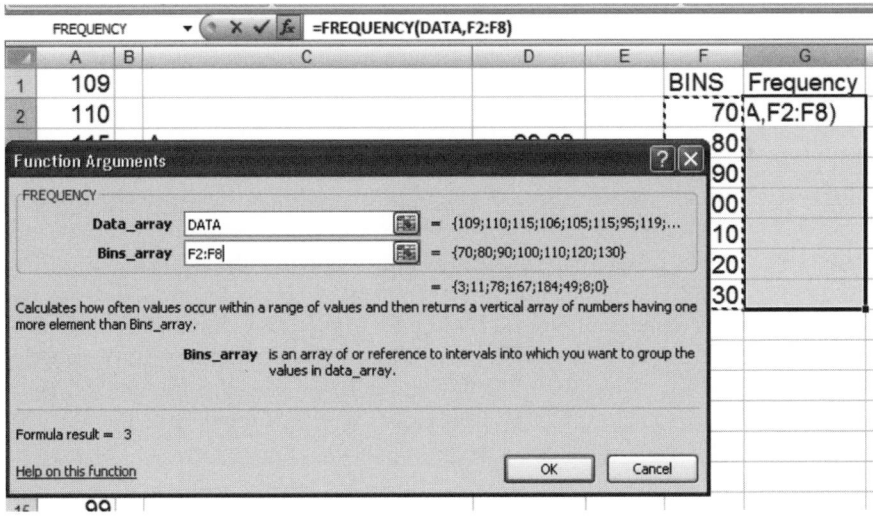

Figure 9.3 The Function Arguments window

This is very important: the Frequency function is an **array** function. When using an **array** function in Excel, you are going to get the answer in more than one cell, cells G2:G8 in our case. This corresponds to the set of bins.

A simple OK or Return cursor will result in a single cell reply (in cell G2). Since we want to know the frequency of **each** of our selected bins, the answers should be filled in the entire range (G2:G8). When the answer appears in a single cell, you cannot drag it down or copy it to the rest of the cells. Dragging does not work in an array function.

To get the results in **all** cells you have to: first make sure that all the cells that you want the answer in are selected *before* entering the Frequency function, and after filling-in the different fields, hold down the CTRL and Shift keys simultaneously—and **while** they are pressed, click the OK button or hit Return. This will calculate the array result in the range G2:G8. It may take some practice. See the results in Figure 9.4.

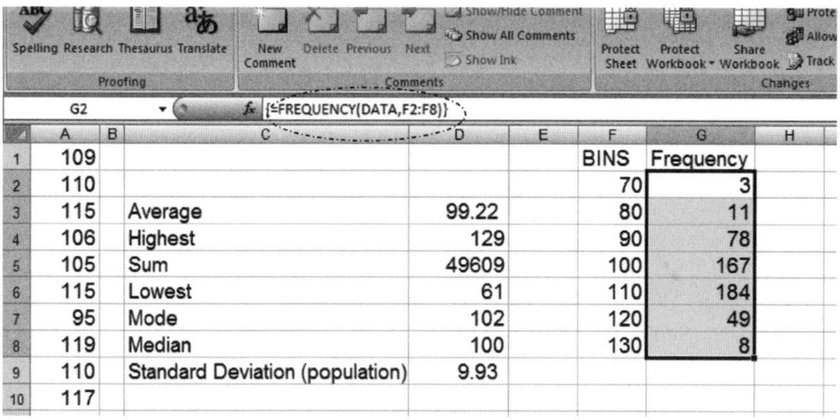

Figure 9.4   The Frequency function in Excel

Note the function in the formula bar in Figure 9.4. The array results cannot be changed. If you visit any of the calculated frequency cells in column G, you will see how the result shows curled brackets, {=FREQUENCY(DATA,F2:F8)}. Curled brackets indicate that results of these functions cannot be altered.

A simple observation of the results: most of the data is distributed around the average (99.21 was the previously calculated average) or the center of the distribution. Having the frequency distribution, we can now create a chart of the frequency distribution using the information in the range F2:G8.

In creating a frequency distribution chart, I want to have a two-dimensional column chart. I want the bin values in column F (70, 80, . . . and 130) on the X axis and the frequency values of column G as Y/columns. If you don't have a header for the X values (in column F), Excel will create the chart where these values will be on the X axis:

- Remove the header (BINS).
- Select the range: CTRL+Shift+*.
- Use Insert 2-D Column Chart as shown in Figure 9.5.

The result is shown in Figure 9.6. Notice how the chart has gaps between the columns. The original data is continuous data and the chart displays the data with gaps. You have to remove the gaps on the chart.

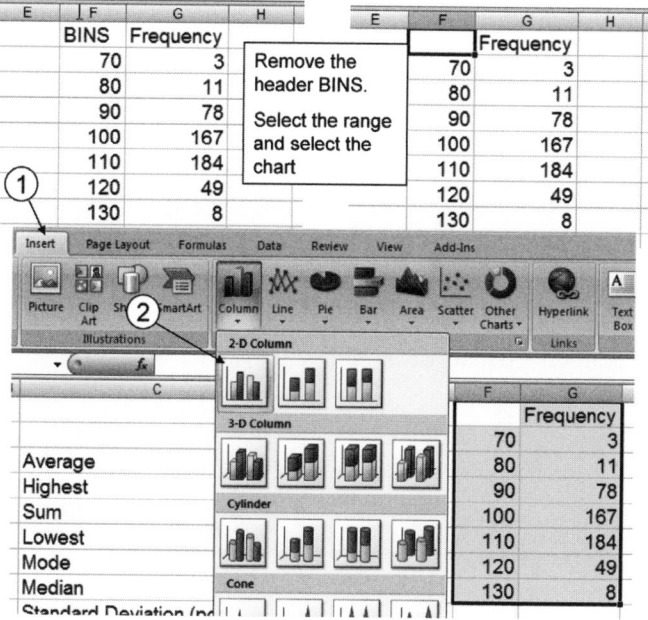

Figure 9.5 Inserting a frequency chart

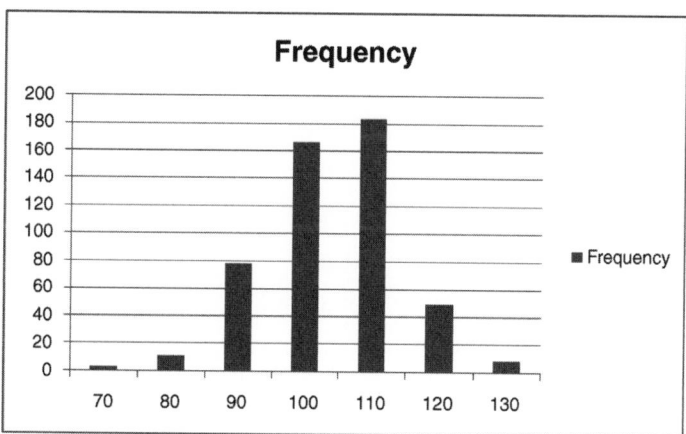

Figure 9.6 The frequency chart with gaps

To remove the gaps in the frequency chart: right-click any one of the columns to select the series. Select Format Data Series. On the menu remove the gap. See Figure 9.7.

This is a common Excel problem: if you don't remove the header BINS in cell F1 before creating the chart, Excel attempts to create chart columns for both the BINS and the

Frequency. If you did not remove the word "BINS" before generating the chart, you would have ended up with the result shown in Figure 9.8. The first part of Figure 9.8 shows two sets of columns. The columns that show the BINS values (data series: 70, 80, 90, . . . 130) and the second set of columns (data series) that correspond to the calculated frequency values. You will have to remove the BINS data series and insert these values (70, 80, 90, . . . 130) on the X-axis. To remove the BINS series and to force the BINS values to appear on the X-axis:

- Right-click the chart.
- Select Data.
- In the Select Data Source dialog box, remove the Bins series from the Y-axis.
- In the same Select Data Source menu, click on Edit to have a pop-up window allowing you to select the Axis Labels.
- Select the data for the X-axis.

The only manipulation left to do is removing the gaps again as you did before. See Figure 9.7.

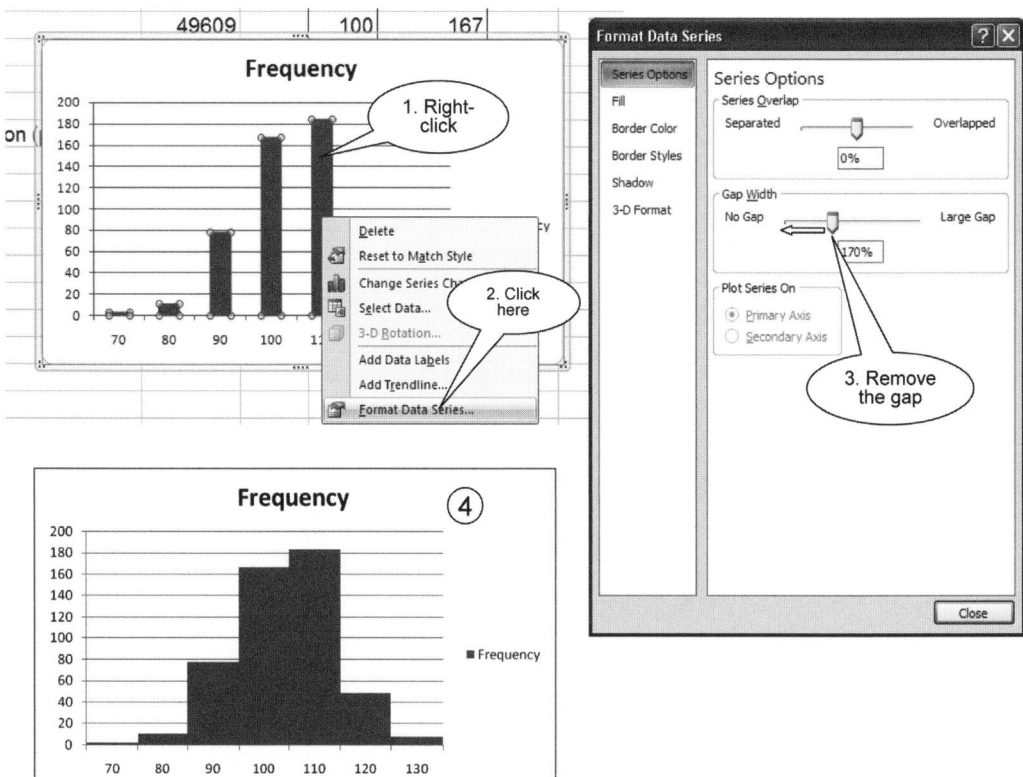

Figure 9.7 Removing the gaps in the chart

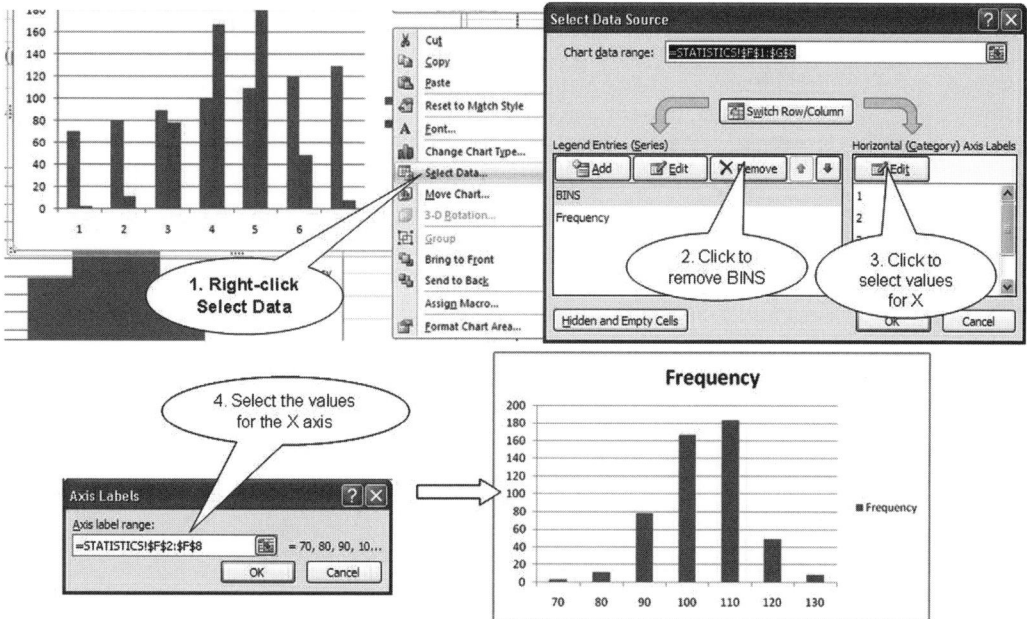

Figure 9.8   Removing the "Bins" data series and adding it to the X-axis

One More Example

On the sheet *HHold Income* in the Excel Chapter 9 file, we have the data of 1,000 customers. What you may want to do is find out the distribution of the data as you did in the example above.

First, start by selecting the range A2:A1001 and name the data Income. After selecting A2:A1001, just type the name Income in the Name box and hit Enter. Proceed to find the highest and lowest values of the range as I did in cells C3 and C4. See Figure 9.9.

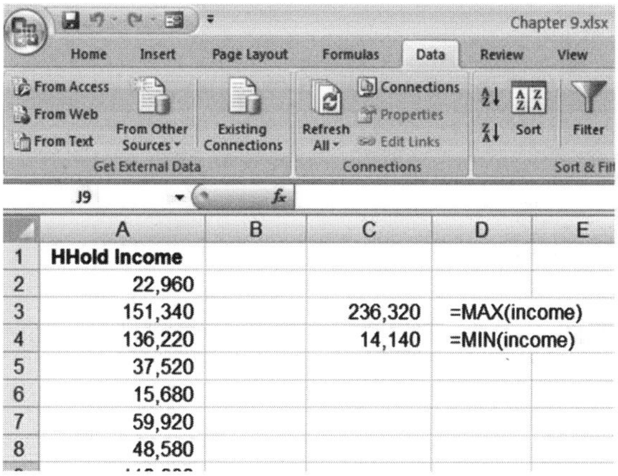

Figure 9.9   The HHold Income example

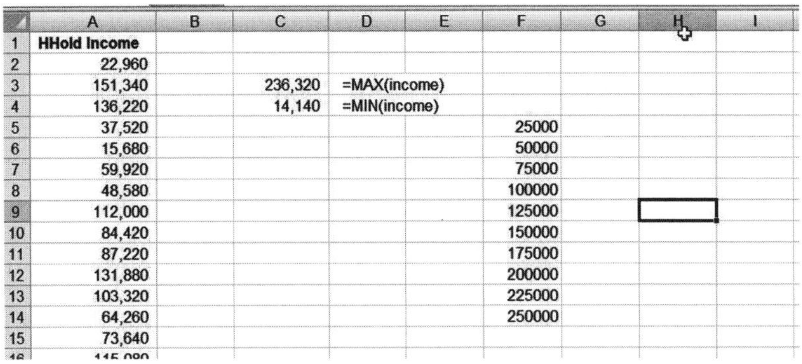

Figure 9.10 Preparing the bins for the frequency calculations

Now you can create the Bins. I chose, after calculating the highest and lowest values, to create bins from 25,000 to 250,000, with increments of 25,000. See Figure 9.10.

Type the word Frequency in G4, then select the range of G5:G14 and activate the Frequency function menu. Remember, this is an array function and you have to calculate all the frequencies in the range at once. See Figure 9.11.

Fill the required fields with the following information: type Income in the Data_array field, then select F5:F14 for the Bin_array field. Remember to apply the array function rule: hold down the CTRL+Shift keys as you hit Enter. When you use the CTRL+Shift+Enter, you will get the frequency distribution, as shown in Figure 9.12. Looking at the results it is notable that the data is not distributed symmetrically. It is skewed data. When you create a chart of the data, the visual impact will be even stronger for presentation purposes.

To create the chart, select the range F4:G14 and create a two-dimensional column chart. The process and the chart are illustrated in Figure 9.13.

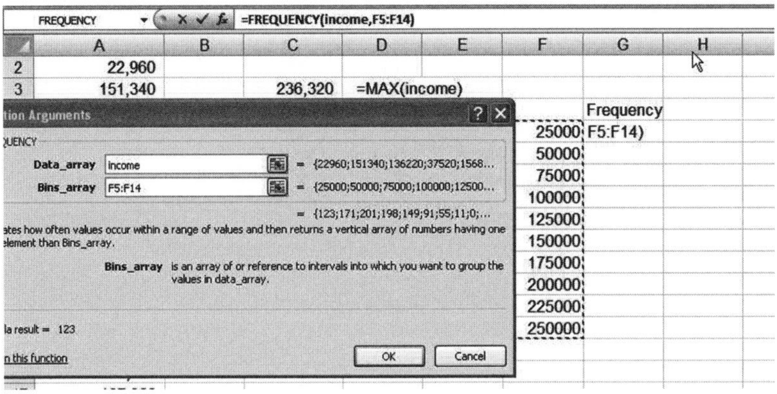

Figure 9.11 Calculating the frequency

	Frequency
25000	123
50000	171
75000	201
100000	198
125000	149
150000	91
175000	55
200000	11
225000	0
250000	1

Figure 9.12   The frequencies

This is continuous data, the gap between columns should be removed. See Figure 9.14.

The final frequency distribution can be seen in Figure 9.15. Notice how the data is skewed and very few people among the 1,000 customers have a household income over $200,000. It can be confirmed by going back to the original data to verify that only 12 households or 1.2 percent have an income over $200,000.

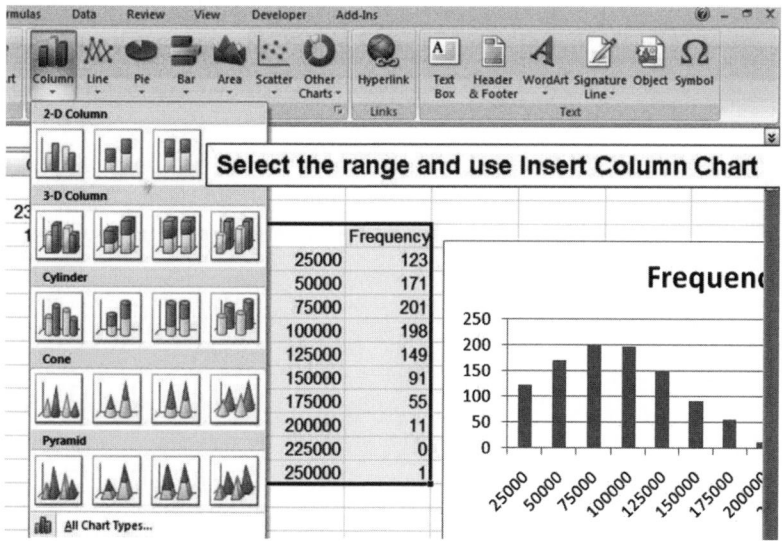

Figure 9.13   Creating the chart

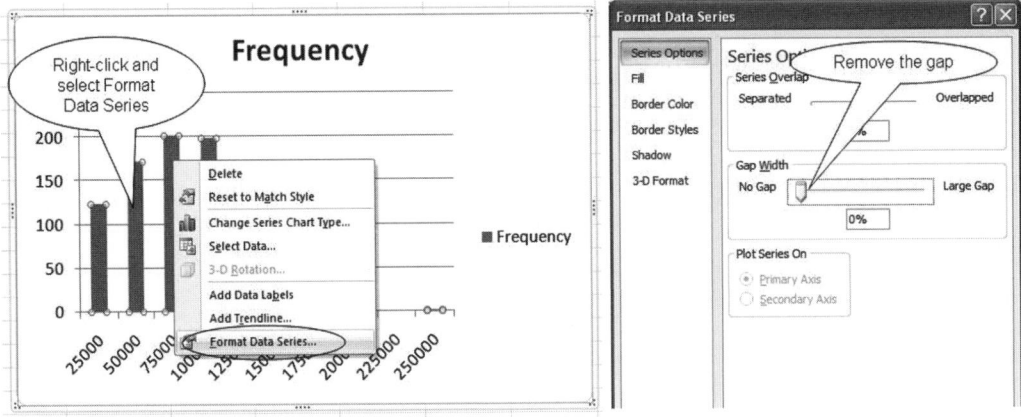

Figure 9.14　Removing the gap in the chart

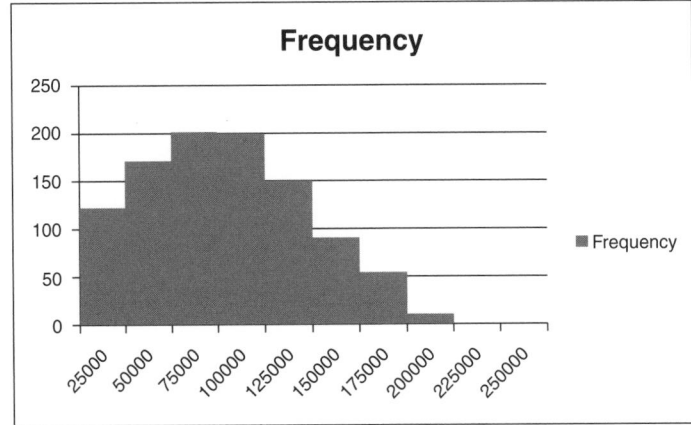

Figure 9.15　Frequency distribution chart

REVIEW QUESTIONS

You will find these examples in the Excel Chapter 9 file:

1. On the *Review* sheet of Chapter 9, construct a frequency distribution table and a frequency distribution chart.
2. Using the *Statistics* sheet of the Chapter 9 file, create a new frequency distribution table and a new frequency distribution chart. This time apply different bin sizes in multiples of 5 starting with 65, 70, and ending with 130.
3. Using the *HHold Income* sheet of the Chapter 9 file, create a new frequency distribution table and a new frequency distribution chart. This time program different bin sizes in multiples of 20,000 starting with 20,000, 40,000, and ending with 240,000.

ANSWERS

1.

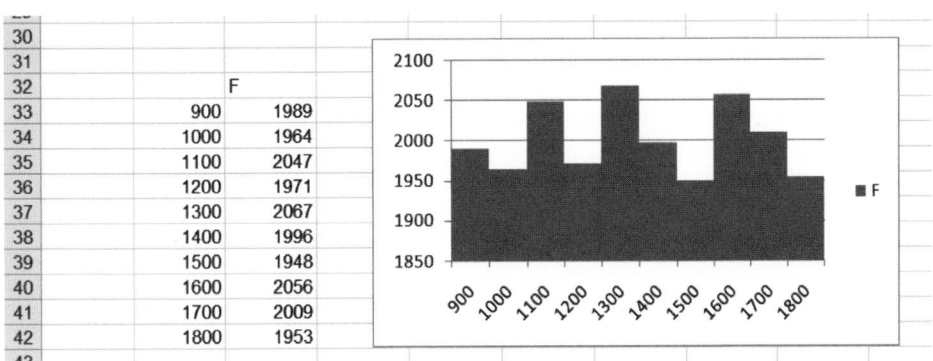

	F	
30		
31		
32		
33	900	1989
34	1000	1964
35	1100	2047
36	1200	1971
37	1300	2067
38	1400	1996
39	1500	1948
40	1600	2056
41	1700	2009
42	1800	1953
43		

2.

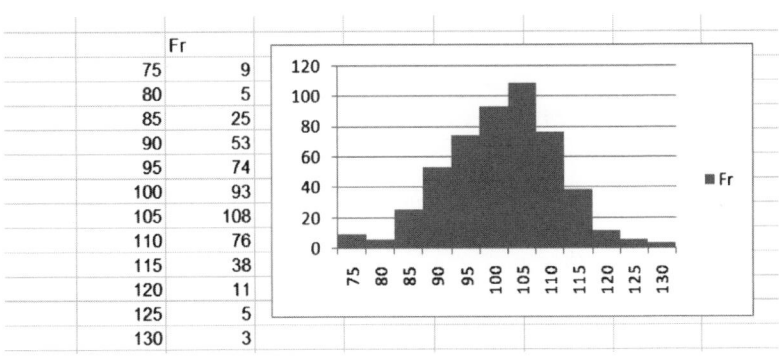

	Fr
75	9
80	5
85	25
90	53
95	74
100	93
105	108
110	76
115	38
120	11
125	5
130	3

3.

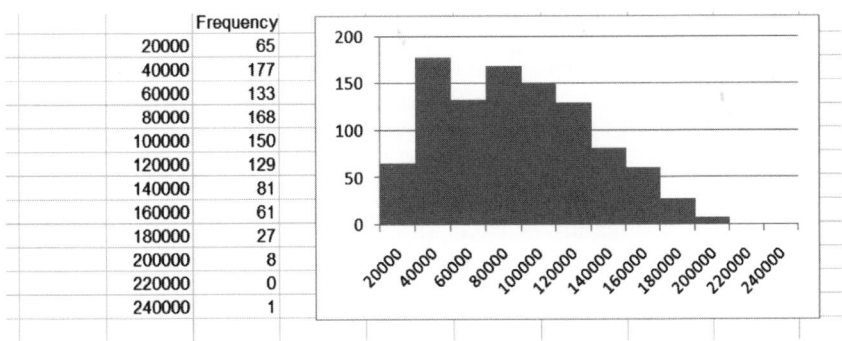

	Frequency
20000	65
40000	177
60000	133
80000	168
100000	150
120000	129
140000	81
160000	61
180000	27
200000	8
220000	0
240000	1

Statistical Regression

Statistical regression is the relation between selected values of x and observed values of y. I am not going to explain or define "regression" as that is beyond the scope of this book. My purpose is to explain how to use Excel to calculate the parameters of a regression line. In the Excel file Chapter 10 under the sheet named *Regression,* you will find a set of data that will be used to demonstrate this feature in Excel. The data (sales over time) is going to create an almost perfectly straight line when you draw it on x y coordinates.

Month	3	4	5	6	7	8	9	10	11	12
Sales	9	15	21	24	32	35	39	45	48	54

USING THE SCATTER CHART IN EXCEL

You can use the chart option of Excel to reveal or demonstrate the relationship between the two data sets. We assume, in this example, that the Sales is our Y variable and that the Month is our X variable. To create a chart, select the Month and Sales data B1:C11 (including the header) and activate the Chart Wizard. When you select, under the Insert ribbon, the very first scatter chart as shown in Figure 10.1, it will result in the XY scatter chart.

To better visualize, you can add a regression line to the chart. Right-click on any of the points in the chart and select Add Trend line in the small drop-down menu. Check the last two boxes on the Format Trend line menu to display the trend line's equation and R^2 (R-squared) value. See Figure 10.2 for the menu and the results of programming the line's equation and R^2 (R-squared) value. The equation of the regression line is reversed.

The regression line is y $=-4.3455 + 4.8727$x.

The slope is 4.8727 and the intercept is -4.3455. R^2 is 0.9945.

This Add Trend line feature of Excel allows you to find linear and other relationships between data sets without using other calculations and functions. Once you find a relationship, you can, at a single glance, analyze whether the data and the relationship between the variables is meaningful or not. I will further demonstrate in other examples how understanding these relationships can be an advantage.

What do the results mean? The intercept is -4.35. Theoretically, when x was 0 (at time zero) sales were -4.35. It does not make sense; however, it does work for the equation of the range of x between 3 and 12.

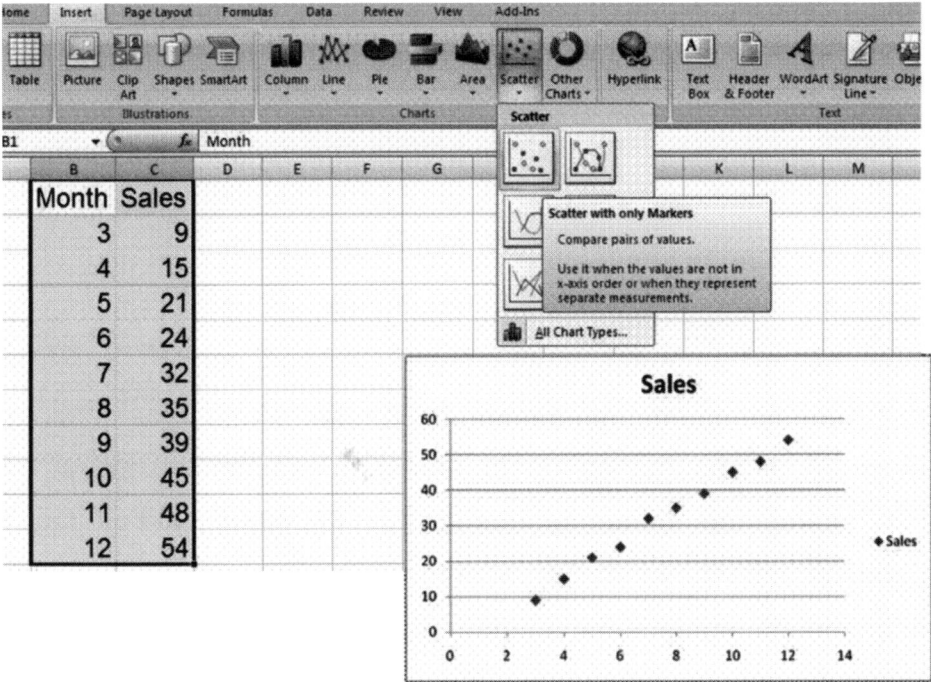

Figure 10.1   Creating the XY scatter chart

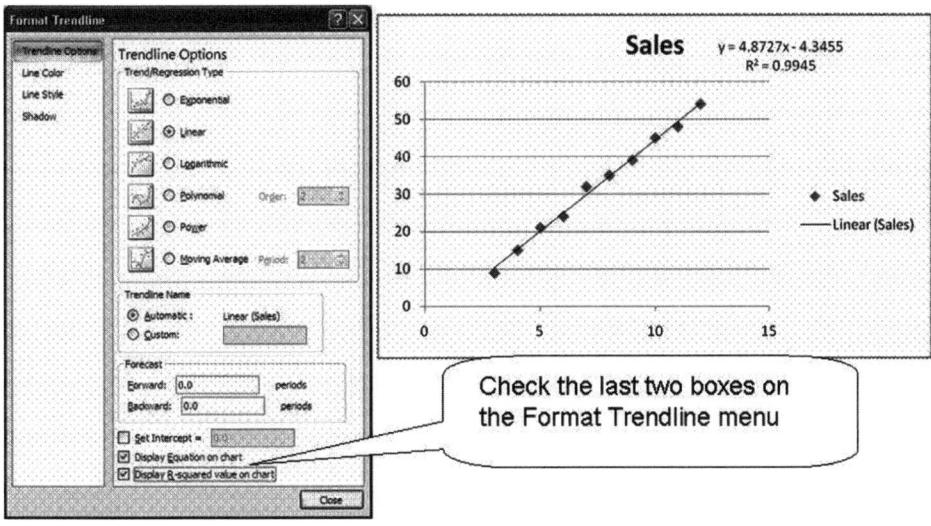

Figure 10.2   Displaying the regression line on a chart

The slope is 4.87. In the time range from 3 to 12, sales went up on average by 4.87 units every month.

R^2 is 0.9945. R^2 is the coefficient of determination. The values of R^2 always range between 0 and 1.

R^2 is used in statistical models of forecasting/regressions to measure how accurate the model is to predict the future values, using the existing regression formula applied to the current data. In the above example, R^2 is close to 1, which means that the regression line is excellent. If it is close to 0 you cannot use the data for forecasting.

LINEAR REGRESSION—USING EXCEL FUNCTIONS

In addition to the chart feature that allowed you to add the equation and R^2, you can calculate the following three values using Excel conventional functions: the slope, the intercept, and R^2. We can use the functions Intercept, Slope, and RSQ (for R^2—R squared) to obtain the same values created on the chart. In addition you can use the Forecast function to predict y values based on given x's. In other words, it allows sales forecasting based on a time value.

In order to save time calculating these functions, you may want to **name** some of the cell ranges that will be used in these calculations. It will make it easier to use the various functions without selecting the ranges again every time you want to calculate one of the parameters.

Select cell range B2:B11 and name it x. Select cells C2:C11 and name them y. I wrote, in cells E4, E5, and E6, the function names I am about to calculate on the regression sheet as shown in Figure 10.3.

You can use the function f_x ⇨ Statistical ⇨ Intercept to calculate the intercept point in cell F4. Use the function f_x ⇨ Statistical ⇨ Slope to calculate the slope in cell F5; and use the function f_x ⇨ Statistical ⇨ RSQ to calculate the R^2 value in cell F6. See figure 10.4.

Notice that we used x and y for our Function Arguments. It saves us the trouble of selecting the ranges of cells again and again.

The three values are the same values you obtained on the chart when you used the Add Trend line menu. You can use the results obtained to forecast y values.

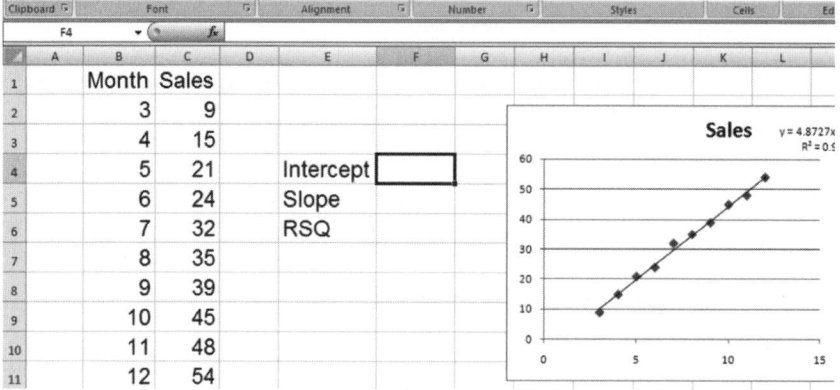

Figure 10.3 Calculating regression parameters

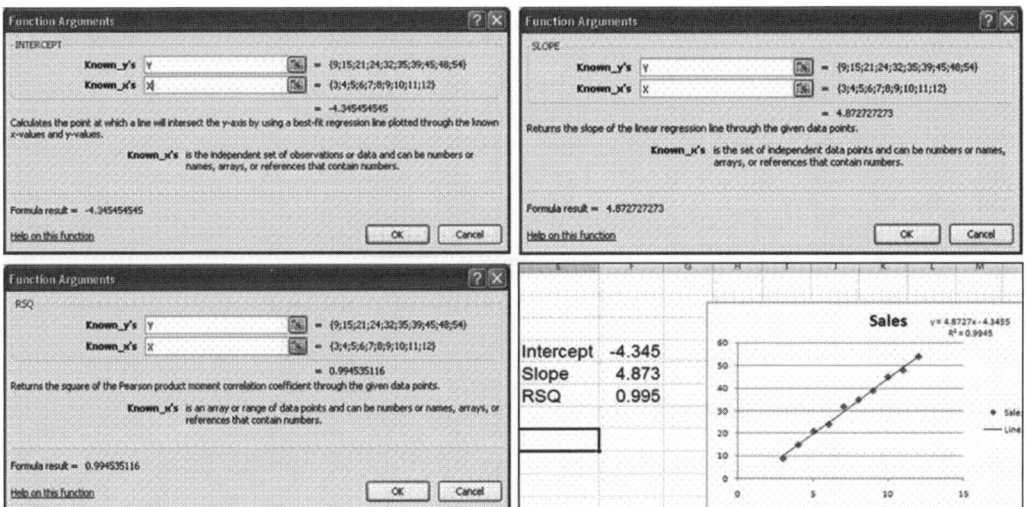

Figure 10.4 Calculating menus

For example, you may want to use them to forecast month 13: $y = -4.345$ (Intercept) $+$ 4.8379 (Slope) $\times$ 13, or use the Forecast function for the following months, as shown in Figure 10.5.

Use: $f_x \Rightarrow$ Statistical $\Rightarrow$ FORECAST

The aim is to forecast sales in month 13, therefore in the x field of the menu, we enter the data point we want to forecast the value for; in this case the value in cell B12, for the 13th month. (For easier differentiation, the font formatting is different for the x values to be forecasted.)

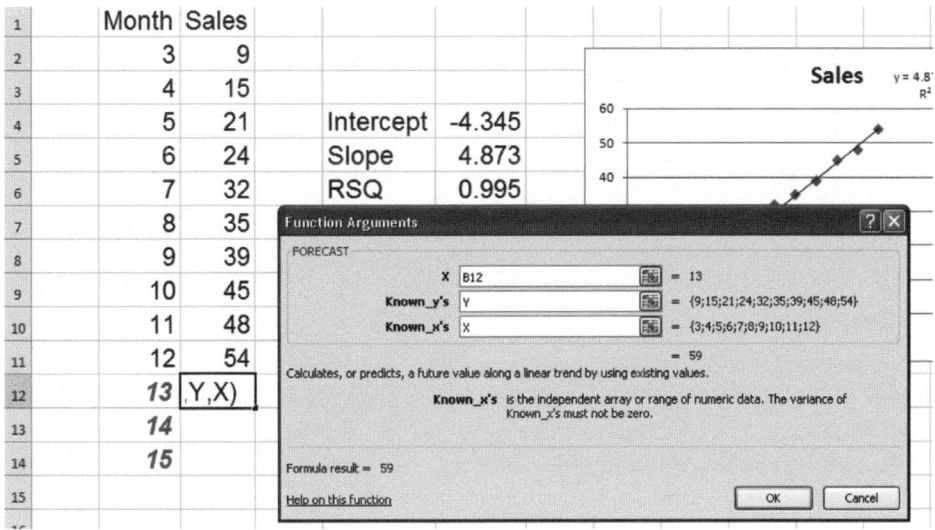

Figure 10.5 Forecast menu

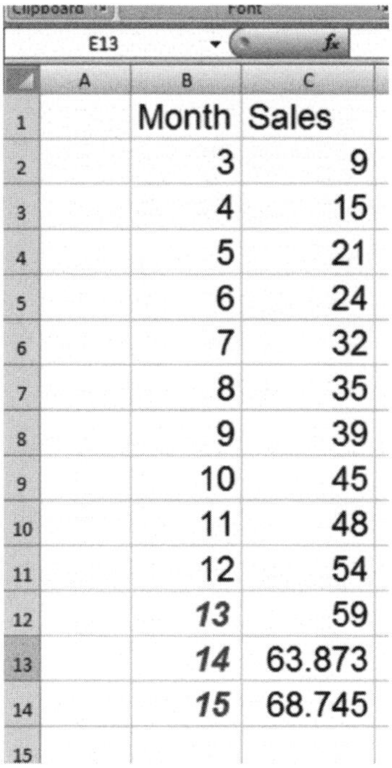

Figure 10.6   The results of using the function Forecast in cells B12:B14

The result for month 13 is 59. The formula can be dragged down to cells C13 and C14, showing the forecast for the following months.

The results of the additional months' calculations using the Forecast function are shown in Figure 10.6.

Some of the conventions or features in Excel can be used to calculate things they were not designed for. The results we just calculated—the values through month 15—can be duplicated without using the Excel Forecast function.

Copy the data to a new sheet. The AutoFill feature can be used to create the regression when the data has the x values in a sequential and equal interval—as we have our months in this example. The AutoFill feature is performing a linear regression on numbers. Select all the values in column C and drag them down. The amazing results are seen in Figure 10.7. You are performing a linear regression using the AutoFill feature.

One More Example

On the sheet *HHold Income* in the Chapter 9 Excel file you can find the household income of a sample of 1,000 customers and the amount of money they used to purchase merchandise from an online appliances sales company. I would like to find the relationship between the household income and purchases, so that I can try and forecast, based on household income, the amount a customer will spend on appliances.

We can create a chart and find the trend line, the linear regression line, and the R^2—of the relationship. In Figures 10.8 and 10.9 you can see the data and the scatter chart I created.

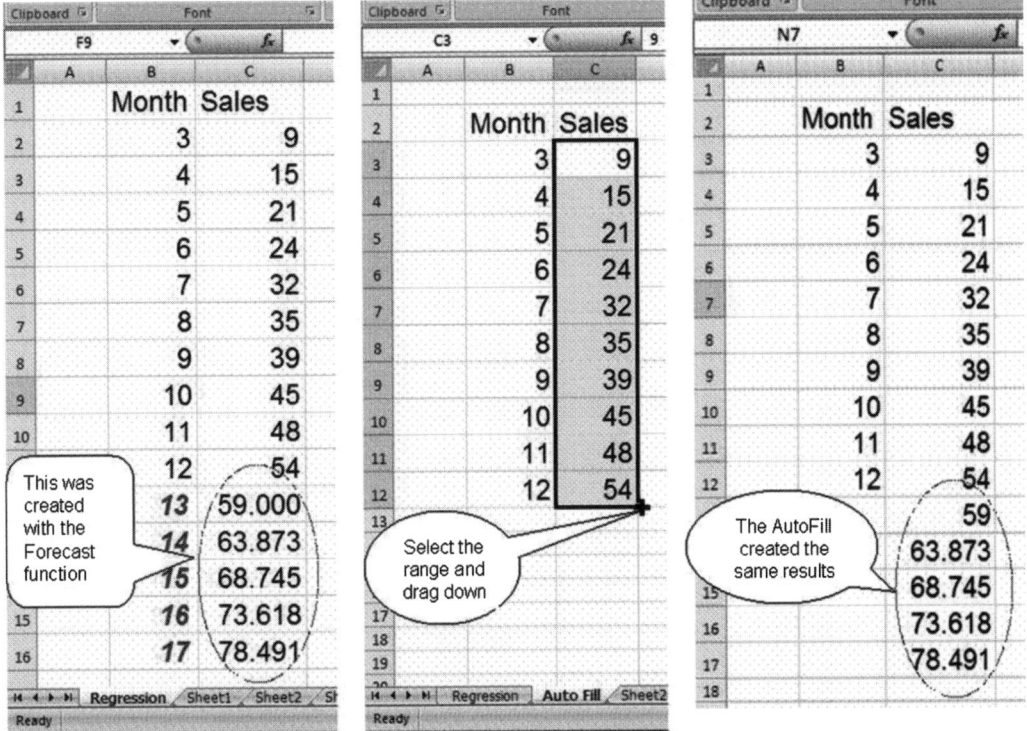

Figure 10.7 Forecast using AutoFill

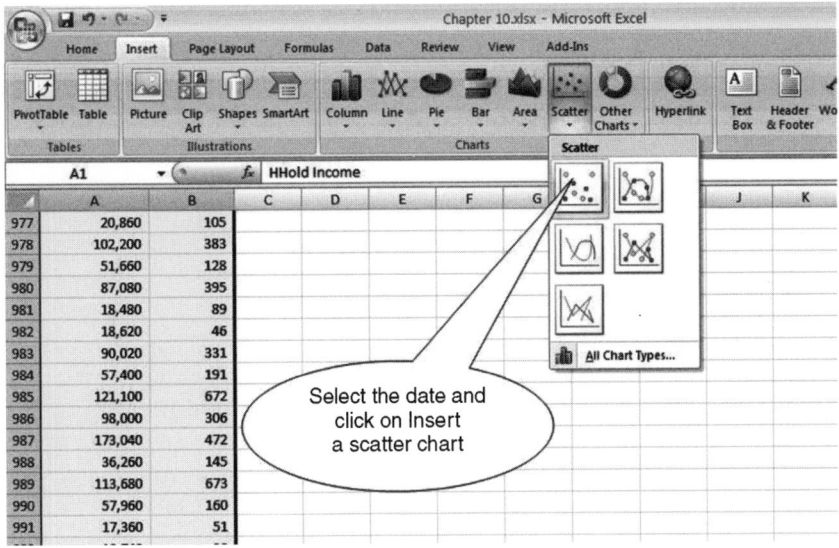

Figure 10.8 The scatter chart

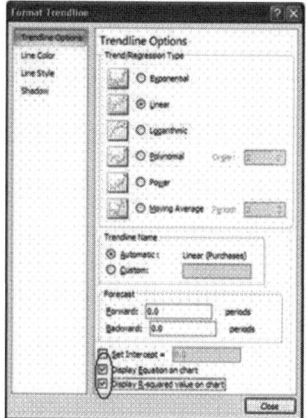 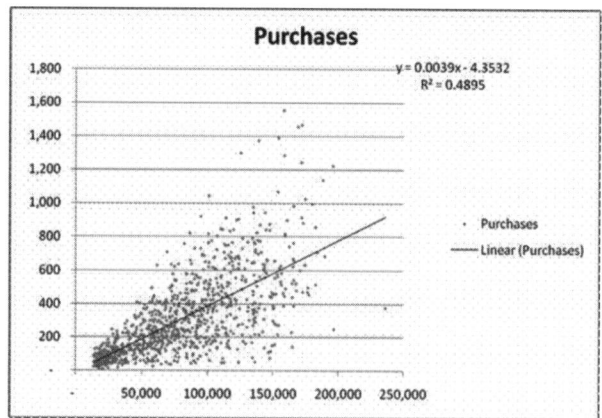

Figure 10.9   Adding the trend line equation to the data

The next step is to create the trend line. You can right-click any of the points, then add the regression line and R^2. I used the same procedure as before. The results are shown in Figure 10.9. $y = 0.0039x - 4.3532$ and $R^2 = 0.4895$. (I formatted the data points to be smaller on the chart.)

The slope of 0.0039 indicates that theoretically every additional dollar in the household income increases the potential purchasing of an individual of our population by $0.0039. If you wanted to forecast the potential purchases of an individual with a household income of $100,000 using the equation $y = 0.0039x - 4.3532$ you would forecast:

$$y = 0.0039 * (100,000) - 4.3532 = \$365.65$$
This result is not accurate since R^2 is low ($R^2 = 0.4895$).

As explained before, since R^2 is not close to 1, you cannot use the regression line to forecast accurately purchase as a function of income. The forecast model would be trustworthy as a forecast tool if the R^2 was above 0.8.

APPENDIX—USING THE CHART FEATURE TO CREATE A TREND LINE IN EXCEL 2003

In the Excel 2003 Chapter 10 file, use the data in the sheet called *Regression* to create an XY scatter chart. Select the data B1:C11, click on the Chart Wizard, and select XY (scatter). Or use the Insert menu ⇨ Chart, and the Wizard will pop-up. See Figure 10.10.

On the XY chart you just created, right-click any of the points and in the drop-down menu, choose Add Trend line. Click on the Options tab in the Add Trend line menu. Check the boxes for Display equation on the chart and Display R-squared value on chart. See Figure 10.11.

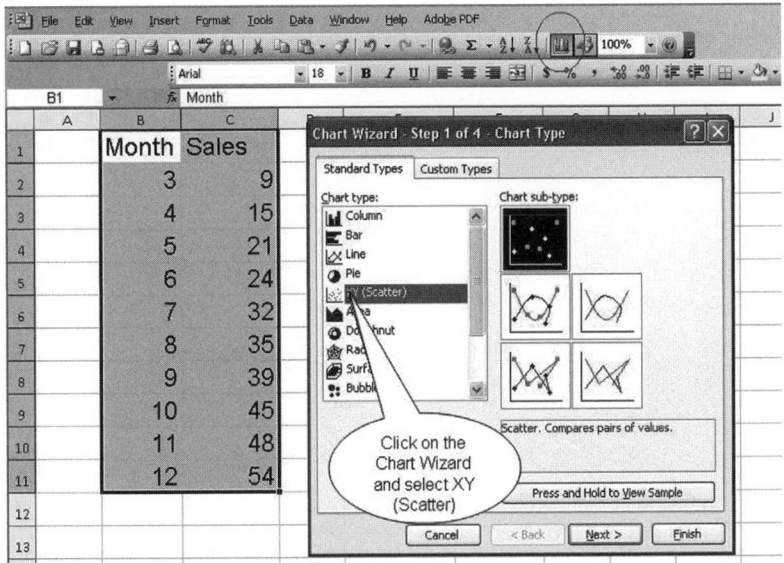

Figure 10.10 Scatter chart

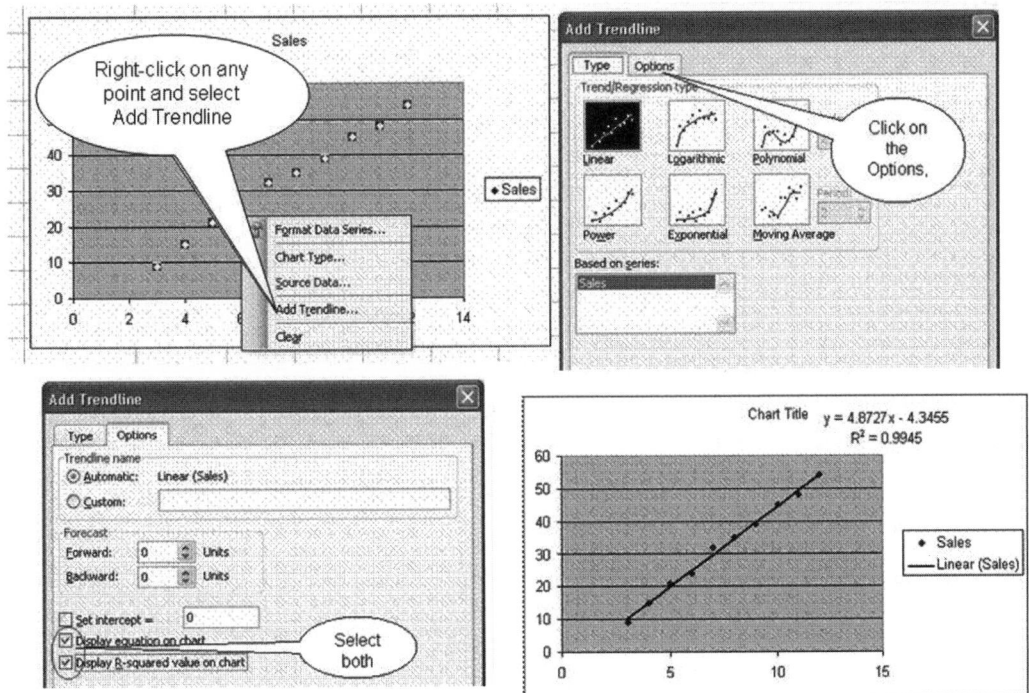

Figure 10.11 Adding the trend line and formulas

REVIEW QUESTIONS

You will find these examples in the Excel Chapter 10 file:

1. On the *HHold Income* sheet, create names for the ranges A2:A1001 (HHold_Income) and B2:B1001 (Purchases).
2. Use the names HHold_Income and Purchases you just created and calculate the Slope, Intercept, and RSQ, using the Excel function Shift+F3.
3. Use the Forecast function to calculate the forecasted value if the Household income is $60,000 and $150,000.

ANSWERS

1. You may want to select the entire range A1:B1001 by pressing the CRTL+Shift+* keys, and apply Create from selection with Excel 2007 under the Formula ribbon or Insert ⇨ Name ⇨Create with Excel 2003 or earlier versions.
2. Slope = 0.0039. Intercept = − 4.3532. RSQ = 0.4895.
3. $229.65 and $463.65.

CHAPTER 11

Data Analysis—The Excel Easy to Use Statistics Add-in

Excel has several add-ins that are useful in a business environment. An Excel add-in is a file/ workbook (usually with an extension .xlas in Excel 2007 or .xla with earlier versions) that can be activated when you open Excel. The file contains VBA code (macro) that adds more features to Excel; usually it is in the form of new functions.

Add-ins provide an excellent way of increasing the power of Excel and they are the ideal vehicle for distributing your custom functions or procedures. Excel is shipped with a variety of add-ins ready for you to load and start using, and many third-parties' add-ins are available to download from a variety of sites.

One of the pre-programmed add-ins in Excel is called Data Analysis (called Analysis ToolPak before installation and/or activation). The ToolPak contains a variety of statistical functions—I will demonstrate a couple of them here.

First, check to see if the Analysis ToolPak is activated in your Excel. Look for [Data Analysis] on the right side of the Data ribbon. If it is not there, you will need to activate it. In previous Excel versions, it is the last item in the Tools menu.

First things first: If you have to install the Analysis ToolPak, follow these steps:

1. Click on the Office ■ icon.
2. In the menu click on Excel Options.
3. In the Excel Options menu select Add-Ins on the left.
4. In the Add-Ins menu choose the Analysis ToolPack and click on Go.
5. Choose again the Analysis ToolPack in the small menu and click OK.
6. Click on Yes when you are asked to install it.

It will take Excel a few seconds to install the Analysis ToolPak. See Figure 11.1. All the other Excel add-ins can be activated/installed with the same procedure.

DESCRIPTIVE STATISTICS

Now that the Data Analysis ToolPak add-in is on the right side of the Data ribbon, I can use it to easily perform many of the calculations that were carried out in the previous chapters. I am going to calculate the same set of statistical functions one more time using the Data Analysis add-in. The data can be found On the *Statistics* sheet in the chapter 11 Excel file.

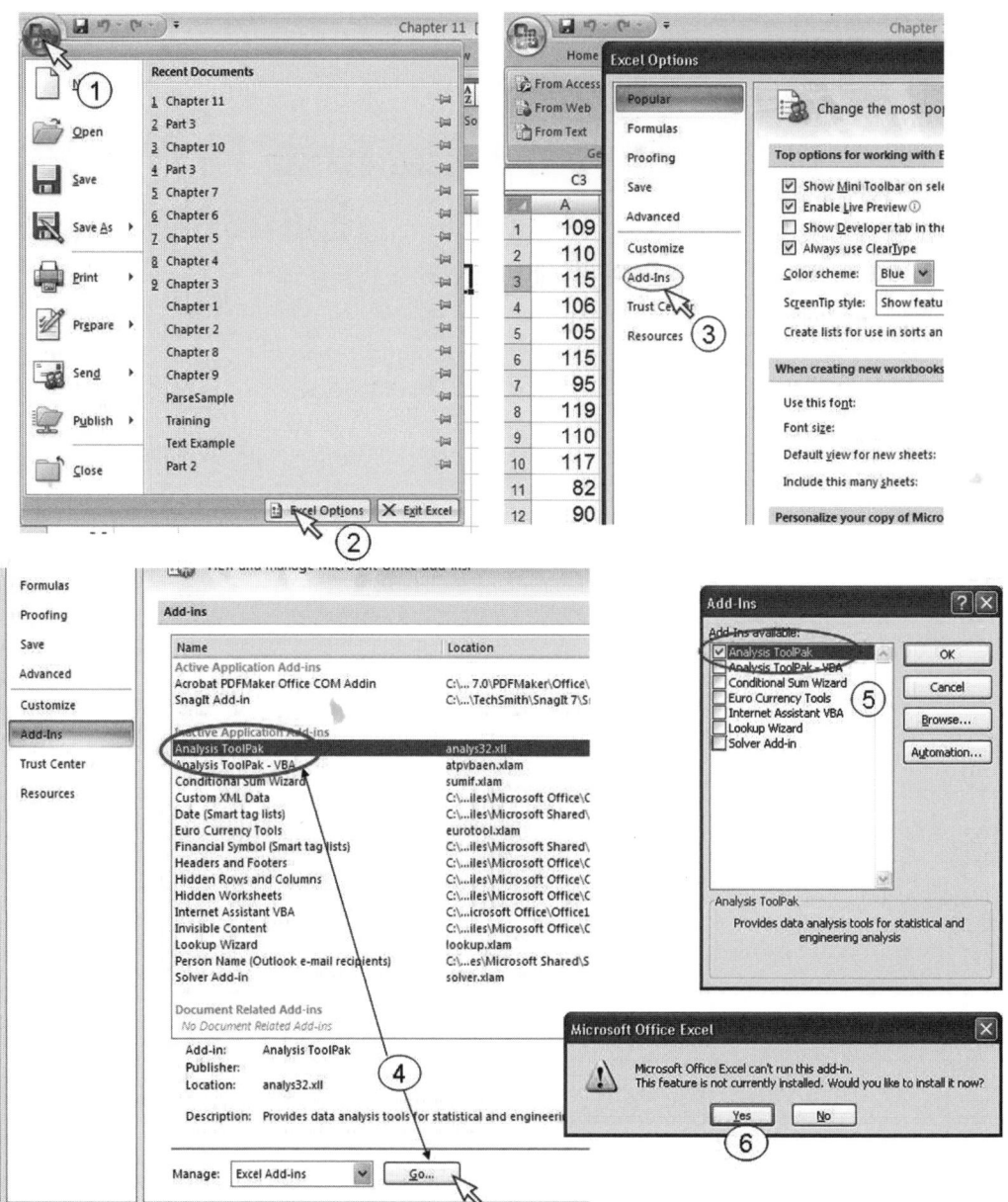

Figure 11.1   To activate the add-in

First, select Data Analysis under the Data ribbon. When you click on the Data Analysis button, the Data Analysis menu will pop up as shown in Figure 11.2. Select Descriptive Statistics and confirm (OK or Enter).

In the Descriptive Statistics window, you can use our data set for the input range by typing DATA or by selecting A1:A500 (the range A1:A500 was named DATA ahead of

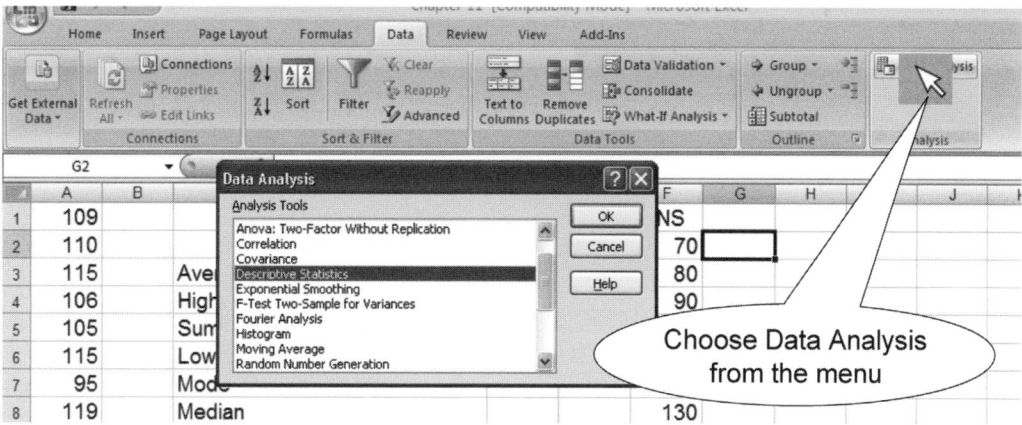

Figure 11.2   Data Analysis is under the Data ribbon

time). You can now check the last four boxes on the bottom left of the menu and click OK. See Figure 11.3 for the menu and the results.

Please note: When you are using the Analysis ToolPak, the results are not linked any more to the original data. Unlike the other Excel functions, the results will not change if you change the original data. You will have to calculate them again.

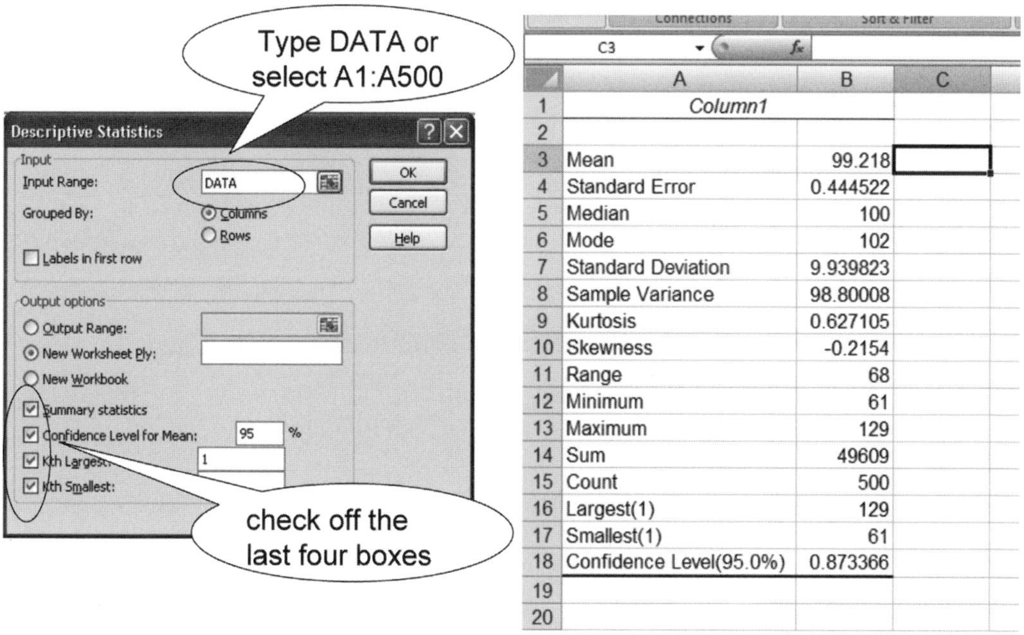

Figure 11.3   The Descriptive Statistics menu

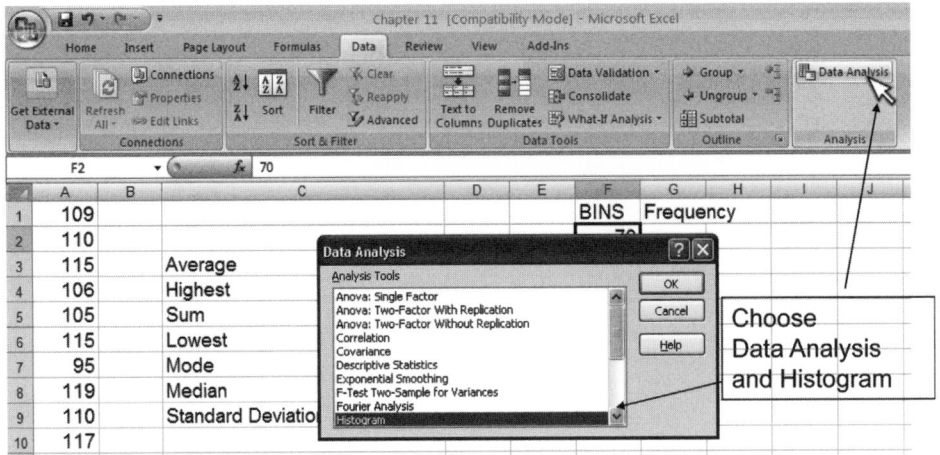

Figure 11.4   To activate the Data Analysis menu, click on the Data Analysis icon

FREQUENCY DISTRIBUTION USING "HISTOGRAM"

You can also calculate the frequencies and create the frequency chart using the Histogram feature of the Analysis ToolPack. Choose Data Analysis and select Histogram. See Figure 11.4.

In the Histogram dialog box, type DATA for the Input Range and select F2:F8 for the Bin Range. The only selection needed is the last box on the bottom left called Chart Output. See Figure 11.5. It will create the results you want. The results are shown in Figure 11.6.

You may want to format the chart as we did before to eliminate the gap between the columns. Remember? This is continuous data. Figure 11.7 describes the three steps needed to format the chart.

One more example

On the sheet *HHold Income* in the Chapter 9 file, you will find the household income of a sample of 1,000 customers and the amount of money they spent to purchase merchandise from an online appliances sales company.

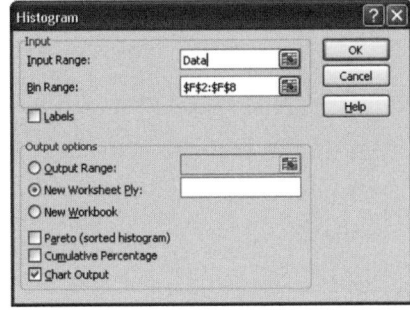

Figure 11.5   The Histogram menu

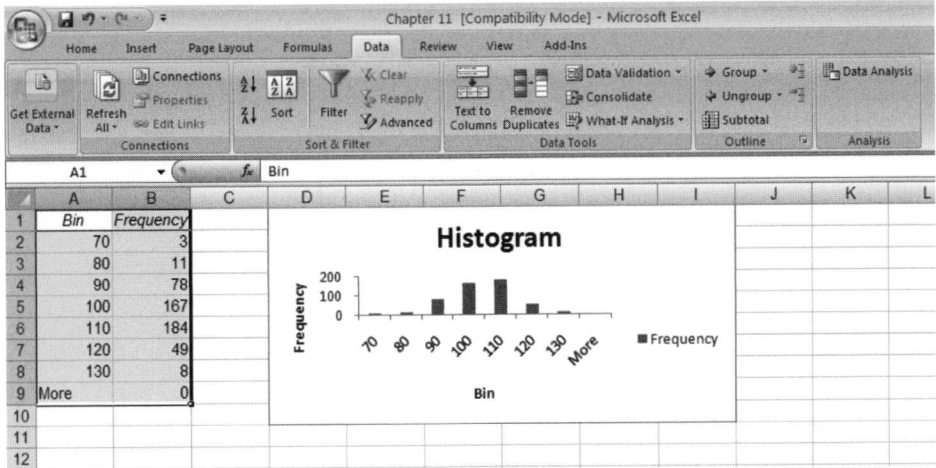

Figure 11.6   The Histogram output

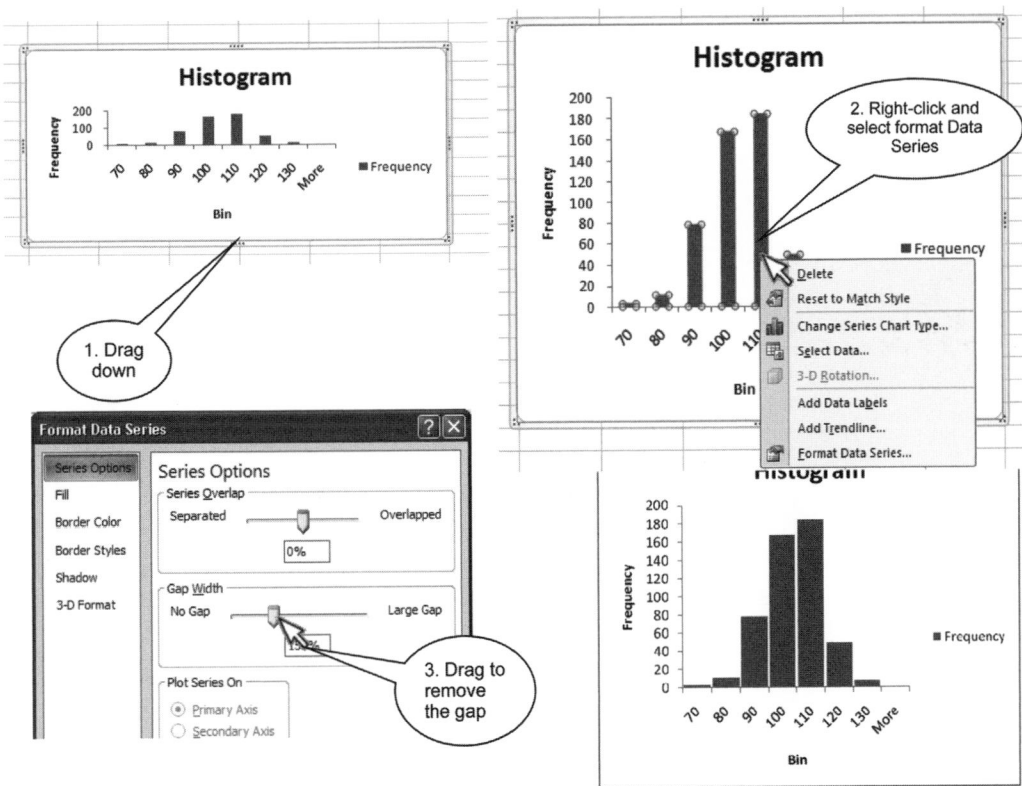

Figure 11.7   Steps needed to format the chart

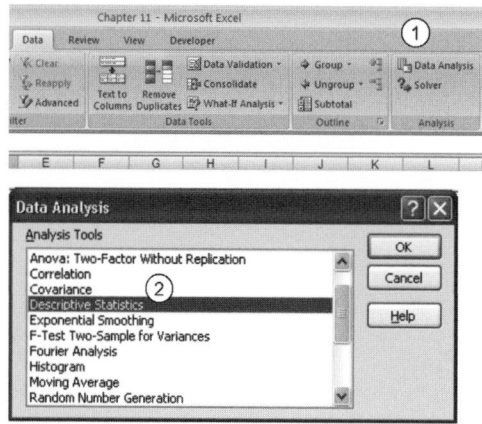
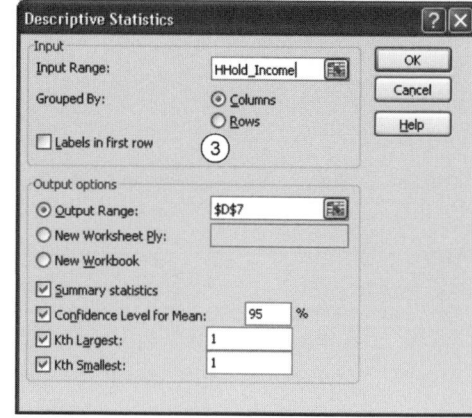

Figure 11.8 Using the Descriptive Statistic menu

You can name the two data sets. I used the menu and named the range A2:A1001 as HHold_Income, and the range B2:B1001 as Purchases. I will use these two sets using the data analysis.

First, I am going to use the descriptive statistics. In Figure 11.8, you can see the procedure I used.

	A	B	C	D	E	F	G
2	22,960	54					
3	151,340	658					
4	136,220	761					
5	37,520	108					
6	15,680	26					
7	59,920	189		*Column1*			
8	48,580	403					
9	112,000	496		Mean	78545.46		
10	84,420	522		Standard Error	1355.442038		
11	87,220	661		Median	75180		
12	131,880	302		Mode	101080		
13	103,320	779		Standard Deviation	42862.84076		
14	64,260	104		Sample Variance	1837223118		
15	73,640	443		Kurtosis	-0.560981818		
16	115,080	379		Skewness	0.419094988		
17	107,380	133		Range	222180		
18	111,160	49		Minimum	14140		
19	93,660	305		Maximum	236320		
20	17,360	57		Sum	78545460		
21	73,640	263		Count	1000		
22	39,620	233		Largest(1)	236320		
23	75,460	296		Smallest(1)	14140		
24	40,460	207		Confidence Level(95.0%)	2659.840048		
25	22,260	101					

Figure 11.9 Descriptive Statistics output

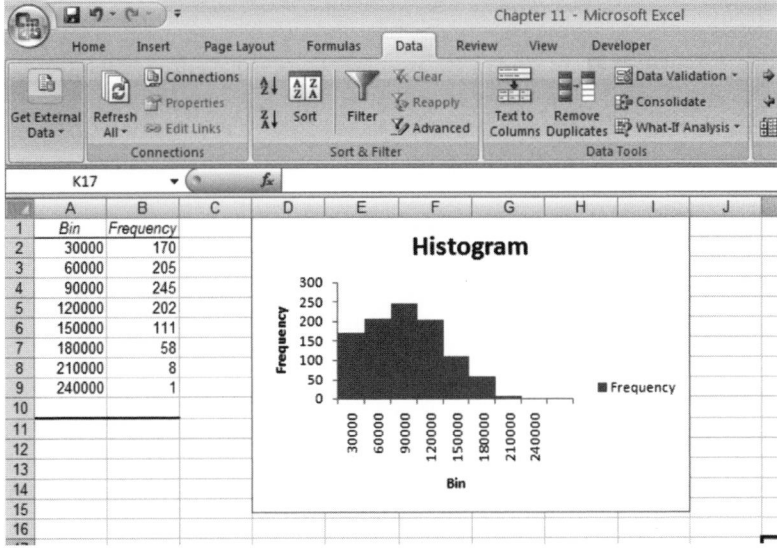

	A	B	C	D	E	F	G	H	I	J
2	22,960	54								
3	151,340	658								
4	136,220	761								
5	37,520	108								
6	15,680	26					236320		30000	
7	59,920	189		Column1			14140		60000	
8	48,580	403	Histogram						90000	
9	112,000	496	Input						120000	
10	84,420	522	Input Range:	HHold_Income		OK			150000	
11	87,220	661	Bin Range:	$I$6:$I$13		Cancel			180000	
12	131,880	302	Labels			Help			210000	
13	103,320	779							240000	
14	64,260	104	Output options							
15	73,640	443	○ Output Range:							
16	115,080	379	◉ New Worksheet Ply:							
17	107,380	133	○ New Workbook							
18	111,160	49								
19	93,660	305	☐ Pareto (sorted histogram)							
20	17,360	57	☐ Cumulative Percentage							
21	73,640	263	☑ Chart Output							
22	39,620	233	Largest(1)		236320					

Figure 11.10　The Histogram menu

1. I clicked on the Data Analysis under the Data ribbon.
2. I chose the Descriptive Statistics option in the Data Analysis menu.
3. I entered the data set (I used F3 for paste-name) HHold_Income for the Input Range. I indicated D7(absolute value) in the Output Range. I also checked all the boxes on the left bottom part of the menu.

See the results in Figure 11.9. The results start in cell D7.

Figure 11.11　Formatted chart

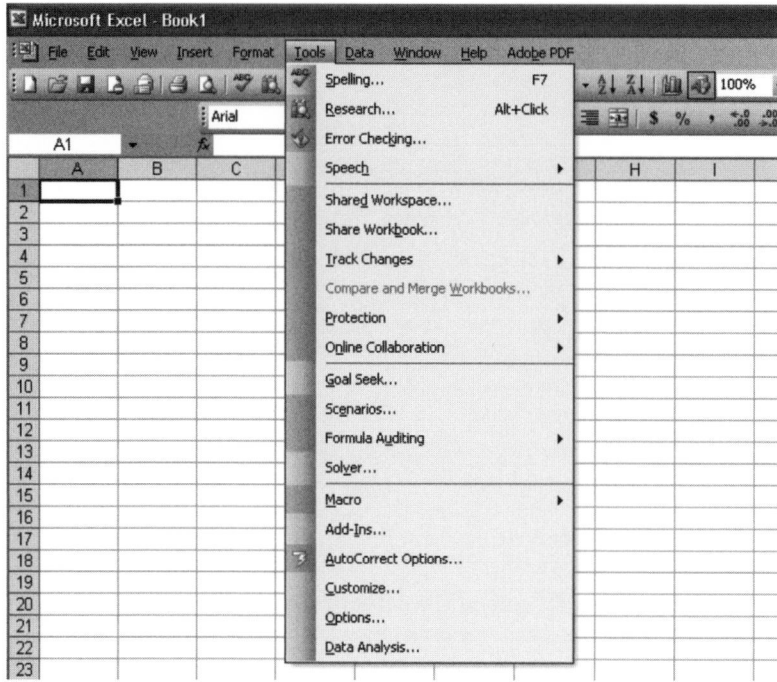

Figure 11.12 Data Analysis is under the Tools menu

To use the histogram, we need to establish it. We calculated the lowest and highest numbers to be 14,140 and 236,326; therefore, we need to create bins as shown in Figure 11.10. We can use Data Analysis to create the histogram.

The formatted output is shown in Figure 11.11.

APPENDIX—USING DATA ANALYSIS IN EXCEL 2003

The Analysis ToolPak works exactly the same way in previous versions of Excel. The only notable differences are in how to launch and activate it, if it is not pre-installed when you start Excel.

To use the Data Analysis in Excel 2003 or other versions, go to Tools ⇨ Data Analysis. See Figure 11.12.

If the Data Analysis is not on your Tools menu, you have to activate it. To activate the Data Analysis, go to Tools ⇨ Add-Ins, and check the Analysis ToolPakv option as shown in Figure 11.13. Now you are ready to go and use the Data Analysis.

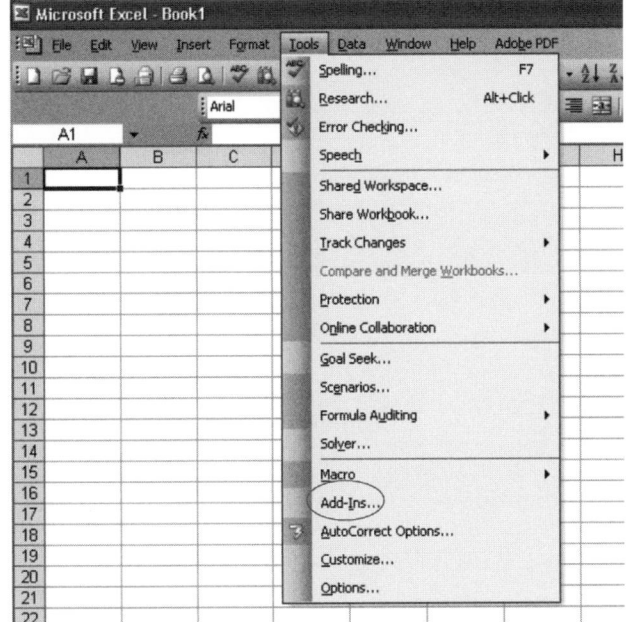
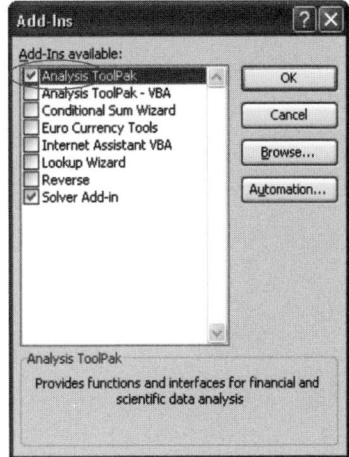

Figure 11.13 Data Analysis in Excel 2003

REVIEW QUESTIONS

You will find these examples in the Excel Chapter 11 file:

1. On the *HHold Income* Sheet, create names for the ranges A2:A1001 (HHold_Income) and B2:B1001 (Purchases).
2. Use the Descriptive Statistics feature of Data Analysis to get the statistics for the Purchases.
3. As you see in problem 2, the lowest value is 9 and the highest is 1,545. Create a Frequency Distribution table and chart.

ANSWERS

1. You may want to select the entire range A1:B1001 by pressing the CRTL+Shift+* keys, and apply Create from Selection with Excel 2007 under the Formula ribbon or Insert ➪ Name ➪ Create with Excel 2003 or earlier versions.

2.

Column1	
Mean	303.694
Standard Error	7.598075751
Median	240
Mode	112
Standard Deviation	240.2722521
Sample Variance	57730.75512
Kurtosis	2.973972391
Skewness	1.469255633
Range	1545
Minimum	9
Maximum	1554
Sum	303694
Count	1000
Largest(1)	1554
Smallest(1)	9
Confidence Level (95.0%)	14.91001873

3.

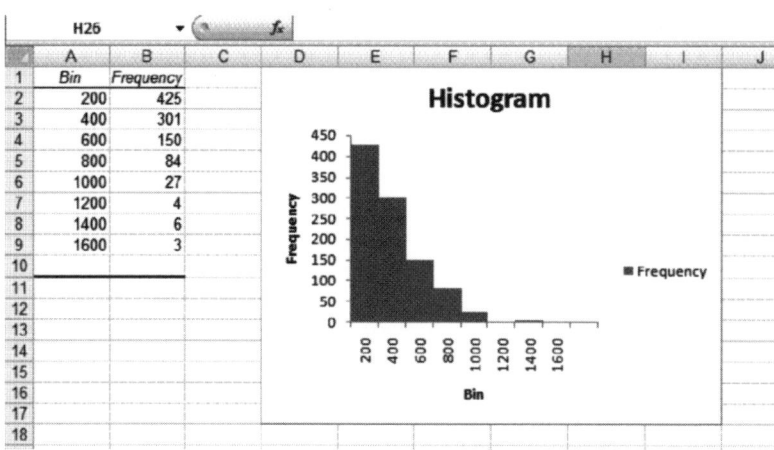

Four

What-if Analysis

What-if analysis enables the user to find out what will be the impact of change. It can be a change of input data or a change in assumptions. The change can be presented in incremental modification of key values.

This part of the book will show you how to take advantage of these What-if tools in the decision-making process. This part demonstrates features such as naming cells for modeling, the Goal Seek, data tables (one- and two-way tables), and the effective use of scroll bars.

Goal Seek allows you to change one variable at a time in the decision models you build in spreadsheets. You can gain insight into the impact of inputs on the final goal. You will find out what the optimal input should be in order to reach a specific goal.

Data Tables enable you to evaluate the incremental change of specific input values on the results. You can change one or two variables simultaneously and watch the impact of these changes on your decision-influencing results.

This section also introduces the use of scroll bars as tools for changing inputs in a model. These scroll bars allow examining changes in more than two variables in a model simultaneously.

Naming Cells—for Meaningful Decision Making and Modeling

When you use Excel for modeling and decision making, one of the challenges you face is the ability to follow the logic or understand the meaning of the functions and the model. The following examples illustrate this problem.

In Figure 12.1, you can see an example of a car loan. The example is in the *Car Loan no names* sheet of the Excel file Chapter 12. If you read the formulas and functions on the model, it is not immediately clear what was meant when the functions or the formulas were created. The formulas are revealed on the right. I used CTRL+` or CTRL+~ to show the formulas.

This is the example: You are purchasing a car for $22,000. You are required to pay $4,000 as a down payment. The annual interest rate is 8 percent and the loan duration is three years. The payments are made at the end of period. Some loans require a beginning of the period payment, such as a mortgage, and others, as in this example, require it at the end. The payments are monthly payments.

The loan formula in cell B4 is clear. It is the price minus the down payment. To calculate the Payment amount, you have to use the Excel financial function called PMT, which returns the periodic payment for an annuity. (As the Excel menu defines it, PMT: "calculates the payment for a loan based on a constant interest rate.") Figure 12.1 illustrates the function. Note that for the Rate Argument, I used B5/12 (the monthly interest rate divided by 12 months) and for the number of periods, B6∗ 12 (the number of years times 12), since I am calculating monthly payments. Also I used -B4, minus the Loan (minus sign B4). The payment function requires a minus sign for the loan so that the monthly payment will be positive; this is part of Excel's requirements for the Payment function (otherwise, it will result in a negative value).

	A	B	C
1	Item	Car	
2	Price	$ 22,000.00	
3	Down Payment	$ 4,000.00	
4	Loan	$ 18,000.00	
5	Rate	8.00%	
6	Years	3	
7	Payment	$564.05	
8	Total Payments	$ 20,305.96	
9	Total Interest	$ 2,305.96	
10			

	A	B
1	Item	Car
2	Price	22000
3	Down Payment	4000
4	Loan	=B2-B3
5	Rate	0.08
6	Years	3
7	Payment	=PMT(B5/12,B6*12,-B4)
8	Total Payments	=B7*12*B6
9	Total Interest	=B8-B4

Figure 12.1   Functions and formulas without names

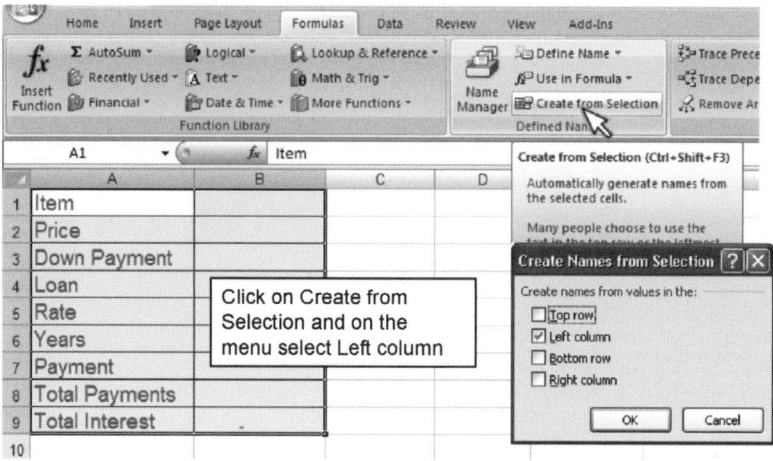

Figure 12.2   Creating a name in Excel

What you really want to see are functions or formulas that convey the information to the analyst or to any other potential audience. The way to make the models meaningful is to change the names of the cells in columns B to be meaningful names. This will make the model very clear and transparent to any potential reader.

To change the names of the cells in column B, simply apply the following procedure:

- Select the two columns with the model A1:B9 on the sheet Car Loan.
- Under the Formulas ribbon, click Create from Selection in the Name Manager sub-category.

See Figure 12.2 for the way it is done.

Once you create the names and enter the formulas and functions, your model will make much more sense. See Figure 12.3.

One More Example—If You Have a Ready Model

In the following example, I received a ready-made Projections Statement where the formulas were already created. See the sheet *BEP Example no names* in the Chapter 12 Excel file. I wanted to change the names of the cells in column C. However, I did not want to recreate the formulas after I changed the names. See Figure 12.4 for the example.

	A	B			A	B
1	Item	Car		1	Item	Car
2	Price	$ 22,000.00		2	Price	22000
3	Down Payment	$ 4,000.00		3	Down Payment	4000
4	Loan	$ 18,000.00		4	Loan	=Price-Down_Payment
5	Rate	8.00%		5	Rate	0.08
6	Years	3		6	Years	3
7	Payment	$ 564.05		7	Payment	=PMT(Rate/12,Years*12,-Loan)
8	Total Payments	$ 20,305.96		8	Total Payments	=Payment*12*Years
9	Total Interest	$ 2,305.96		9	Total Interest	=Total_Payments-Loan

Figure 12.3   Functions and formulas with names

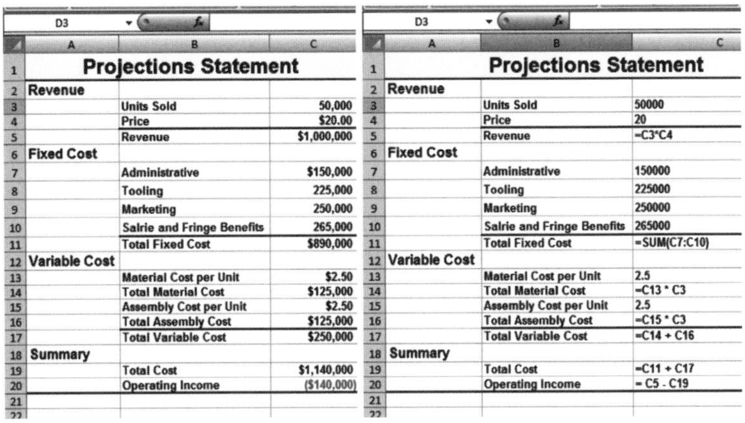

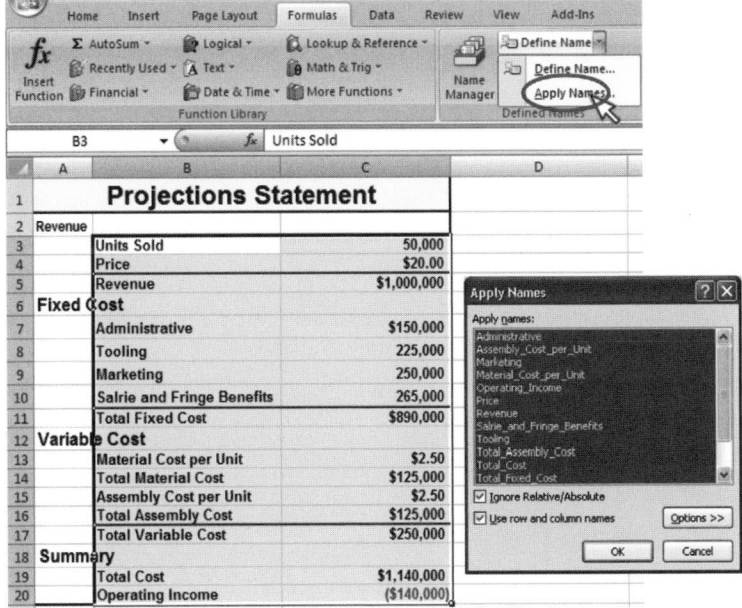

Figure 12.4   Functions and formulas without names

Changing the names in column C is not going to change the formulas. Recreating the formulas would be very time-consuming. The efficient way to do it is to first rename the cell—as we did before—and then apply the name to reflect this renaming. This is the way to do it:

- Create the names by selecting B3:C20 and using Formulas ⇨ Create from Selection.
- Select B3:C20 again and under the Formulas ribbon, click on the drop-down menu next to Define Name and select Apply Names. When you click OK in the dialog box, your model will automatically apply all these cells' names and show them in the formulas. See Figure 12.5.

Figure 12.5   Applying names

	A	B	C
1		Projections Statement	
2	Revenue		
3		Units Sold	50000
4		Price	20
5		Revenue	=Units_Sold*Price
6	Fixed Cost		
7		Administrative	150000
8		Tooling	225000
9		Marketing	250000
10		Salrie and Fringe Benefits	265000
11		Total Fixed Cost	=SUM(Administrative:Salrie_and_Fringe_Benefits)
12	Variable Cost		
13		Material Cost per Unit	2.5
14		Total Material Cost	=Material_Cost_per_Unit * Units_Sold
15		Assembly Cost per Unit	2.5
16		Total Assembly Cost	=Assembly_Cost_per_Unit * Units_Sold
17		Total Variable Cost	=Total_Material_Cost + Total_Assembly_Cost
18	Summary		
19		Total Cost	=Total_Fixed_Cost + Total_Variable_Cost
20		Operating Income	= Revenue - Total_Cost

Figure 12.6 Formulas with names

You can see the final results in Figure 12.6. Now the model makes much more sense. Any reader can understand what functions are at play, and what is being analyzed.

We are going to use these two examples in the following chapters.

APPENDIX—CREATE AND APPLY NAMES IN EXCEL 2003

In the example shown in Figure 12.7, you can see the same example of a car loan. The example is in the *Car Loan no names* sheet of the Chapter 12 Excel 2003 file. If you read the formulas and functions on the model, it is not clear at all what was meant when the functions or the formulas were created. The formulas are revealed on the right. I used CTRL+` or CTRL+~ to show the formulas.

What you really want to see are functions or formulas that convey the information to the analyst or to any other potential audience.

To change the names in the cells in column B, apply the following procedure:

- Select the two columns with the model A1:B9 on the sheet named *Car Loan.*
- Use Insert ⇨ Name ⇨ Create.
- In the Create Names window, select Left column.

	A	B
1	Item	Car
2	Price	$ 22,000.00
3	Down Payment	$ 4,000.00
4	Loan	$ 18,000.00
5	Rate	8.00%
6	Years	3
7	Payment	$564.05
8	Total Payments	$ 20,305.96
9	Total Interest	$ 2,305.96

	A	B
1	Item	Car
2	Price	22000
3	Down Payment	4000
4	Loan	=B2-B3
5	Rate	0.08
6	Years	3
7	Payment	=PMT(B5/12,B6*12,-B4)
8	Total Payments	=B7*12*B6
9	Total Interest	=B8-B4

Figure 12.7 Formulas without names

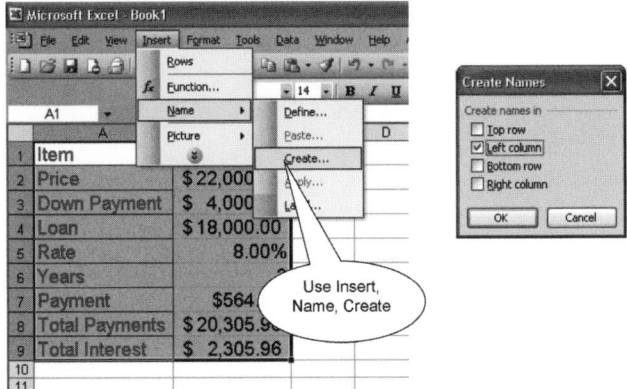

Figure 12.8   Creating names in Excel 2003

See Figure 12.8 for the way it is done.
Now look at the results in Figure 12.9.

One More Example—If You Have a Ready Model

In the second example, we already have all the formulas. What we want to do is change the formulas to reflect the names. See the sheet *BEP Example no names* in the Chapter 12 Excel 2003 file. I wanted to change the names in the cells in column C. However, I did not want to recreate the formulas after I changed the names. See Figure 12.10 for the example.

We have to take two steps as we did before. First, we have to select the two columns, B and C, and use Insert ➪ Name ➪ Create. The same procedure you see in Figure 12.8. The cell will be named. However, the formulas will not have the names as part of them. In order to APPLY the names to the formulas, you have to select the two columns again, B and C, and use Insert ➪ Name ➪Apply. See Figure 12.11 for the procedure.

See the results in Figure 12.12. Now the model makes much more sense.

	A	B
1	Item	Car
2	Price	22000
3	Down Payment	4000
4	Loan	=Price-Down_Payment
5	Rate	0.08
6	Years	3
7	Payment	=PMT(Rate/12,Years*12,-Loan)
8	Total Payments	=Payment*Years*12
9	Total Interest	=Total_Payments-Loan

Figure 12.9   Model with names in formulas

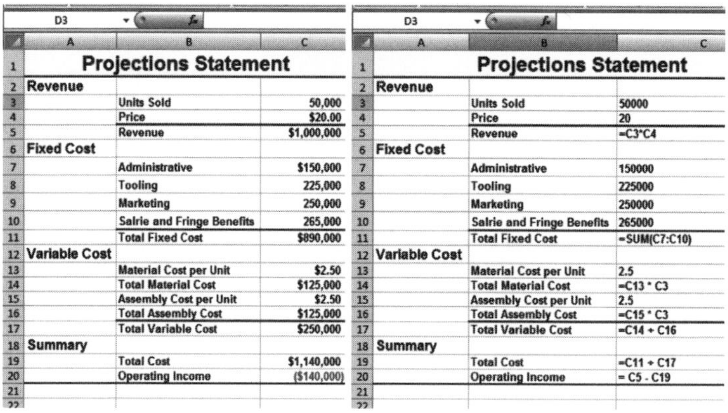

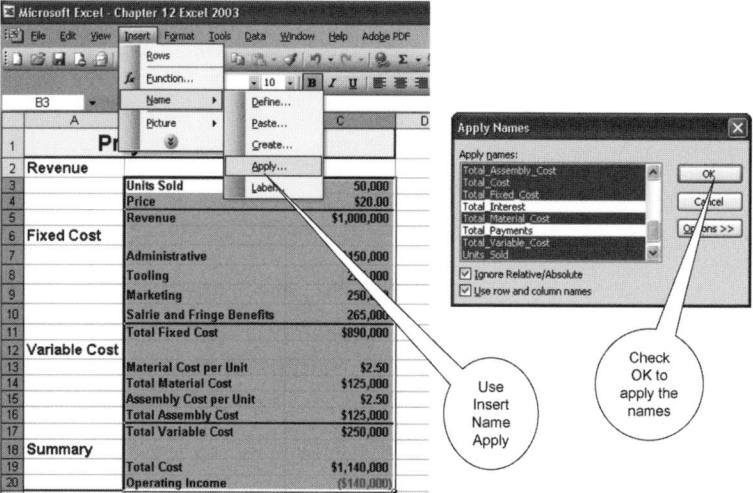

Figure 12.10   Formulas without names

Figure 12.11   Apply Names menu

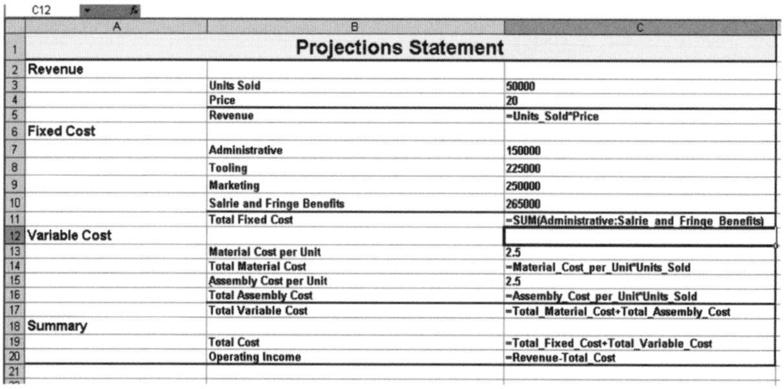

Figure 12.12   Formulas with names

REVIEW QUESTIONS

You will find these examples in the Excel Chapter 12 file:

1. On the *Review* sheet of the Chapter 12 file, you will see the following example, where the formulas are revealed on the right side.

	A	B			A	B
1	Units	10,000		1	Units	10000
2	Sales Price per Unit:	$12		2	Sales Price per Unit:	12
3	Manufacturing Cost per Unit:	$8		3	Manufacturing Cost per Unit:	8
4	Fixed Monthly Expense:	$25,000		4	Fixed Monthly Expense:	25000
5	Revenue	$120,000		5	Revenue	=B1*B2
6	Expenses	$105,000		6	Expenses	=B4+B3*B1
7	Profit	$15,000		7	Profit	=B5-B6

Create the cell names in column B. Use the names in column A.

2. **Apply** the names you just created to the formulas in column B.

ANSWERS

1. Select A1:B7 and under the Formulas ribbon, click on Create from Selection. On the Create Names from Selection menu, select Left column. See figure below. In Excel 2003 use Insert ➪ Name ➪ Create.

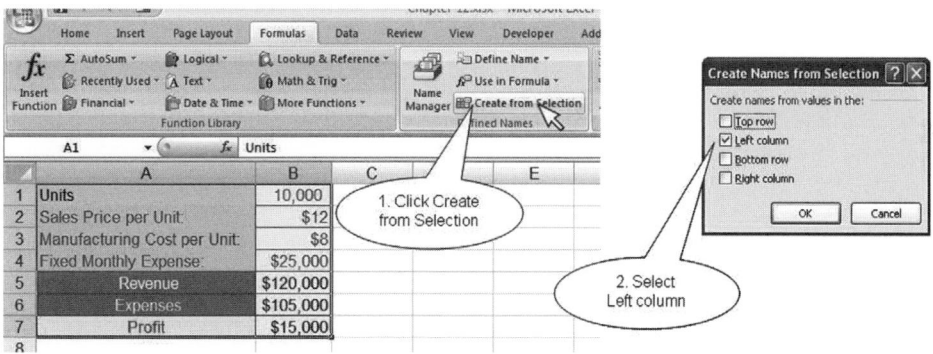

2. Select A1:B7, click on the drop-down menu next to Define Names and use Apply Names. See the figures for the procedure and the results.

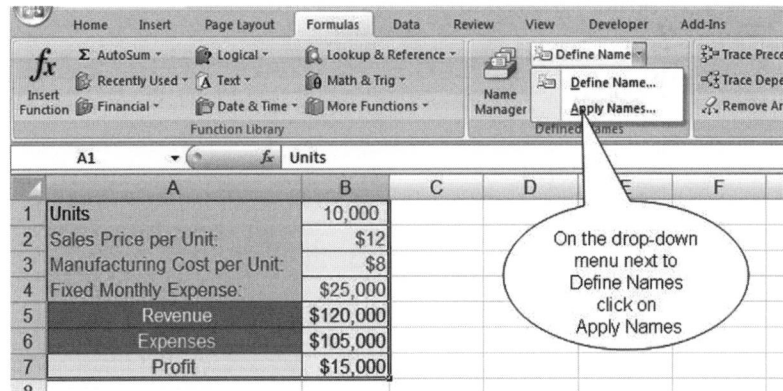

	A	B
1	Units	10,000
2	Sales Price per Unit:	$12
3	Manufacturing Cost per Unit:	$8
4	Fixed Monthly Expense:	$25,000
5	Revenue	$120,000
6	Expenses	$105,000
7	Profit	$15,000

	A	B
1	Units	10000
2	Sales Price per Unit:	12
3	Manufacturing Cost per Unit:	8
4	Fixed Monthly Expense:	25000
5	Revenue	=B1*B2
6	Expenses	=B4+B3*B1
7	Profit	=B5-B6

	A	B
1	Units	10000
2	Sales Price per Unit:	12
3	Manufacturing Cost per Unit:	8
4	Fixed Monthly Expense:	25000
5	Revenue	=Units*Sales_Price_per_Unit
6	Expenses	=Fixed_Monthly_Expense+Manufacturing_Cost_per_Unit*Units
7	Profit	=Revenue-Expenses

CHAPTER 13

What-if Analysis and Goal Seek

What-if analysis allows the user to test the impact on the outcome of a model by changing values in certain cells. This chapter describes one aspect of the What-if analysis procedure—the Goal Seek. The following chapters will continue with other What-if analysis such as analysis with data tables and scroll bars.

This Goal Seek concept is demonstrated with the same car loan example that was introduced in chapter 12. See Figure 13.1 for the model and formulas.

Let me go over the example again. You are purchasing a car for $22,000. You are required to pay $4,000 as a down payment. The annual interest rate is 8.00 percent and the loan duration is three years. The payments are made at the end of period. Some loans require a beginning of the period payment, such as a mortgage, and others, as in this example, require it at the end. The payments are monthly payments.

The loan formula in cell B4 is clear. It is the price minus the down payment. To calculate the Payment amount, you have to use the Excel financial function called PMT, which returns the periodic payment for an annuity. (As the Excel menu defines it, PMT: "calculates the payment for a loan based on a constant interest rate.") Figure 13.2 illustrates the function. Note that for the Rate Argument, I used Rate/12 and for the number of periods, the Years*12, since I am calculating monthly payments. Also I used -Loan (minus sign Loan). The payment function requires a minus sign for the loan so that the monthly payment will be positive; this is part of Excel's requirements for the Payment function (otherwise it will result in a negative value). See Figure 13.2.

The function calculates the monthly payment for the loan to be $564.05. I calculated the last two cell values B8 and B9. For the Total Payments we used=Payment*Years*12 and for the Total Interest: =Total_Payments -Loan. The results are shown on the left side of Figure 13.1. When you use CTRL+` (left apostrophe) or CRTL+~ (tilde), you can see all the formulas on the sheet. These formulas are shown again on the right side of Figure 13.3.

	A	B			A	B
1	Item	Car		1	Item	Car
2	Price	$ 22,000.00		2	Price	22000
3	Down Payment	$ 4,000.00		3	Down Payment	4000
4	Loan	$ 18,000.00		4	Loan	=Price-Down_Payment
5	Rate	8.00%		5	Rate	0.08
6	Years	3		6	Years	3
7	Payment	$ 564.05		7	Payment	=PMT(Rate/12,Years*12,-Loan)
8	Total Payments	$ 20,305.96		8	Total Payments	=Payment*12*Years
9	Total Interest	$ 2,305.96		9	Total Interest	=Total_Payments-Loan

Figure 13.1 Car loan example model used for analysis

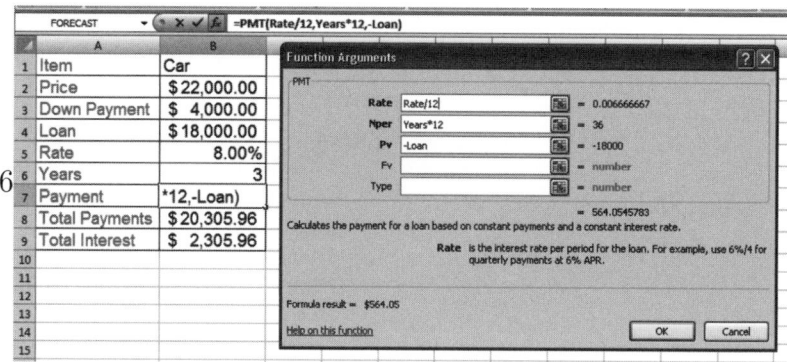

Figure 13.2   The Payment Function Arguments window

The values and the formulas				
Item Purchased	Car	Item Purchased		Car
Price	$ 22,000.00	Price		22000
Down Payment	$ 4,000.00	Down Payment		4000
Loan	$ 18,000.00	Loan		=Price-Down_Payment
Rate	8.00%	Rate		0.08
Years	3	Years		3
Payment	$564.05	Payment		=PMT(Rate/12,Years*12,-Loan)
Total Payments	$ 20,305.96	Total Payments		=Payment*Years*12
Total Interest	$ 2,305.96	Total Interest		=Total_Payments-Loan

Figure 13.3   The results and the formulas of the model

GOAL SEEK

Goal Seek is used to check what would happen to an input or an assumption if we wanted the **end result** to be different from the result obtained. In our example, we will fine-tune the monthly payment of $564.05 to obtain a different solution or value. What would happen if you could not afford the amount of $564.05 as your payments? What should you do if you could pay only $530 a month?

You can use Goal Seek to evaluate various possible inputs, generating different scenarios:

- You can try and purchase a less expensive car.
- You can put down a larger down payment.
- You can repay the loan over a longer period (more than three years).
- You may negotiate a lower interest rate.

Goal Seek will allow you to change only ONE parameter at a time, all the other parameters need to remain the same as originally defined. We will see later on how to use other

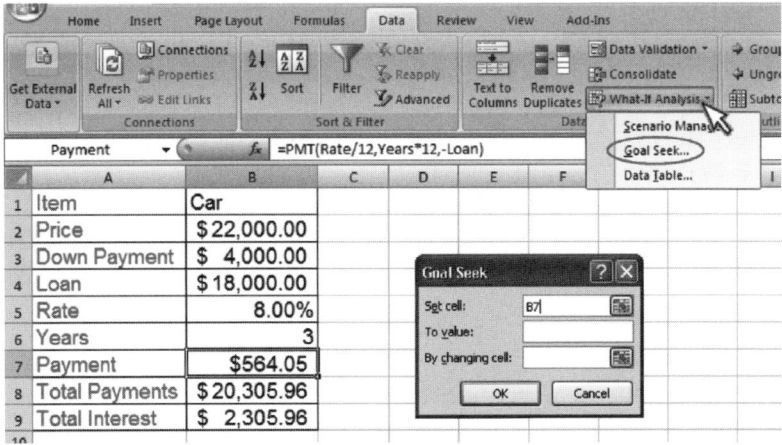

Figure 13.4 Goal Seek can be found under the Data ribbon

Excel tools for a What-if analysis, allowing more than one parameter to change in order to achieve a desired outcome.

Start with the option of purchasing a less expensive car. Select the Payment cell B7. Select Goal Seek from the What-If Analysis menu on the Data ribbon. See Figure 13.4.

As you would like to pay only $530 per month, use the Goal Seek to assist you. If you try it, the Goal Seek tells you that you could, under these circumstances, purchase a car for $20,913.26, keeping in mind that all other factors (loan payback time period, down-payment, interest rate) are presumed to remain the same. Only the monthly payment has changed compared to our original proposition. (See Figure 13.5.) This is powerful; the Goal Seek calculates that if you want to buy a car under those conditions, and all you can reimburse is $530 a month, you have to go out and buy yourself a $20,913.26 car.

If you really want the same car, you may want to cancel the Goal Seek and try it again with a different option. You can choose the down payment for the variable cell. What kind of a down payment do you have to come up with if you wish to buy the same car and pay only $530 a month over the course of three years, at an 8 percent interest rate? Try it. The answer is $5,086.74.

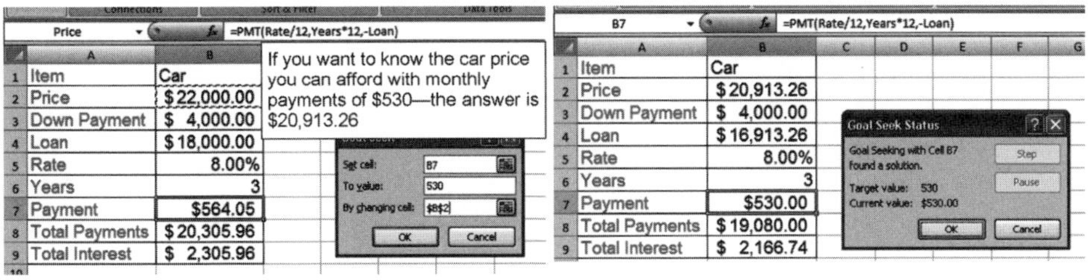

Figure 13.5 Goal Seek for a new price

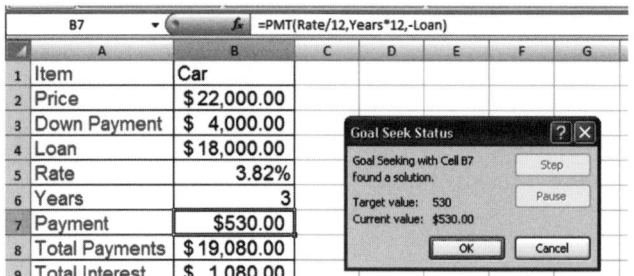

Figure 13.6   Using Goal Seek for a new interest rate

Try a different option. Try adjusting the number of years it will take to pay off the same loan in order to achieve our goal of a $530 monthly payment. If you use the Goal Seek again, it will turn out to be 3.22 years—close to 39 months.

In Figure 13.6, you can see that I checked the impact on the interest rate of paying only $530 a month. As you can see, the desired interest rate to meet this goal is 3.82 percent.

The Goal Seek is a powerful, useful, and easy-to-use feature. Try one more example. This is the same example we used before.

One More Example—Break Even Point Analysis

In Figure 13.7, I show the second example that will demonstrate the same Goal Seek concepts shown above. In the example, our projections show $140,000 losses in the statement. The operating income is negative.

Operating_Income	= Revenue - Total_Cost		
A	B	C	C
Projections Statement			nt
Revenue			
	Units Sold	50,000	50000
	Price per Unit	$20.00	20
	Revenue	$1,000,000	=Units_Sold*Price_per_Unit
Fixed Cost			
	Administrative	$150,000	150000
	Tooling	225,000	225000
	Marketing	250,000	250000
	Salrie and Fringe Benefits	265,000	265000
	Total Fixed Cost	$890,000	=SUM(Administrative:Salrie_and_Fringe_Benefits)
Variable Cost			
	Material Cost per Unit	$2.50	2.5
	Total Material Cost	$125,000	=Material_Cost_per_Unit * Units_Sold
	Assembly Cost per Unit	$2.50	2.5
	Total Assembly Cost	$125,000	=Assembly_Cost_per_Unit * Units_Sold
	Total Variable Cost	$250,000	=Total_Material_Cost + Total_Assembly_Cost
Summary			
	Total Cost	$1,140,000	=Total_Fixed_Cost + Total_Variable_Cost
	Operating Income	($140,000)	= Revenue - Total_Cost

Figure 13.7   Second model—break even point analysis

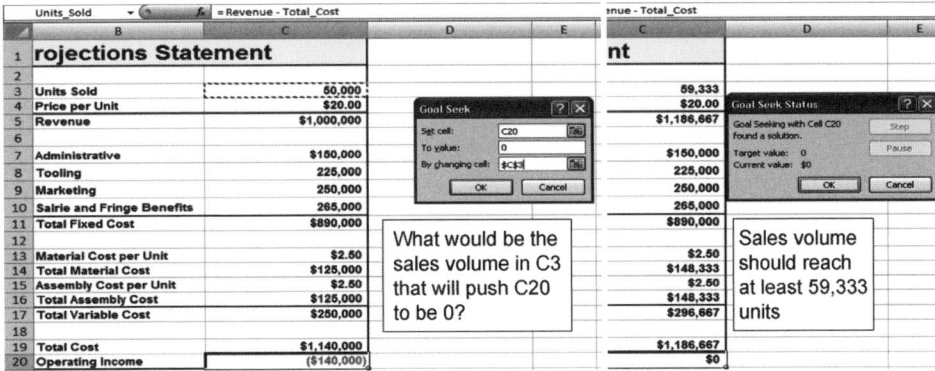

Figure 13.8   The sales volume should reach at least 59,333 units to break even

The objective here is to have this statement break even. In other words: what do you have to change to eliminate the $140,000 in losses and make it at least 0? The tool to use again is Goal Seek. You can use Goal Seek and calculate the impact of the changes of a few of the inputs: Sales Volume/Units Sold, Price per Unit, or any one of the other inputs in the statement.

Start with the number of units sold. How many units do you have to sell in order to break even? If you use Goal Seek you will find out, as you see in Figure 13.8, that the sales volume would have to reach at least 59,333 units.

You can try Goal Seek by yourself. I tried Goal Seek for the Price per Unit as you can see in Figure 13.9. Keeping all other inputs fixed, you would have to sell the product for at least $22.80 in order to break even.

I also tried reducing the marketing budget. See Figure 13.10. When I used Goal Seek, it indicated that we can break even if the marketing budget is reduced to $110,000.

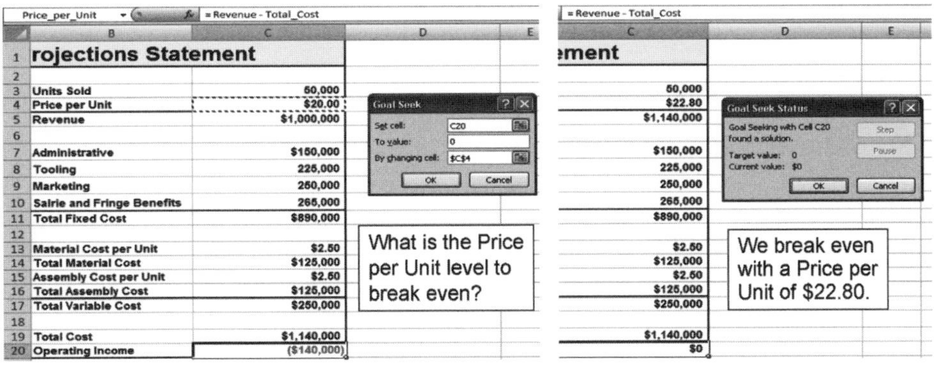

Figure 13.9   The price has to be $22.80 to break even

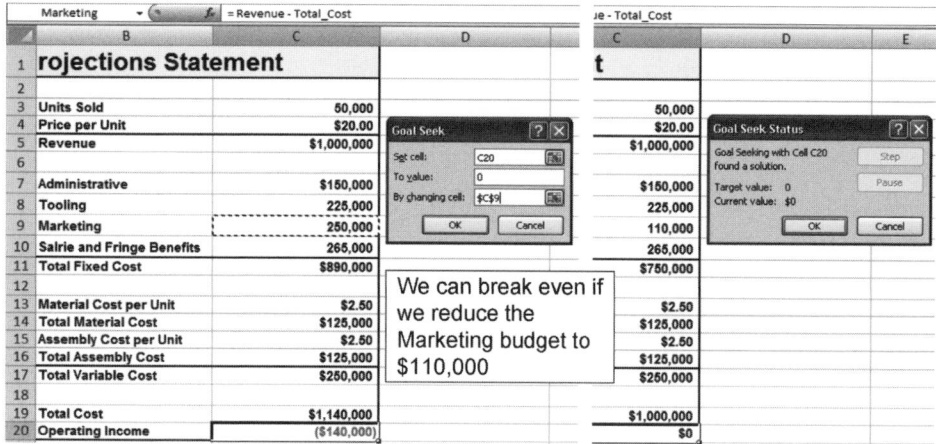

Figure 13.10 The marketing budget has to reach $110,000 to break even

APPENDIX—GOAL SEEK IN EXCEL 2003

In previous versions of Excel, the operation of Goal Seek is identical to the 2007 interface. The only difference is in the way to find it. In Excel 2003 or previous versions, Goal Seek can be found in the list under the Tools menu heading. See Figure 13.11.

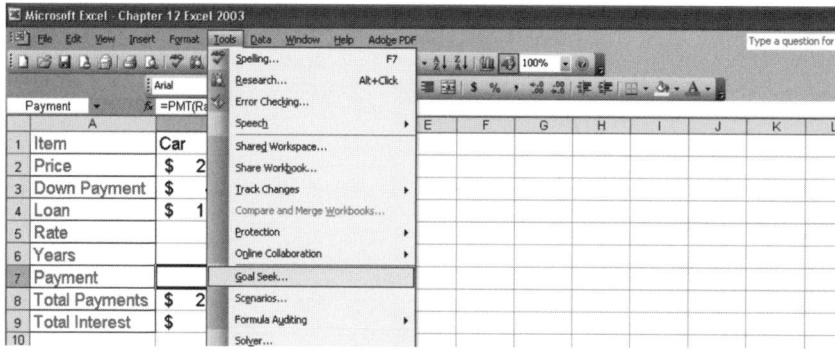

Figure 13.11 Finding Goal Seek under the Tools menu

REVIEW QUESTIONS

You will find these examples in the Excel Chapter 13 file:

1. On the *Review* sheet for the Excel file called Chapter 13, you will see the example below. The right side of the figure shows the formulas used to calculate the sheet.

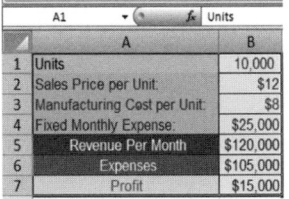 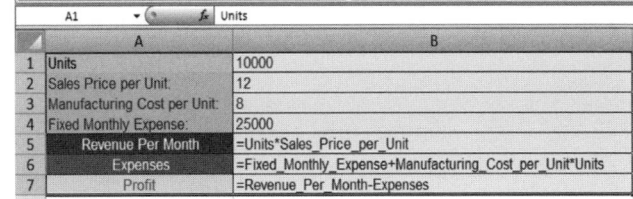

Use Goal Seek to find the break even price for this sheet.

2. On the same sheet, calculate the minimum number of units the firm has to sell in order to break even.
3. On the same sheet, figure out what should be the maximum Manufacturing Cost per Unit in order to break even.
4. What is the highest Fixed Monthly Expenses possible in the same statement to break even?

ANSWERS

1. $11
2. 6,250 units
3. $10
4. $40,000

CHAPTER 14

Sensitivity Analysis—One- and Two-way Data Tables

A data table is a range of cells that shows how changing certain inputs in your model affect the outcome. A data table provides a tool for recalculating multiple options in one operation while showing them together on your worksheet. A data table is also referred to by analysts and decision makers as a "Sensitivity Analysis" table. Sensitivity analysis is a way to investigate the impact of changes in the input of the decision-making models.

Using the same car loan example used in the last two chapters, you will explore the impact on the results of changing some of the inputs in the model. The inputs may be the price, the number of years of the loan, the interest rate, and so on. The results/output, in this example, may be the payment, the total payments, or the total interest.

The first example will investigate the use of a data table to demonstrate our sensitivity analysis using the interest rate. The initial model has a rate of 8.00 percent. I want to try a range of rates from 3 percent to 9 percent—see Figure 14.1. First, I must set up the table. In this example, the range of rates is placed down the column to the left of the planned table. I am going to investigate the impact of changes in the rate on the last three output items on the sheet in cells B7:B9, the payment, total payments, and the total interest.

The rest of the table is set up to the right of the varying rates column. Starting with cell F2, type "=" and select cell B7 (now called Payment since it was named previously); then click Enter to transfer the information to that cell. (See Figure 14.2.)

Repeat this procedure for the values in cells B8 and B9. In cell G2: type = and select B8 (or Total Payments value). In cell H2: type = and select Total Interest value (B9). The results are shown in Figure 14.3.

	C13		*fx*						
	A	B	C	D	E	F	G	H
1	Item	Car			Rate	Payment	Total Payments	Total Interest
2	Price	$ 22,000.00						
3	Down Payment	$ 4,000.00			3%			
4	Loan	$ 18,000.00			4%			
5	Rate	8.00%			5%			
6	Years	3			6%			
7	Payment	$564.05			7%			
8	Total Payments	$ 20,305.96			8%			
9	Total Interest	$ 2,305.96			9%			

Figure 14.1 The car loan model

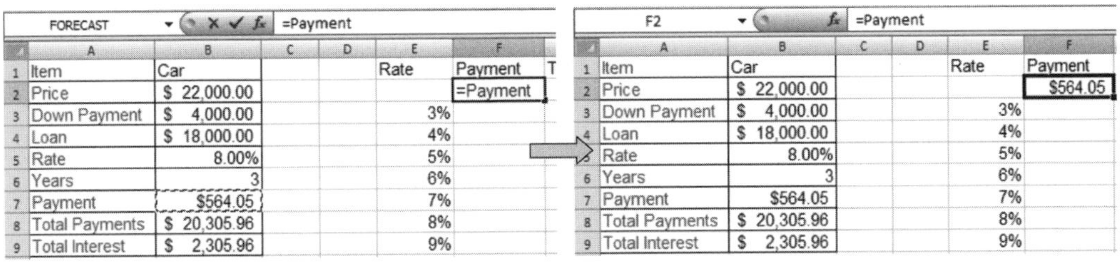

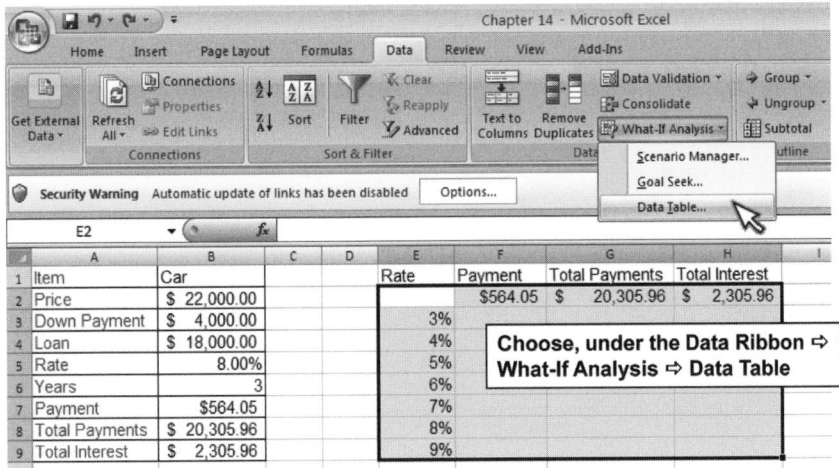

Figure 14.2   Preparing the data table—transfer the parameters to the table

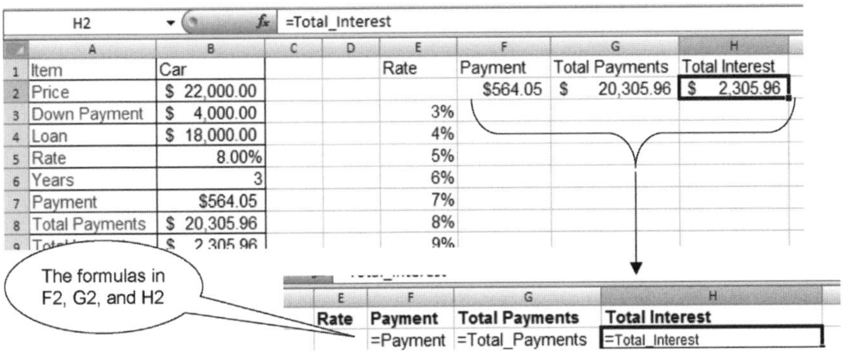

Figure 14.3   Preparing the data table

The data table can then be filled with the desired sensitivity analysis results. The first step is to select the area of the table where the results should appear (E2:H9). The second step is to activate the Data Table menu item. Under the Data ribbon, on the drop-down menu of the What-If Analysis, choose Data Table. See Figure 14.4. (In Excel 2003 or earlier, Data menu ⇨ Table.)

Figure 14.4   Creating a one-way data table

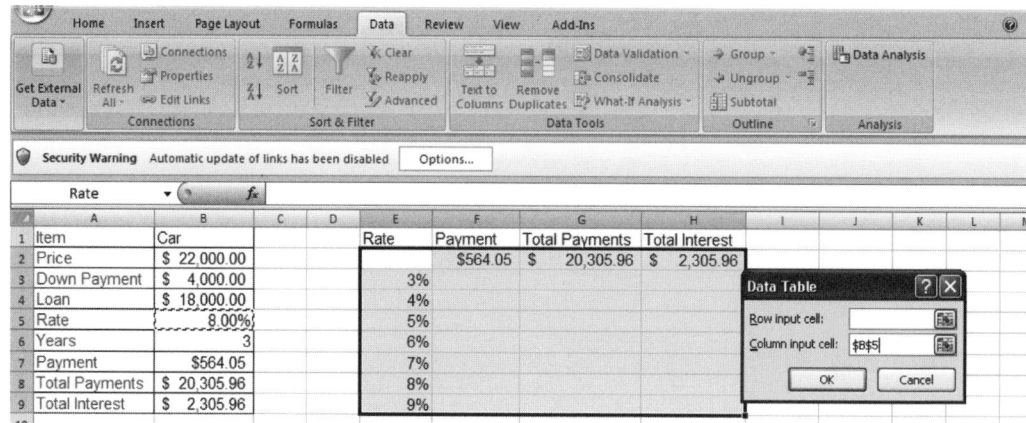

Figure 14.5   Click on the original rate in B5

In the data table dialog box, on the right side of Figure 14.5, select the Column input cell (remember, the input data—the Rate, is changing down the column) and click on cell B5—the cell containing the original rate. Click OK.

The function argument can be interpreted as "**WHAT** happens to payments, total payments, and so on, **IF** the interest rate changes." Hence, "what-if" analysis.

This will result in the desired sensitivity analysis table of Figure 14.6. Note how the row that belongs to the rate of 8 percent matches the results of the original model.

You may repeat this process with different input variables and create other sensitivity analysis tables; for example, you could check the output when the number of years changes as you see in Figure 14.7. The results are shown in Figure 14.8.

Two-way Table

In the tables above, you saw how you can vary one of the inputs in the column, (interest rate, the number of years, or the price) and view, in the table, the impact of these input changes on the outcome. (This is the sensitivity analysis or the what-if analysis.)

	Security Warning	Automatic update of links has been disabled	Options...					
	F8		▾	{=TABLE(,B5)}				
	A	B	C	D	E	F	G	H
1	Item	Car			Rate	Payment	Total Payments	Total Interest
2	Price	$ 22,000.00				$564.05	$ 20,305.96	$ 2,305.96
3	Down Payment	$ 4,000.00			3%	$ 523.46	$ 18,844.62	$ 844.62
4	Loan	$ 18,000.00			4%	$ 531.43	$ 19,131.54	$ 1,131.54
5	Rate	8.00%			5%	$ 539.48	$ 19,421.14	$ 1,421.14
6	Years	3			6%	$ 547.59	$ 19,713.42	$ 1,713.42
7	Payment	$564.05			7%	$ 555.79	$ 20,008.36	$ 2,008.36
8	Total Payments	$ 20,305.96			8%	$ 564.05	$ 20,305.96	$ 2,305.96
9	Total Interest	$ 2,305.96			9%	$ 572.40	$ 20,606.23	$ 2,606.23
10								

The row that belongs to the rate of 8 percent matches the results of the original model

Figure 14.6   The original value row gives the same results as the original model

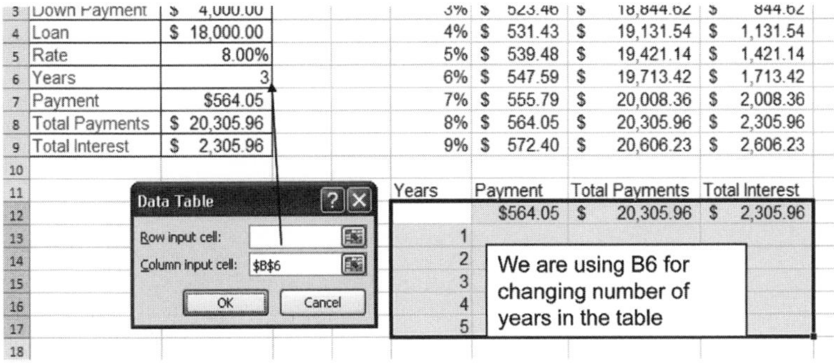

3	Down Payment	$ 4,000.00			3%	$	523.46	$	18,844.62	$	844.62
4	Loan	$ 18,000.00			4%	$	531.43	$	19,131.54	$	1,131.54
5	Rate	8.00%			5%	$	539.48	$	19,421.14	$	1,421.14
6	Years	3			6%	$	547.59	$	19,713.42	$	1,713.42
7	Payment	$564.05			7%	$	555.79	$	20,008.36	$	2,008.36
8	Total Payments	$ 20,305.96			8%	$	564.05	$	20,305.96	$	2,305.96
9	Total Interest	$ 2,305.96			9%	$	572.40	$	20,606.23	$	2,606.23

Data Table dialog box:
Row input cell: [ ]
Column input cell: $B$6
OK   Cancel

Years / Payment / Total Payments / Total Interest
$564.05 $ 20,305.96 $ 2,305.96

1
2   We are using B6 for
3   changing number of
4   years in the table
5

Figure 14.7 Use B6, the number of years, for the Column input

It is also possible to vary two inputs and view their impact on one output. This is called a "two-way sensitivity table." For the following example, I will vary two inputs: the number of years on the row side and the interest rate on the column side; and observe their impact on the monthly payments.

To set-up the table, list the rates (on the column side) and the number of years (on the row) while the payment is at the intersection of the two (top left cell of the table.) In cell E20 I have =Payment, and the value $564.05 is displayed. See Figure 14.9.

Below the Payment value in E20, I listed the desired interest rates. To the right of the Payment, I listed the number of years. This time when I use the data table, I will input entries in both cells of the dialog box: the row input cell and the column input cell.

For the row input cell, click on the cell containing the number of years in the original model (cell B6) and for the column input cell, click on the cell with the original interest rate (cell B5). See Figure 14.10.

Figure 14.11 shows the resulting output. Note that the original Payment value in the cell corresponds to the intersection of three years and 8 percent interest. It is the same as the Payment value of the original model. This is a good way to verify that the table was correctly set-up and that the parameters were accurately filled.

Data Tables—One More Example

Let's now illustrate the use of the data table for the Projections Statement example used in the last two chapters. See Figure 14.12. In this example, the break even point was

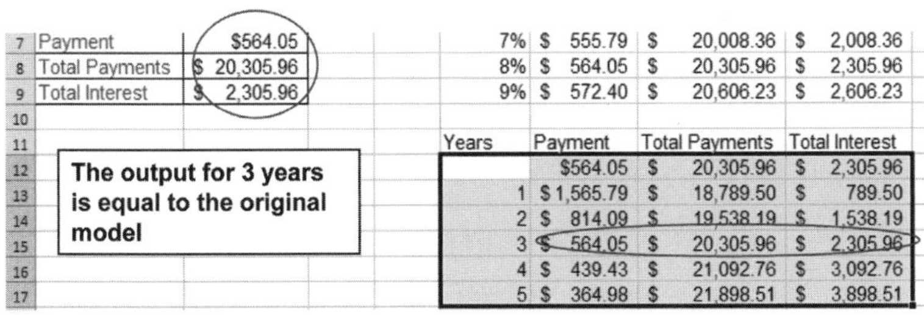

7	Payment	$564.05			7%	$	555.79	$	20,008.36	$	2,008.36
8	Total Payments	$ 20,305.96			8%	$	564.05	$	20,305.96	$	2,305.96
9	Total Interest	$ 2,305.96			9%	$	572.40	$	20,606.23	$	2,606.23

The output for 3 years is equal to the original model

Years / Payment / Total Payments / Total Interest
$564.05 $ 20,305.96 $ 2,305.96

1	$1,565.79	$	18,789.50	$ 789.50
2	$ 814.09	$	19,538.19	$ 1,538.19
3	$ 564.05	$	20,305.96	$ 2,305.96
4	$ 439.43	$	21,092.76	$ 3,092.76
5	$ 364.98	$	21,898.51	$ 3,898.51

Figure 14.8 The data table for changing the number of years

	A	B			E	F	G	H	I	J	K
3	Down Payment	$ 4,000.00			3%	$ 523.46	$ 18,844.62	$ 844.62			
4	Loan	$ 18,000.00			4%	$ 531.43	$ 19,131.54	$ 1,131.54			
5	Rate	8.00%			5%	$ 539.48	$ 19,421.14	$ 1,421.14			
6	Years	3			6%	$ 547.59	$ 19,713.42	$ 1,713.42			
7	Payment	$564.05			7%	$ 555.79	$ 20,008.36	$ 2,008.36			
8	Total Payments	$ 20,305.96			8%	$ 564.05	$ 20,305.96	$ 2,305.96			
9	Total Interest	$ 2,305.96			9%	$ 572.40	$ 20,606.23	$ 2,606.23			
10											
11					Years	Payment	Total Payments	Total Interest			
12						$564.05	$ 20,305.96	$ 2,305.96			
13					1	$ 1,565.79	$ 18,789.50	$ 789.50			
14					2	$ 814.09	$ 19,538.19	$ 1,538.19			
15					3	$ 564.05	$ 20,305.96	$ 2,305.96			
16					4	$ 439.43	$ 21,092.76	$ 3,092.76			
17					5	$ 364.98	$ 21,898.51	$ 3,898.51			
18											
19							Two Way Table				
20					=Payment		2	3	4	5	
21					5%						
22				Rate	6%		Number of years				
23					7%						
24					8%						
25					9%						
26					10%						

Figure 14.9 Entering the parameters in a two-way table

either 59,333 units or a selling price of $22.80. I used Goal Seek to figure this out in chapter 13.

I prepared two tables: one to investigate the impact of changes in the number of units sold on the Revenue, Expenses, and Income and a second table to examine the effect of changes of the selling price on the same output.

In the first table, I transferred the Revenue, Expenses, and Income to the top of the table using the following procedure: in cell F3, I typed = and selected C5, which is named

	A	B			E	F	G	H	I	J	K
4	Loan	$ 18,000.00			4%	$ 531.43	$ 19,131.54	$ 1,131.54			
5	Rate	8.00%			5%	$ 539.48	$ 19,421.14	$ 1,421.14			
6	Years	3			6%	$ 547.59	$ 19,713.42	$ 1,713.42			
7	Payment	$564.05			7%	$ 555.79	$ 20,008.36	$ 2,008.36			
8	Total Payments	$ 20,305.96			8%	$ 564.05	$ 20,305.96	$ 2,305.96			
9	Total Interest	$ 2,305.96			9%	$ 572.40	$ 20,606.23	$ 2,606.23			
10											
11					Years	Payment	Total Payments	Total Interest			
12						$564.05	$ 20,305.96	$ 2,305.96			
13		Data Table	? X		1	$ 1,565.79	$ 18,789.50	$ 789.50			
14					2	$ 814.09	$ 19,538.19	$ 1,538.19			
15		Row input cell:	$B$6		3	$ 564.05	$ 20,305.96	$ 2,305.96			
16		Column input cell:	$B$5		4	$ 439.43	$ 21,092.76	$ 3,092.76			
17					5	$ 364.98	$ 21,898.51	$ 3,898.51			
18		OK	Cancel								
19							Two Way Table				
20					$564.05	1	2	3	4	5	
21					5%						
22					6%						
23					7%						
24					8%						
25					9%						
26					10%						

Figure 14.10 Enter the rate for the column and the number of years for the row

	Two Way Table				
$564.05	1	2	3	4	5
5%	$1,540.93	$ 789.69	$ 539.48	$414.53	$ 339.68
6%	$1,549.20	$ 797.77	$ 547.59	$422.73	$ 347.99
7%	$1,557.48	$ 805.91	$ 555.79	$431.03	$ 356.42
8%	$1,565.79	$ 814.09	$ 564.05	$439.43	$ 364.98
9%	$1,574.13	$ 822.33	$ 572.40	$447.93	$ 373.65
10%	$1,582.49	$ 830.61	$ 580.81	$456.53	$ 382.45

Figure 14.11 The original output is identical to the original model

Revenue. I repeated the process for cells G3 and H3, resulting in the information shown in Figure 14.13.

Now you can select the data table range E3:H13 and use the Data Table menu as shown in Figure 14.14. Remember that you are trying to analyze the impact of varying the number of units, therefore it is necessary to use the original number of units as the Column Input cell. The results are the values in the figure. Notice where the break even point is. In chapter 13, we determined, using Goal Seek, that it was at 59,333 units; the sensitivity analysis returns the same result as the Income goes from negative to positive between the 50,000 and 60,000 units mark.

Break Even Point (BEP) Chart

To generate an easy-to-read visual aid, create a BEP chart. After selecting the table E3:H13, use the Chart Wizard with the Scatter XY chart to create the BEP chart (Scatter with data

Figure 14.12 Projections statement model

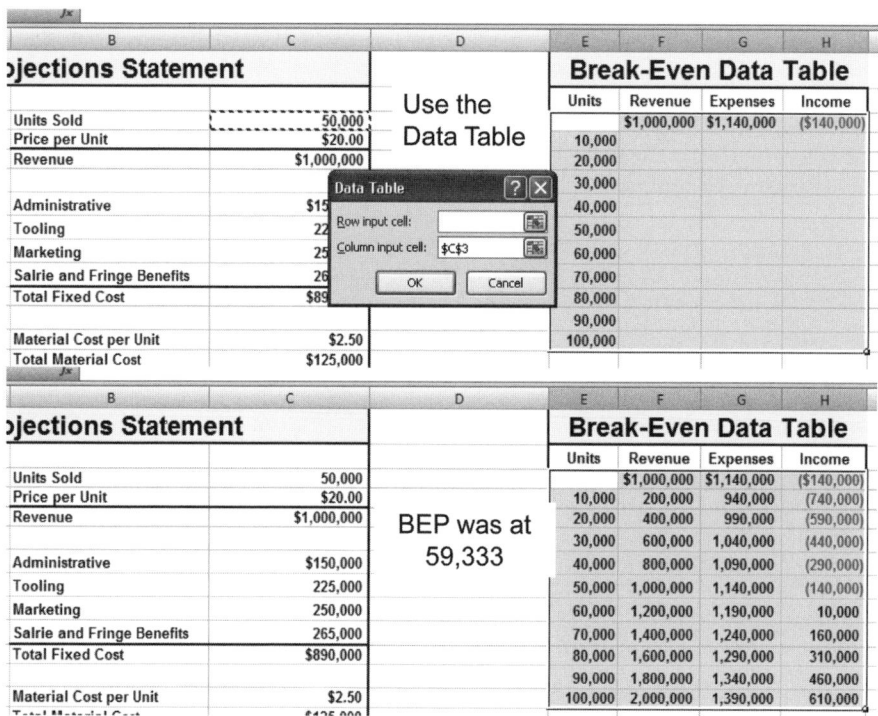

				Break-Even Data Table			
			Units	Revenue	Expenses	Income
Units Sold	50,000				$1,000,000	$1,140,000	($140,000)
Price per Unit	$20.00		10,000			
Revenue	$1,000,000		20,000			
			30,000			
Administrative	$150,000		40,000			
Tooling	225,000		50,000			
Marketing	250,000		60,000			
Salrie and Fringe Benefits	265,000		70,000			

The data table has the information in cells F3:G3

	Break-Even Data Table		
Units	Revenue	Expenses	Income
	=Revenue	=Total_Cost	=Operating_Income
10000			
20000			
30000			
40000			
50000			
60000			
70000			
80000			
90000			
100000			

Figure 14.13   Data table when the number of units sold is changing

Figure 14.14   Use Units Sold for the Column input cell

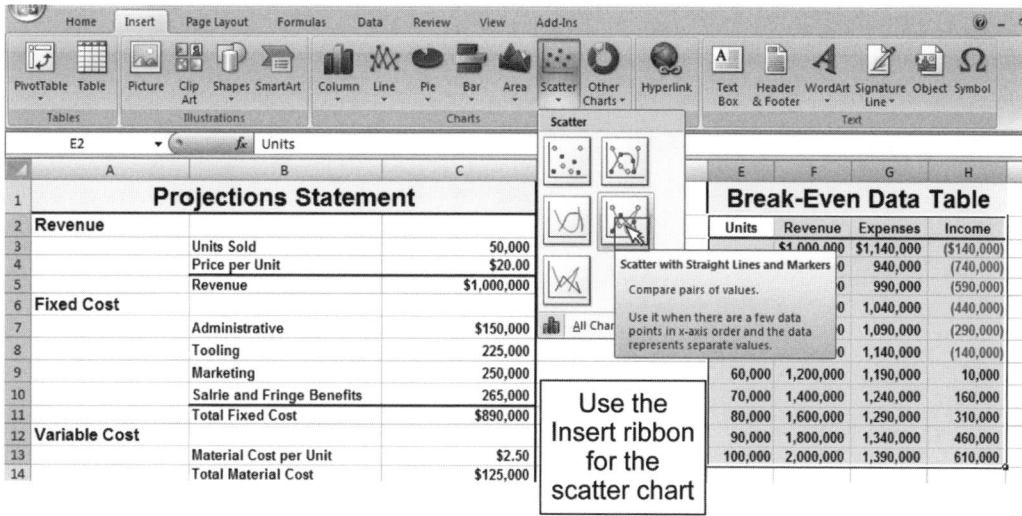

Figure 14.15   Creating the Break Even chart

points connected by lines, Excel calls it "Scatter with Straight Lines and Markers"). See Figure 14.15. You can use the Insert ribbon for the chart.

Excel 2003: Select the table ⇨ Insert menu ⇨ Chart ⇨ Scatter. Or use the Chart Wizard.

The Break Even Point chart is shown in Figure 14.16. Depending on your audience, the visual impact might be stronger with a graph than with numbers only. The break even point is easily found on the chart.

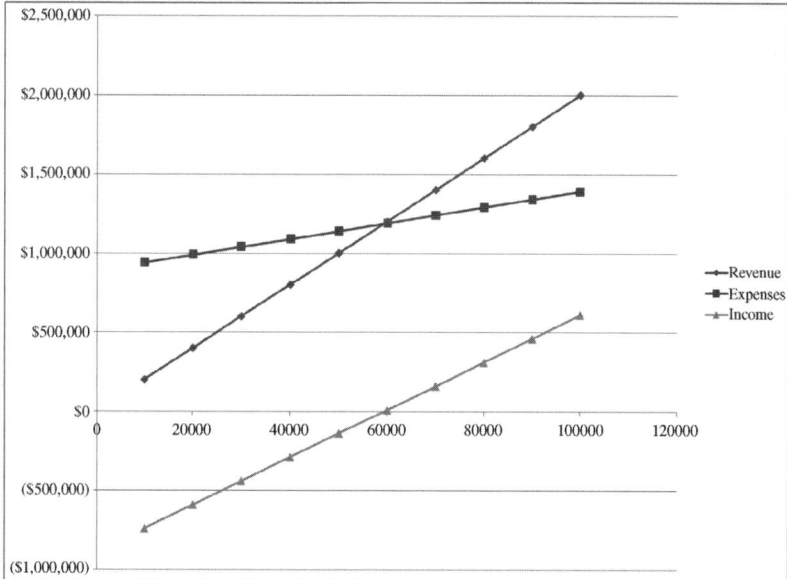

Figure 14.16   Break Even Point chart

REVIEW QUESTIONS

You will find these examples in the Excel Chapter 14 file:

1. Set up a data table for the Projections Statement example, where you vary the Price.

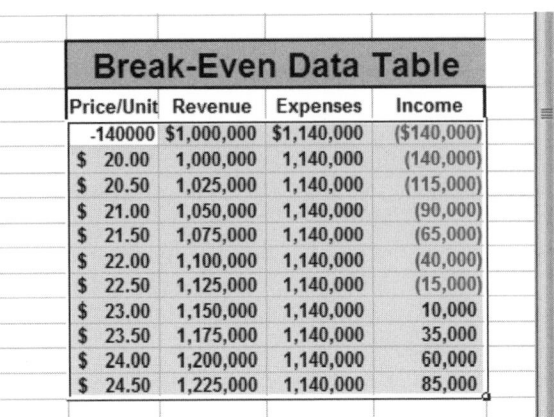

Break-Even Data Table			
Price/Unit	Revenue	Expenses	Income
-140000	$1,000,000	$1,140,000	($140,000)
$ 20.00	1,000,000	1,140,000	(140,000)
$ 20.50	1,025,000	1,140,000	(115,000)
$ 21.00	1,050,000	1,140,000	(90,000)
$ 21.50	1,075,000	1,140,000	(65,000)
$ 22.00	1,100,000	1,140,000	(40,000)
$ 22.50	1,125,000	1,140,000	(15,000)
$ 23.00	1,150,000	1,140,000	10,000
$ 23.50	1,175,000	1,140,000	35,000
$ 24.00	1,200,000	1,140,000	60,000
$ 24.50	1,225,000	1,140,000	85,000

2. Set up a two-way table for the Projections Statement example of the chapter as shown in the figure below. You want to find out the impact on Operating Income of varying the unit price and the number of units.

fx =Operating_Income											
K	L	M	N	O	P	Q	R	S	T	U	
-140000	$ 20.00	$ 20.50	$ 21.00	$ 21.50	$ 22.00	$ 22.50	$ 23.00	$ 23.50	$ 24.00	$ 24.50	
10,000											
20,000											
30,000											
40,000											
50,000											
60,000											
70,000											
80,000											
90,000											
100,000											

3. Create a two-way data table as shown in the figure below.

{=TABLE(C4,C3)}

K	L	M	N	O	P	Q	R	S	T	U
-140000	$ 20.00	$ 20.50	$ 21.00	$ 21.50	$ 22.00	$ 22.50	$ 23.00	$ 23.50	$ 24.00	$ 24.50
10,000	(740,000)	(735,000)	(730,000)	(725,000)	(720,000)	(715,000)	(710,000)	(705,000)	(700,000)	(695,000)
20,000	(590,000)	(580,000)	(570,000)	(560,000)	(550,000)	(540,000)	(530,000)	(520,000)	(510,000)	(500,000)
30,000	(440,000)	(425,000)	(410,000)	(395,000)	(380,000)	(365,000)	(350,000)	(335,000)	(320,000)	(305,000)
40,000	(290,000)	(270,000)	(250,000)	(230,000)	(210,000)	(190,000)	(170,000)	(150,000)	(130,000)	(110,000)
50,000	(140,000)	(115,000)	(90,000)	(65,000)	(40,000)	(15,000)	10,000	35,000	60,000	85,000
60,000	10,000	40,000	70,000	100,000	130,000	160,000	190,000	220,000	250,000	280,000
70,000	160,000	195,000	230,000	265,000	300,000	335,000	370,000	405,000	440,000	475,000
80,000	310,000	350,000	390,000	430,000	470,000	510,000	550,000	590,000	630,000	670,000
90,000	460,000	505,000	550,000	595,000	640,000	685,000	730,000	775,000	820,000	865,000
100,000	610,000	660,000	710,000	760,000	810,000	860,000	910,000	960,000	1,010,000	1,060,000

4. On the *Review* sheet of the File Chapter 14 (see the figure below) create the following data tables:

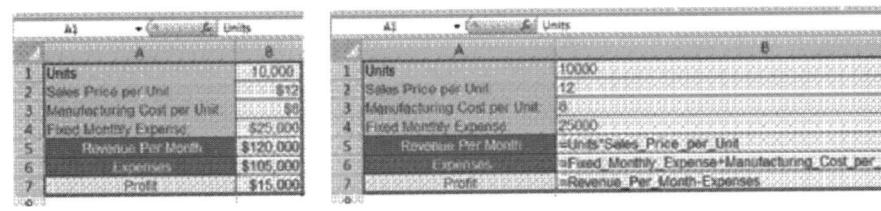

- A one-way vertical data table with the column headers Revenue Per Month, Expenses, and Profit. The column input cell should be the Sales Price per Unit.

Price	Revenue Per Month	Expenses	Profit
	120000	105000	$15,000
9.0			
9.5			
10.0			
10.5			
11.0			
11.5			
12.0			
12.5			
13.0			

■ A one-way vertical data table with the column headers Revenue Per Month, Expenses, and Profit. The column input cell should be the Manufacturing Cost per Unit

Cost	Revenue Per Month	Expenses	Profit
	120000	105000	$15,000
6.0			
6.5			
7.0			
7.5			
8.0			
8.5			
9.0			
9.5			
10.0			

■ A two-way data table evaluating the Profit. The column input cell should be the Manufacturing Cost per Unit and the row input cell should be the Sales Price per Unit.

$ 15,000	9.0	9.5	10.0	10.5	11.0	11.5	12.0	12.5	13.0
6.0									
6.5									
7.0									
7.5									
8.0									
8.5									
9.0									
9.5									
10.0									

ANSWERS

1. Type the headers Price/Unit, Revenue, Expenses, and Income in the first row of the table E18:H18. Follow by typing the values 20.00 and 20.50 in cell E20 and E21. Select these two values and using the AutoFill feature drag the values down to 24.50.

In cell F19 type = and click on cell C5. It will result in the value $1,000,000—the revenue. In cell G19 type = and click on cell C19. It will result in the value $1,140,000—the total expenses. In cell H19 type = and select cell C20. It will result in the value-$140,000—the operating income.

Select the entire table E19:H29. From the Data ribbon, click on the drop-down menu of the What-If Analysis and choose Data Table. See figure below. (In Excel 2003 choose Data ⇨ Data Table.) In the Data Table menu, select C4 in the Column Input cell.

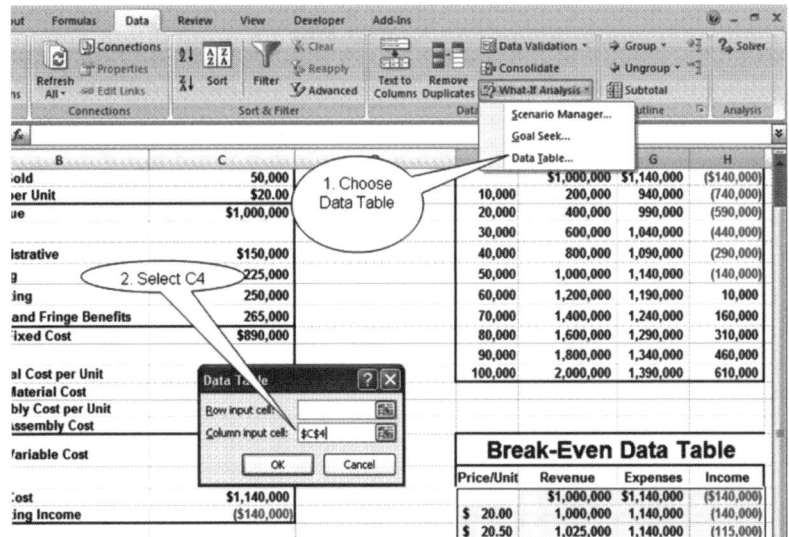

2. Create the table shown in the figure above. Type or copy and paste the Units Sold from 10,000 to 100,000 with increments of 10,000. Type or copy and paste the Unit Price along the top row of the table. In the intersection cell K3, type = and click on cell C20. It will result in -140,000, the net operation income.

3. Select the table K3:U13. From the Data ribbon click on the drop-down menu of the What-If Analysis and choose Data Table. See figure below. (In Excel 2003 choose Data ⇨ Data Table.) In the Data Table menu, select C4 in the Row Input cell and C3 in the Column Input cell. See figure below. The result is shown in the figure of the question.

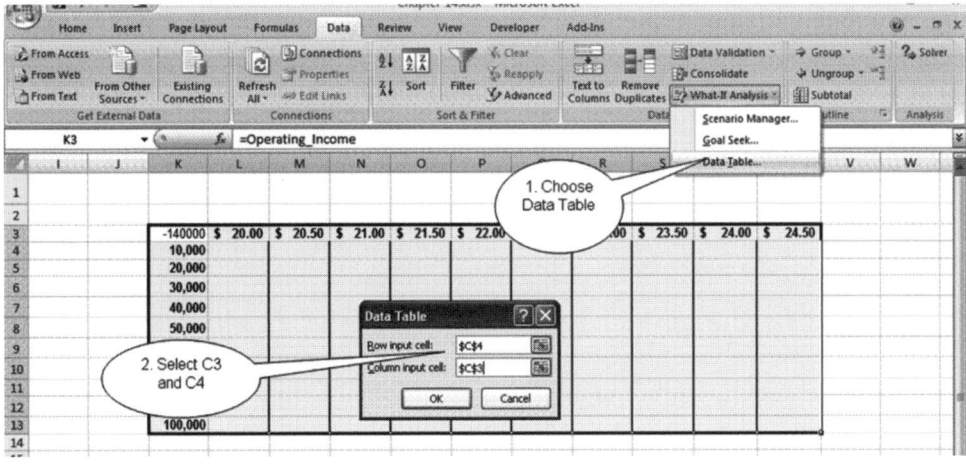

In the first table, I use the price B2 as the column input price. See figure below for results.

	D	E	F	G
	Price	Revenue Per Month	Expenses	Profit
		120000	105000	$15,000
	9.0	120000	115000	5000
	9.5	120000	120000	0
	10.0	120000	125000	-5000
	10.5	120000	130000	-10000
	11.0	120000	135000	-15000
	11.5	120000	140000	-20000
	12.0	120000	145000	-25000
	12.5	120000	150000	-30000
	13.0	120000	155000	-35000

In the second table, I use the cost per unit B3 as the column input price. See figure below for results.

Cost	Revenue Per Month	Expenses	Profit
	120000	105000	$15,000
6.0	120000	85000	35000
6.5	120000	90000	30000
7.0	120000	95000	25000
7.5	120000	100000	20000
8.0	120000	105000	15000
8.5	120000	110000	10000
9.0	120000	115000	5000
9.5	120000	120000	0
10.0	120000	125000	-5000

In the third two-way table, I used the price B2 for the row input cell and the cost per unit B3 for the column input cell. See the figure below for the results.

$ 15,000	9.0	9.5	10.0	10.5	11.0	11.5	12.0	12.5	13.0
6.0	5000	10000	15000	20000	25000	30000	35000	40000	45000
6.5	0	5000	10000	15000	20000	25000	30000	35000	40000
7.0	-5000	0	5000	10000	15000	20000	25000	30000	35000
7.5	-10000	-5000	0	5000	10000	15000	20000	25000	30000
8.0	-15000	-10000	-5000	0	5000	10000	15000	20000	25000
8.5	-20000	-15000	-10000	-5000	0	5000	10000	15000	20000
9.0	-25000	-20000	-15000	-10000	-5000	0	5000	10000	15000
9.5	-30000	-25000	-20000	-15000	-10000	-5000	0	5000	10000
10.0	-35000	-30000	-25000	-20000	-15000	-10000	-5000	0	5000

CHAPTER 15

Using Scroll Bars for Sensitivity Analysis

Data tables, as shown in the last chapter, are excellent tools for sensitivity analysis. One of the problems you may encounter when using them—especially if you want to analyze many inputs' parameters—is that you have to create a number of tables to have an extensive analysis. As data tables are limited to a maximum of two variables for any output, it may be difficult to view a few or all the tables simultaneously, and it might become a difficult undertaking.

A different solution to modify the input is to use scroll bars. Scroll bars were created in Excel for changing values in forms. You are going to harness the power of these scroll bars to change input values in the financial statements of decision making models, analyzing the impact of these changes on the output.

To illustrate this idea go back to our car loan example used in the last couple of chapters. See Figure 15.1. This loan example has a number of inputs: price, down payment, years, and

Item	Car
Price	$ 22,000.00
Down Payment	$ 4,000.00
Loan	$ 18,000.00
Rate	8.00%
Years	3
Payment	$564.05
Total Payments	$ 20,305.96
Total Interest	$ 2,305.96

Rate	Payment	Total Payments	Total Interest
	$564.05	$ 20,305.96	$ 2,305.96
3%	$ 523.46	$ 18,844.62	$ 844.62
4%	$ 531.43	$ 19,131.54	$ 1,131.54
5%	$ 539.48	$ 19,421.14	$ 1,421.14
6%	$ 547.59	$ 19,713.42	$ 1,713.42
7%	$ 555.79	$ 20,008.36	$ 2,008.36
8%	$ 564.05	$ 20,305.96	$ 2,305.96
9%	$ 572.40	$ 20,606.23	$ 2,606.23

Years	Payment	Total Payments	Total Interest
	$564.05	$ 20,305.96	$ 2,305.96
1	$ 1,565.79	$ 18,789.50	$ 789.50
2	$ 814.09	$ 19,538.19	$ 1,538.19
3	$ 564.05	$ 20,305.96	$ 2,305.96
4	$ 439.43	$ 21,092.76	$ 3,092.76
5	$ 364.98	$ 21,898.51	$ 3,898.51

Two Way Table

$564.05	1	2	3	4	5
5%	$ 1,540.93	$ 789.69	$ 539.48	$414.53	$ 339.68
6%	$ 1,549.20	$ 797.77	$ 547.59	$422.73	$ 347.99
7%	$ 1,557.48	$ 805.91	$ 555.79	$431.03	$ 356.42
8%	$ 1,565.79	$ 814.09	$ 564.05	$439.43	$ 364.98
9%	$ 1,574.13	$ 822.33	$ 572.40	$447.93	$ 373.65
10%	$ 1,582.49	$ 830.61	$ 580.81	$456.53	$ 382.45

The car loan example used previously to illustrate Goal Seek and Data Tables

Figure 15.1 The car loan example

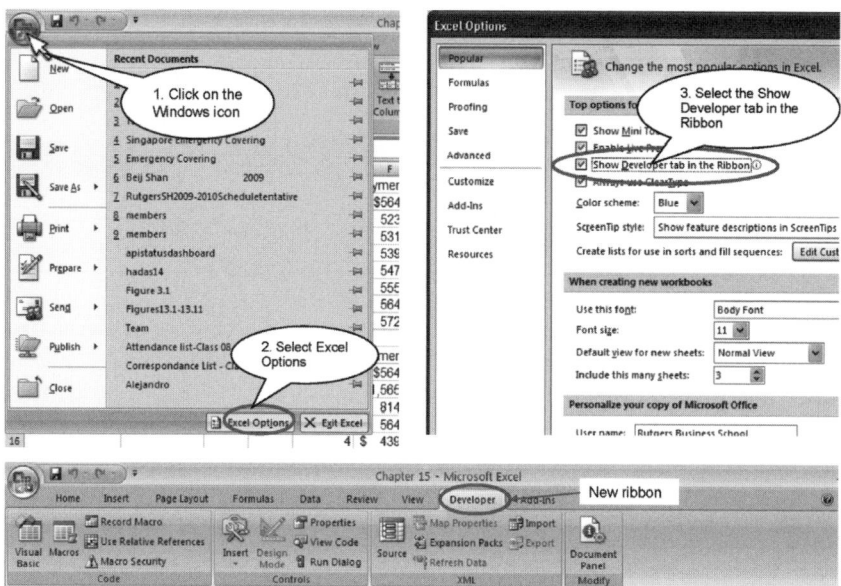

Figure 15.2   Adding the Developer ribbon

interest rate. We used the data tables varying the rate and the number of years to explore the effect of their changes on the output.

I will demonstrate the way to use the scroll bar instead of—or in addition to—the data table. The first value you are going to link to a scroll bar is the number of years or the duration of the loan.

To create scroll bars in Excel 2007—you have to first add the Developer tab to your ribbons. Click on the Office icon 🔵 and select Excel Options at the bottom of the menu. See Figure 15.2. In the Option menu, choose the Show Developer tab in the ribbon. Developer now appears in your ribbons header.

The Developer ribbon has an Insert Controls icon that you will use to draw and use the scroll bars. When you click on the Insert Controls icon, you will see four lines of icons. The first two lines' icons are used for Forms and the last two lines' icons are used for Macros (called ActiveX Controls). See Figure 15.3.

You are going to use the Forms Control on the first two lines. On the second line of the Controls, belonging to the Forms Controls icons, select the Scroll Bar. See Figure 15.4.

When you select the Scroll Bar icon, your mouse pointer will become a thin crosshair cursor (+). You can draw the scroll bar by dragging the cursor, keeping the mouse button pressed down. It may take some practice the first time to get the desired shape and size of your scroll bar. I chose to draw the scroll bar next to the number of years in cell B6, since the number of years is the first cell that I want to control. Because scroll bars cannot be named or otherwise identified, it is best to position them next to the cells that they will control.

The scroll bar is now next to the number of years in cell B6. You are going to set up some of its parameters. Right-click on the scroll bar and choose Format Control—the last entry on the local menu in Figure 15.5. In the new Format Control menu, you will enter the values you want to control.

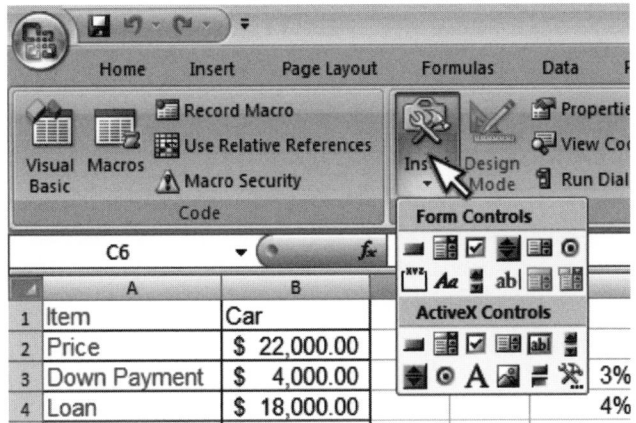

Figure 15.3   The Control icon and toolbars on the Developer ribbon

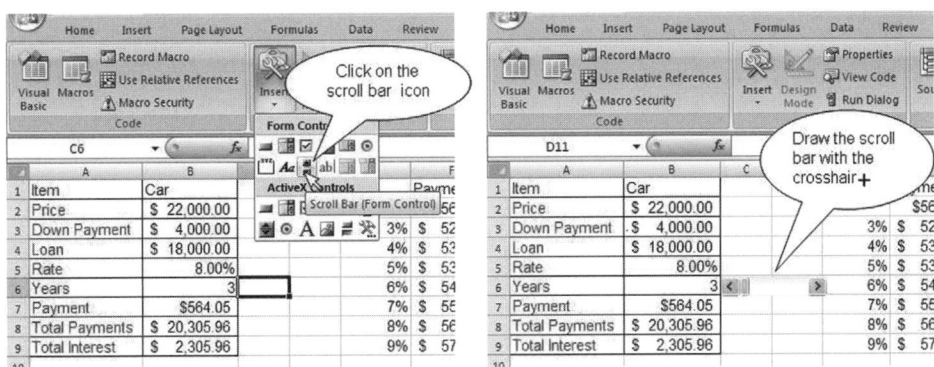

Figure 15.4   Click on the Scroll Bar icon and draw the scroll bar

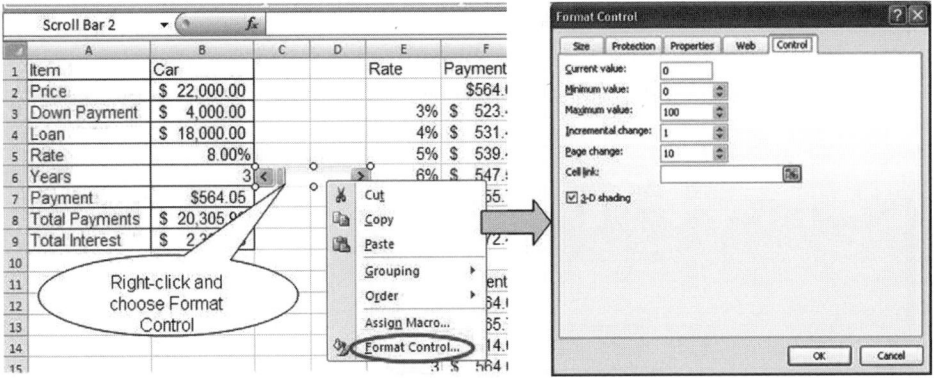

Figure 15.5   Scroll Bar Format Control menu

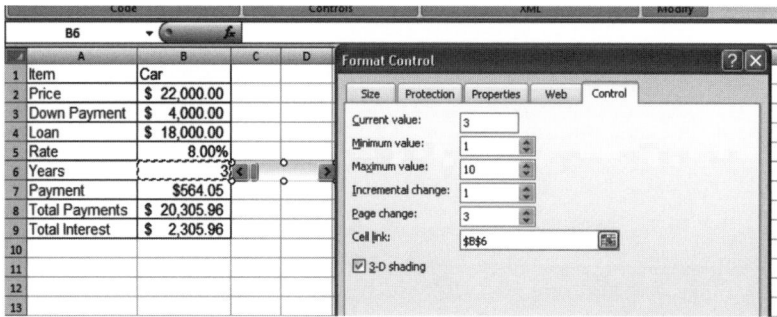

Figure 15.6   Scroll bar attributes

Fill in all the entries in the Format Control menu as follows:

- The Current value is that of the parameter you want to control (enter 3, the number of years currently in cell B6).
- The Minimum and Maximum values define the range between which the scroll bar will have effect. (I chose 1 and 10 years—but you can choose other values.) This would be the equivalent of the range created in the data table.
- Incremental change is the value by which the variable will change when a single click is performed on either of the end arrows of the scroll bar. (I chose to enter 1.)
- Page change is the incremental change when you click on the gray area of the scroll bar between the arrows and the center scroll bar. (I chose 3.)
- Cell link designs the original cell I want to control with the scroll bar. Since we are defining for the number of years, select B6.

See Figure 15.6.

Complete the form and click OK. Then click on any cell in your worksheet and you may use the scroll bar.

When you click on either arrow of the scroll bar, it will change the number of years by one. It will vary the number of years from one to 10. The page change was set to be three. When you click in the grey area of the scroll bar, it will change the value by three. See Figure 15.7.

When you complete the scroll bar for the number of years, you will understand how simple and powerful it is. It is also a great tool for dynamic presentation purposes. Your

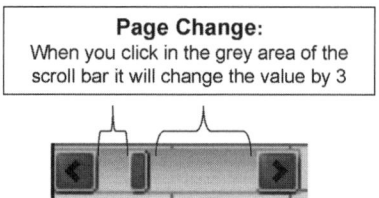

Figure 15.7   Page change on scroll bar

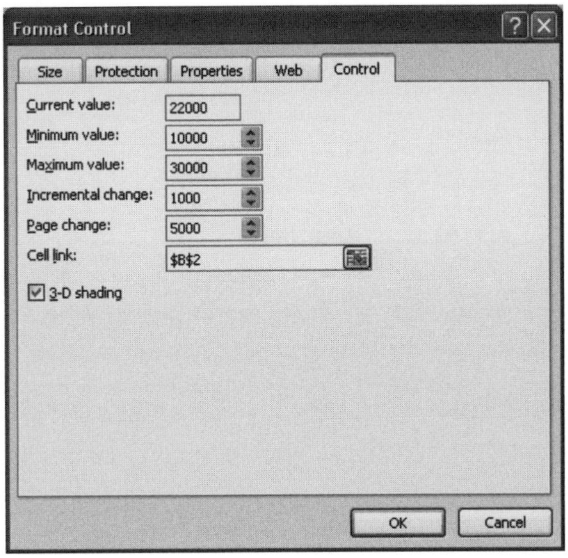

Figure 15.8   Scroll bar for price

audience can see the impact of the change in your input as you slide the scroll bar. You can try the scroll bar on other input parameters.

Now try the scroll bar on cell B2, the price. You can vary the price from $10,000 to $30,000 with an Incremental change of $1,000 and Page change of $5,000. See Figure 15.8. Remember, Incremental change is the single programmed value evolution any time you click on the scroll bar arrows and Page change is the incremental change when you click on the gray area of the scroll bar between the arrows and the center scroll bar.

Now you have two scroll bars, one for the number of years and one for the price. You may want to try and change the down payment of the loan with a new scroll bar. Try to vary it from 2,000 to 6,000 with increments of 500 and a page change of 1,000. You may discover that changing the interest rate does not work.

Scroll Bar Limitations

The Format Control menu will only allow values that are between 0 and 30,000. Furthermore, it will not accept any fractions of an integer, such as the interest rate for example. In other words, the values for the scroll bar have to be integers from 0 to 30,000. If you want to use fractions or percentages—as you will need in our model—or values above 30,000, you will have to bypass the scroll bar limitations. How do you do that?

For values over 30,000 you will need to control a separate/dummy cell.

I created a scroll bar on the sheet named *Large Numbers*. The scroll bar controls the cell B5. For demonstration purposes, I did not change any of the values in the Format Control menu, and used the default values, varying B5 from 0 to 100.

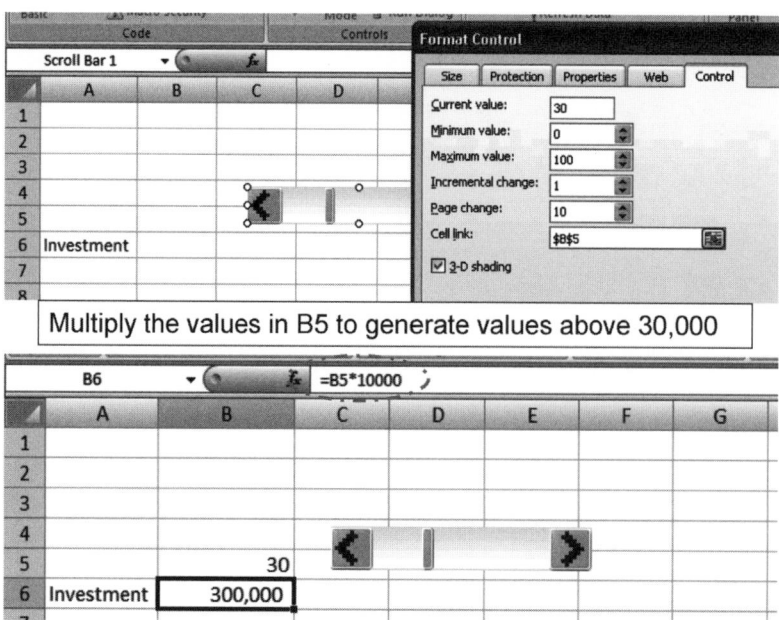

Figure 15.9   Scroll bar for values over 30,000

I used a formula in cell B6 ("dummy cell") to multiply the value of B5 by 10,000. The effect of this formula is that the values in cell B6 vary from 0 to 1,000,000 with increments of 10,000 (1,000,000 = 100 x 10,000). This enables me to bypass the 30,000 limitations of the scroll bar. See Figure 15.9.

The same logic applies for using the scroll bar to vary values of fractions or percentages. This time you should create a formula to divide the values of a controlled cell instead of multiplying them.

Going back to the car loan example—create a scroll bar next to cell C5 as shown in Figure 5.10. As you control cell C5, you can use the formula C5/100 in cell B5, which will effectively allow you to vary the interest rate in cell B5 indirectly. If you use C5/400—you will be able to vary the rate with increments of 0.25 percent.

To move the scroll bar, you need to right-click on it first. Activate the scroll bar you just created for the rate and move it over cell C5—so that when you make your presentation the value in cell C5 is hidden from the viewers.

APPENDIX—THE SCROLL BAR IN EXCEL 2003

To create the scroll bar go to: View ⇨ Toolbars and select Forms toolbar. This is the only difference when using the scroll bar for the 2003 version. In Figure 15.11, you can see the way it is selected. You can also check the Excel file Chapter 15 Excel 2003.

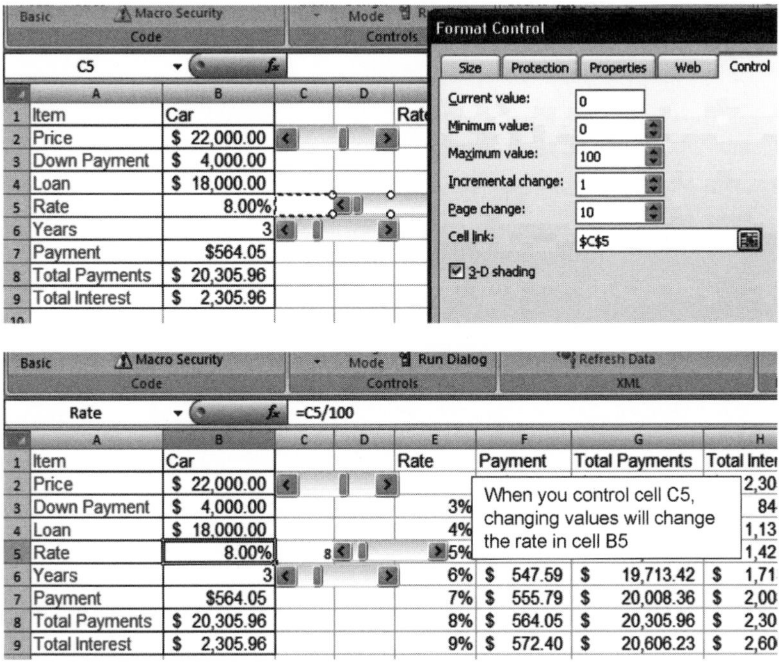

Figure 15.10 Changing the rate

Figure 15.12 illustrates the Forms toolbar. The scroll bar is circled on the figure. Everything else is the same as Excel 2007. Just to remind you, when you select the Scroll Bar icon, your mouse pointer will become a thin crosshair (+). You can draw the scroll bar by dragging the cursor, keeping the mouse button pressed down. It may take some practice the first time to get the desired shape and size of your scroll bar.

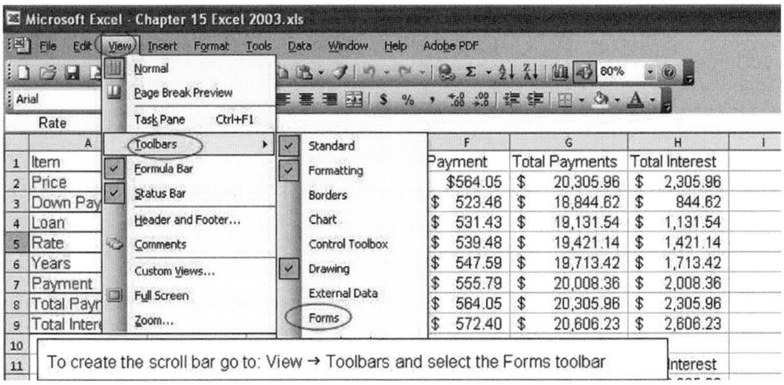

Figure 15.11 Using the View Toolbars menu for the Forms toolbar

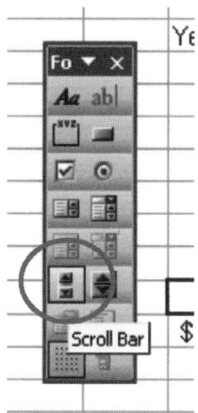

Figure 15.12 Click on the Scroll Bar icon and draw the scroll bar

REVIEW QUESTIONS

You will find these examples on the Excel Chapter 15 file:

1. On the *Review* sheet for the Excel file called Chapter 15, you will see the small figure below. This is the same example we used in the previous chapters. The right side of the figure shows the formulas used to calculate the sheet.

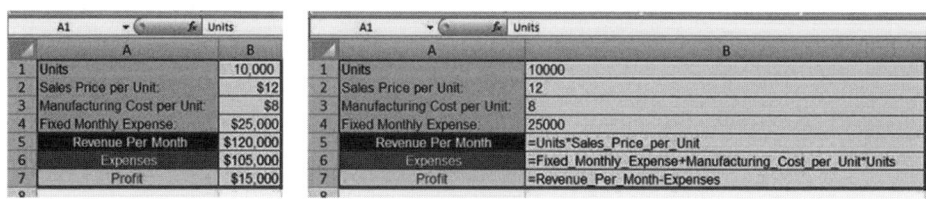

Create a scroll bar to control the Sales Price per Unit from $9 to $15.

2. Create a second scroll bar to vary the Manufacturing Cost per Unit from $5 to $12, using $1 increments.
3. Create a third scroll bar to vary the Fixed Monthly Expenses from $20,000 to $30,000 with increments of $1,000 and a page change of $2,000.

ANSWERS:

1.

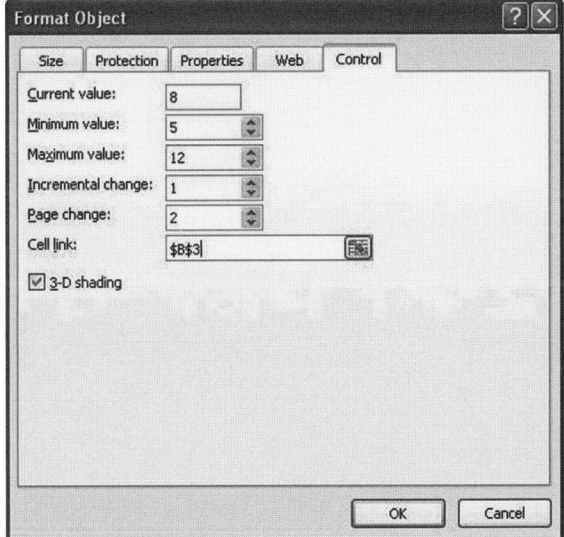

2.

3.

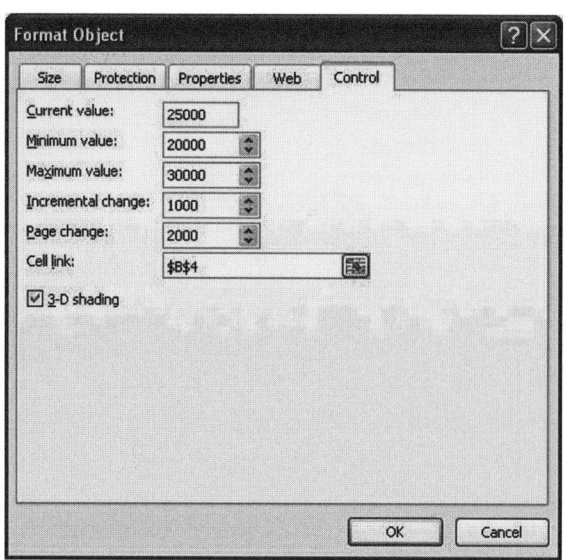

Multi-Page Systems and Lookups

Two topics are discussed in Part V: multi-page systems and lookup functions.

Most Excel users either keep their entire model or information on one worksheet or—when they use a number of sheets—do not take advantage of structuring the workbook/system so that can use Excel more effectively. The first portion of this part will cover this topic.

The second portion of this part will discuss lookup functions. It will demonstrate how to perform an exact lookup and how to perform range lookups. After you have understood the lookup function described, you will be able to perform any of the other lookup functions.

CHAPTER 16

Multi-Page Budgets—Going to the Third Dimension

This chapter will be using Excel with more than just rows and columns. The objective is to use sheets, in addition to rows and columns, in the same workbook.

So far, most spreadsheets in this book used models with rows and columns only. You are now going to utilize the third dimension in the model, namely sheets. You may want to prepare Payroll reports for four or five weeks on separate sheets and compile the results (going to the third dimension) into the last sheet for a summary. Other possible applications include summing four quarters' sheets into an annual report, inventory reports of different locations consolidated into a corporate total inventory report, or a summary budget for a number of departments.

The first part of this chapter will illustrate the preparation of the multidimensional Excel workbook. What you want to do is make all the sheets in the workbook identical in format. You will also be inserting the same basic information on all the sheets. After these preparations, you will finally compile the results of all the sheets in the summary sheet.

A Payroll Example

This example is going to demonstrate how to set up a monthly payroll report for five weeks on five separate sheets. After you have the data for the five weeks, you are going to sum the data into the totals sheet. First, you are going to format six sheets, one for each week and one for the totals, in an Excel workbook. It is like preparing a template.

If you open a new workbook, you probably have the default number of sheets, three. In this example, you will need six sheets, one for each week and one for the totals compilation. You will have to add three sheets. Use Shift+F11 to add sheets. Make it a total of six. Rename the sheets Week1, Week2, Week3, Week4, Week5, and Totals by double-clicking on each tab. See Figure 16.1. The Excel workbook is named *Chapter 16A*.

Since most of the information and the formatting on all six sheets will be the same, you will have to select all six sheets so that you can do it on all of them at once. When all the sheets are selected, you will be able to enter the data simultaneously on all of them.

There are two ways to select all the sheets. The first way is to click on the sheet tab Week1, hold the CTRL key, and click to select each and every one of the other sheet tabs. The second option is to right-click any sheet tab and choose Select All Sheets in the local

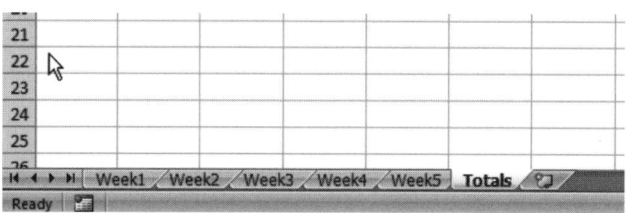

Figure 16.1   Creating six sheets

menu. All the sheets are selected. You will see the word "Group" in brackets—warning you that all sheets are selected. See Figure 16.2.

When you enter data or format, it will enter the data, the formats, and the formulas on all sheets. Notice that the Excel Workbook name indicates that the sheets are grouped and that all the sheets are selected. See Figure 16.2.

When all sheets are selected, you can input the information in all sheets on the workbook simultaneously. The same data and formulas will appear on all the sheets. Figure 16.3 shows the information and formulas for the weekly salaries' calculations entered on all sheets. When I created the template for all sheets, I used 0 for the number of hours. As I enter the data in later, these 0's will be replaced with the actual hours worked.

In Figure 16.3, you can see the information, formats, and formulas that will appear on all six sheets. The sheets are completed with the sum of the salaries as you can see in Figure 16.4.

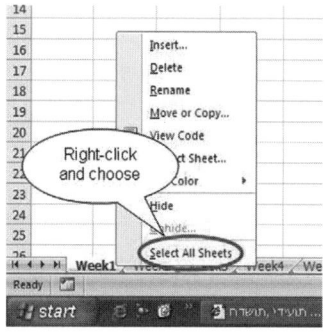
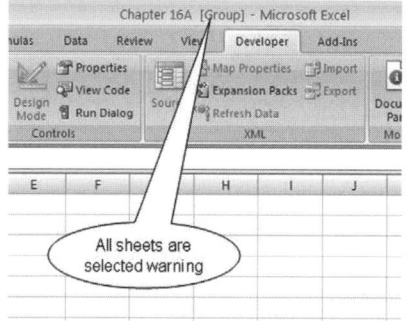

Figure 16.2   Selecting all sheets

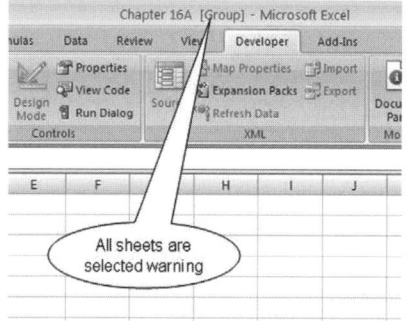

Figure 16.3   The formulas will show up on all sheets

FORECAST	▼	✕ ✓ ƒ	=SUM(E2:E5)		
	A	**B**	**C**	**D**	**E**	**F**
1	**Last Name**	**First Name**	**Rate**	**Hours**	**Salary**	
2	Alfano	Vincenzo	17.63	0.00	0.00	
3	Bai	Ye	12.73	0.00	0.00	
4	Barile	Brad	11.05	0.00	0.00	
5	Bedard	Greg	11.90	0.00	0.00	
6					=SUM(E2:E5)	

Figure 16.4 Sum off all salaries

All six sheets will be identical as long as they stay grouped. If you click on any one sheet tab, this will de-select the group. The group will be released. You can check and see that the same information, data, formulas, and formats appear on each of the individual sheets. They are identical.

The next part is to enter the hours worked for each one of the five weeks. This data is displayed in Figure 16.5. As you enter the hours worked, the formulas will calculate the salaries and the totals for each one of the individual weeks.

You have to **sum** the Hours of the first employee, Vincenzo Alfano, for all five weeks into the totals sheet. The significant part of this sum is "drilling" vertically through all five sheets and summing the information on the last sheet, named the totals sheet. See Figure 16.6.

What you want to do is to select cell D2 on the totals sheet and sum the hours worked for Vincenzo Alfano from all the others, the five individual weeks' sheets.

Week 1

	A	**First Name**	**Rate**	**Hours**	**Salary**
1	**Last Name**			**Hours**	**Salary**
2	Alfano	Vincenzo	17.63	11.00	193.93
3	Bai	Ye	12.73	17.00	216.41
4	Barile	Brad	11.05	21.00	232.05
5	Bedard	Greg	11.90	13.00	154.70
6					797.09

Week 2

	A	**First Name**	**Rate**	**Hours**	**Salary**
1	**Last Name**			**Hours**	**Salary**
2	Alfano	Vincenzo	17.63	38.00	669.94
3	Bai	Ye	12.73	40.00	509.20
4	Barile	Brad	11.05	40.00	442.00
5	Bedard	Greg	11.90	35.00	416.50
6					2037.64

Week 3

	A	**First Name**	**Rate**	**Hours**	**Salary**
1	**Last Name**			**Hours**	**Salary**
2	Alfano	Vincenzo	17.63	40.00	705.20
3	Bai	Ye	12.73	40.00	509.20
4	Barile	Brad	11.05	25.00	276.25
5	Bedard	Greg	11.90	38.00	452.20
6					1942.85

Week 4

	A	**First Name**	**Rate**	**Hours**	**Salary**
1	**Last Name**			**Hours**	**Salary**
2	Alfano	Vincenzo	17.63	33.00	581.79
3	Bai	Ye	12.73	22.00	280.06
4	Barile	Brad	11.05	39.00	430.95
5	Bedard	Greg	11.90	40.00	476.00
6					1768.80

Week 5 (D6)

	A	**First Name**	**Rate**	**Hours**	**Salary**
1	**Last Name**	**First Name**	**Rate**	**Hours**	**Salary**
2	Alfano	Vincenzo	17.63	20.00	352.60
3	Bai	Ye	12.73	21.00	267.33
4	Barile	Brad	11.05	18.00	198.90
5	Bedard	Greg	11.90	22.00	261.80
6					1080.63

This is the information entered on the five sheets

Figure 16.5 The five weeks' payrolls

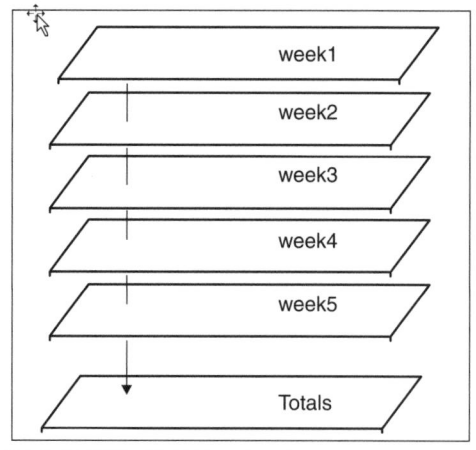

Figure 16.6   Summing, the third dimension

After you select the cell D2, click on the Auto-sum icon Σ. Next, click on the Week1 sheet tab. Your formula bar will read = SUM(Week1!). Next, press Shift + click on the Week5 sheet tab.

Your formula bar will read = SUM(Week1:Week5!). This indicates that you are going to sum the values from week1 to week5. The only thing that is left to do is select the cell where you want the result to appear, namely cell D2 on the Totals sheet. Click on D2 and the formula bar will read = SUM(Week1:Week5!D2). When you hit Enter, you will get the desired sum; the sum of the total number of hours Mr. Alfano worked for the five weeks. It should be 142.00. The salary is computed automatically for the entire month. See Figure 16.7.

When you drag the values down—or double click the drag handle—Excel will complete the information for the rest of the employees. Figure 16.8 illustrates the results.

Note all the formulas on the sheet (using CTRL+~) in Figure 16.9.

	FORECAST	=SUM(Week1:Week5!D2)				
	A	B	C	D	E	F	G
1	**Last Name**	**First Name**	**Rate**	**Hours**	**Salary**		
2	Alfano	Vincenzo	17.63	=SUM(Week1:Week5!D2)		
3	Bai	Ye	12.73	0.00	0.00	
4	Barile	Brad	11.05	0.00	0.00	
5	Bedard	Greg	11.90	0.00	0.00	
6					2503.46	

	D2	=SUM(Week1:Week5!D2)				
	A	B	C	D	E	F	G
1	**Last Name**	**First Name**	**Rate**	**Hours**	**Salary**		
2	Alfano	Vincenzo	17.63	142.00	2503.46	
3	Bai	Ye	12.73	0.00	0.00	
4	Barile	Brad	11.05	0.00	0.00	
5	Bedard	Greg	11.90	0.00	0.00	
6					2503.46	

Figure 16.7   Hours were summed for all sheets

Figure 16.8 All sheets are summed in the totals sheet

Figure 16.9 Formulas for the total sheet

A Second Example—Bakers' Supplies

Good Taste Bakers' Supplies has four sales centers, located in Miami, New York, Los Angeles, and Denver. The sales manager in the company's headquarters wants to aggregate the sales information for the four different locations. The sales manager prepared this workbook, containing five sheets (Excel workbook, *Chapter 16B*). The sheets are similar in their format and structure. The workbook contains the information for the four sites and a company sheet. See Figure 16.10 for details of one of the four locations, as well as the summary sheet.

The sales manager would like you to sum the information of the four locations into the summary sheet. To do so, select cell B5 in the company's sheet, so that you can sum the other four sheets' B5 cells into it. When B5 is selected, click on the Auto-sum icon Σ. Now proceed by clicking on the first sheet's tab—Miami. The formula bar will read = SUM(Miami!). Use Shift + click on the last sheet tab you want to include in the sum—Denver. The formula bar will read = SUM(Miami:Denver!). Now click on cell B5 in the company's sales sheet. When you click the B5 cell it will sum all the B5 cells from the Miami through the Denver sheets. The formula bar will read = SUM(Miami: Denver!B5). You can drag the result down to transfer the formula to the rest of the cells in column B. See Figure 16.11.

	A2	▾	*fx*	New York's Sales		

	A	B	C	D	E	F	G
1	**Good Taste Bakers' Supplies**						
2	New York's Sales						
3							23-May-2009
4	Item kg.	Units On Hand	Average Unit Cost	Total Cost	Average Unit Price	Total Value	Profit Potential
5	flour	6,732	$0.37	$2,490.84	$0.52	$3,500.64	$1,009.80
6	dry yeast	101	56.00	5,656.00	78.00	7,878.00	2,222.00
7	sugar	3,000	0.52	1,560.00	0.93	2,790.00	1,230.00
8	baking soda	120	1.21	145.20	1.56	187.20	42.00
9	dill seed	54	3.21	173.34	5.12	276.48	103.14
10	margarine	1,800	0.32	576.00	0.56	1,008.00	432.00
11	cocoa	190	0.65	123.50	0.92	174.80	51.30
12	Total	11,997		$10,724.88		$15,815.12	$5,090.24

	A2	▾	*fx*	Company's Sales		

	A	B	C	D	E	F	G
1	**Good Taste Bakers' Supplies**						
2	Company's Sales						
3							23-May-2009
4	Item kg.	Units On Hand	Average Unit Cost	Total Cost	Average Unit Price	Total Value	Profit Potential
5	flour		$0.37	$0.00	$0.52	$0.00	$0.00
6	dry yeast		56.00	0.00	78.00	0.00	0.00
7	sugar		0.52	0.00	0.93	0.00	0.00
8	baking soda		1.21	0.00	1.56	0.00	0.00
9	dill seed		3.21	0.00	5.12	0.00	0.00
10	margarine		0.32	0.00	0.56	0.00	0.00
11	cocoa		0.65	0.00	0.92	0.00	0.00
12	Total		-	$0.00		$0.00	$0.00

Figure 16.10   Bakers' Supplies example

	B5	▾	*fx*	=SUM(Miami:Denver!B5)	

	A	B	C	D
1	**Good Taste Bakers**			
2			Company's Sales	
3				
4	Item kg.	Units On Hand	Average Unit Cost	Total Cost
5	flour	26,432	$0.37	$9,779.84
6	dry yeast	-	56.00	0.00
7	sugar	-	0.52	0.00

Figure 16.11   Sum of all sheets for flour

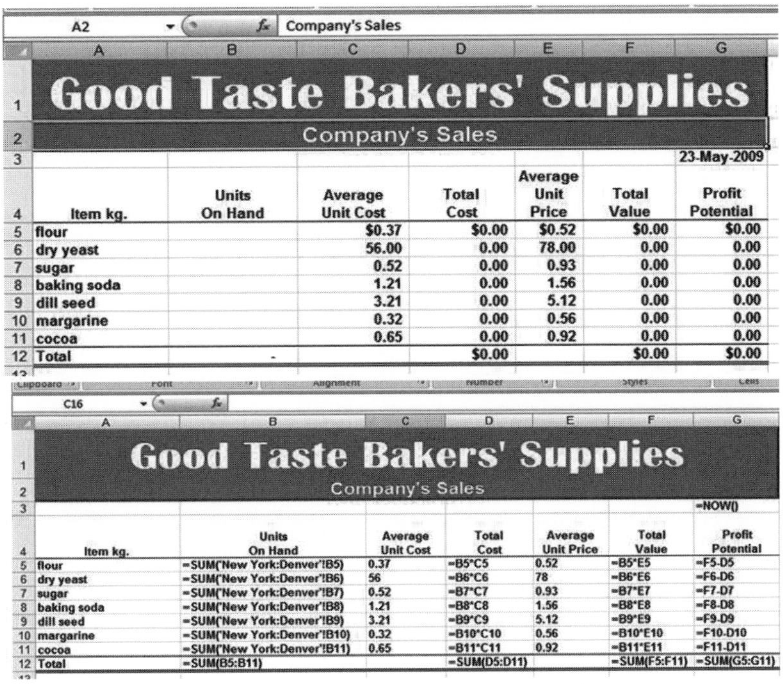

Figure 16.12 The results and the formulas of the summation

Figure 16.12 displays the results. The bottom figure displays the calculated values and the formulas.

REVIEW QUESTIONS

1. File Chapter 16 *Review* has five sheets. Four sheets have sales data for the four regions, North, West, South, and East. Sum the four sheets into the Total sheet.

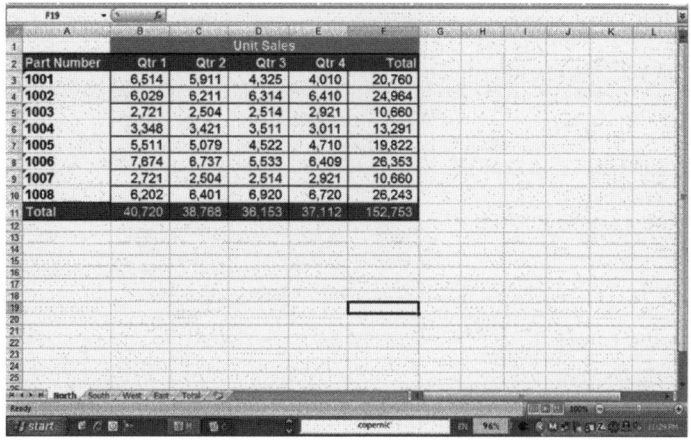

2. In the file *Chapter 16 Annual*, you will find 13 sheets for the 12 months January through December and a total sheet. Sum the sheets into the total one.

Year	
Month	
Revenue	
Products	
Services	
Total Revenues	
Expenses	
Rent	
Salaries	
Supplies	
Travel	
Utilities	
Total Expenses	
Net Income	

ANSWERS

1.

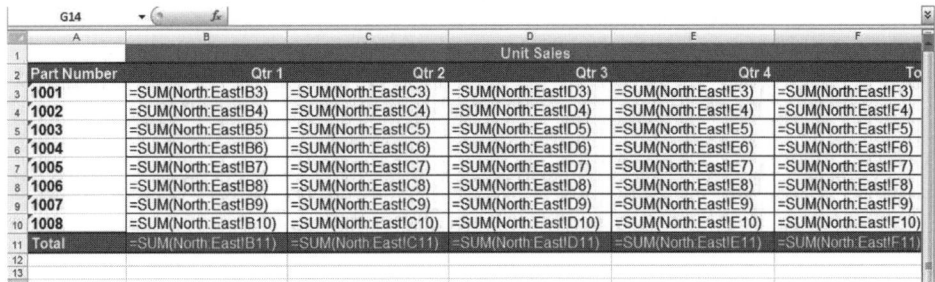

	Part Number	Qtr 1	Qtr 2	Qtr 3	Qtr 4	Total
1				Unit Sales		
2	Part Number	Qtr 1	Qtr 2	Qtr 3	Qtr 4	Total
3	1001	26,056	22,825	16,404	15,460	80,745
4	1002	23,459	24,025	24,360	25,060	96,904
5	1003	10,227	9,197	9,160	11,104	39,688
6	1004	12,735	12,865	13,148	11,464	50,212
7	1005	21,387	19,497	17,192	18,260	76,336
8	1006	30,039	26,129	21,236	25,056	102,460
9	1007	10,227	9,197	9,160	11,104	39,688
10	1008	24,151	24,785	26,784	26,300	102,020
11	Total	158,281	148,520	137,444	143,808	588,053

G14

	A	B	C	D	E	F
1				Unit Sales		
2	Part Number	Qtr 1	Qtr 2	Qtr 3	Qtr 4	To
3	1001	=SUM(North:East!B3)	=SUM(North:East!C3)	=SUM(North:East!D3)	=SUM(North:East!E3)	=SUM(North:East!F3)
4	1002	=SUM(North:East!B4)	=SUM(North:East!C4)	=SUM(North:East!D4)	=SUM(North:East!E4)	=SUM(North:East!F4)
5	1003	=SUM(North:East!B5)	=SUM(North:East!C5)	=SUM(North:East!D5)	=SUM(North:East!E5)	=SUM(North:East!F5)
6	1004	=SUM(North:East!B6)	=SUM(North:East!C6)	=SUM(North:East!D6)	=SUM(North:East!E6)	=SUM(North:East!F6)
7	1005	=SUM(North:East!B7)	=SUM(North:East!C7)	=SUM(North:East!D7)	=SUM(North:East!E7)	=SUM(North:East!F7)
8	1006	=SUM(North:East!B8)	=SUM(North:East!C8)	=SUM(North:East!D8)	=SUM(North:East!E8)	=SUM(North:East!F8)
9	1007	=SUM(North:East!B9)	=SUM(North:East!C9)	=SUM(North:East!D9)	=SUM(North:East!E9)	=SUM(North:East!F9)
10	1008	=SUM(North:East!B10)	=SUM(North:East!C10)	=SUM(North:East!D10)	=SUM(North:East!E10)	=SUM(North:East!F10)
11	Total	=SUM(North:East!B11)	=SUM(North:East!C11)	=SUM(North:East!D11)	=SUM(North:East!E11)	=SUM(North:East!F11)

2. The values are shown on the left side of the figure and the formulas on the right.

	A	B
1	Annual	
2		
3	Revenue	
4	Products	327
5	Services	330
6	Total Revenues	657
7	Expenses	
8	Rent	96
9	Salaries	97
10	Supplies	101
11	Travel	102
12	Utilities	96
13	Total Expenses	492
14	Net Income	165
15		

	A	B
1	Annual	
2		
3	Revenue	
4	Products	=SUM(Jan:Dec!B4)
5	Services	=SUM(Jan:Dec!B5)
6	Total Revenues	=SUM(Jan:Dec!B6)
7	Expenses	
8	Rent	=SUM(Jan:Dec!B8)
9	Salaries	=SUM(Jan:Dec!B9)
10	Supplies	=SUM(Jan:Dec!B10)
11	Travel	=SUM(Jan:Dec!B11)
12	Utilities	=SUM(Jan:Dec!B12)
13	Total Expenses	=SUM(Jan:Dec!B13)
14	Net Income	=SUM(Jan:Dec!B14)
15		

CHAPTER 17

Lookup Tables

Lookup tables are a good way to search for information and to return specific data relating to the information you introduce or look for. The Lookup function is a quick way to find the information one needs, and is particularly efficient when dealing with large databases that would be extremely time-consuming to search manually. This chapter will introduce a vertical lookup table in two ways or configurations. The first one is when you are looking to return a single value within a certain data range. The second way will demonstrate a request for an exact match.

When you create a vertical lookup table, the left column of the table is where you define the information you want to look up. The first column contains the unique values on which you base the lookup search.

Range—Approximate Match Lookup

This lookup is a way to find a value that does not have an exact match, but would fall within a certain range. Consider an example of assigning grades to students based on their scores on an exam. The table in H2:J6, in Figure 17.1, indicates the range of values for exam grades. The left column has the scores and the other two columns specify the grades in two formats. This lookup is called, by Excel, a range lookup—since you will get the grade if you are within a certain range. For example, if the student has a score in the range of 76 to 85, then the letter grade received should be a "B." Note that the B or the letter grade is in the second column and the grade in a word version is in the third column of the table. This table does not need an exact match. For another example, any score that equals to 66, but is less than 76, will result in a grade of C or Satisfactory. **This is why it is not an exact match.** The example

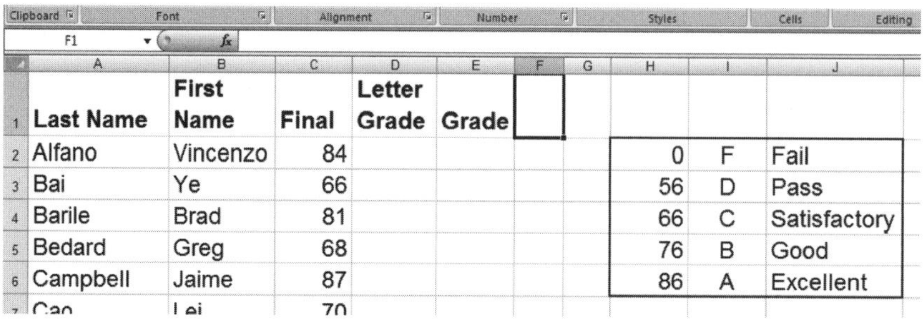

Figure 17.1   Grade sheet lookup table

H	I	J
0	F	Fail
56	D	Pass
66	C	Satisfactory
76	B	Good
86	A	Excellent

Figure 17.2   Grade ranges

shows students and their exam scores. You want to look up their scores in the table and assign them the appropriate grades.

In Figure 17.2, you see the lookup table only. This is the table you are going to get the information from. The lookup table in Figure 17.2 is in the range of H2:J6. It is always a better idea to give the range a name. You avoid, as pointed out before, having to use absolute addressing and it also provides a better feel for the lookup range.

The first step is to name the range H2:J6. You will call it "Table" as you can see in Figure 17.3. The reason you assign a name to the range is that it is more convenient and less confusing to use a name than absolute addressing when you refer to the data. Select the data in H2:J6 and type the name Table in the Name box and hit Enter. The range is now called Table. See Figure 17.3.

Now you can use the VLOOKUP function, which is the very last function under the Lookup & Reference functions list. Refer to Figure 17.4. The function is called VLOOKUP because the table in the range H2:J6 is vertical. You would be using HLOOKUP if the table was horizontal. Select the cell D2 where you want the answer and use the function f_x or try the Shift+F3 shortcut for the Function menu.

You are planning to lookup the score in cell C2 in the table and program how it converts to a letter grade.

This is how to fill in the Function Arguments window fields:

- In this example, the **Lookup value** is the grade in cell C2 (84).
- **Table array**: is our lookup table. You called it Table. Use F3 to get the name.

	A	B	C	D	E	F	G	H	I	J
Table			fx	0						
1	**Last Name**	**First Name**	**Final**	**Letter Grade**	**Grade**					
2	Alfano	Vincenzo	84	Select the data in				0	F	Fail
3	Bai	Ye	66	H2:J6 and type the				56	D	Pass
4	Barile	Brad	81	name Table in the				66	C	Satisfactory
5	Bedard	Greg	68	Name box.				76	B	Good
6	Campbell	Jaime	87					86	A	Excellent

Figure 17.3   Naming the range "Table"

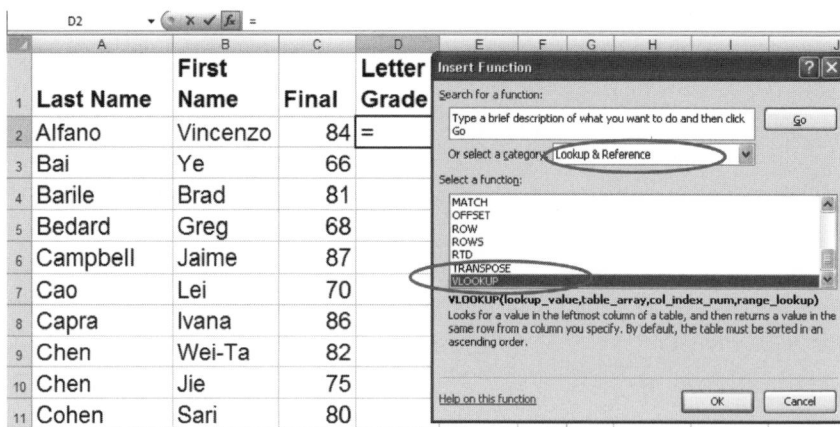

Figure 17.4 Using the VLOOKUP function

■ **Col index num**: Which column in the table has the value you want?
The answer is "**2**." The second column of the lookup table will result in the letter grade.

■ **Range lookup**: Do you want only an exact match? Is an approximate match okay? If you use TRUE as the last argument, or omit the last argument, an approximate match will be returned. In this case, you do not insist on an EXACT match, therefore, you will leave it blank. See Figure 17.5.

Once you obtain one grade you may copy and paste, drag down the results, or double-click the drag handle to fill the rest of the list in the column as you can see in Figure 17.6.

You will use this function again to obtain the worded Grade in column E. This time the Col index num is 3: the third column in the Lookup table as shown in Figure 17.7.

Again, once the first cell has the function formula, you can double-click the crosshair cursor when your mouse hovers over the grab handle to fill the information in the rest of the column. See Figure 17.8.

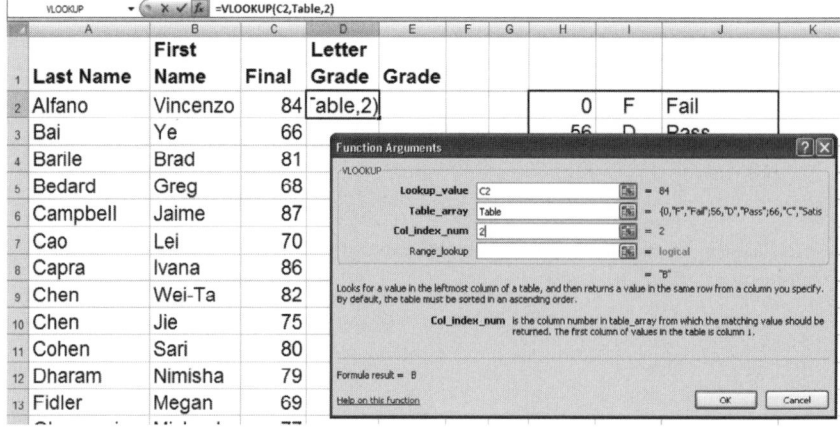

Figure 17.5 The VLOOKUP menu

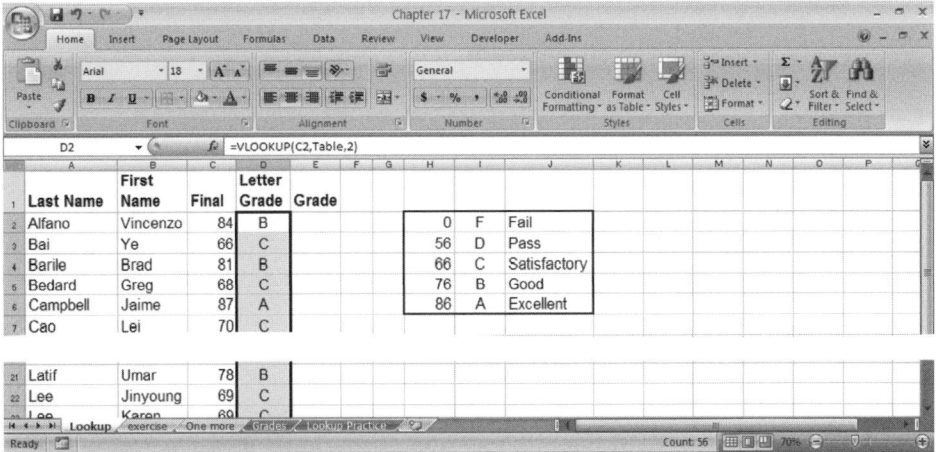

Figure 17.6 The results of VLOOKUP

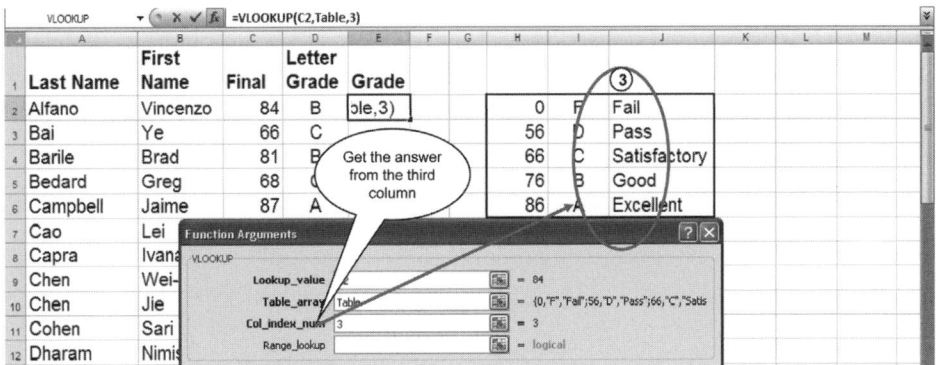

Figure 17.7 The grades are obtained from the third column

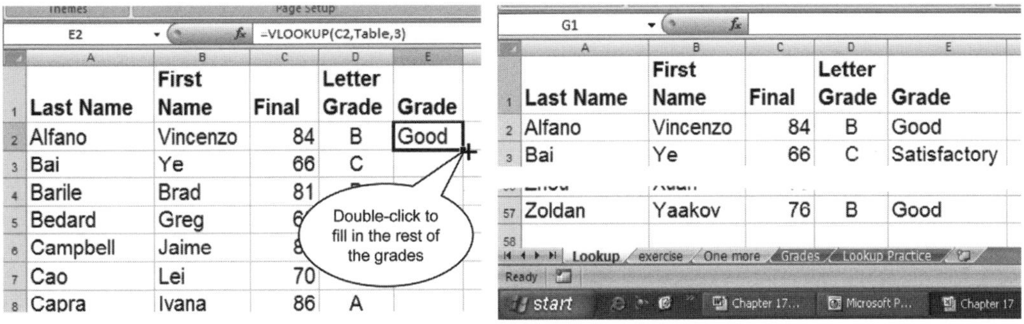

Figure 17.8 Getting the results for the rest of the database

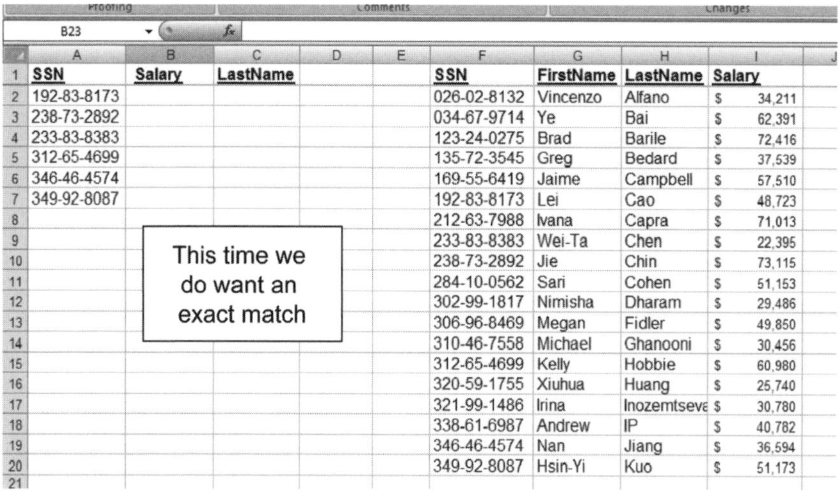

SSN	Salary	LastName			SSN	FirstName	LastName	Salary
192-83-8173					026-02-8132	Vincenzo	Alfano	$ 34,211
238-73-2892					034-67-9714	Ye	Bai	$ 62,391
233-83-8383					123-24-0275	Brad	Barile	$ 72,416
312-65-4699					135-72-3545	Greg	Bedard	$ 37,539
346-46-4574					169-55-6419	Jaime	Campbell	$ 57,510
349-92-8087					192-83-8173	Lei	Cao	$ 48,723
					212-63-7988	Ivana	Capra	$ 71,013
					233-83-8383	Wei-Ta	Chen	$ 22,395
					238-73-2892	Jie	Chin	$ 73,115
					284-10-0562	Sari	Cohen	$ 51,153
					302-99-1817	Nimisha	Dharam	$ 29,486
					306-96-8469	Megan	Fidler	$ 49,850
					310-46-7558	Michael	Ghanooni	$ 30,456
					312-65-4699	Kelly	Hobbie	$ 60,980
					320-59-1755	Xiuhua	Huang	$ 25,740
					321-99-1486	Irina	Inozemtseva	$ 30,780
					338-61-6987	Andrew	IP	$ 40,782
					346-46-4574	Nan	Jiang	$ 36,594
					349-92-8087	Hsin-Yi	Kuo	$ 51,173

Figure 17.9 The need for an exact match lookup

An Exact Match Lookup

When you require an exact match of the values you look up, you need to indicate in the last argument of the lookup table (called "Range look up") that you do not want an approximate value. This time—as you want an exact match—you need to enter the word "False" to indicate it in the VLOOKUP menu.

To facilitate manipulations later on, give the data range a name. Select the range F2:I20 and type the word "Range" in the name box. Do not forget to hit Enter to create the name. See Figure 17.10.

Then use the VLOOKUP function to locate the desired values.

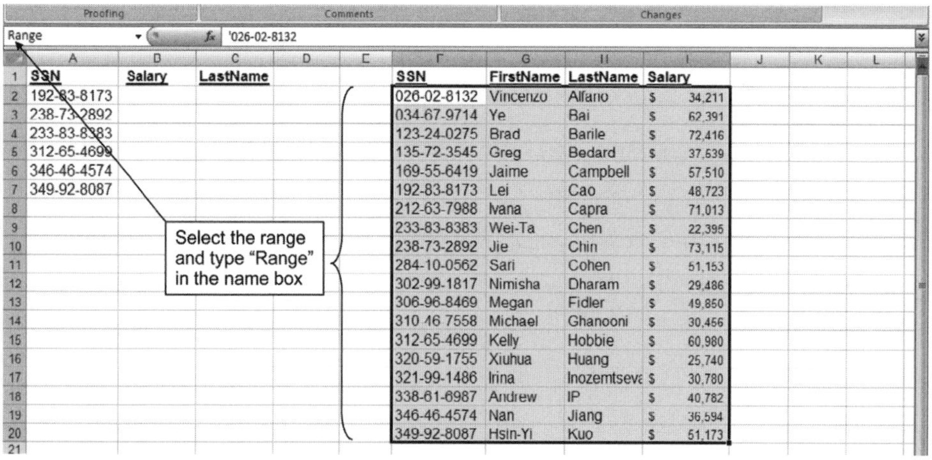

SSN	Salary	LastName			SSN	FirstName	LastName	Salary
192-83-8173					026-02-8132	Vincenzo	Alfano	$ 34,211
238-73-2892					034-67-9714	Ye	Bai	$ 62,391
233-83-8383					123-24-0275	Brad	Barile	$ 72,416
312-65-4699					135-72-3545	Greg	Bedard	$ 37,539
346-46-4574					169-55-6419	Jaime	Campbell	$ 57,510
349-92-8087					192-83-8173	Lei	Cao	$ 48,723
					212-63-7988	Ivana	Capra	$ 71,013
					233-83-8383	Wei-Ta	Chen	$ 22,395
					238-73-2892	Jie	Chin	$ 73,115
					284-10-0562	Sari	Cohen	$ 51,153
					302-99-1817	Nimisha	Dharam	$ 29,486
					306-96-8469	Megan	Fidler	$ 49,850
					310-46-7558	Michael	Ghanooni	$ 30,456
					312-65-4699	Kelly	Hobbie	$ 60,980
					320-59-1755	Xiuhua	Huang	$ 25,740
					321-99-1486	Irina	Inozemtseva	$ 30,780
					338-61-6987	Andrew	IP	$ 40,782
					346-46-4574	Nan	Jiang	$ 36,594
					349-92-8087	Hsin-Yi	Kuo	$ 51,173

Figure 17.10 Naming the lookup table "Range"

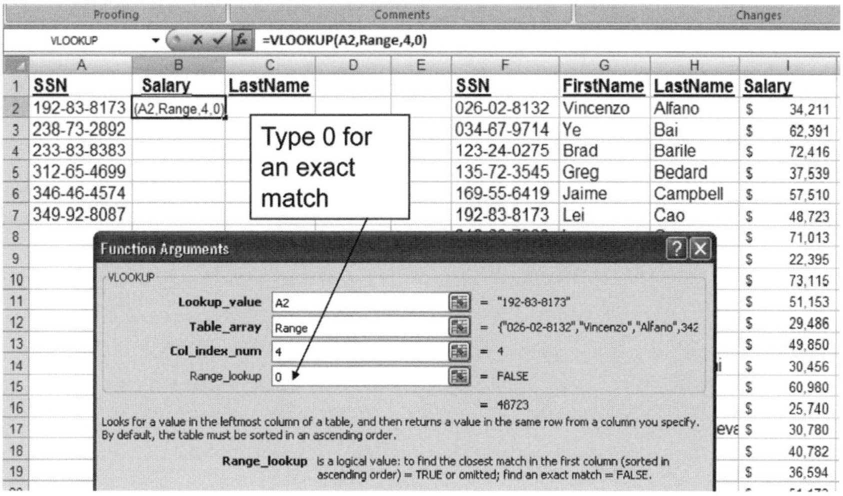

Figure 17.11 Type 0 (zero) or false for an exact match

In Figure 17.11, you look up the salaries in the table based on SSN, the Social Security Number.

- **Lookup value**: the value you want to look up. In this example, the SSN is in A2.
- **Table array**: is our lookup table. You called it Range.
- **Col index num**: in which column of the table is the value you want located? 4: the forth column of the lookup table.
- **Range lookup**: Do you want an exact match? Is an approximate match okay?

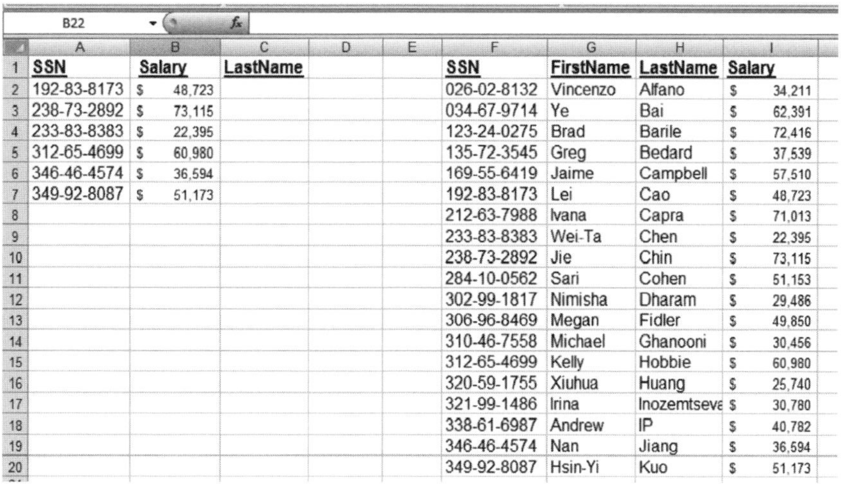

	A	B	C	D	E	F	G	H	I
1	SSN	Salary	LastName			SSN	FirstName	LastName	Salary
2	192-83-8173	$ 48,723				026-02-8132	Vincenzo	Alfano	$ 34,211
3	238-73-2892	$ 73,115				034-67-9714	Ye	Bai	$ 62,391
4	233-83-8383	$ 22,395				123-24-0275	Brad	Barile	$ 72,416
5	312-65-4699	$ 60,980				135-72-3545	Greg	Bedard	$ 37,539
6	346-46-4574	$ 36,594				169-55-6419	Jaime	Campbell	$ 57,510
7	349-92-8087	$ 51,173				192-83-8173	Lei	Cao	$ 48,723
8						212-63-7988	Ivana	Capra	$ 71,013
9						233-83-8383	Wei-Ta	Chen	$ 22,395
10						238-73-2892	Jie	Chin	$ 73,115
11						284-10-0562	Sari	Cohen	$ 51,153
12						302-99-1817	Nimisha	Dharam	$ 29,486
13						306-96-8469	Megan	Fidler	$ 49,850
14						310-46-7558	Michael	Ghanooni	$ 30,456
15						312-65-4699	Kelly	Hobbie	$ 60,980
16						320-59-1755	Xiuhua	Huang	$ 25,740
17						321-99-1486	Irina	Inozemtseva	$ 30,780
18						338-61-6987	Andrew	IP	$ 40,782
19						346-46-4574	Nan	Jiang	$ 36,594
20						349-92-8087	Hsin-Yi	Kuo	$ 51,173

Figure 17.12 Lookup results for salary

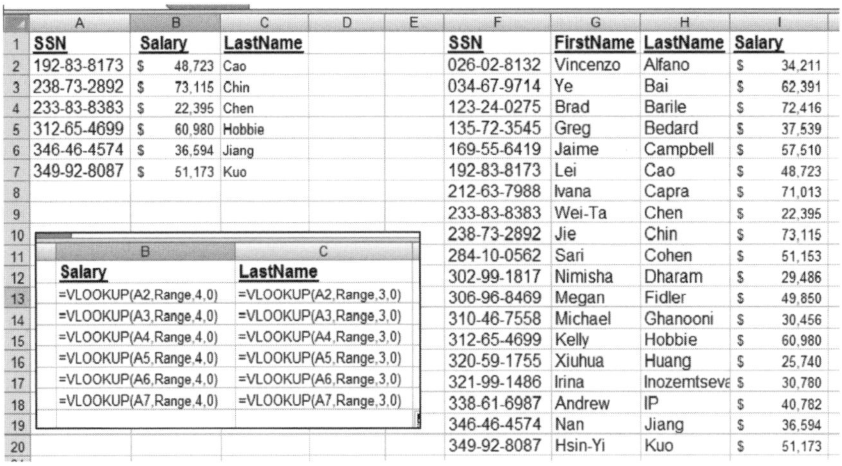

	A	B	C	D	E	F	G	H	I
1	SSN	Salary	LastName			SSN	FirstName	LastName	Salary
2	192-83-8173	$ 48,723	Cao			026-02-8132	Vincenzo	Alfano	$ 34,211
3	238-73-2892	$ 73,115	Chin			034-67-9714	Ye	Bai	$ 62,391
4	233-83-8383	$ 22,395	Chen			123-24-0275	Brad	Barile	$ 72,416
5	312-65-4699	$ 60,980	Hobbie			135-72-3545	Greg	Bedard	$ 37,539
6	346-46-4574	$ 36,594	Jiang			169-55-6419	Jaime	Campbell	$ 57,510
7	349-92-8087	$ 51,173	Kuo			192-83-8173	Lei	Cao	$ 48,723
8						212-63-7988	Ivana	Capra	$ 71,013
9						233-83-8383	Wei-Ta	Chen	$ 22,395
10						238-73-2892	Jie	Chin	$ 73,115
11						284-10-0562	Sari	Cohen	$ 51,153
12						302-99-1817	Nimisha	Dharam	$ 29,486
13						306-96-8469	Megan	Fidler	$ 49,850
14						310-46-7558	Michael	Ghanooni	$ 30,456
15						312-65-4699	Kelly	Hobbie	$ 60,980
16						320-59-1755	Xiuhua	Huang	$ 25,740
17						321-99-1486	Irina	Inozemtseva	$ 30,780
18						338-61-6987	Andrew	IP	$ 40,782
19						346-46-4574	Nan	Jiang	$ 36,594
20						349-92-8087	Hsin-Yi	Kuo	$ 51,173

	B	C
12	Salary	LastName
13	=VLOOKUP(A2,Range,4,0)	=VLOOKUP(A2,Range,3,0)
14	=VLOOKUP(A3,Range,4,0)	=VLOOKUP(A3,Range,3,0)
15	=VLOOKUP(A4,Range,4,0)	=VLOOKUP(A4,Range,3,0)
16	=VLOOKUP(A5,Range,4,0)	=VLOOKUP(A5,Range,3,0)
17	=VLOOKUP(A6,Range,4,0)	=VLOOKUP(A6,Range,3,0)
18	=VLOOKUP(A7,Range,4,0)	=VLOOKUP(A7,Range,3,0)

Figure 17.13 Results and formulas

If you use TRUE or omit the last argument, an approximate match can be returned. In this case, you DO want an EXACT match. Use: **False** or type **0.** (The value "0" is the same as "False" in Excel functions.) The results are shown in Figure 17.12.

Now repeat this procedure and use an exact match in the VLOOKUP to obtain the last names in column C. This time the Col index num is in column 3. Compare your results to the values in Figure 17.13. The figure shows the outcome and the functions.

REVIEW QUESTIONS

You will find these examples in the Excel Chapter 17 file:

1. On the sheet called *Exercise*, you will find a list of transactions and part numbers. You also have a table with part numbers and product names on the table on the right. Select the table and give it a name. Use the VLOOKUP function to obtain the product names from the table.

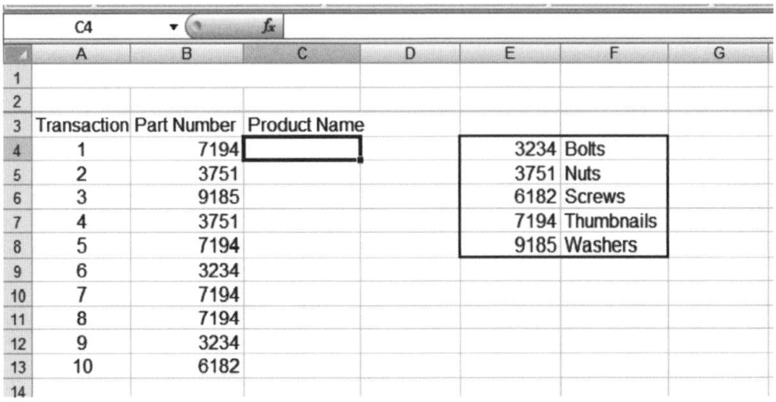

C4

	A	B	C	D	E	F	G
1							
2							
3	Transaction	Part Number	Product Name				
4	1	7194			3234	Bolts	
5	2	3751			3751	Nuts	
6	3	9185			6182	Screws	
7	4	3751			7194	Thumbnails	
8	5	7194			9185	Washers	
9	6	3234					
10	7	7194					
11	8	7194					
12	9	3234					
13	10	6182					
14							

2. Use the VLOOKUP function to complete the table on the *Lookup Practice* sheet.

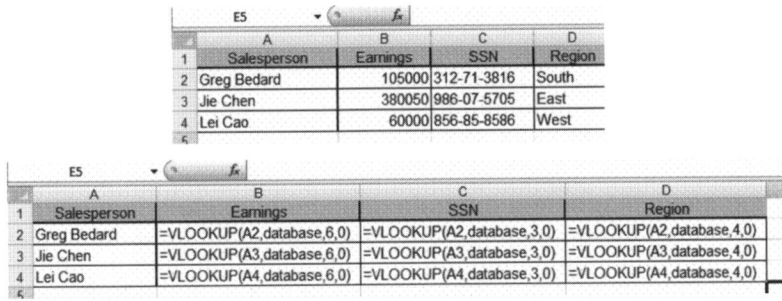

	A	B	C	D	E	F	G
1	Salesperson	Earnings	SSN	Region			
2	Greg Bedard						
3	Jie Chen						
4	Lei Cao						
5							
6							
7							
8	Salesperson	Employee ID	SSN	Region	Department	Earnings	
9	Vincenzo Alfano	EM001	816-17-3312	East	Accounting	$72,000.00	
10	Ye Bai	EM002	799-70-8097	South	Accounting	$80,000.00	
11	Brad Barile	EM003	336-68-4467	South	Accounting	$95,000.00	
12	Greg Bedard	EM004	312-71-3816	South	Accounting	$105,000.00	
13	Jaime Campbell	EM005	534-98-7549	East	Accounting	$90,000.00	
14	Lei Cao	EM006	856-85-8586	West	Accounting	$60,000.00	
15	Ivana Capra	EM007	456-78-8906	East	Accounting	$87,000.00	

ANSWERS

1. Name the range E4:F8 "tools" and use the function =VLOOKUP(B4,tools,2) in the cell C4 returning "Thumbnails."
2. Name the range A9:F48 "database." Use the VLOOKUP function as shown, below and drag the results to the rest of the table.

	A	B	C	D
1	Salesperson	Earnings	SSN	Region
2	Greg Bedard	105000	312-71-3816	South
3	Jie Chen	380050	986-07-5705	East
4	Lei Cao	60000	856-85-8586	West

	A	B	C	D
1	Salesperson	Earnings	SSN	Region
2	Greg Bedard	=VLOOKUP(A2,database,6,0)	=VLOOKUP(A2,database,3,0)	=VLOOKUP(A2,database,4,0)
3	Jie Chen	=VLOOKUP(A3,database,6,0)	=VLOOKUP(A3,database,3,0)	=VLOOKUP(A3,database,4,0)
4	Lei Cao	=VLOOKUP(A4,database,6,0)	=VLOOKUP(A4,database,3,0)	=VLOOKUP(A4,database,4,0)

The Data Menu and Ribbon

This part of the book will deal with the Data menu features of Excel. It will discuss and cover the following topics:

- Sorting data
- Filters
- Creating and using Data Forms
- Grouping data
- Subtotals
- Pivot Tables.

In order to make the best use of all Excel features when using lists or tables, the databases must be set-up in a specific way.

Following are some basic rules for the set-up before starting the actual data processing:

- The first row of the database must contain headers.
- All these headers have to be unique headers—avoid using the same header names.
- The list can have any number of columns and any number of rows within the sheet boundaries.
- The databases should not have blank rows or columns within the database/range.
- If the list/database doesn't start in row 1, there must be at least one blank row above the headers.
- If the list doesn't start in column A, you should have at least one blank column to the left of the list.

Sorting Data

Sorting data in Excel is done using the menus and icons under the Data ribbon. This section deals with sorting. The Sort icons are shown in Figure 18.1.

Consider the following example of a simple database. The data for the example is on the sheet named *Database* in the Chapter 18 Excel file. The table is shown in Figure 18.2. Initially, the data is in the order of (or sorted by) the employee number in column B.

If you wish to sort the entire table by a single parameter/column, you have to select a single cell in that column and click on the Sort icon. For example, if you wish to sort the table

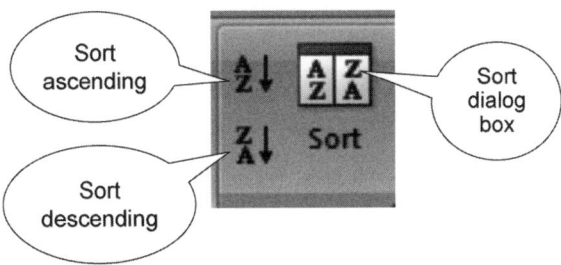

Figure 18.1   The Sort icons

	A	B	C	D	E	F	G
1	Employee	Employee No.	Gender	Dep	Job	Seniority	Age
2	Alfano, Vincenzo	1101	M	4	Electrician	7	48
3	Bai, Ye	1102	M	3	Machinist	5	32
4	Barile, Brad	1103	M	2	Electrician	12	36
5	Bedard, Greg	1104	M	1	Carpenter	15	35
6	Campbell, Jaime	1105	F	3	Carpenter	13	32
7	Cao, Lei	1106	F	1	Electrician	4	23
8	Capra, Ivana	1107	F	2	Electrician	23	45
9	Chen, Wei-Ta	1108	M	3	Machinist	7	25
10	Chen, Jie	1109	M	1	Carpenter	0	48
11	Cohen, Sari	1110	F	2	Electrician	0	22
12	Dharam, Nimisha	1111	F	3	Carpenter	15	35
13	Fidler, Megan	1112	F	1	Electrician	6	45
14	Ghanooni, Michael	1113	M	2	Electrician	3	34
15	Hobbie, Kelly	1114	F	3	Machinist	2	28
16	Huang, Xiuhua	1115	M	1	Carpenter	8	41
17	Inozemtseva, Irina	1116	F	4	Electrician	11	45
18	IP, Andrew	1117	M	4	Carpenter	3	33
19	Jiang, Nan	1118	M	1	Carpenter	0	38

Figure 18.2   Database example

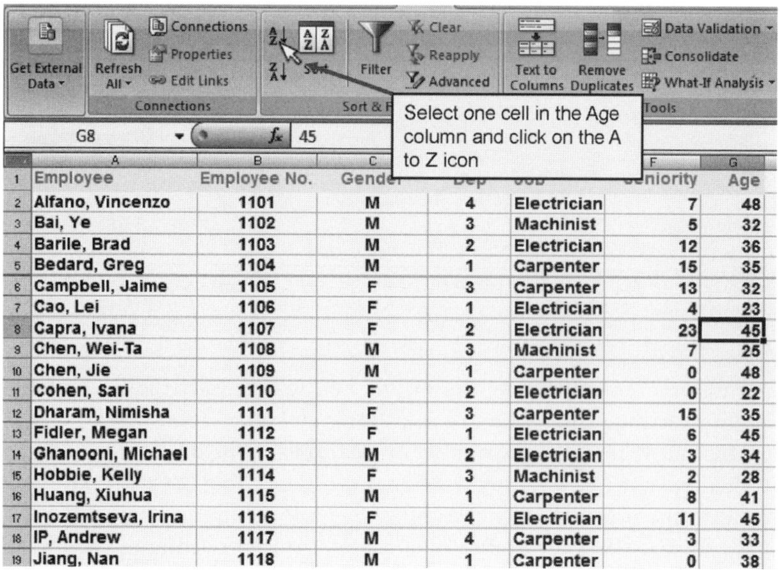

Figure 18.3   Sort Ascending

by age, click on a single cell in the Age column and click on the Sort A to Z icon ![icon]. See Figure 18.3.

You may use the A to Z icon for ascending order and the Z to A icon for descending order. You should try any one of the other columns. Clicking on the icon when you select a single cell will sort the entire table/database using the parameter/column you chose. Figure 18.4 shows the data sorted by ascending value of age.

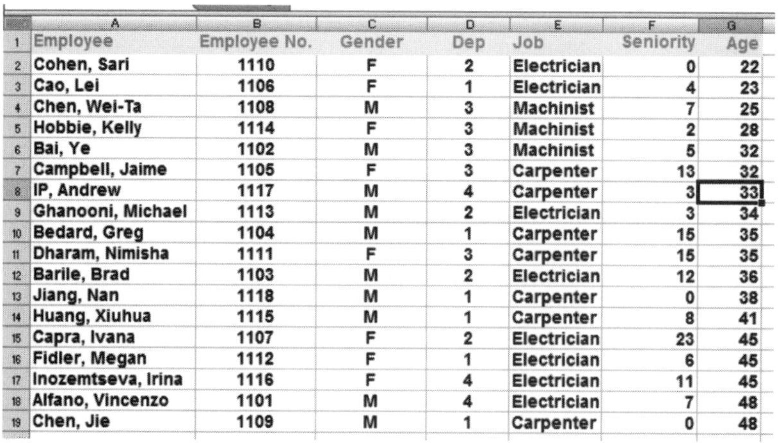

Figure 18.4   Data sorted by age

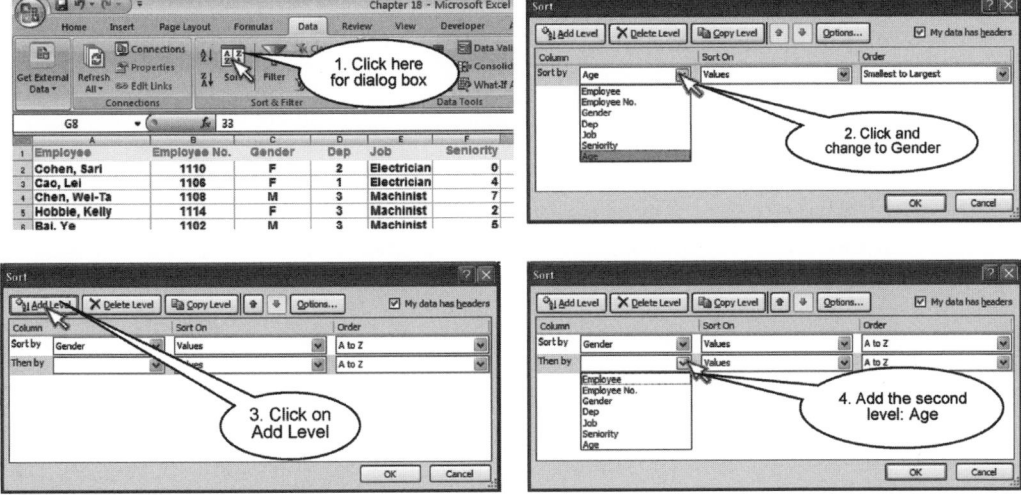

Figure 18.5 Sorting by more than one parameter

Sorting by multiple parameters

If you wish to sort by more than one parameter, you have to use the Sort dialog box.

For example, should you want to sort by gender and by age within the gender, follow the example in Figure 18.5.

In the dialog box, you have to select the Sort by cell and select the column header you want the sorting to occur in. Then, under the Sort On category, choose the type of sort you want to use (value, color, and so on). The third drop-down menu allows you to choose whether you wish to apply ascending or descending sorting. Click on Add Level when you want to add the secondary sorting parameter/header. The secondary level implies that this sorting will occur *within* the first sorted category. You may continue this way with more headers, up to a maximum of three.

Notice how, in Figure 18.6 the ages are sorted *within* the gender. You may sort, using this function, by up to three parameters, in ascending or descending order.

More about sorting There are two more ways to access the sort features in Excel. One way is through the Home ribbon. On the right side of the ribbon you will see the Sort and Filter icon. See Figure 18.7.

Another way is to right-click after selecting a cell or to use a shortcut for right-click, Shift+F10. The local menu allows you to use the sort features as you can see in Figure 18.8.

Sort by Color in Excel 2007 Excel 2007 has a new feature that allows you—among other features—to sort by color or format. On the sheet named *Colors*, you can try and sort the data by color. When you click on the Sort icon, you can proceed with sorting the data using cell colors. Figure 18.8 illustrates starting the sort by color. Figure 18.9 shows how to add

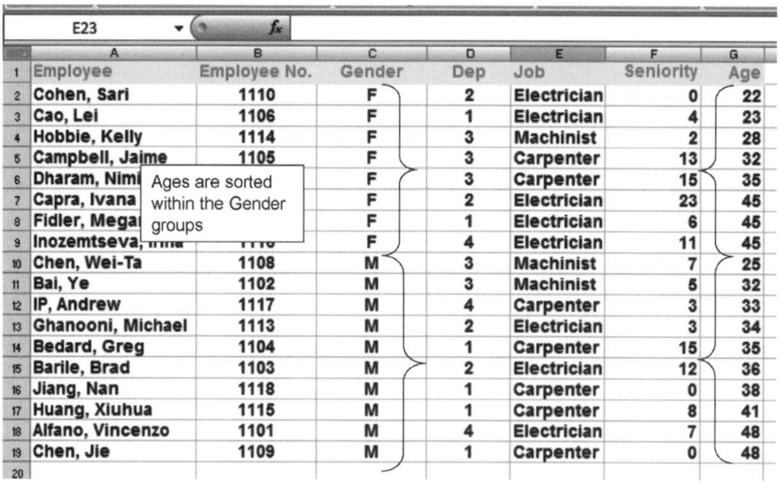

	Employee	Employee No.	Gender	Dep	Job	Seniority	Age
2	Cohen, Sari	1110	F	2	Electrician	0	22
3	Cao, Lei	1106	F	1	Electrician	4	23
4	Hobbie, Kelly	1114	F	3	Machinist	2	28
5	Campbell, Jaime	1105	F	3	Carpenter	13	32
6	Dharam, Nimi		F	3	Carpenter	15	35
7	Capra, Ivana		F	2	Electrician	23	45
8	Fidler, Mega		F	1	Electrician	6	45
9	Inozemtseva,		F	4	Electrician	11	45
10	Chen, Wei-Ta	1108	M	3	Machinist	7	25
11	Bai, Ye	1102	M	3	Machinist	5	32
12	IP, Andrew	1117	M	4	Carpenter	3	33
13	Ghanooni, Michael	1113	M	2	Electrician	3	34
14	Bedard, Greg	1104	M	1	Carpenter	15	35
15	Barile, Brad	1103	M	2	Electrician	12	36
16	Jiang, Nan	1118	M	1	Carpenter	0	38
17	Huang, Xiuhua	1115	M	1	Carpenter	8	41
18	Alfano, Vincenzo	1101	M	4	Electrician	7	48
19	Chen, Jie	1109	M	1	Carpenter	0	48

Figure 18.6 Data sorted by age within the gender sort

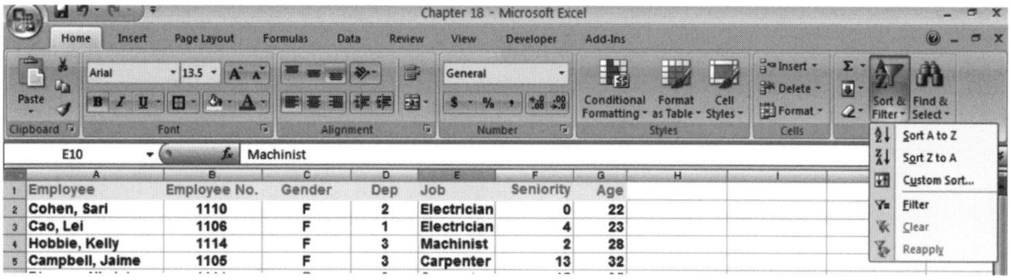

Figure 18.7 Sorting through the Home ribbon icon

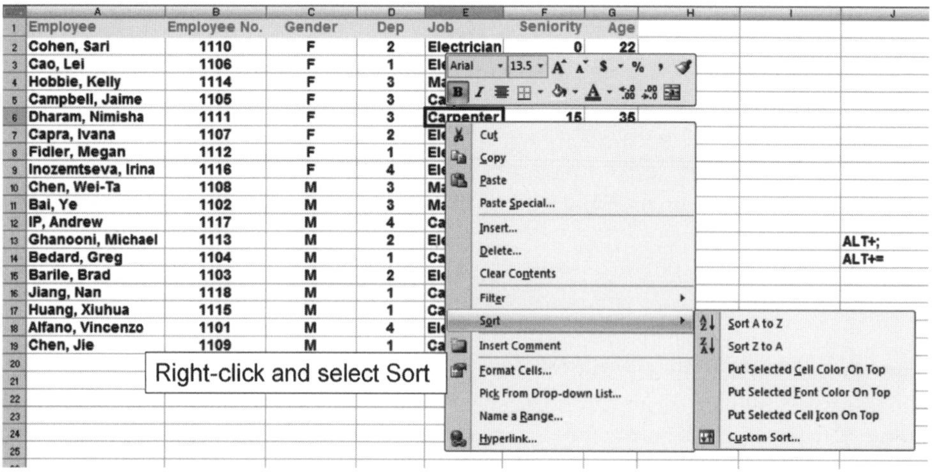

Figure 18.8 Right-click or use a shortcut, Shift+F10

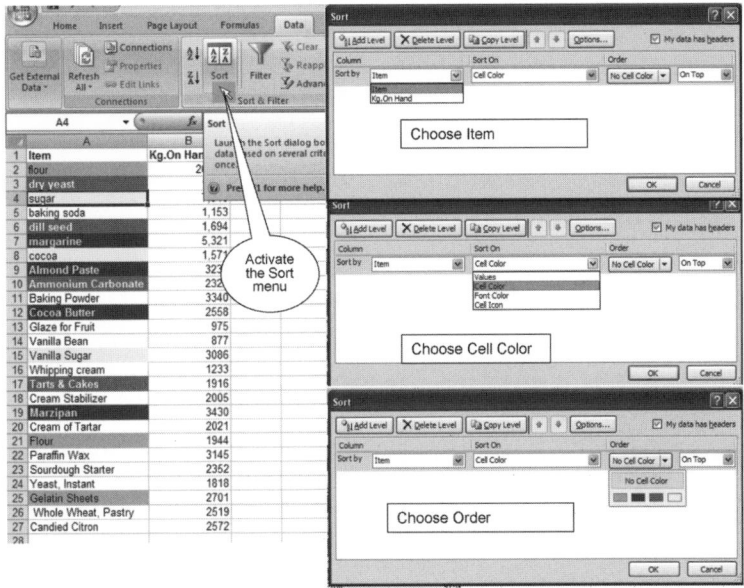

Figure 18.9 Sorting by color

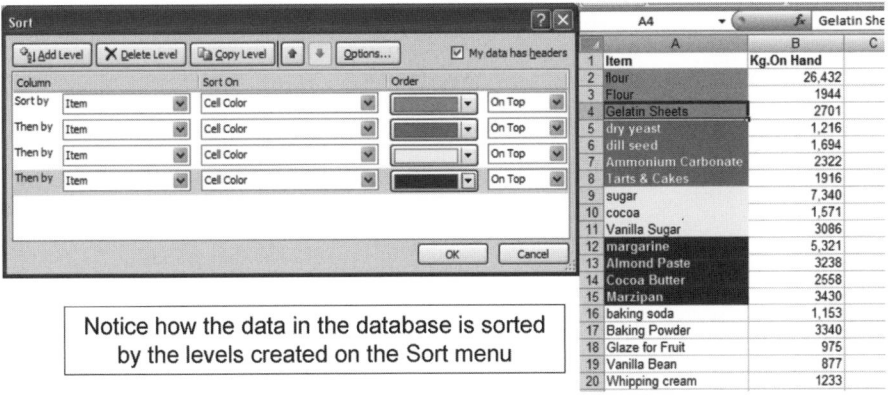

Figure 18.10 Data sorted by color in column A

levels and sorting the data by cell colors. The color option is under Sort By as illustrated in Figure 18.9.

Note how, in Figure 18.10 the data is sorted by color.

APPENDIX—SORTING IN EXCEL 2003 OR EARLIER VERSIONS OF EXCEL

Excel 2003 has the same icons to sort by. See Figure 18.11. The icons are similar to the Excel 2007 icons.

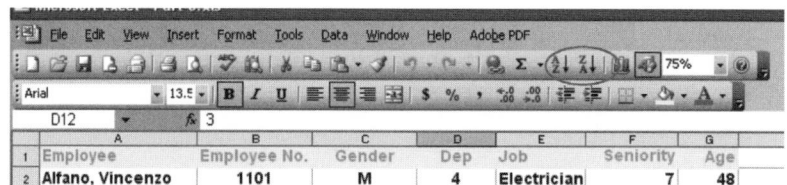

Figure 18.11   Sorting icons for Excel 2003

To sort by more than one parameter, you can use the Data menu. The menu is shown in Figure 18.12.

The Data menu for sorting, as shown in Figure 18.13, has up to three levels. Each level gives you the option to sort the parameters by either ascending or descending order.

Figure 18.12   Date Sort menu in Excel 2003

Figure 18.13   The Sort menu in Excel 2003

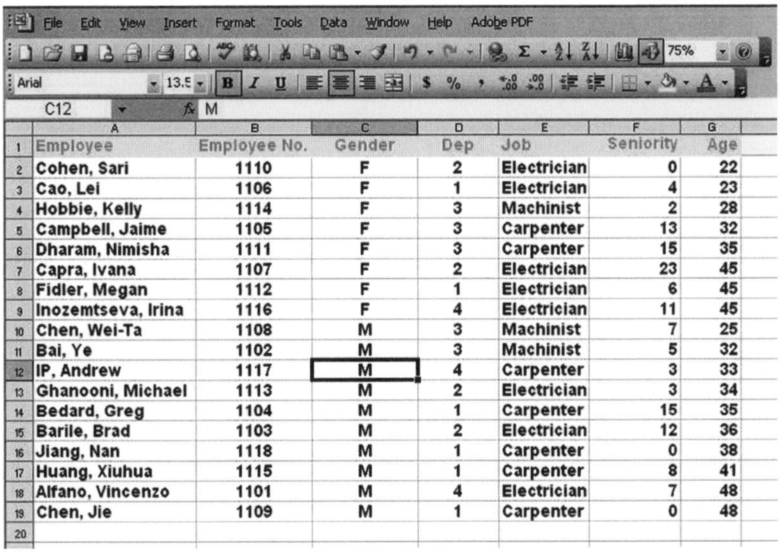

Figure 18.14 Data sorted by age within the gender sort

Note how in Figure 18.14 the ages are sorted within the gender. You may sort, using this function, by up to three parameters, each in ascending or descending order.

REVIEW QUESTIONS

You will find these examples in the Excel Chapter 18 file:

1. In the *Review* sheet, sort the data by the Income level. Sort it again by Purchases.

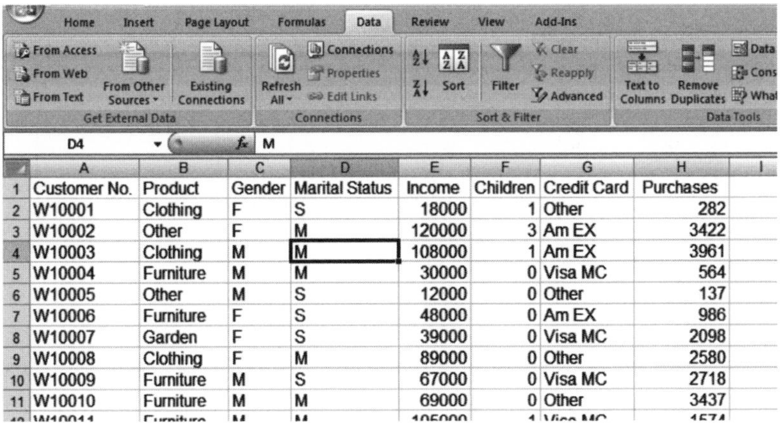

2. Sort the database by the Credit Card name and by Gender within the Credit Card category.
3. Sort the database on the sheet *Review Color* by the colors in column A.

ANSWERS

1. Click on any cell in the range in column E and click on the Sort icon A to Z to sort the database. Repeat with any cell in column H, Purchases, and click on the Sort icon A to Z to sort the database.

2.

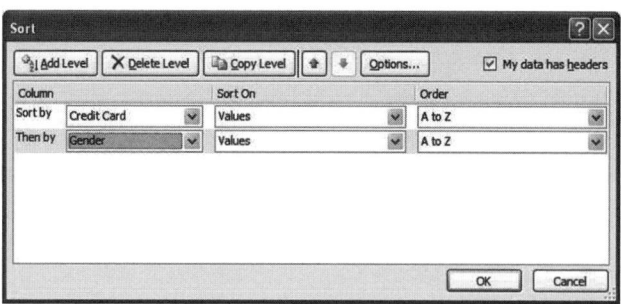

	A	B	C	D	E	F	G	H
1	Employee	Employee No.	Gender	Dep	Job	Seniority	Age	
2	Alfano, Vincenzo	1101	M	4	Electrician	7	48	
3	Bai, Ye	1102	M	3	Machinist	5	32	
4	Barile, Brad	1103	M	2	Electrician	12	36	
5	Bedard, Greg	1104	M	1	Carpenter	15	35	
6	Campbell, Jaime	1105	F	3	Carpenter	13	32	
7	Cao, Lei	1106	F	1	Electrician	4	23	
8	Capra, Ivana	1107	F	2	Electrician	23	45	
9	Chen, Wei-Ta	1108	M	3	Machinist	7	25	
10	Chen, Jie	1109	M	1	Carpenter	0	48	
11	Cohen, Sari	1110	F	2	Electrician	0	22	
12	Dharam, Nimisha	1111	F	3	Carpenter	15	35	
13	Fidler, Megan	1112	F	1	Electrician	6	45	
14	Ghanooni, Michael	1113	M	2	Electrician	3	34	
15	Hobbie, Kelly	1114	F	3	Machinist	2	28	
16	Huang, Xiuhua	1115	M	1	Carpenter	8	41	
17	Inozemtseva, Irina	1116	F	4	Electrician	11	45	
18	IP, Andrew	1117	M	4	Carpenter	3	33	
19	Jiang, Nan	1118	M	1	Carpenter	0	38	

3.

Sort				
Add Level	Delete Level	Copy Level	Options...	☑ My data has headers
Column		**Sort On**		**Order**
Sort by	Credit Card	Values		A to Z
Then by	Gender	Values		A to Z

OK   Cancel

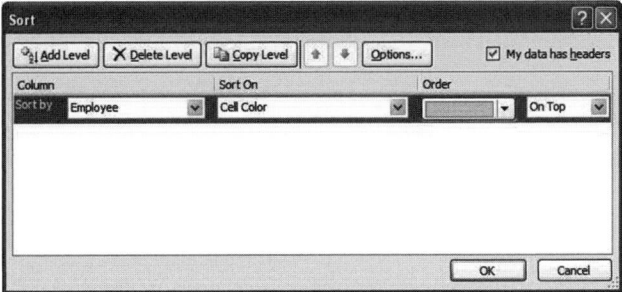

AutoFilter

Filtering is an easy and very fast way to find—and work—with subsets of data in a table and/or database. A filtered table displays only the rows that meet the conditions you itemize or specify for a column or a number of columns. There are several improvements with Excel 2007 AutoFilter with new options that allow you to filter by color or cell formatting.

To activate the AutoFilter, first select a single cell or a region in the table/database, as shown in Figure 19.1 for the sheet named *Database* in the Chapter 19 workbook file. There are three ways to activate the AutoFilter:

1. Under the Data ribbon, click on the AutoFilter icon.
2. Under the Home ribbon, click on the Sort and Filter icon and select Filter.

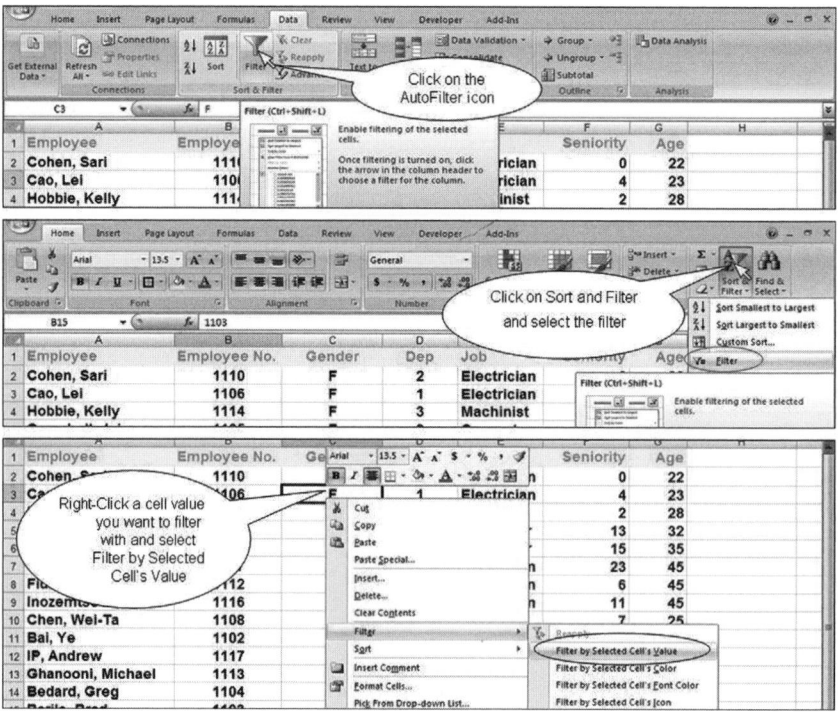

Figure 19.1 Three ways to activate the AutoFilter

3. Right-click a cell value you want to filter with, and select Filter by Selected Cell's Value in the local menu.

Filtered data will display only the rows that meet criteria or conditions you specify in your query/filter. It will hide rows that you do not want displayed.

Using the AutoFilter feature, you can create different types of filters: value, format/color, text, dates, and so on.

A drop-down arrow ⏷ means that filtering is enabled but not applied. A Filter button ▼ means that a filter was applied.

Try not mix formats like text and numbers or numbers and dates in the same columns when entering the initial data.

In Figure 19.2, we filtered the database for females only.

There are other ways to filter data with the AutoFilter in Excel—you can master them yourself once you understand the concept. I will mention only a few of them.

Dates

To activate the AutoFilter on a date column, after you click on the Filter button, click one of the comparison commands (Equals, Before, After, or Between) or click Custom Filter to get a dialog box.

For example—try to create a filter for a date later than "2/1/2008" and where the date is before "6/1/2008." See Figure 19.3 to see how it can be done for the sheet named *Example*. You can try using different dates.

Below and above average

These are very much self-explanatory: to filter by numbers above the average, click Above Average; to filter by numbers that are below the average, click Below Average. The important thing to note is that Excel will calculate by itself the average of your values list, you do not need to fill in this value anywhere in the sheet. See Figure 19.4.

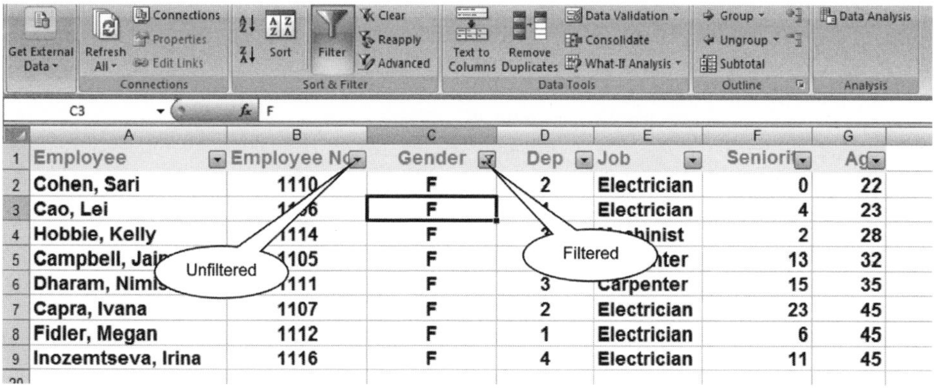

Figure 19.2 Filtered and unfiltered columns

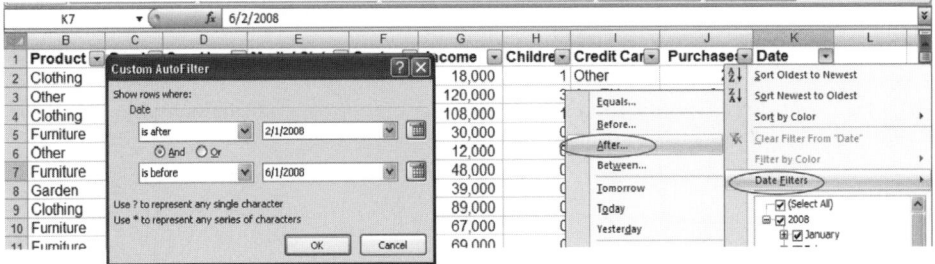

Figure 19.3   Filter by date

You may want to reapply/refresh a filter after you make changes in the data. Click any cell in the range or table, and then click Reapply on the Data ribbon, in the Sort & Filter group.

Filter by Color

If you formatted a range of cells manually or by conditional formatting, you can also filter the data by formatted colors. It is also possible to filter by an icon set created through a conditional format.

In the data of the sheet called *Color* in the Chapter 19 file, select a cell in the column containing cells formatted by color, as shown in Figure 19.5. On the Data ribbon, click on the AutoFilter, and then click on the arrow in the column header and select Filter by Color. You can now apply Filter by Cell Color. (You can also Filter by Font Color or Filter by Cell Icon.)

Remember: To reapply a filter after you change the data, click a cell in the range or table, and then click Reapply in the Data ribbon, under the Sort & Filter group.

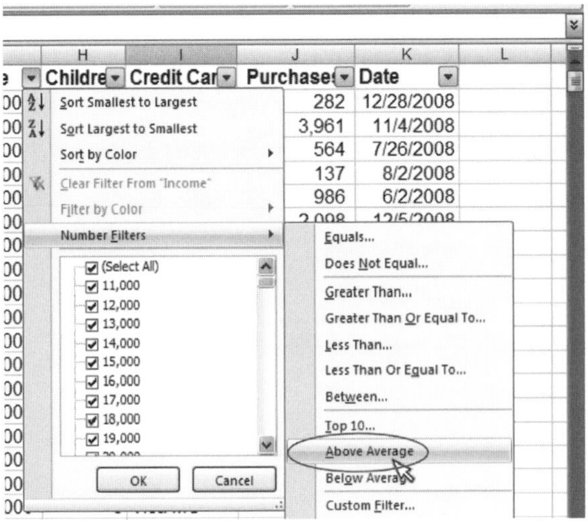

Figure 19.4   Filter all values above the average

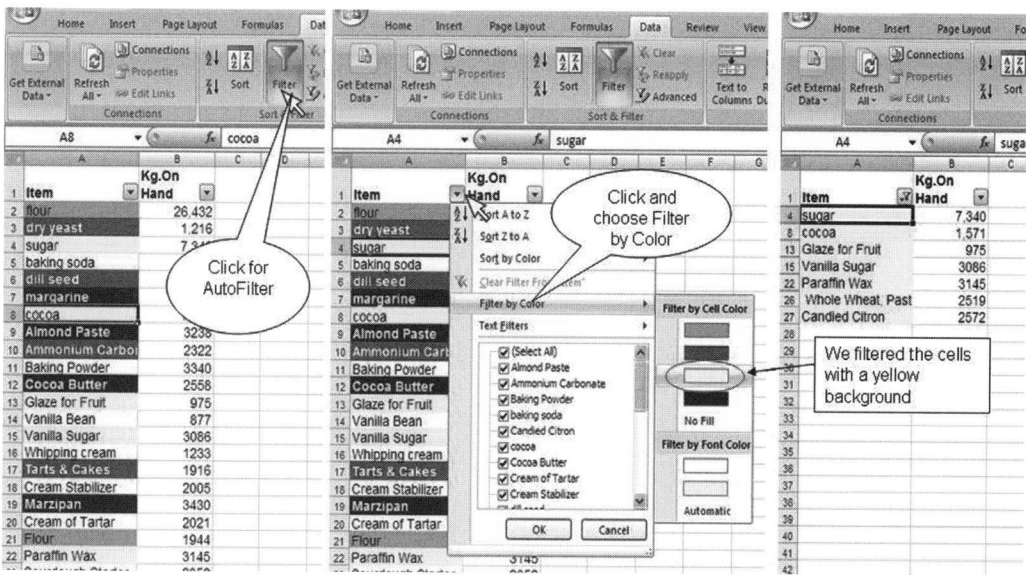

Figure 19.5   Filter by color

APPENDIX—AUTOFILTER IN EXCEL 2003

Filtering in previous versions of Excel is done through the Data menu. To activate filtering, click on the Data menu and select AutoFilter.

When you use Data ⇨ Filter ⇨ AutoFilter, arrows will appear to the right of the headers in the filtered range ▼ (see Figure 19.6).

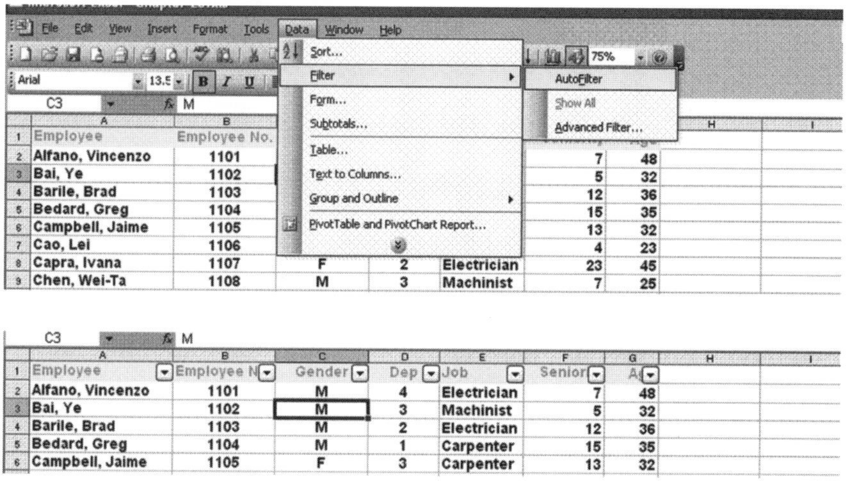

Figure 19.6   Filter in Excel 2003

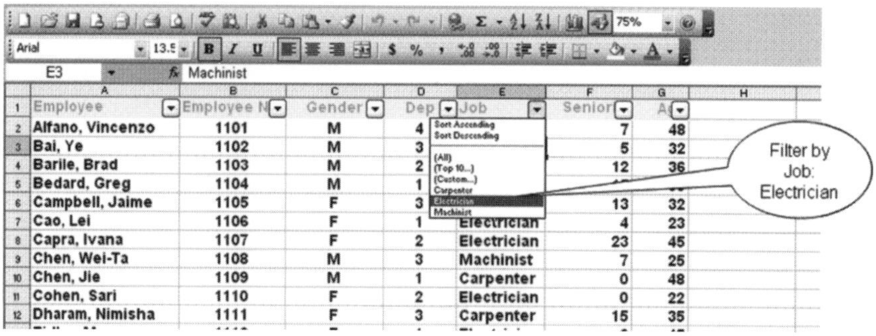

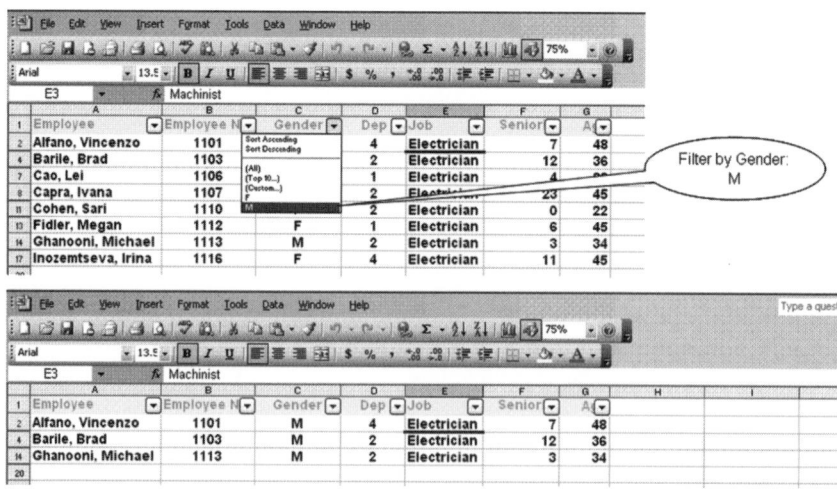

Figure 19.7 Filtering the database for Electricians

When you choose to apply one of the filters, Excel indicates the filtered columns with blue highlighting. Try to filter the Job column for Electrician; and in the Gender column for M (male). See Figure 19.7.

Look at the results in Figure 19.8; the table is filtered: all the male electricians.

You can also use Custom AutoFilter. For example, filter all the records for Age older than 40. See Figure 19.9.

Filtering is a fast way to find and work with subsets of data in a table/database. A filtered table displays only the rows that meet the conditions you itemize or specify for a column.

Figure 19.8 Filter by gender and job

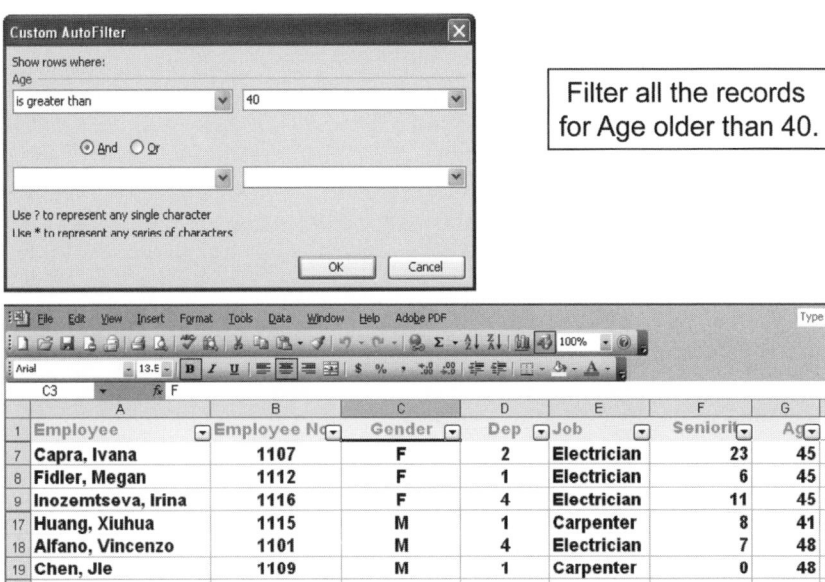

Filter all the records for Age older than 40.

Figure 19.9   Custom AutoFilter for Age above 40

REVIEW QUESTIONS

You will find these examples in the Excel Chapter 19 file:

1. Open the Excel sheet named *Review*. You may be familiar with the data; you used this sheet earlier in this chapter. Use the AutoFilter to choose female married customers with no children.

2. Using the same sheet, filter for all customers with an annual income over $80,000 with purchases below $100.
3. On the sheet *Review Color* select all the employees with a yellow background in column A, using the AutoFilter.

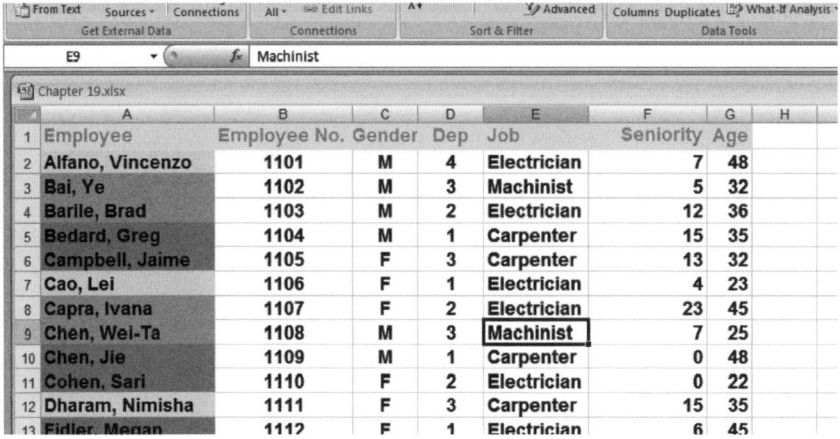

ANSWERS

1. Use the AutoFilter icon and filter as shown here:

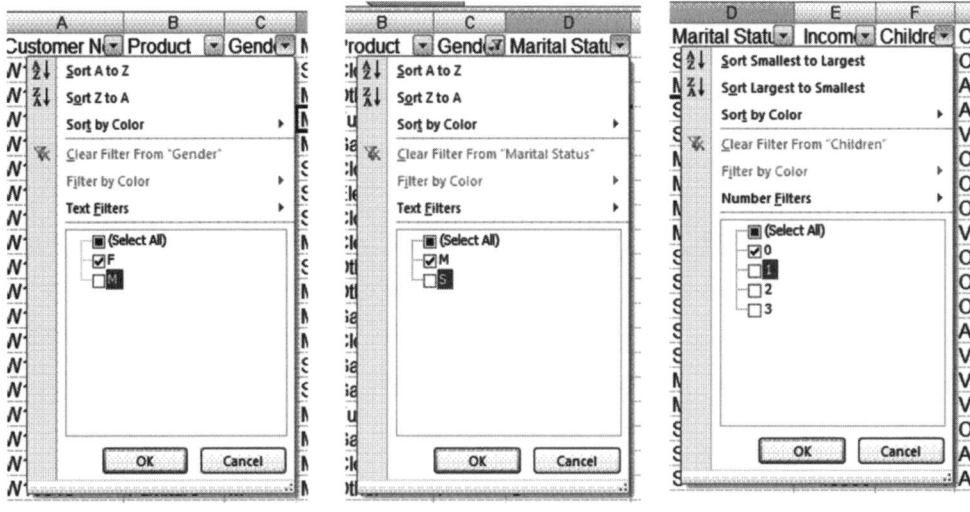

2. Use the AutoFilter icon and filter for Income Greater than $80,000 as shown in the figure below. Repeat the procedure for purchases below $100.

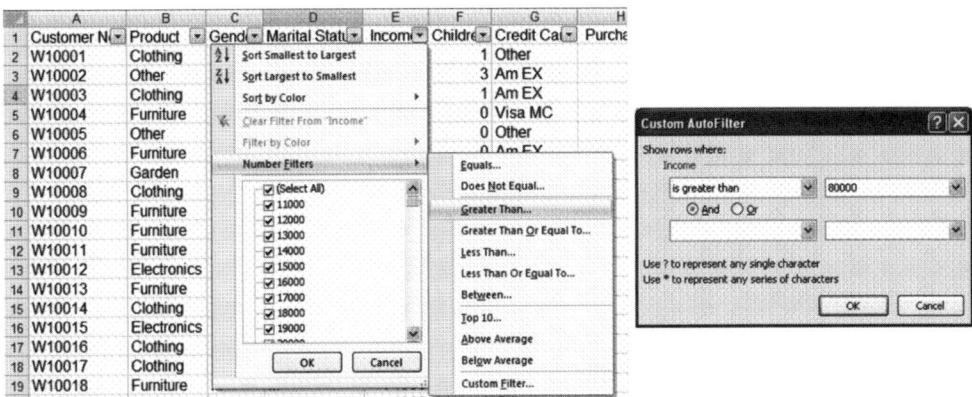

3. Use the AutoFilter icon and filter as shown here by color, selecting yellow.

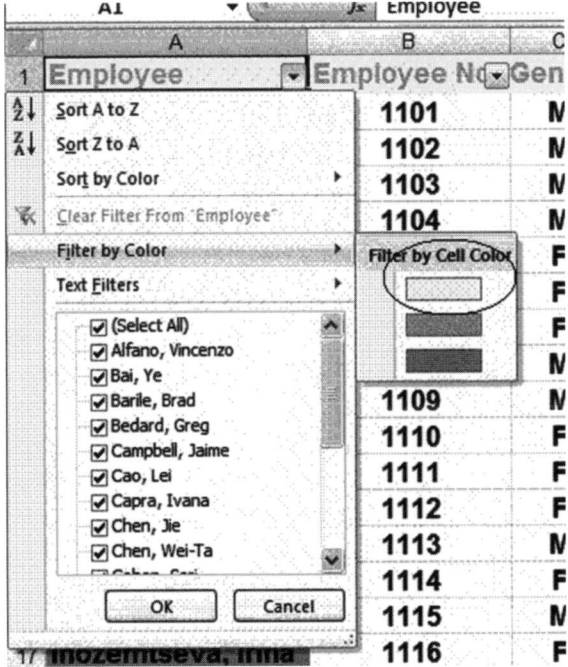

CHAPTER 20

Data Forms and Features Eliminated in Excel 2007

This chapter gives me an opportunity to explain how to add features that were eliminated in Excel 2007. A few elements disappeared in this version. One of them is the Data Form.

A data form is a dialog box that gives you a convenient way to enter or display one complete row of information, or "record," in a range or list. The Data Form feature was eliminated in Excel 2007. However, the Data Form and other features that were eliminated can still be activated through the Quick Access menu.

To get the Data Form menu or any other Excel commands that were not carried through in Excel 2007:

- Click on the Customize Quick Access toolbar.
- Select More Commands.
- Change the type of commands requested to Commands not in the Ribbon.
- Select Forms and click on Add.

The Quick Access menu will now show the Forms icon. See Figure 20.1.

To activate the Data Form, select any cell in the range/table and click on the **Data Form** icon in the Quick Access menu. **If you are familiar with Excel 2003 shortcuts, you can use the keyboard shortcut ALT + D + O.**

Figure 20.2 displays the menu.

Using the form you can do one or more of the following:

- Add a record:
  - Click New.
  - Type the information for the new record.
  - When you finish, press Enter to add the record.
- Change a record:
  - Find the record you want to change.
  - To move through records, use the scroll bar arrows in the dialog box. To move through 10 records at a time, click the scroll bar between the arrows. To move to the next record in the range or list, click Find Next.
  - To move to the previous record in the range or list, click Find Prev.
- Search a record using conditions:

- Click Criteria, and then enter the criteria into the form.
- To find records that match the criteria, click Find Next or Find Prev.
- To return to the data form without searching for records based on the criteria, you specified, click Form.
- Delete a record:
  - Find the record and press Delete.
- Move fast within a form:
  - Moving down from one field (Selection button on the right side of the menu) to the other, use Tab. Moving up one field at a time, use Shift+Tab.

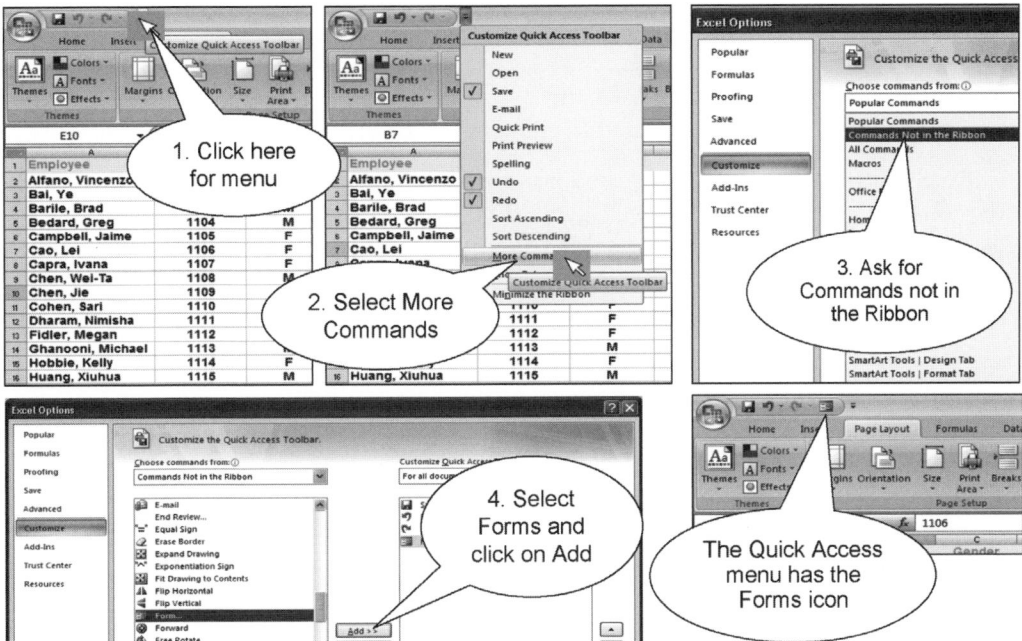

Figure 20.1 Adding command icons to the Quick Access menu

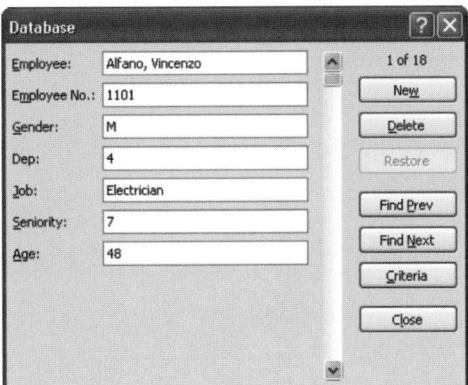

Figure 20.2 The Database Form menu

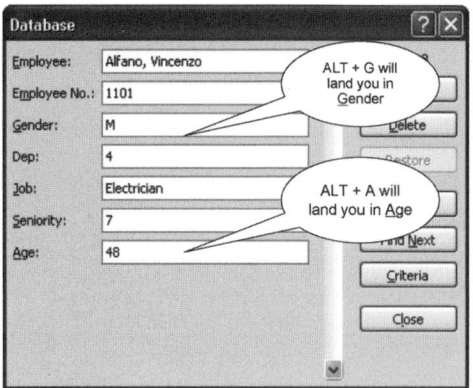

Figure 20.3. Moving within a form

Excel has the different fields in the form marked with underlining one unique letter for every field within the form. Look at Figure 20.2. Employee (E), Employee No. (m), Gender (G), Dep(D), Job (J), Seniority (S), and Age (A). To move to a specific field, use ALT + underlined letter. ALT + A will land you in Age. ALT + G will land you in Gender. See Figure 20.3.

Note: Data Forms can display a maximum of 32 fields at one time.

APPENDIX—THE DATA FORM IN EXCEL 2003 OR EARLIER VERSIONS

The only difference with Excel 2003 is the way to access the form:

Select a cell in the range/table and under the Data menu, select Form.
Figure 20.4 displays the Data menu.
Figure 20.5 displays the form.

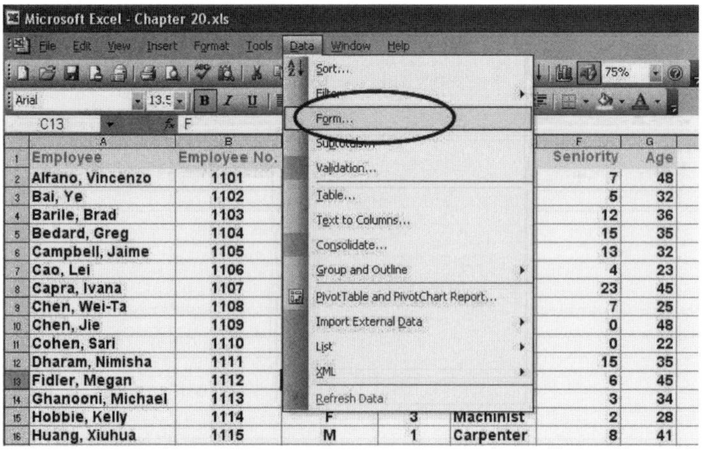

Figure 20.4 Data Form in Excel 2003

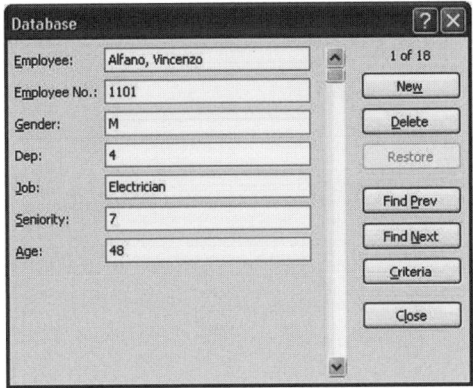

Figure 20.5 Database menu in Excel 2003

REVIEW QUESTIONS

You will find these examples in the Excel Chapter 20 file:

1. Activate the Data Form on the Quick Access toolbar.
2. Use the *Review* sheet and activate the Data Form. Use the Criteria and find Mr. IP.

	A	B	C	D	E	F
1	Employee Numbe	Last Name	First Name	Address	City	State
2	E10001	Alfano	Vincenzo	1 Carlisle Court	Florham Park	NJ
3	E10002	IP	Ye	101 Woodbine Circle	Elizabeth	NJ
4	E10003	Barile	Brad	103 Lindner Place	Livingston	NY
5	E10004	Bedard	Greg	1048 Fairmount Ave	Newark	NJ
6	E10005	Campbell	Jaime	109 Rockdale Lane	Newark	SC
7	E10006	Cao	Lei	120 Burnet Crescent	Lawrenceville	NJ
8	E10007	Capra	Ivana	1605 Sun Valley Way	Summit	NJ
9	E10008	Chen	Wei-Ta	2 Silvia Place	Elizabeth	NY
10	E10009	Chen	Jie	21 Elmwood Drive	Union City	NJ
11	E10010	Cohen	Sari	224 45th St	Robbinsville	NJ
12	E10011	Dharam	Nimisha	250 Gorge Rd 27-K	North Arlington	NJ
13	E10012	Fidler	Megan	326 Edgar Ave.	Elizabeth	NJ
14	E10013	Ghanooni	Michael	51 Clifton Avenue Apt C-191	Highland Mills	NJ
15	E10014	Hobbie	Kelly	7231 Town Court South	South Plainfield	NJ
16	E10015	Huang	Xiuhua	77 Bleeker St. Apt 7	Goose Creek	NJ
17	E10016	Inozemtseva	Irina	815 Floral Avenue	Cliffside Park	NJ
18	E10017	IP	Andrew	856 Westfield Ave.	New Providence	NJ
19	E10018	Jiang	Nan	86 New England Ave. Apt 45	Malverne	NJ
20						

3. Add a new customer to the database using the form.

Employee Number	Last Name	First Name	Address	City	State
E10019	Gottlieb	Isaac	180 University Av	Newark	NJ

ANSWERS

1. Click on the Windows icon. Under Excel options, use Customize and add the Forms icon to the Quick Access menu.

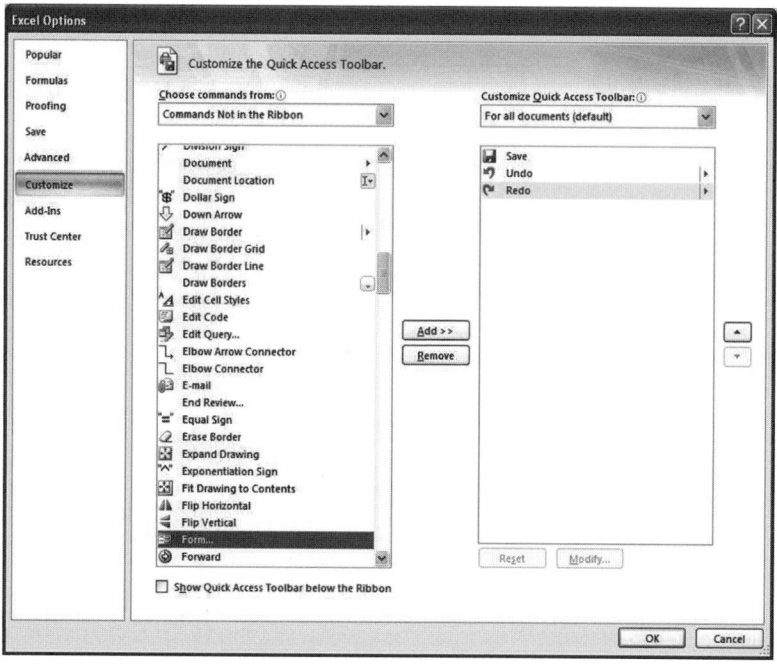

2. Click on the Forms icon in the Quick Access menu and on the form click on Criteria and type IP. You will find the record when you select Find Next.

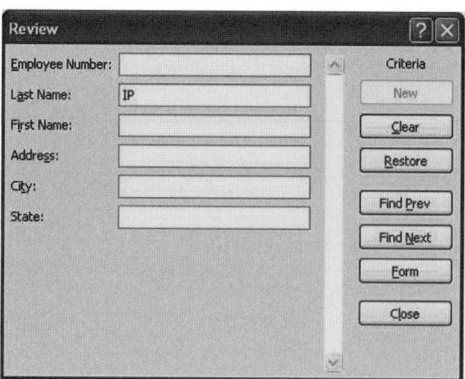

3. Click on the Forms icon. Click on New and fill the information in. When you click on Close, the data will be added to the database.

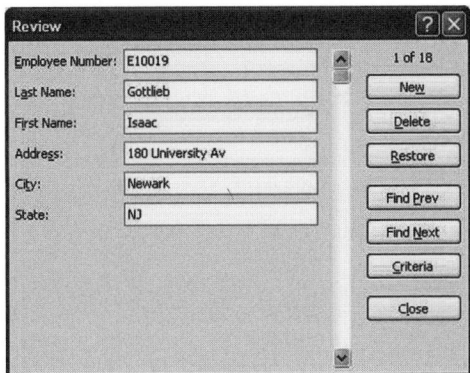

CHAPTER 21

Group and Outline Data

Grouping and outlining in Excel enables you as an analyst to view different levels of information on demand. You can either reveal all the information or hide certain levels of information by collapsing different levels of data. When you have a large spreadsheet you can collapse the data and show only the subtotals. This is an effective tool for presentation and analysis.

You can create these outlines for your data so that you can show or hide levels of detail with a single click. You can click the outline symbols, [1|2|3], ⊞, ⊟ and display only the rows or columns that present summaries or headings for sections of your data. You can also use the symbols to see details for individual summaries or headings. Excel allows you to create an outline of up to eight levels.

This is important for the preparation of the data:

- The data for an outline should be a continuous range. Each column should have a label in the first row and there should not be blank rows or columns within that range.
- When the range contains a function, such as SUM, you can automatically outline the data.
- If you wish to outline columns, make sure that the range has labels in the first column on the left.

The procedure is simple:

- Select a cell or a range of cells you want to outline in the database.
- On the Data ribbon, click on the Group drop-down menu. Choose Auto Outline.

The file Chapter 21 contains data you can use to group and outline. Each QTR row sums the data above it. The quarters are totaled again in row 18. In column J, we sum the data horizontally for each of the rows. See Figure 21.1.

Select the Auto Outline option from the Group drop-down menu. See Figure 21.2. The result is shown in Figure 21.3.

You can click the outline symbols [1|2|3], ⊞, ⊟ to display only the rows or columns that present summaries or headings for sections of your data, or you can use the symbols to see details for individual summaries or headings.

If you click on level 2 on the left icon, [1|2|3], it will group the data as you see in Figure 21.4.

To expand the group and show some of the details, click on ⊞. Following the same logic, you can use ⊟ to hide/collapse them. See Figures 21.3, 21.4, and 21.5.

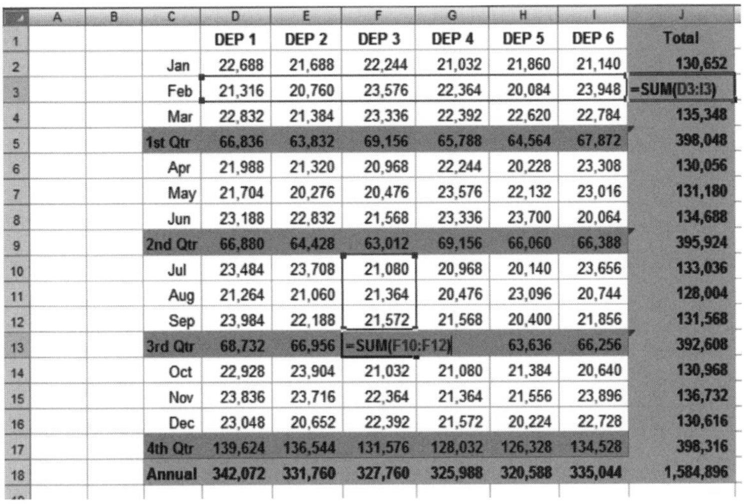

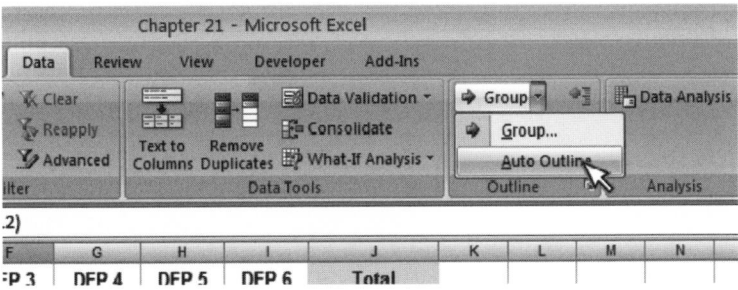

Figure 21.1 The data for group and outline

Figure 21.2 Group drop-down menu

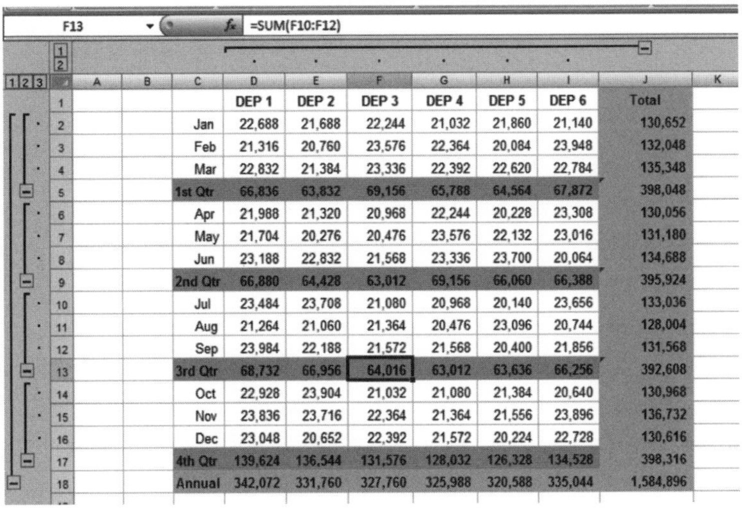

Figure 21.3 Data with grouping features

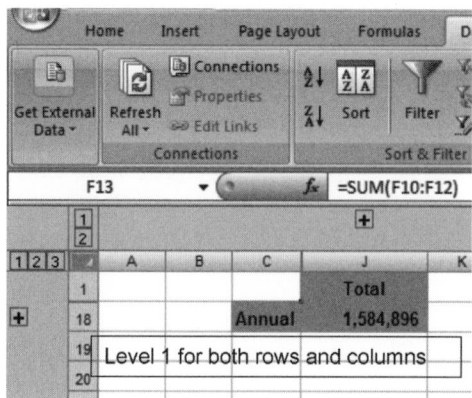

		DEP 1	DEP 2	DEP 3	DEP 4	DEP 5	DEP 6	Total
5	1st Qtr	66,836	63,832	69,156	65,788	64,564	67,872	398,048
9	2nd Qtr	66,880	64,428	63,012	69,156	66,060	66,388	395,924
13	3rd Qtr	68,732	66,956	64,016	63,012	63,636	66,256	392,608
17	4th Qtr	139,624	136,544	131,576	128,032	126,328	134,528	398,316
18	Annual	342,072	331,760	327,760	325,988	320,588	335,044	1,584,896

Click on level 2 and it collapses the outline to that level

Figure 21.4   Collapsing the data

Click to expand group

		DEP 1	DEP 2	DEP 3	DEP 4	DEP 5	DEP 6	Total
5	1st Qtr	66,836	63,832	69,156	65,788	64,564	67,872	398,048
9	2nd Qtr	66,880	64,428	63,012	69,156	66,060	66,388	395,924
13	3rd Qtr	68,732	66,956	64,016	63,012	63,636	66,256	392,608
17	4th Qtr	139,624	136,544	131,576	128,032	126,328	134,528	398,316
18	Annual	342,072	331,760	27,760	325,988	320,588	335,044	1,584,896

		DEP 1	DEP 2	DEP 3	DEP 4	DEP 5	DEP 6	Total
2	Jan	22,688	21,688	22,244	21,032	21,860	21,140	130,652
3	Feb	21,316	20,760	23,576	22,364	20,084	23,948	132,048
4	Mar	22,832	21,384	23,336	22,392	22,620	22,784	135,348
5	1st Qtr	66,836	63,832	69,156	65,788	64,564	67,872	398,048
9	2nd Qtr	66,880	64,428	63,012	69,156	66,060	66,388	395,924
13	3rd Qtr	68,732	66,956	64,016	63,012	63,636	66,256	392,608
17	4th Qtr	139,624	136,544	131,576	128,032	126,328	134,528	398,316
18	Annual	342,072	331,760	327,760	325,988	320,588	335,044	1,584,896

Figure 21.5   Group or collapse with the + and − signs

F13   =SUM(F10:F12)

	A	B	C	J	K
1				Total	
18			Annual	1,584,896	
19	Level 1 for both rows and columns				
20					

Figure 21.6   Collapsed data at level 1

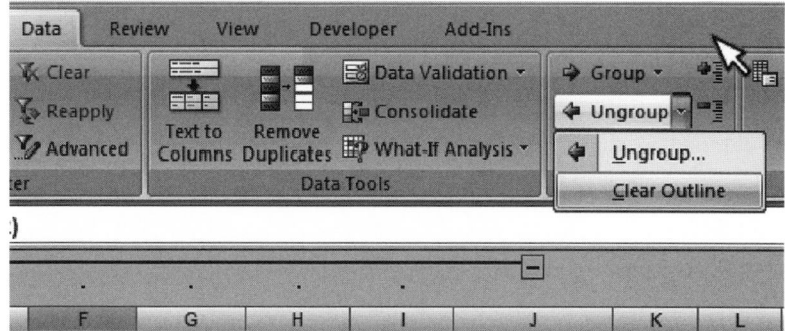

Figure 21.7 Returning to a normal view: Clear Outline

You can hide or show data on either the columns or rows. You could hide all the data using the level 1 for both directions. See Figure 21.6.

Try different groupings for the columns and the rows.

To return to a normal view: on the Data ribbon, point to Ungroup, and in the drop-down menu, select Clear Outline. See Figure 21.7.

APPENDIX—GROUP AND OUTLINE DATA EXCEL 2003 OR EARLIER VERSIONS

The only difference with Excel 2003 is the way to access the Group and Outline Data. Use Data ➪ Group and Outline ➪ Auto Outline. See Figure 21.8. Clearing the outline or the grouping is also done using the same menu. All the other features are identical to the Excel 2007 version.

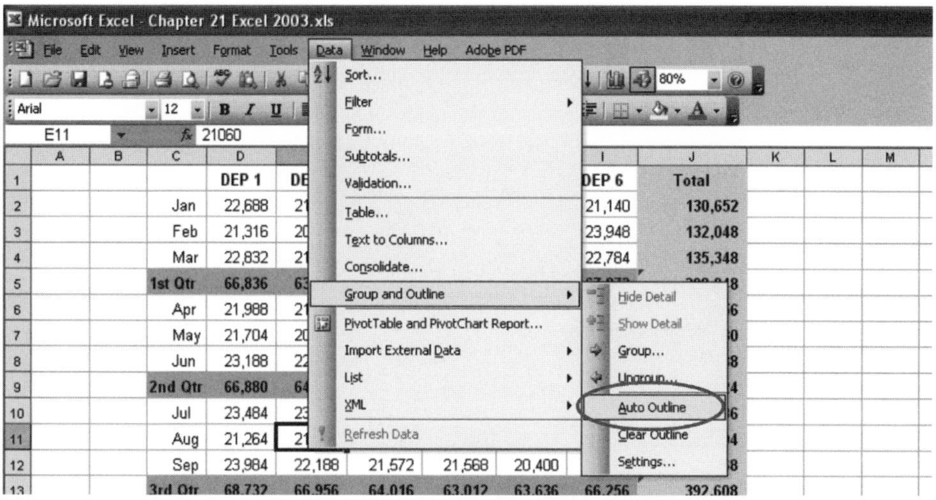

Figure 21.8 The Auto Outline menu in Excel 2003

REVIEW QUESTIONS

You will find these examples in the Excel Chapter 21 file:

1. On the *Summary Income Statement* sheet, you will find a detailed summary for the years 2006 and 2007. The data is summarized by categories of income and expenses. In the other direction, the quarters are totaled annually.

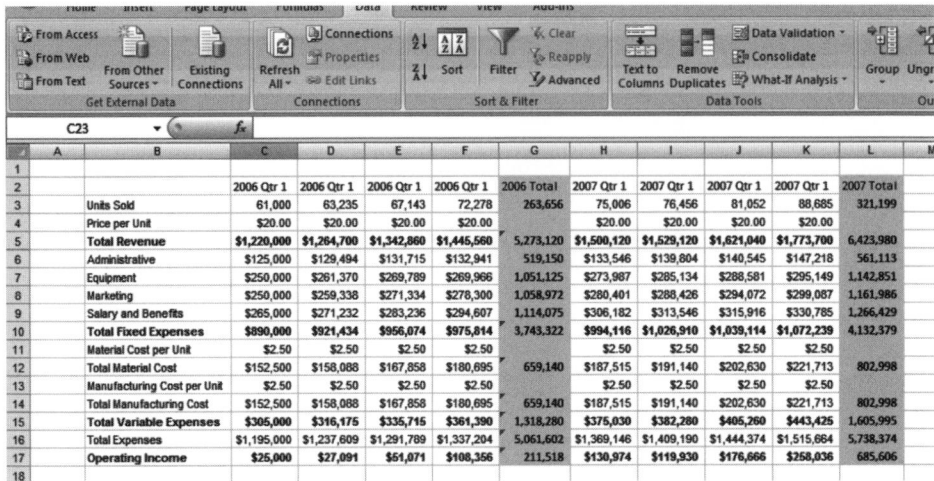

Use the Grouping feature to summarize the data as shown below:

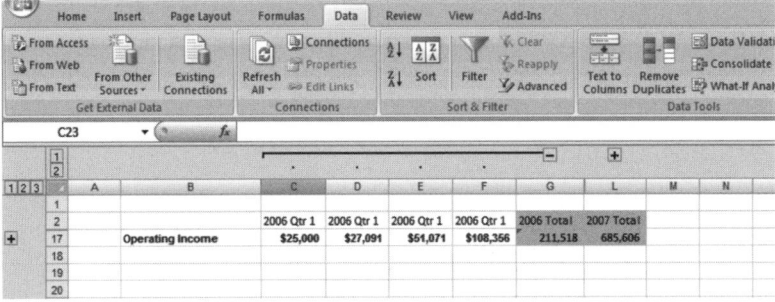

2. When the data is grouped, try out the icons next to the GROUP and UNGROUP icons. The two very last icons. ⬛ and ⬛.

ANSWERS

1. Click on the drop-down menu next to the Group icon on the Data menu and select Auto Outline. Click on the grouping button 1 on the left side of the data.

CHAPTER 22

Subtotals

The Subtotal feature in Excel is an additional way to summarize data. The Subtotal—which does not necessarily apply to numerical sums only—can summarize and display your data in a logical way.

Excel can automatically calculate subtotal and grand total values in a table. When you insert automatic subtotals, Excel outlines the table so that you can display and hide the rows' details for each subtotal. This is the same concept as was explored in the previous chapter about outlines.

Subtotals are calculated with a summary function. (Examples of summary functions include Sum, Count, and Average.) **Subtotal** calculates subtotal values with one of 11 different functions. It is possible to utilize more than one type of summary function for each column.

To insert subtotals, you have to organize the table so that the rows you want to subtotal are grouped together by a certain parameter or type of information. You can calculate subtotals for any column that contains numerical values. However, only the Count function can be applied to nonnumeric data. If you attempt to calculate any other function for nonnumeric data, the result will be zeros for the sum and errors for all other functions.

Grand total values are derived from the data, not from the values in the subtotal rows. If you use the Average Summary function, the grand total displays an average of all the rows' details in the list, not an average of the values in the subtotal rows (it is not the average of the averages).

Excel recalculates subtotal and grand total values automatically as you edit the detail data.

The following exercise will make use of the same data used in previous chapters. The data is shown in Figure 22.1.

Before proceeding with the Subtotal function, you need—as I said before—to sort the data. If you wish to get the averages for the ages of females and males, that data needs to first be sorted by gender. See Figure 22.2, in which the data is sorted by gender.

In the Data ribbon, use Subtotal to get the average age of females and males. The process is shown in Figure 22.3.

- Click on the Subtotal icon in the Data ribbon.
- In the resulting menu, choose Gender for the At each change in. This is the parameter the original data was sorted by.
- The function you are interested in is the Average.

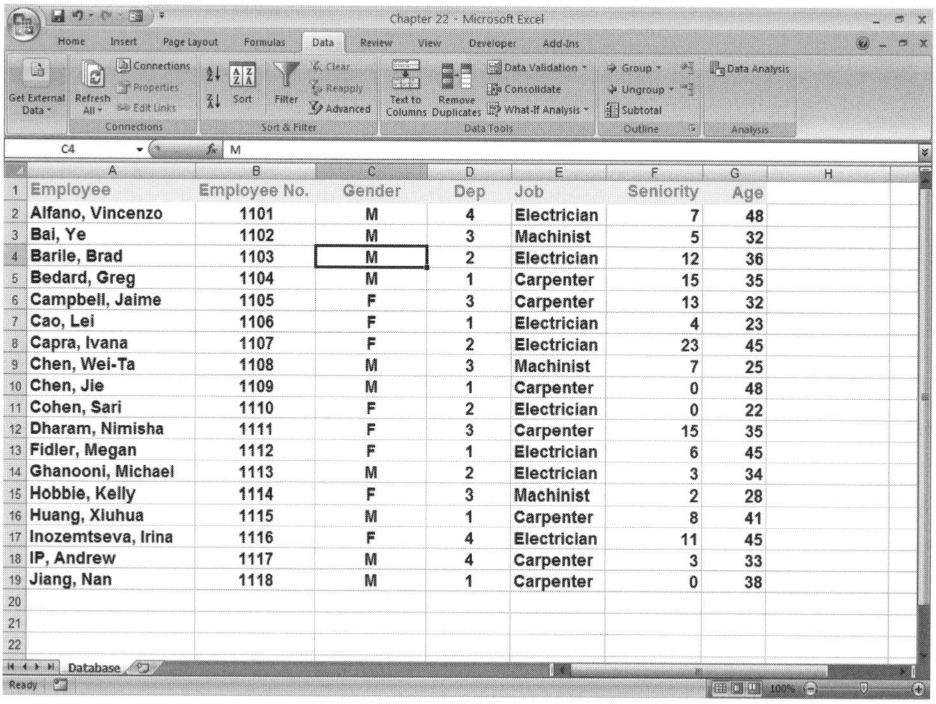

Figure 22.1   The data on the sheet *Database* in the Excel file Chapter 22

■ Check the appropriate box to indicate which columns or data you wish to apply the Average function to. In our example, select the Age. You could have asked for the Seniority as well. I just chose the age.

You can see the subtotals created in Figure 22.4. The averages are for the grouped data for females and males.

Figure 22.2   Data sorted by gender

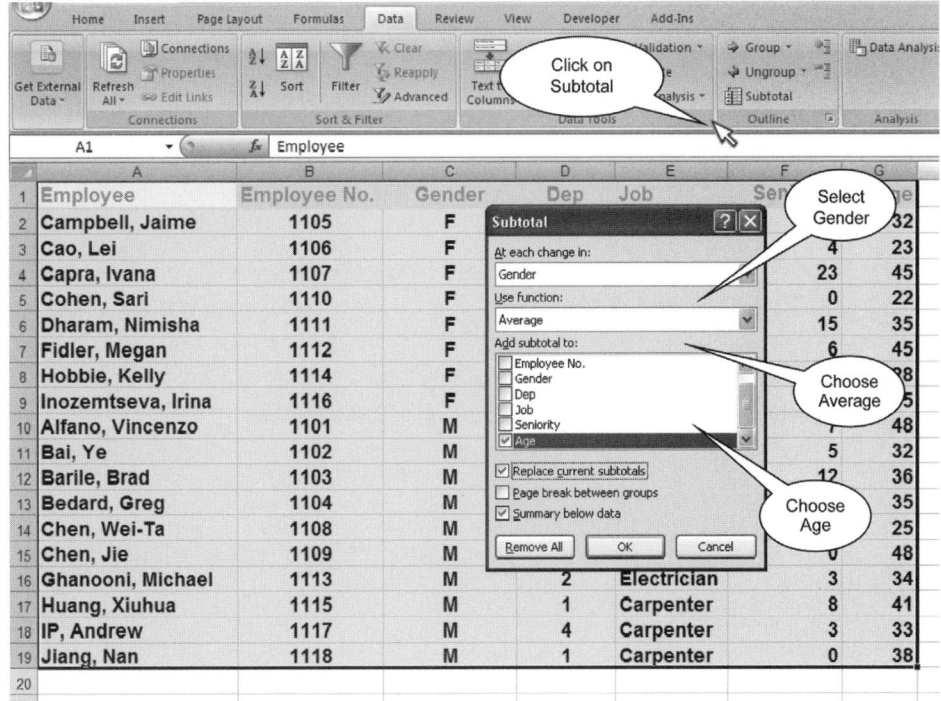

Figure 22.3   Subtotal menu

1 2 3		A	B	C	D	E	F	G
	1	Employee	Employee No.	Gender	Dep	Job	Seniority	Age
	2	Campbell, Jaime	1105	F	3	Carpenter	13	32
	3	Cao, Lei	1106	F	1	Electrician	4	23
	4	Capra, Ivana	1107	F	2	Electrician	23	45
	5	Cohen, Sari	1110	F	2	Electrician	0	22
	6	Dharam, Nimisha	1111	F	3	Carpenter	15	35
	7	Fidler, Megan	1112	F	1	Electrician	6	45
	8	Hobbie, Kelly	1114	F	3	Machinist	2	28
	9	Inozemtseva, Irina	1116	F	4	Electrician	11	45
	10			F Average				34.375
	11	Alfano, Vincenzo	1101	M	4	Electrician	7	48
	12	Bai, Ye	1102	M	3	Machinist	5	32
	13	Barile, Brad	1103	M	2	Electrician	12	36
	14	Bedard, Greg	1104	M	1	Carpenter	15	35
	15	Chen, Wei-Ta	1108	M	3	Machinist	7	25
	16	Chen, Jie	1109	M	1	Carpenter	0	48
	17	Ghanooni, Michael	1113	M	2	Electrician	3	34
	18	Huang, Xiuhua	1115	M	1	Carpenter	8	41
	19	IP, Andrew	1117	M	4	Carpenter	3	33
	20	Jiang, Nan	1118	M	1	Carpenter	0	38
	21			M Average				37
	22			Grand Average				35.833

Figure 22.4   Subtotaled data with grouping buttons

		A	B	C	D	E	F	G
	1	Employee	Employee No.	Gender	Dep	Job	Seniority	Age
+	10	When you click on level 2		F Average				34.375
+	21	you get the summary		M Average				37
−	22			Grand Average				35.833
	23							

Figure 22.5   Collapsed data

Note, by looking at Figure 22.4, how the data is grouped and outlined. You can use the outline symbols ▮1▮2▮3▮, ⊞, and ⊟ to either display or collapse the groupings, according to your presentation needs. I clicked on the level 2 button, as you can see in Figure 22.5.

One More Example—Function Applied to Multiple Categories

Using the same data set, call up the same menu to remove the subtotals. Sort by a different parameter and start again:

- Click on Subtotal again and in the pop-up menu, select Remove All. Figure 22.6 displays how to do it.
- Sort the data again—this time sort it by Job.
- Create a new Subtotal—this time choose Max for both Age and Seniority.

   Collapse the report using the grouping menu. See Figure 22.7.

Copying Grouped Data

When data is grouped or filtered—as in the case of using the Subtotal function—many of the rows are hidden. Lines 2–8 are hidden in Figure 22.7. So are lines 10-17 and 19-21. If you attempt to copy the data and paste it somewhere else, the **complete** data set will be pasted, including the hidden data. See Figure 22.8.

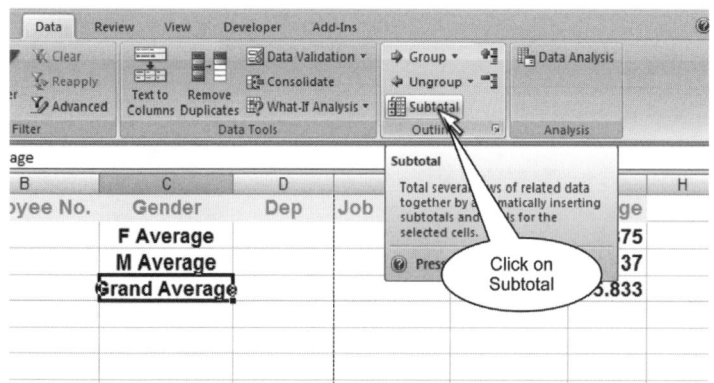

Figure 22.6   Removing the subtotal

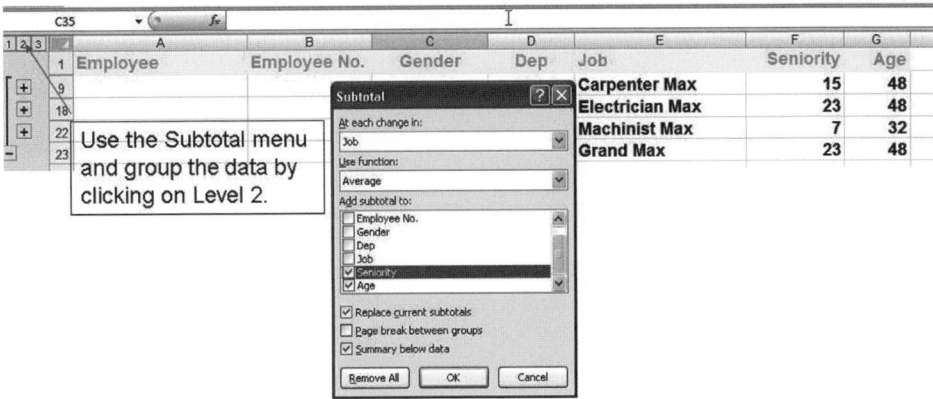

Figure 22.7 Data subtotaled by job

What you really want to do is to copy only the visible data!
To overcome this common problem, you need to copy the visible cells only.
There are a few ways to do it:

1. Select the data E1:G23 and use the Excel menu to select the visible cells only.
   a. Home ➾ Find & Select ➾ Go To Special and choose Visible cells only (or use shortcut CTRL+G) Go To Special.
   b. Copy or **CTRL+C**.
   c. Paste at destination with **CTRL+V**. See Figure 22.9.

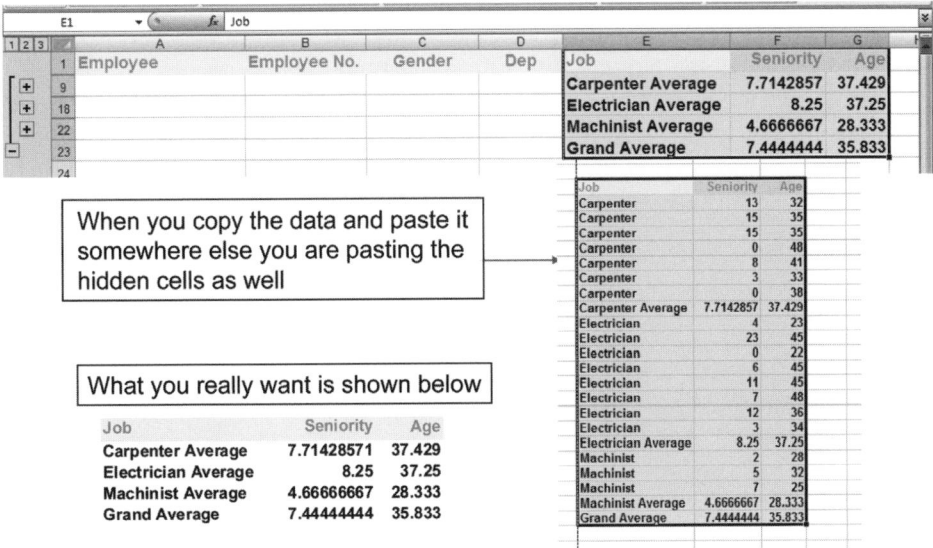

Figure 22.8 The problem when you copy grouped data

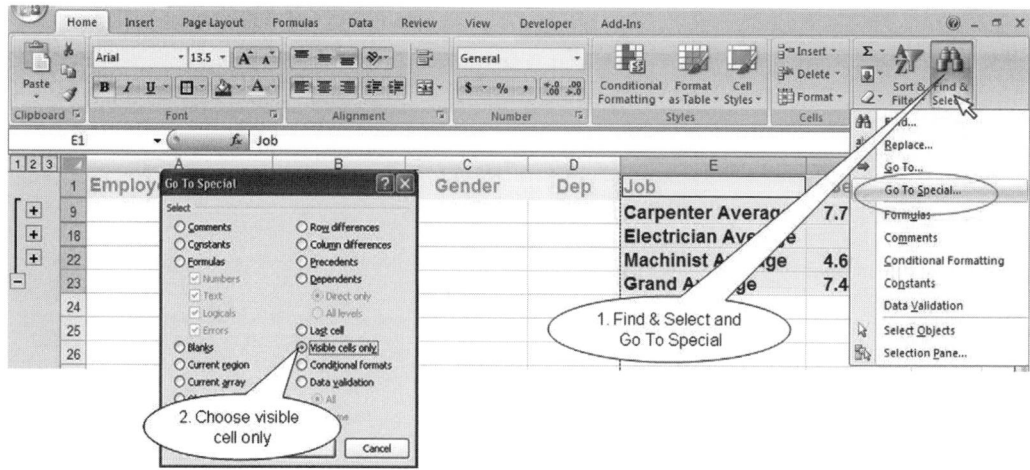

Figure 22.9   Selecting Visible cells only through the menu

2. A second way is using a shortcut: Select the data E1:G23.
   a. Use **ALT+;** (which is equivalent to Go To Visible Cells only).
   b. Copy or **CTRL+C**.
   c. Paste at destination with **CTRL+V.**

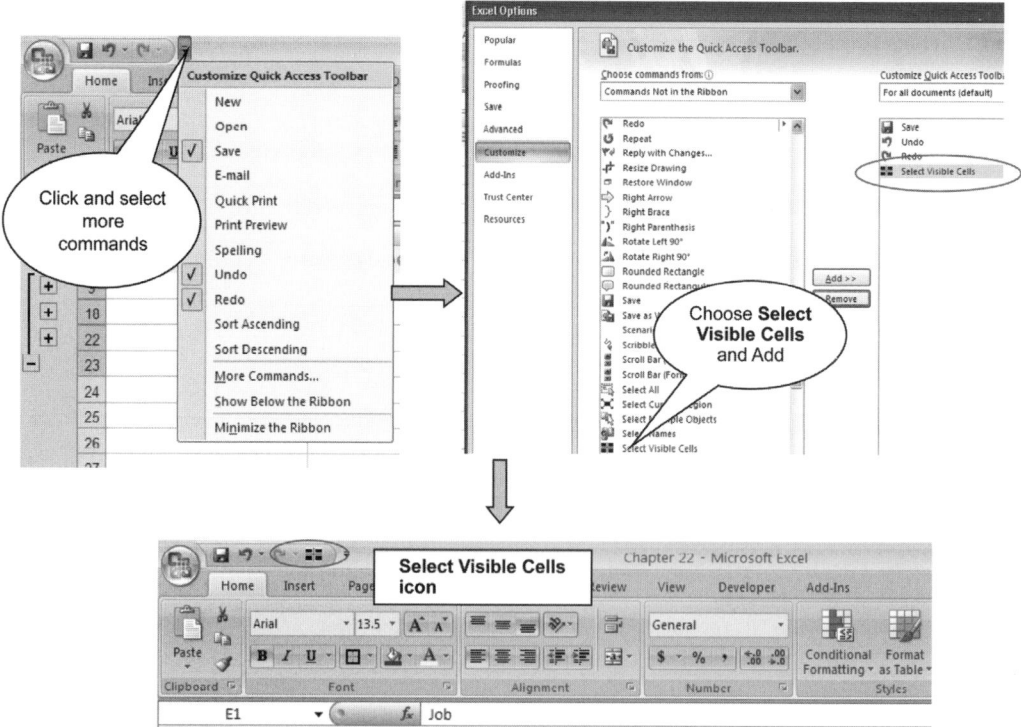

Figure 22.10   Adding the icon to the Quick Access menu

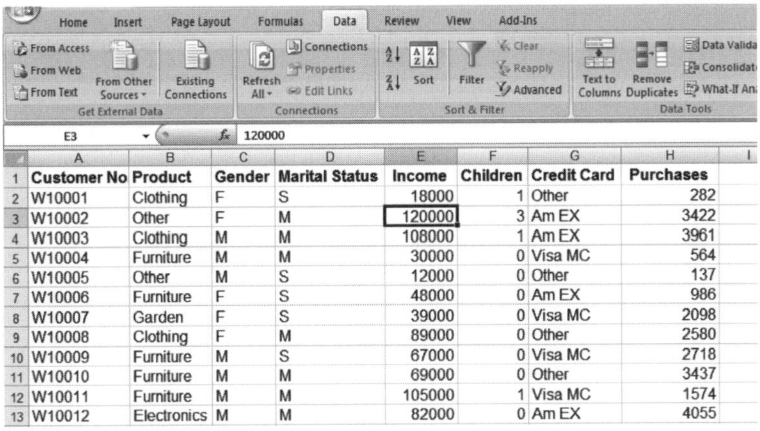

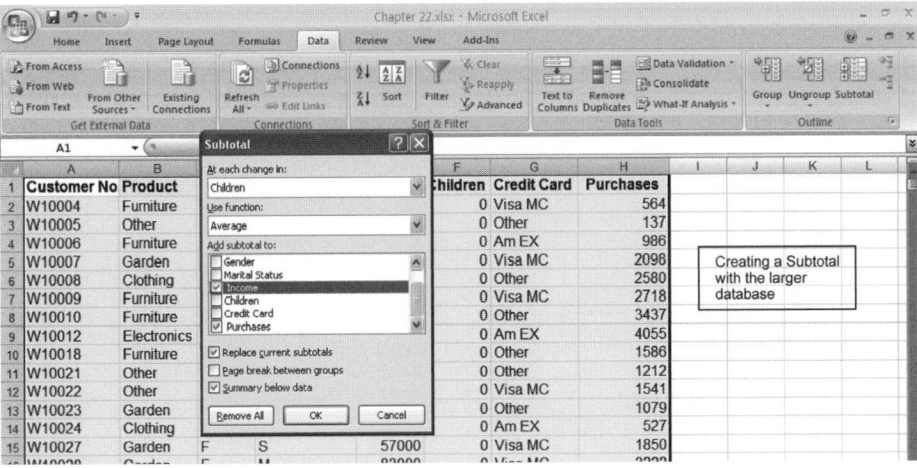

Figure 22.11 Second database

3. If you have to do it very often, activate the Select Visible Cells only icon  so that it appears in the Quick Access menu.

   a. Choose Customize Access Toolbar.

   b. In the drop-down menu choose More Commands.

   c. Choose all commands.

   d. Click on Select Visible Cells, click on Add and OK. See Figure 22.10.

   e. You can then click on the icon (Select Visible Cells), which appears in the Quick Access menu.

   f. Copy the region and Paste in destination.

SECOND EXAMPLE—LARGER DATABASE

On the *Second Example* worksheet in the Excel Chapter 22 file, you will find the data we used in previous chapters. The data, shown in Figure 22.11, contains information about 1,000

Figure 22.12 Subtotal menu grouped by number of children

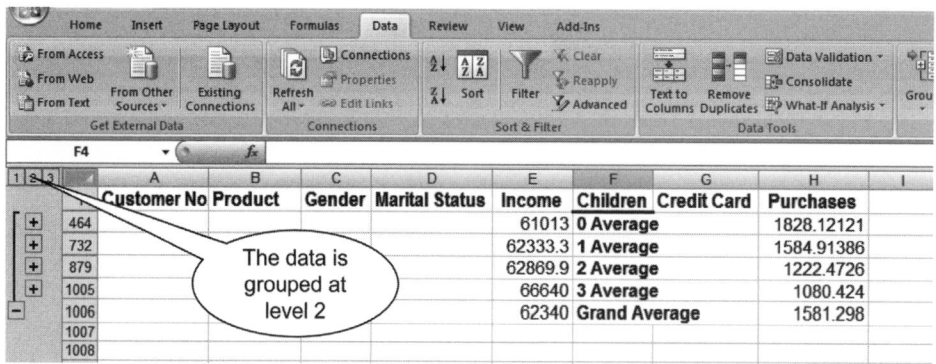

Figure 22.13 Grouped data

customers. What I want to find out is the average income and the average amount spent by customers with 0 children, 1 child, 2 children, and so on.

The first step is to sort data by the number of children. After the database is sorted, you can use the Subtotal menu.

In the Subtotal menu, for the At each change in field, select Children. For the Function use the Average and for the Add subtotal choose both Income and Purchases as shown in Figure 22.12.

The final result is shown in Figure 22.13. I used the grouping level number 2 on the left to show only the relevant summarized data.

APPENDIX—CREATING SUBTOTALS IN EXCEL 2003

The only difference in Excel 2003 is the way to activate the Subtotal.

Open the Excel 2003 file *Chapter 22 Excel 2003*. Use Data ⇨ Subtotal. See Figure 22.14. All the rest is the same as described above.

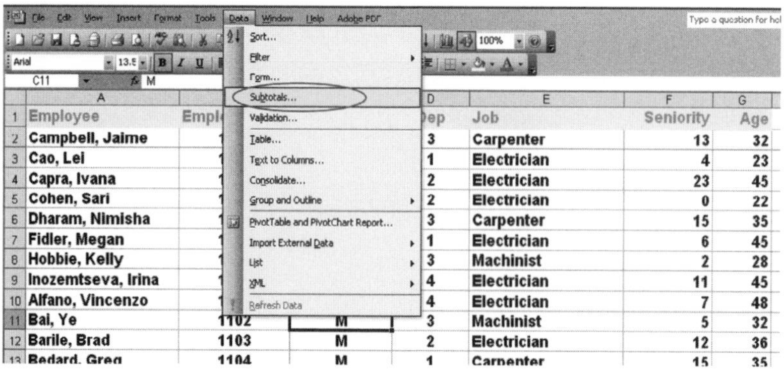

Figure 22.14 The Subtotal menu in Excel 2003

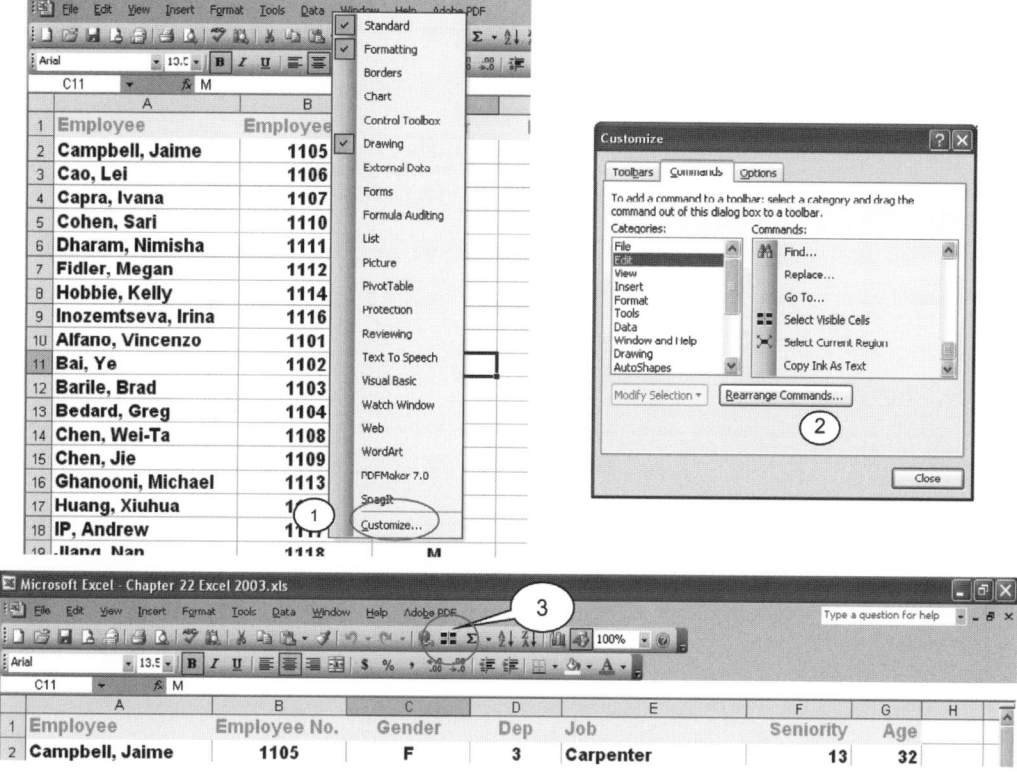

Figure 22.15   Adding the Visible Cell Only icon to your menus

Visible Cells Only icon in Excel 2003

In Excel 2003, to add the Select Visible Cells command, do the following:

1. Right-click on the **toolbar** or on any menu and click **Customize**.
2. Go to the **Commands** tab and select **Edit** under **Categories**.
3. Scroll down the list under **Commands** and click on **Select Visible Cells.** Drag the icon to your menus area. The icon will be there to select visible cells only. See Figure 22.15.

REVIEW QUESTIONS

You will find these examples in the Excel Chapter 22 file:

1. On the *Second Example* worksheet, you will find the data we used in this chapter. Use the Subtotal function to find total purchases by category of credit card: American Express, Visa/MC, and other cards.
2. Find out, using the same data, the maximum amount spent by any customer for each one of the Product categories: Clothing, Electronics, Furniture, Garden, or Other.
3. Repeat the exercise. This time, find the total Income by Gender.

ANSWERS

1.

		A	B	C	D	E	F	G	H
	1	Customer No	Product	Gender	Marital Status	Income	Children	Credit Card	Purchases
+	318							Am EX Total	508,025
+	686							Other Total	583,379
+	1004							Visa MC Total	489,894
−	1005							Grand Total	1,581,298
	1006								
	1007								

G7 cell reference, 1 2 3 outline controls

2.

		A	B	C	D	E	F	G	H
	1	Customer No	Product	Gender	Marital Status	Income	Children	Credit Card	Purchases
+	193		Clothing Max						8,082
+	402		Electronics Max						6,771
+	609		Furniture Max						7,233
+	806		Garden Max						7,578
+	1006		Other Max						7,641
−	1007		Grand Max						8,082
	1008								

B12 cell reference, 1 2 3 outline controls

3. Females $674,213 and Males $907,085.

CHAPTER 23

Pivot Tables

When you have a large database and you want to discover trends and patterns at a glance, you can use PivotTable reports to help you. Pivot tables allow you to:

- summarize the data contained in large tables into a compact layout;
- find relationships within the data that are hard to evaluate because of a vast amount of data;
- organize the data into a format that can be charted easily.

First you have to decide what questions you want the data to answer. To construct a pivot table you need to identify these two elements in your data:

- which parameters or data fields are the variables you want to summarize;
- what column fields are the variables that will "organize" the data summary.

Certain constraints exist:

- In the first row of the data, each one of the columns should have a unique header (or label).
- There should be no empty rows or columns within the range of data used for the report. Each column should contain only one type of data: text in one column and numeric values in a separate column.

PivotTable Example

This section will start with a simple example using the database employed previously. See Figure 23.1 for the database. In this example, you will want to calculate the average age by gender and job.

To start the PivotTable, select any cell (or range of cells) in the database and click on the PivotTable icon in the Insert ribbon. Click OK on the Create PivotTable menu. See Figure 23.2.

In Excel 2007, the layout and feel is slightly different than in previous versions of Excel, but the functionality is the same. Once you activate the PivotTable, it will appear as in Figure 23.3. I dragged the PivotTable field list closer to the PivotTable area.

	A	B	C	D	E	F	G	H
1	Employee	Employee No.	Gender	Dep	Job	Seniority	Age	
2	Alfano, Vincenzo	1101	M	4	Electrician	7	48	
3	Bai, Ye	1102	M	3	Machinist	5	32	
4	Barile, Brad	1103	M	2	Electrician	12	36	
5	Bedard, Greg	1104	M	1	Carpenter	15	35	
6	Campbell, Jaime	1105	F	3	Carpenter	13	32	
7	Cao, Lei	1106	F	1	Electrician	4	23	
8	Capra, Ivana	1107	F	2	Electrician	23	45	
9	Chen, Wei-Ta	1108	M	3	Machinist	7	25	
10	Chen, Jie	1109	M	1	Carpenter	0	48	
11	Cohen, Sari	1110	F	2	Electrician	0	22	
12	Dharam, Nimisha	1111	F	3	Carpenter	15	35	
13	Fidler, Megan	1112	F	1	Electrician	6	45	
14	Ghanooni, Michael	1113	M	2	Electrician	3	34	
15	Hobble, Kelly	1114	F	3	Machinist	2	28	
16	Huang, Xiuhua	1115	M	1	Carpenter	8	41	
17	Inozemtseva, Irina	1116	F	4	Electrician	11	45	
18	IP, Andrew	1117	M	4	Carpenter	3	33	
19	Jiang, Nan	1118	M	1	Carpenter	0	38	

Figure 23.1   Simple database used in a PivotTable

Before you start using pivot tables you may want to make them look and—more importantly—feel like the classic pivot table that enables you to drag and drop the fields into the table. This has to be done only once. Right-click anywhere in the PivotTable area, and choose the classic layout in the PivotTable options. See Figure 23.4.

After you change the layout to the classic layout and move the parameter list closer to the pivot table, your Excel screen will resemble Figure 23.5.

To create the PivotTable, you want to have one parameter, say Job, on the left as Row Labels and the other parameter, maybe Gender, as Column Labels on the top.

The PivotTable report will have four areas as shown in Figure 23.6:

1. The Report filter will be on top of the report. This is the area you use to filter the complete data.
2. The Row Labels is the area where you move fields you want on the horizontal part of the table.
3. The Column Labels is the area where you move fields you want on the vertical part of the table.
4. The center, Σ Values area is where your data will be summarized.

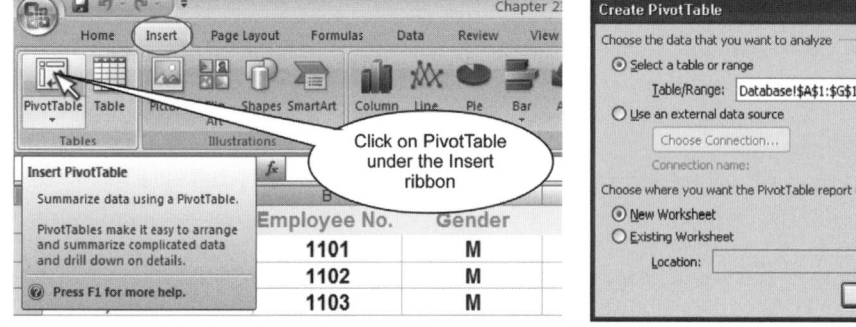

Figure 23.2   For the PivotTable, click on the PivotTable icon under the Insert ribbon

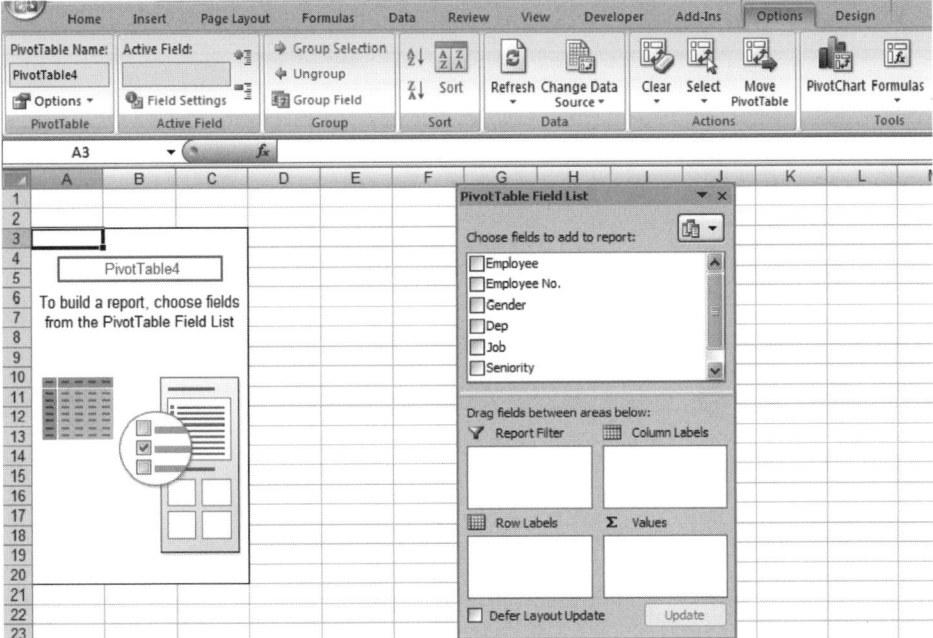

Figure 23.3 Initial PivotTable layout and look

In our example, we will move the Gender to the Row Labels area on the left and the Job field to the Column Labels at the top. There are a few ways this can be achieved. The easiest way with Excel 2007 or previous versions (in the classic layout) is to drag and drop the fields. Drag the Gender to the Row Field area on the left of the table and the Job to the Column Field area. See Figure 23.7.

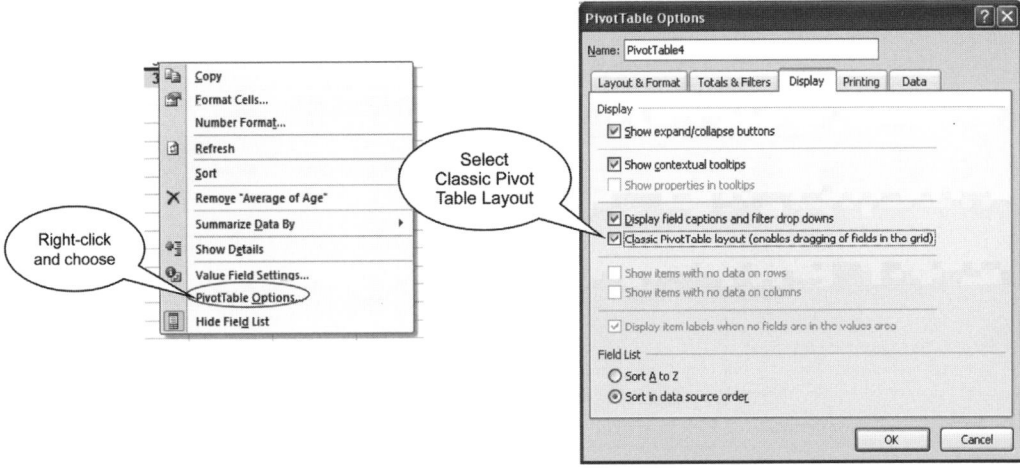

Figure 23.4 Activate the Classic Layout of the PivotTable

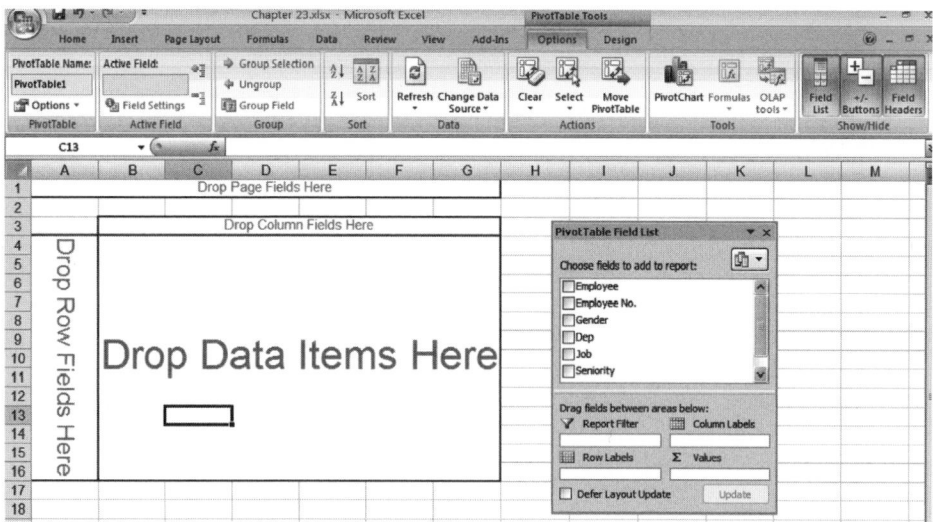

Figure 23.5 PivotTable Field List

Now drag the Age to the center of the table (it reads "Drop Data Items Here"). See the result in Figure 23.8.

By default, the PivotTable calculates the sums of all values. For example, the sum of all the ages of all the Female Carpenters is 67. The sum of the ages of all Machinists is 85. The sum of the ages of all Males is 370.

The information that would be useful in this case would be the average ages, and not the sum of the ages as the default table resulted in. You need the average not the sum. We have to modify the report settings to instruct the PivotTable Report to calculate and read average. To get the average, double-click on the words "Sum of Ages" in the table (upper left corner) and choose Average on the Value Field Settings list. See Figure 23.9 for the menu and the results.

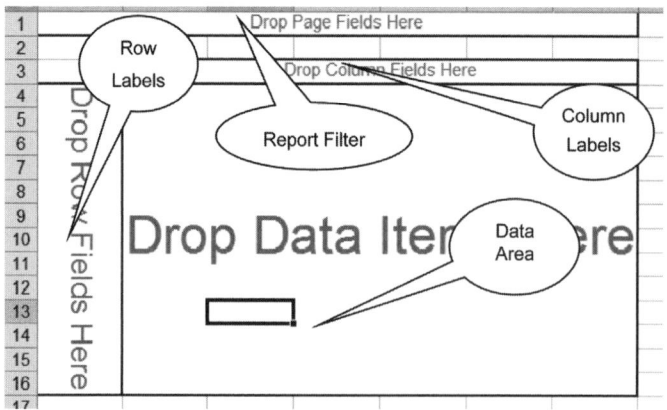

Figure 23.6 The four areas of the PivotTable

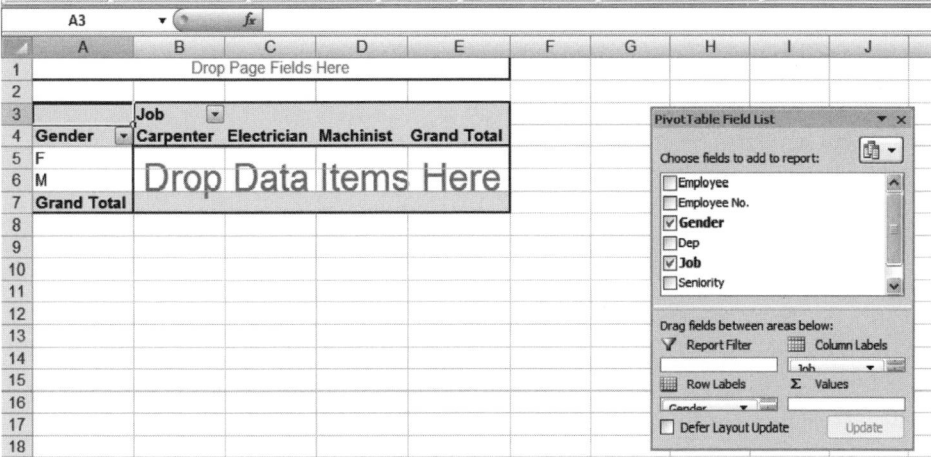

Figure 23.7 Drag the Gender to the left of the table and the Job to the top

You may have noticed already that the resulting table is not formatted. If you attempt to format the table in the conventional way or use **CTRL+1** from the Format menu, it will work only once. Should you modify the PivotTable afterward, the format will be lost.

It is better to use the formatting feature of the PivotTable. When you double-click on the table's Sum of Ages,—activating the Value Field Setting—you will see on the lower left side of the menu the Number Format button. Click on it to enable table formatting. When you use this menu, the **format will not change when you change the table.** Figure 23.10 demonstrates the use of the menu and the results.

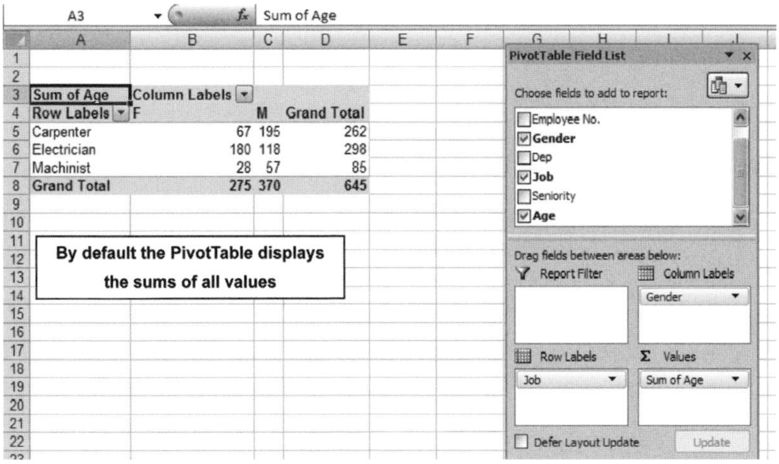

Figure 23.8 PivotTable report

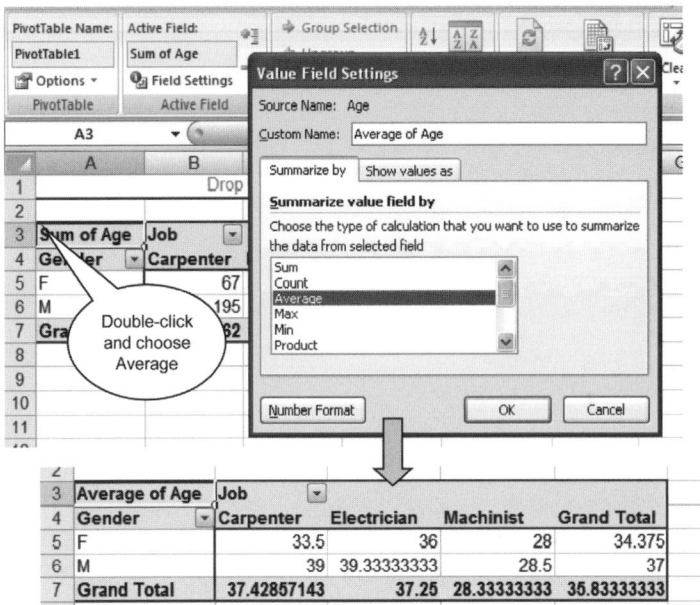

Figure 23.9 Average ages PivotTable report

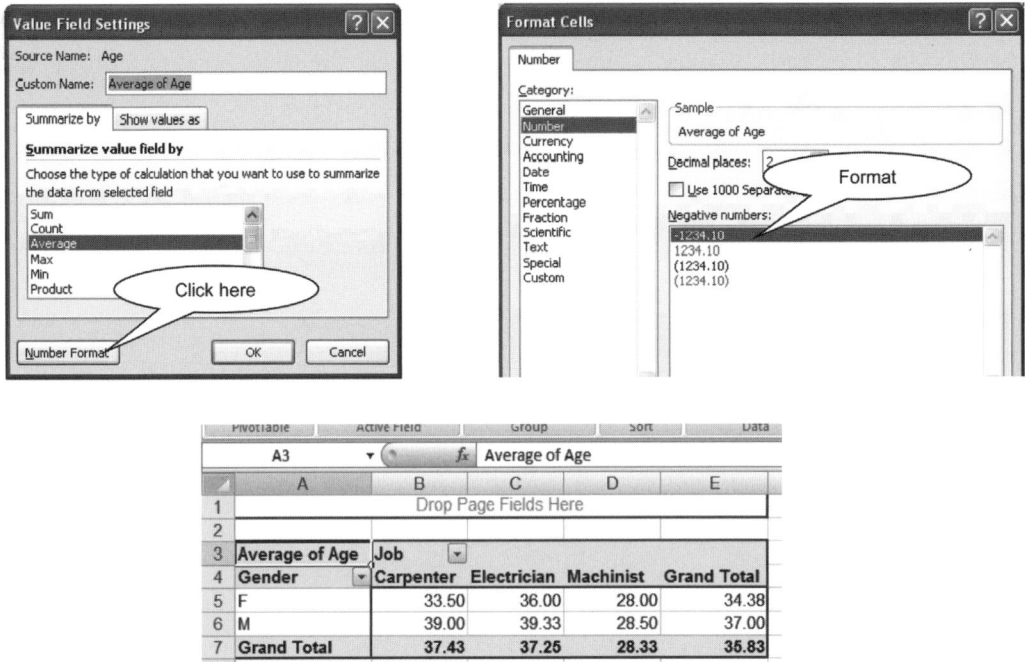

Figure 23.10 Format the PivotTable through the Number Format menu

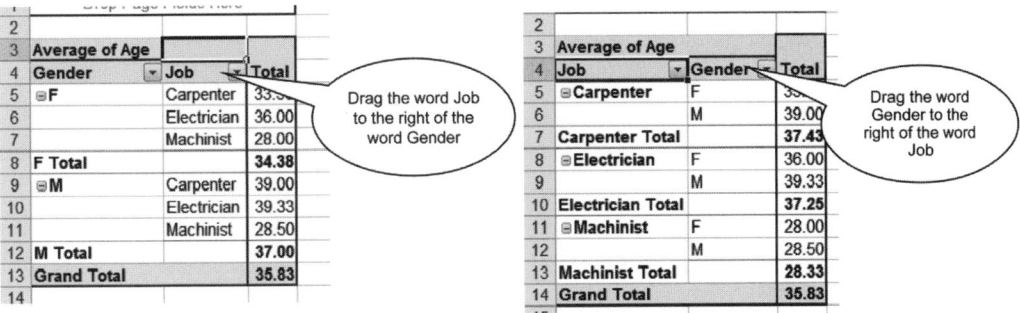

Figure 23.11 Drag and drop the fields to different positions in the table

In the example, the average age of Female Carpenters is 33.50. The average of the ages of all Machinists is 28.33. The average of all Males is 37.00. The average age of all Male Machinists is 28.50.

It is easy to create the type of table that you need for your purposes, using the other feature the PivotTable provides. This feature enables you to drag-and-drop the parameters in different fields/areas.

The first thing is to rearrange the layout. Drag the Gender from the Column Labels area to the Row Labels area. It can be either first or second in the list. I tried both options. Try to change the order yourself. See Figure 23.11.

Now try something else. Drag the Job data to the Column Labels area. The table **PIV-OTED**. This is why it is called a PivotTable. See Figure 23.12. You can explore other options by yourself. Most people think that the Pivot Table is the most powerful feature in Excel.

Before you continue to a more complicated model, try to use some of the filtering elements of the PivotTable on the same example.

First, try to hide the Carpenters on our table. Click on the arrow next to Column Labels and eliminate the Carpenters in the drop-down menu. Notice how, in Figure 23.13, a Filter icon appears, indicating that the fields are filtered.

In addition to filtering or hiding a field through the local menu, Excel has the Filter area above the table. Try to move—drag and drop—the Dep label to the Report Filter area. You can choose to filter this entire report resulting only with the people of Dep 1. Click on the arrow to the right of the Dep label and choose Dep 1. See Figure 23.14.

	First Table			
3	Average of Age	Job		
4	Gender	Carpenter	Electrician	Machinist	Grand Total
5	F	33.50	36.00	28.00	34.38
6	M	39.00	39.33	28.50	37.00
7	Grand Total	37.43	37.25	28.33	35.83

	Pivoted Table			
3	Average of Age	Gender		
4	Job	F	M	Grand Total
5	Carpenter	33.50	39.00	37.43
6	Electrician	36.00	39.33	37.25
7	Machinist	28.00	28.50	28.33
8	Grand Total	34.38	37.00	35.83

Figure 23.12 Pivoted table

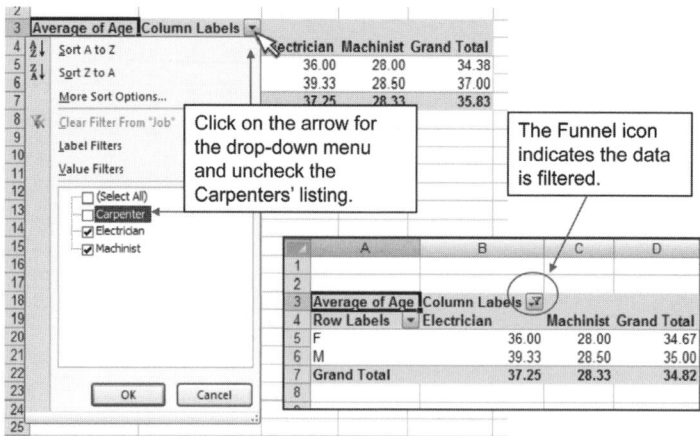

Figure 23.13 Filtered field

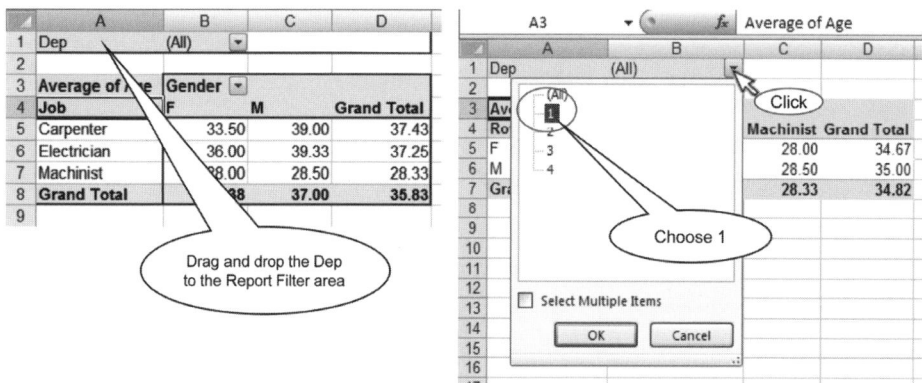

Figure 23.14 Filtering by Department

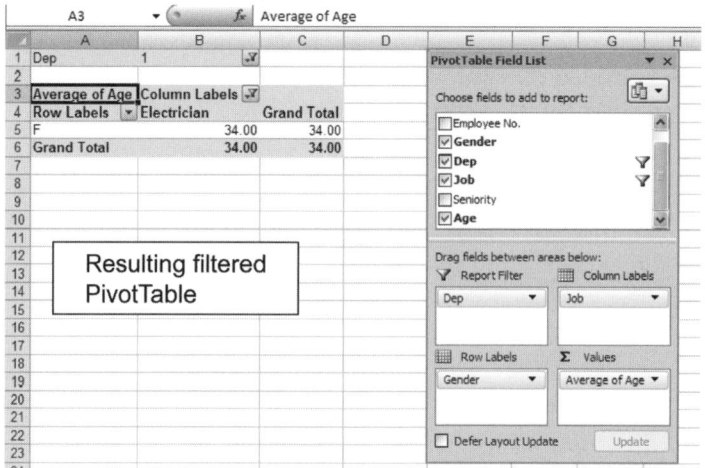

Figure 23.15 Filtered data

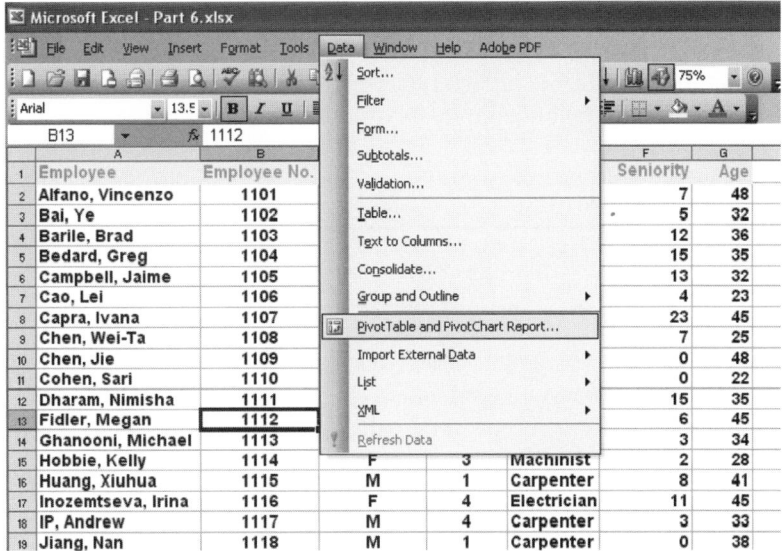

Figure 23.16 The PivotTable in Excel 2003 is under the Data menu

Figure 23.15 displays the resulting filtered PivotTable. I did not filter out the males in our table, but since we don't have males with the attributes filtered, the resulting table shows females only.

APPENDIX—THE PIVOT TABLE IN EXCEL 2003

The only basic difference between pivot tables in Excel 2007 and 2003 is the access path to activate the table. In Excel 2003, you get the PivotTable under the Data menu. See Figure 23.16.

REVIEW QUESTIONS

You will find these examples in the Excel Chapter 23 file:
On the *Review* sheet I sampled the "Executive MBA" database for 2009 students.

1. Use Excel's PivotTable to find the average age of our sample as well as the average age by gender.
2. Count the number of students in each undergraduate discipline.
3. What is the average age by undergraduate discipline and gender?

ANSWERS

1.

2		
3	**Average of Age**	
4	**Gender**	**Total**
5	F	34.50
6	M	35.03
7	**Grand Total**	34.85

2. Drag the undergraduate field to the left where the Raw Data fields are. Drag the field again to the center of the PivotTable where the Data Fields are supposed to be.

2		
3	**Count of Undergraduate**	
4	**Undergraduate**	**Total**
5	Accounting	11
6	Art	2
7	Biology	1
8	Chemistry	1
9	Economics	2
10	Education	3
11	Engineering	14
12	Finance	11
13	Journalism	5
14	Music	1
15	Pharmacy	2
16	Photography	2
17	**Grand Total**	55
18		

3.

Average of Age	Gender		
Undergraduate	**F**	**M**	**Grand Total**
Accounting	32.50	35.22	34.73
Art	36.00	32.00	34.00
Biology		34.00	34.00
Chemistry	33.00		33.00
Economics		36.50	36.50
Education	37.00	34.50	35.33
Engineering	33.60	36.44	35.43
Finance	34.50	33.71	34.00
Journalism	35.00	36.33	35.80
Music		31.00	31.00
Pharmacy	38.00	36.00	37.00
Photography	36.00	31.00	33.50
Grand Total	**34.50**	**35.03**	**34.85**

Data Mining Using Pivot Tables

This chapter is about more advanced PivotTable techniques. After you master the basics of the previous chapter, you can explore many more of the PivotTable features in this chapter.

On the *Example* sheet of the Chapter 24 Excel file, you will see a partial database of 1,000 customers' purchases. Using this sales report, you can try and detect patterns in the data—"mining" as it were—using Excel's PivotTable report. In doing so, you will master many of the possibilities offered by the PivotTable. Figure 24.1 shows a small section of the database. (The sample data has 1,000 sales records.)

As an analyst, you might want to explore relationships between the different variables, for example, between the customers' attributes and purchases. It may help your marketing and salespeople in identifying the type of customers they want to target to increase sales—if you have limited resources, and marketing wants to reach only part of the customer base.

The goal is to try to detect patterns. You can also check the relationship between the number of children and purchases. Try something else: the married/single attribute and purchases. Should marketing target customers with more children? Should they target married or single customers? You can try and find out these relationships using a PivotTable.

Let me start by finding out whether we can find a relationship between the number of children and the amount purchased. Let's verify whether the average purchase value increases or decreases when customers have more children.

	A	B	C	D	E	F	G	H	I	J	K	L
	M7			*fx*								
1	Customer No.	Product	Gender	Own Home	Marital Status	Customer	Income	Children	Credit Card	Purchases	Date	
2	CN1001	Clothing	F	No	S	New	18,000	1	Other	282	12/28/2008	
3	CN1002	Other	F	Yes	M	Repeat	120,000	3	Am EX	3,422	1/8/2008	
4	CN1003	Clothing	M	Yes	M	New	108,000	1	Am EX	3,961	11/4/2008	
5	CN1004	Furniture	M	Yes	M	New	30,000	0	Visa MC	564	7/26/2008	
6	CN1005	Other	M	No	S	New	12,000	0	Other	137	8/2/2008	
7	CN1006	Furniture	F	No	S	New	48,000	0	Am EX	986	6/2/2008	
8	CN1007	Garden	F	No	S	New	39,000	0	Visa MC	2,098	12/5/2008	
9	CN1008	Clothing	F	Yes	M	Repeat	89,000	0	Other	2,580	11/11/2008	
998	CN1997	Garden	F	No	S	New	24,000	0	Visa MC	314	5/4/2008	
999	CN1998	Furniture	M	Yes	M	New	114,000	0	Other	3,309	9/15/2008	
1000	CN1999	Electronics	F	No	M	New	104,000	1	Visa MC	1,977	6/23/2008	
1001	CN2000	Electronics	M	Yes	M	New	114,000	1	Other	3,203	6/2/2008	
1002												

Figure 24.1 A database with 1,000 customers

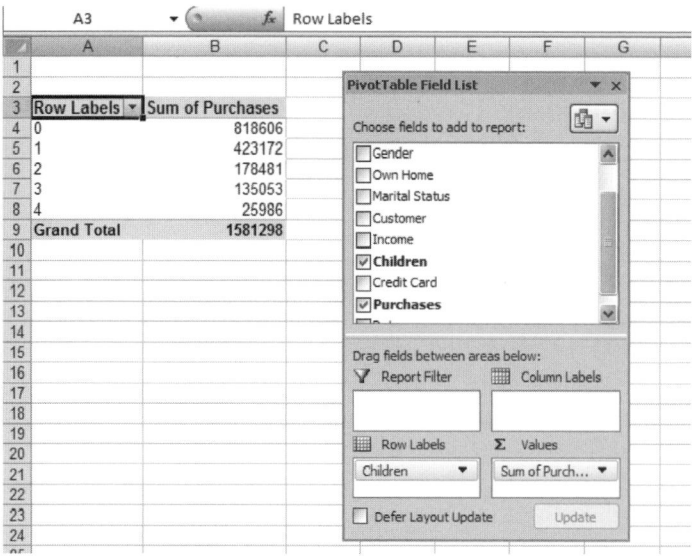

Figure 24.2   Sum of purchases table

Create a PivotTable using the Children field in the Row Labels area. Move (drag and drop) the Purchases field to the Data area. See Figure 24.2. This table is showing the default sum of purchases—which is telling us that, for example, the total amount spent by all customers with 0 children is $818,606.

These are not really numbers that can tell any story about the relationships we are interested in: Is there anything that indicates that an increase in the number of children has an impact on purchases? What you want to know is the *average* amount spent by a customer with 0 children and the *average* amount spent by a customer with 1 child, and so on. This average amount makes more sense than the total amount spent when you try to target the right customers.

You have to change the default Sum in the PivotTable into an Average. A reminder on the procedure (as was done in the previous chapter)—double-click on the word Sum and change it to Average in the menu. See the results in Figure 24.3. Now you can see the average amount spent by customers with 0, 1, 2, 3, and 4 children.

	A	B
1	Drop Page Fields Here	
2		
3	**Average of Purchases**	
4	**Children**	**Total**
5	0	1878
6	1	1585
7	2	1222
8	3	1080
9	4	999
10	**Grand Total**	**1581**

Figure 24.3   The average amount spent by customers with 0, 1, 2, 3, and 4 children

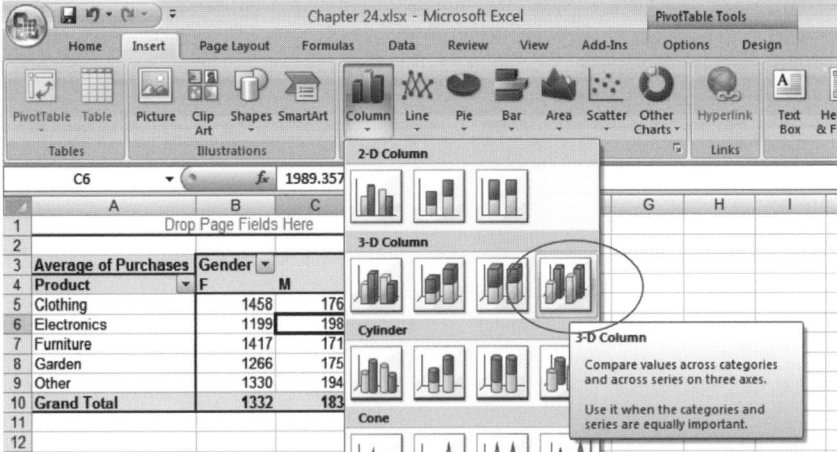

Figure 24.4 The chart to use for pivot tables

There is a clear negative relationship/correlation between the number of children and purchases. The more children a customer has, the less he/she spends. To strengthen the visual impact of Excel, it is preferable to insert a chart.

To insert a chart, go to the Insert ribbon and use the 3-D Column, the one that reads:

"Compare values across categories and across series on three axes. Use it when categories and series are equally important." See Figure 24.4.

This chart is the best when you use pivot tables for data mining.

After inserting a chart, the relationship becomes more instantly obvious. See Figure 24.5.

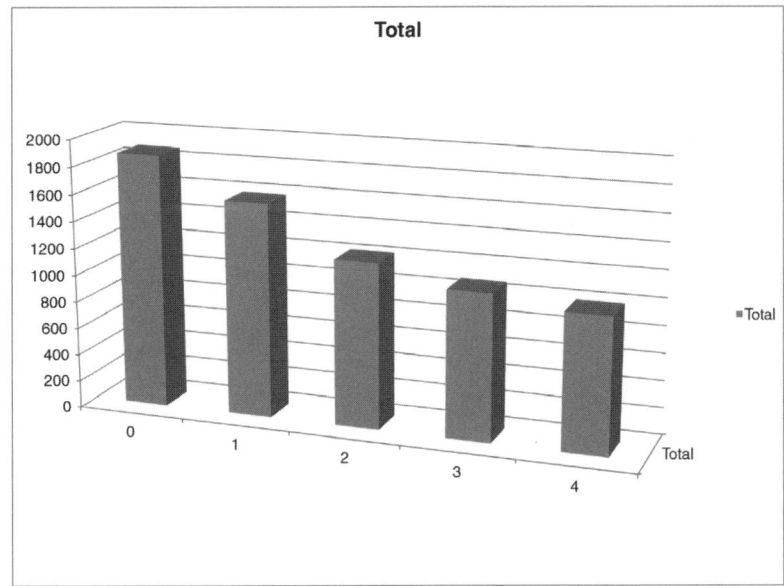

Figure 24.5 Purchase amount in relationship to the number of children

	A	B	C	D	E	F
1	Drop Page Fields Here					
2						
3	**Average of Purchases**					
4	Children	Total				
5	0	1878				
6	1	1585				
7	2	1222				
8	3	1080				
9	4	999				
10	Grand Total	1581				

| Average of Purchases | Own Home | | |
Children	No	Yes	Grand Total
0	1391	2246	1878
1	1142	2136	1585
2	873	1536	1222
3	711	1432	1080
4	683	1712	999
Grand Total	1129	2006	1581

Figure 24.6 Homeowners spend more

You can try something else. Add the Own Home parameter in the Column part of the PivotTable. See Figure 24.6. Drag the field in, and you will see the results. In our data set, homeowners clearly spend much more money than renters. Notice that this is true for any number of children the household has. Whether they have 0, 1, 2, 3, or 4 children, they always spend more if they are owners. The previous relationship also looks to be holding between the decreased spending compared to the increase in number of children.

At first glance, this looks true in Figure 24.6. However, if you look at the chart, you will discover that it is not the case. The chart we created in Figure 24.5 is changing in the background, since the chart is linked to the table. The amount spent by homeowners suddenly increases when you go from 3 to 4 children. It can be difficult to tell from the table, but the charts tell it all. See Figure 24.7.

You can try any of the other parameters: Product type, Gender, Marital Status, Old/New Customer, or the type of Credit Card. It is easy. Drag and drop the different fields into the PivotTable and it will give you the information you need.

What I want to show here is the unconventional, the features that are of more interest. Start with taking out the current parameters (Homeowners and Children), leaving the table with the Average of Purchases only. See Figure 24.8.

Now drag Income to the left where the word Total is (under the Average of Purchases header). The results are overwhelming. It is too much data to look at. See Figure 24.9. The trend is clear if you look at the chart.

To be able to look at the table and make sense of the data, use the Grouping feature of the PivotTable. Right-click a single cell in the Row data (column A) and choose Group. See Figure 24.10. The Grouping menu attempts to group it for you based on the data. It starts from 11,000, the lowest value in the data, and ends at the highest value of 188,000. It will

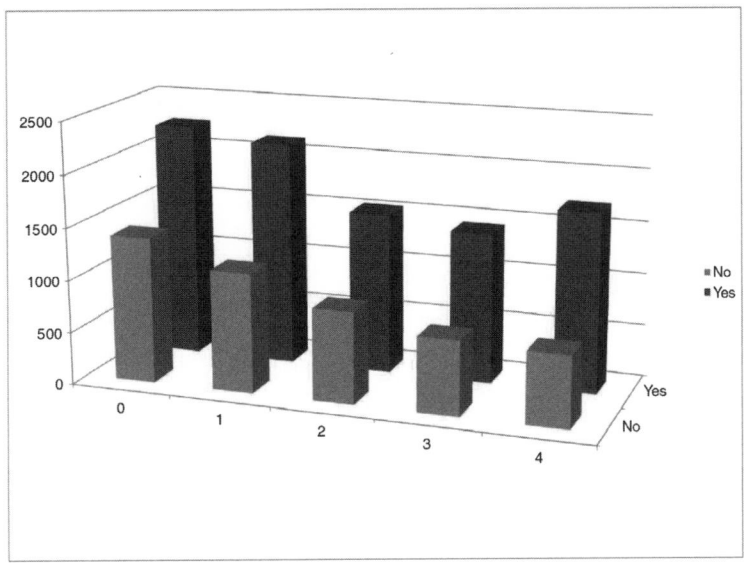

Figure 24.7   The amount spent by owners increases when you move from 3 to 4 children

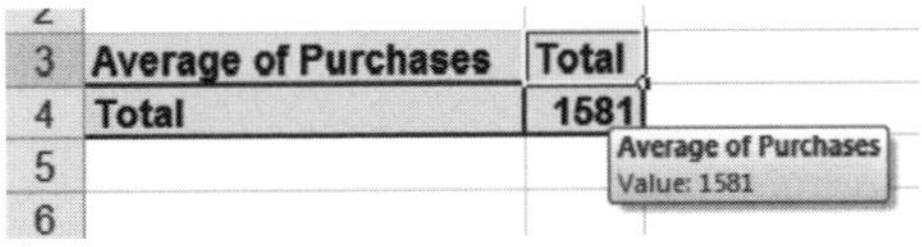

2		
3	**Average of Purchases**	**Total**
4	**Total**	**1581**
5		Average of Purchases
6		Value: 1581

Figure 24.8   Average of Purchases only

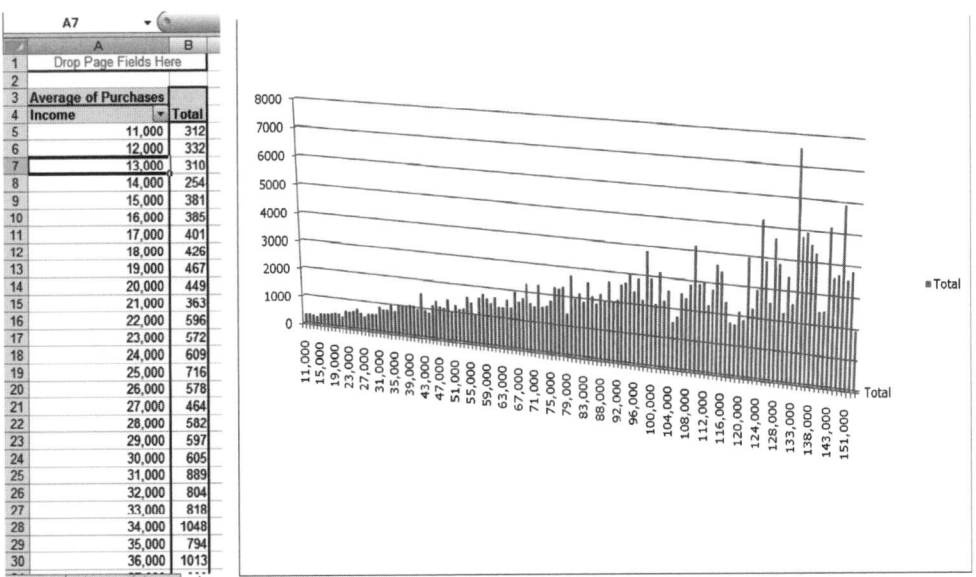

Figure 24.9   The upward trend is clear on the chart. It is difficult to view in the table.

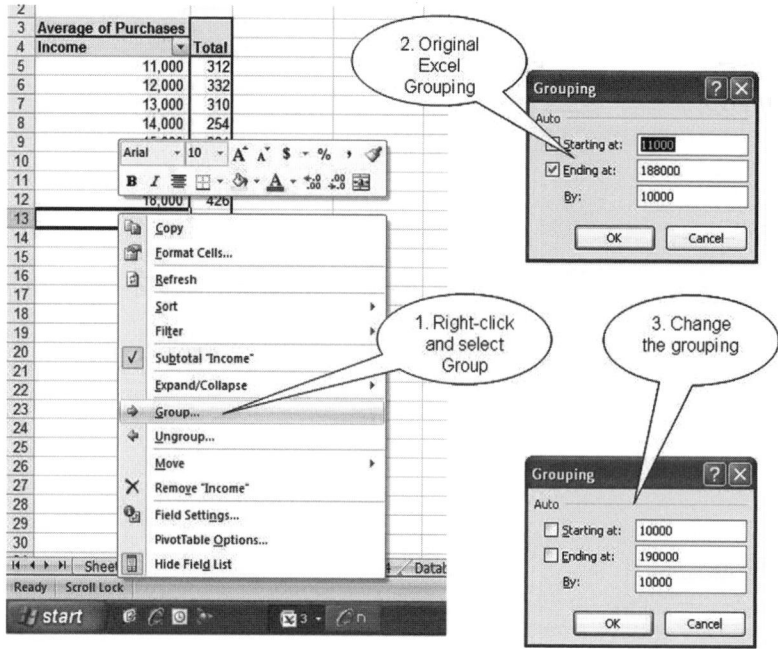

Figure 24.10 Grouping the data

group it by increments of 10,000. I chose the lowest number to be 10,000 and the highest 190,000.

The results of the grouping are shown in Figure 24.11. It is easier to follow. See the results and the chart.

One more thing I want to do is to investigate the relationship between purchases and the time of the year. Pull out (drag and drop) the Income, and replace it with the Date. You are faced with the same problem: too much information. See Figure 24.12 for the results.

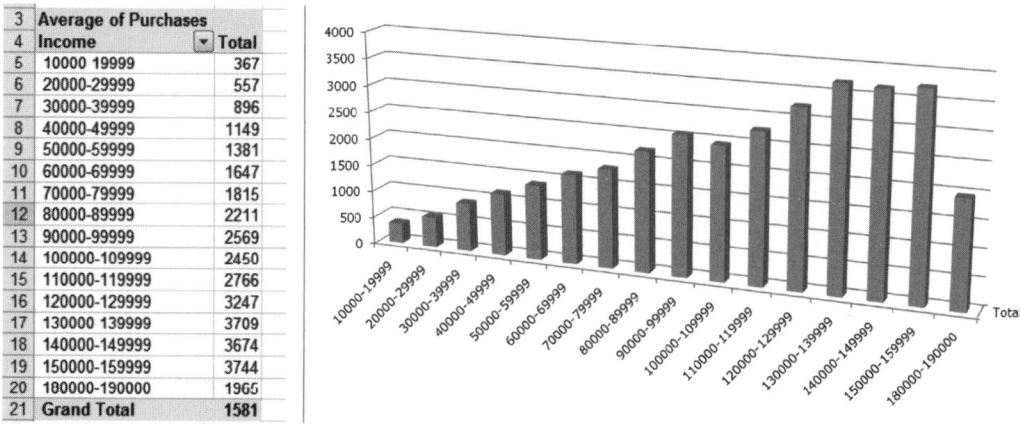

Figure 24.11 Grouped data

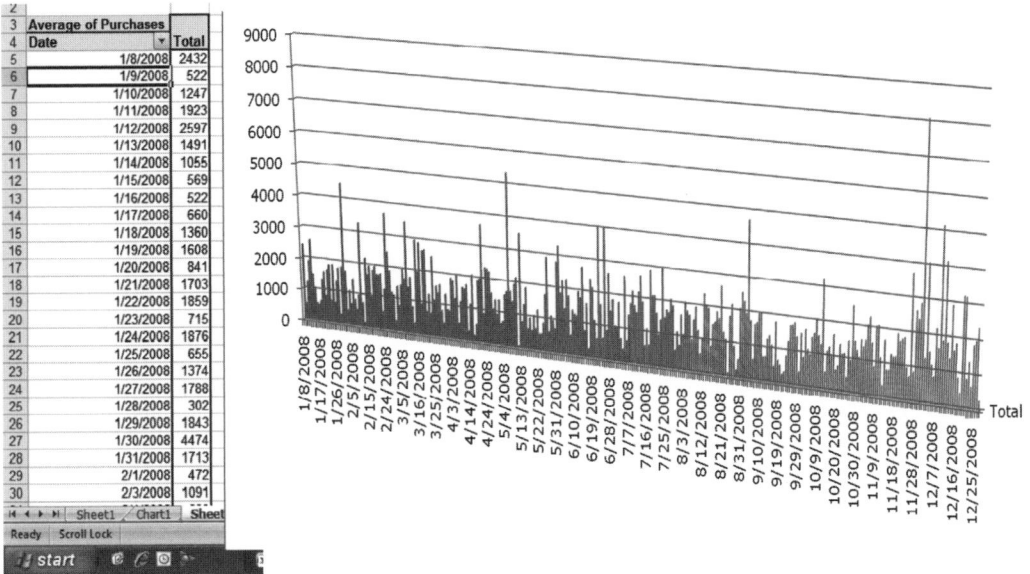

Figure 24.12 Using the dates produces too much information

The solution, again, is to group the data. This time the grouping should be different: Right-click and select Group. The menu—recognizing the fact that you are grouping dates—will suggest time-related grouping categories. The Grouping menu allows you to choose dates. I chose months. See Figure 24.13.

The results are shown in Figure 24.14. Remember the chart is being updated in the background. Sales look slightly higher for June, July, November, and December.

To get even more specific information (the data "mining"), I tried one more thing. I moved the Product to the top of the sheet to the Filter Area, and then filtered the PivotTable

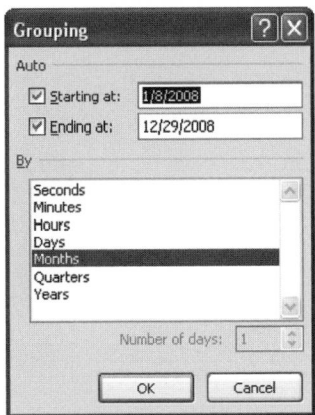

Figure 24.13 Grouping menu for dates

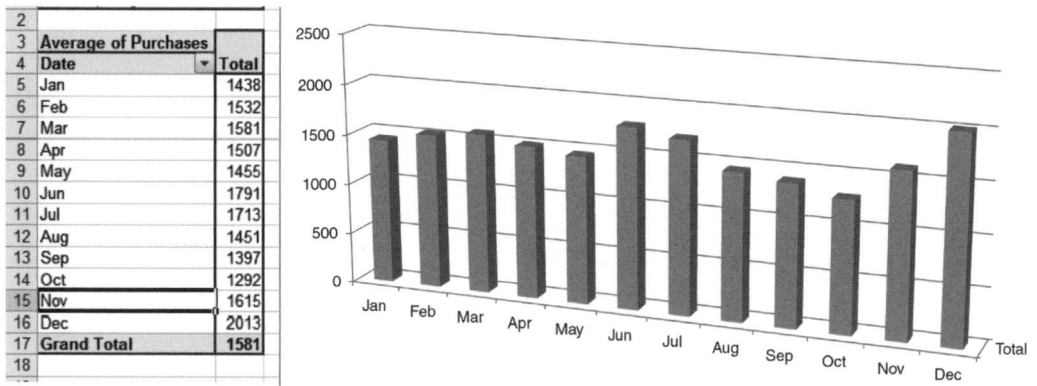

Figure 24.14   Data grouped by month

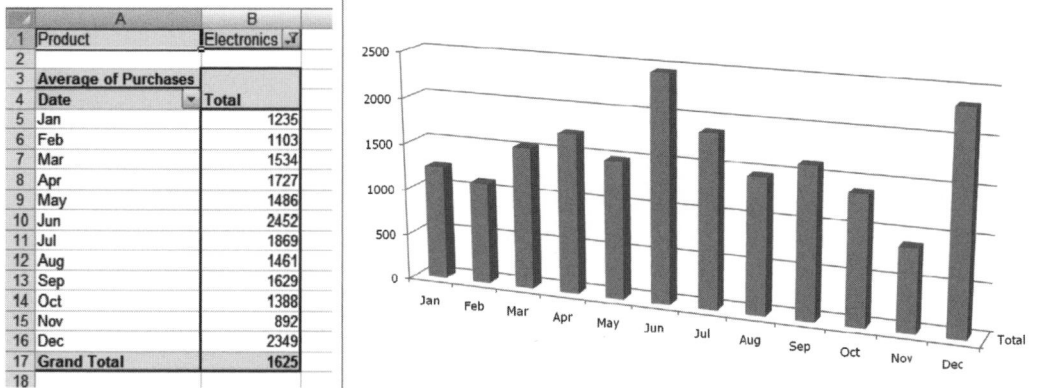

Figure 24.15   Data grouped by month and filtered for electronics

for different products. I discovered that sales were much higher for the months of June and December when the data was narrowed down to electronics only. See Figure 24.15.

APPENDIX—ADVANCED PIVOTTABLE TECHNIQUES IN EXCEL 2003

The only basic difference between pivot tables in Excel 2007 and 2003 is in the path to activate and the way to modify charts. The other menus work the same way.

To create a chart, click on the Chart Wizard on the PivotTable toolbar. See Figure 24.16.

Figure 24.16   The PivotTable toolbar

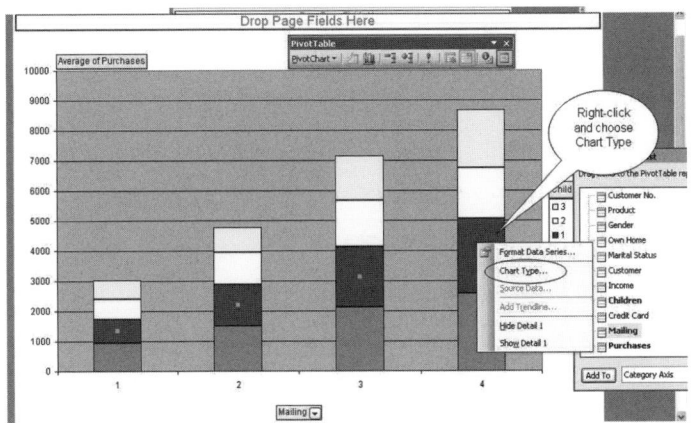

Figure 24.17   Choosing the 3-D chart

If you use the 2-D Column chart, Excel's default chart might not express the situation very eloquently. Right-click on the chart, click on Chart Type, and change to the 3-D Column chart. See Figures 24.17 and 24.18.

This will result in a 3-D chart as in Figure 24.19, which speaks for itself. You will also see a similar chart in the review problems.

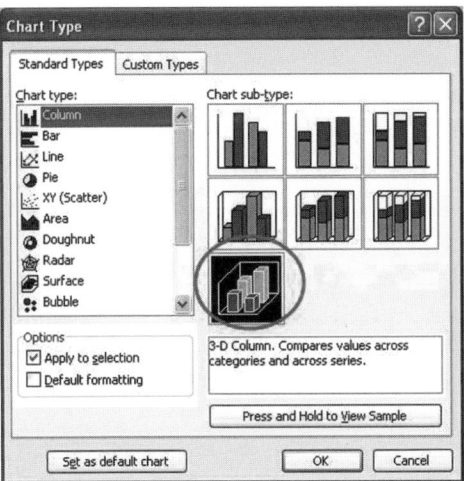

Figure 24.18   Choosing the 3-D chart

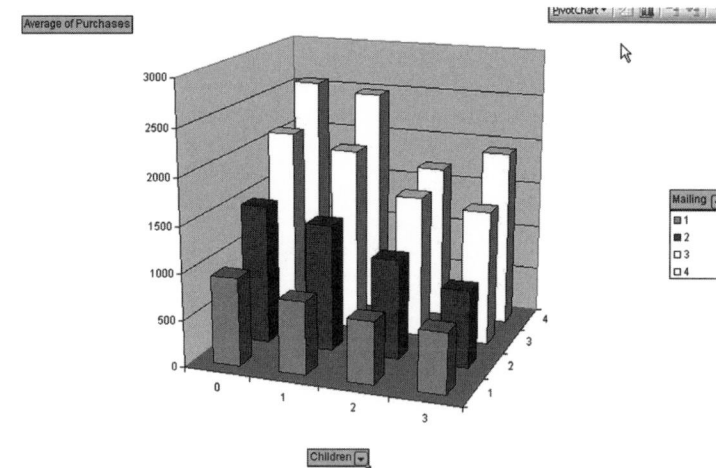

Figure 24.19 A 3-D column chart

REVIEW QUESTIONS

You will find these examples in the Excel Chapter 24 file:

The *Review* sheet of the Chapter 24 file has information regarding the sales of our bakery products in four cities. Use PivotTables to answer the following questions:

1. Which item yields the highest sales?
2. Which city yields the highest sales?
3. Calculate sales by item and by city for January.
4. Use the Percentage feature for the sales per city.
5. Use Charts to present each one of the above.

ANSWERS

1. Flour.

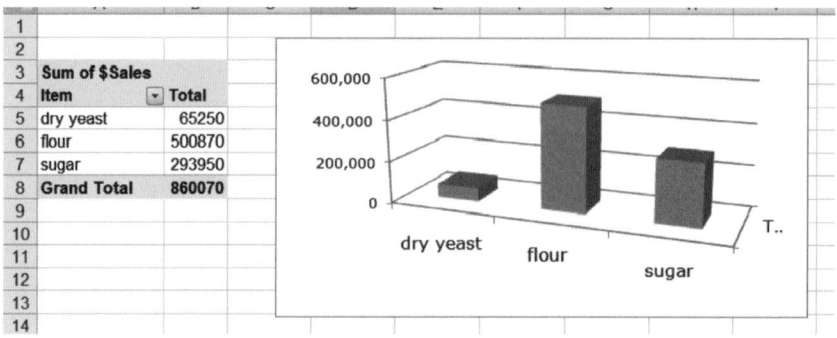

2. NYC.

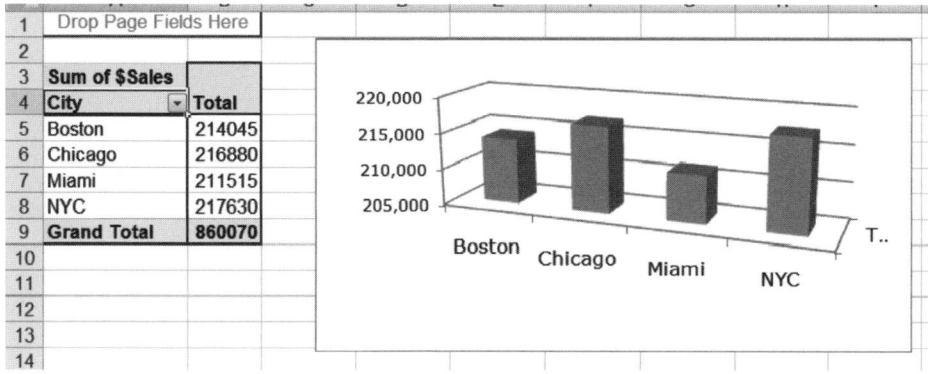

3.

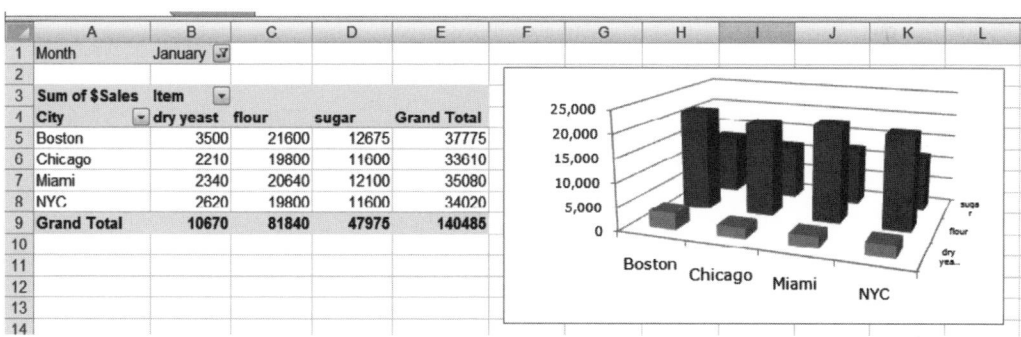

4. Double-click on the Sum, then—under Show Value as in Excel 2007 and under Options in Excel 2003—choose Show Percentage of Column.

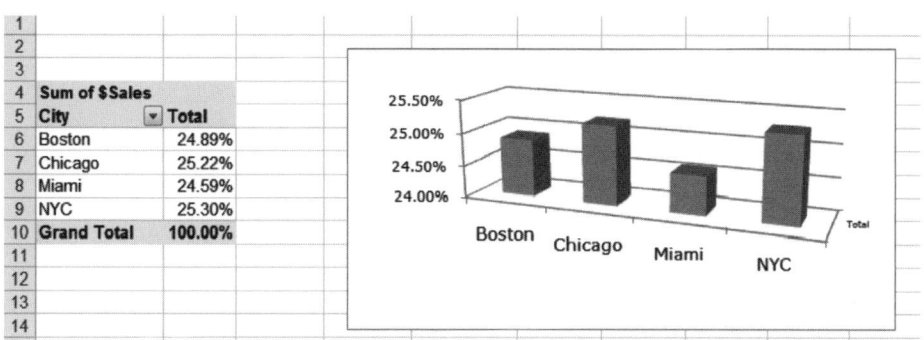

Excel Financial Tools

Microsoft Excel comes equipped with a variety of financial functions. This part will deal with the most frequently used financial formulas that are available, including those in the Analysis ToolPak.

There are many financial principles finance people and other analysts deal with on a regular basis. This section explains how to effectively apply some of these principles using Excel efficiently.

The chapters in this part of the book include:

CHAPTER 25

NPV and IRR—Evaluating Capital Investments

Financial functions in Excel are used to evaluate the financial profitability and effectiveness of investment projects. Most financial procedures involve several payments over the course of carrying out a project, rather than a single payment at a specific point in time. Using the Time Value of Money functions allows you to compare these projects to each other. For example, when financing an asset, the investor will receive future cash flows at different dates in the future. Excel allows you to calculate these financial indicators of investments (NPV—Net Present Value, FV—Future Value, IRR—Internal Rate of Return), which makes it possible to choose the most favorable and gainful investment.

THE TIME VALUE OF MONEY

NPV—Net Present Value

The Net Present Value is an approach/procedure used in long-term capital investment budgeting, where the present value of cash inflows is subtracted from the present value of cash outflows. In other words: the process of calculating the value of an investment by adding the present value of expected future cash flows to the initial cost of the investment. NPV is used to analyze the profitability of an investment/project. NPV compares the value of a dollar today versus the value of that same dollar in the future, taking inflation and return into account. When the NPV of a project is positive, it should be accepted. When it is negative, the project should be rejected because cash flows will be negative.

Calculating the NPV for n periods you will be applying:

$$NPV = CF_0 + CF_1/(1 + r) + CF_2/(1 + r)^2 + CF_3/(1 + r)^3 \cdots + CF_t/(1 + r)^n \qquad (25.1)$$

Excel NPV—Net Present Value Function

When using the NPV function, keep in mind that the function **does not** take into consideration the initial investment at time 0. You will have to subtract it from the result (add the initial investment if it has a minus sign in front of it, in other words, if your initial investment is shown as a negative value) once you complete your function. The function used by Excel is:

$$NPV = \sum_{i=1}^{n} \frac{values_i}{(1 + rate)^i} \tag{25.2}$$

You will have to enter the discount rate and the cash flows. Cash flows should be timed equally to occur at the end of each period.

An example using the NPV function Open the *NPV* sheet for the Chapter 25 file/workbook to see the project examples (Figure 25.1). We have three different projects with an initial investment of $5,000. The discount rate is in cell G1. Using Create Name from Selection, I named the cell Rate.

I chose to first use the formula (25.1) to calculate the NPV. As you see in columns J, K, and L, after calculation of the NPV, the result is $7,164.66. If you add to it the initial investment, the result is $2,164.66.

$$NPV = -5000 + 1000/(1 + .12)1 + 2000/(1 + .12)2 + 3000/(1 + 1.2)3$$

$$+4000/(1 + .12)4 = 2,164.66$$

Using the Excel NPV function, we select the Rate in the first field of the Function Arguments menu, and enter the cash flows range B3:B6 in the Value 1 field (See Figure 25.2). The result is the same as in the formula calculations.

If you drag the results to the right or copy and paste the function, Excel will calculate the NPV for the three projects. As you can see in Figure 25.3, project 3 has the highest NPV.

You have to add the initial (negative) investment to the NPV function to get the real NPV, Net Present Value, results as shown in Figure 25.4.

If you had to choose one investment/project, based on the Net Present Value, your choice would be Project 3 with the highest NPV.

IRR—INTERNAL RATE OF RETURN

Internal rate of return is the discount rate that makes the present value of the future cash flows of an investment equal the cost of the investment. In other words, the objective is to find the discount rate which will make NPV equal to zero.

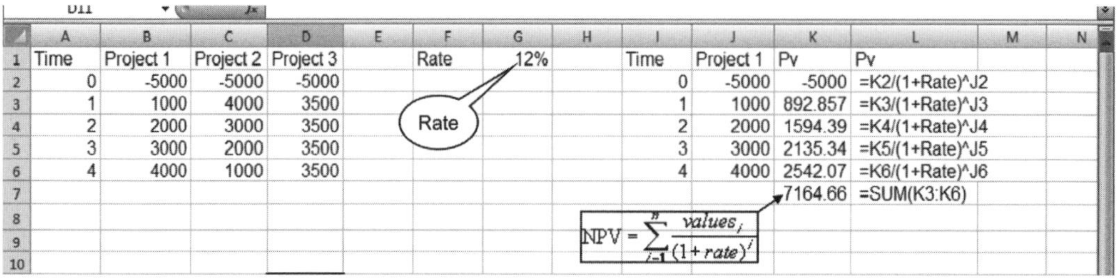

Figure 25.1 Calculating the NPV with formulas

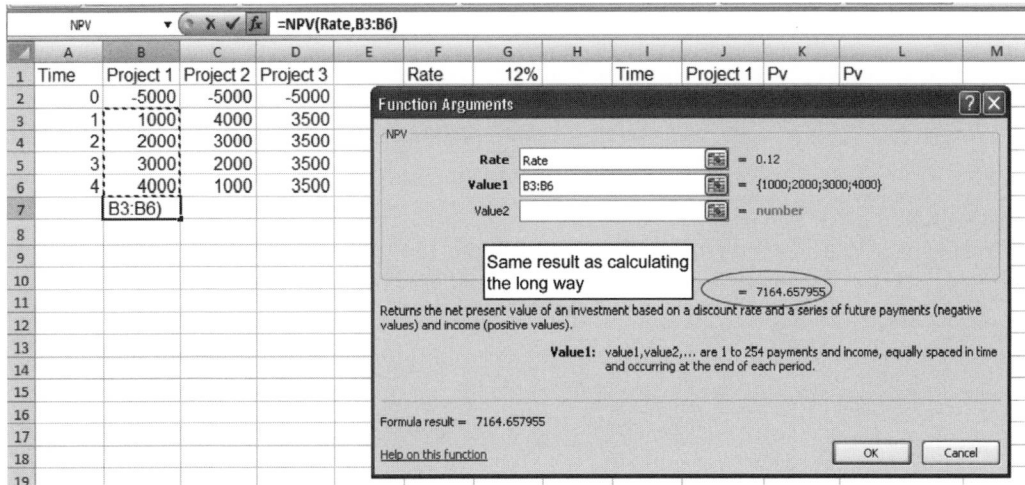

Figure 25.2 The Excel NPV function

	A	B	C	D	E	F	G	H
1	Time	Project 1	Project 2	Project 3		Rate	12%	
2	0	-5000	-5000	-5000				
3	1	1000	4000	3500				
4	2	2000	3000	3500				
5	3	3000	2000	3500				
6	4	4000	1000	3500				
7		$7,164.66	$8,022.09	$10,630.72				
8								
9								

Figure 25.3 NPV for the three projects

	A	B	C	D	E	F	G
1	Time	Project 1	Project 2	Project 3		Rate	12%
2	0	-5000	-5000	-5000			
3	1	1000	4000	3500			
4	2	2000	3000	3500			
5	3	3000	2000	3500			
6	4	4000	1000	3500			
7		$7,164.66	$8,022.09	$10,630.72			
8	NPV	$2,164.66	$3,022.09	$5,630.72			
9			You have to add the initial investment				
10		=B7+B2					
11							
12							

Figure 25.4 Add the initial (negative) investment

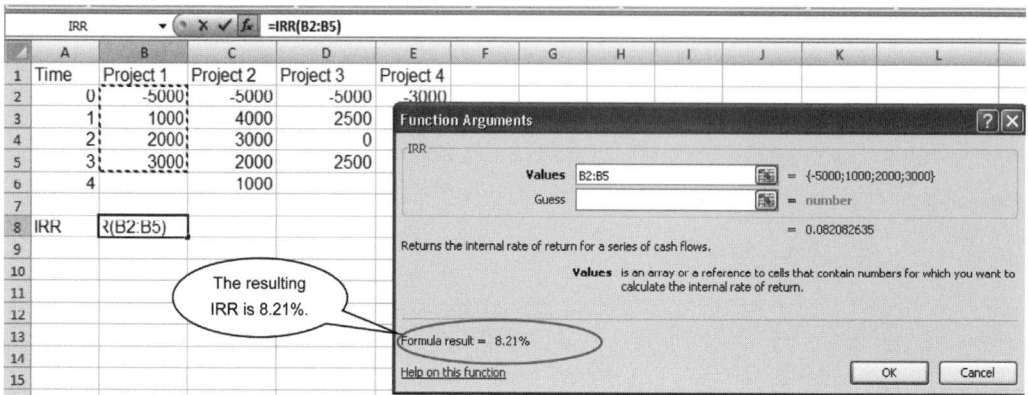

Figure 25.5 An IRR example

	A	B	C	D	E	F	G	H	I	J	K	L
1	Time	Project 1	Project 2	Project 3	Project 4							
2	0	-5000	-5000	-5000	-3000							
3	1	1000	4000	2500								
4	2	2000	3000	0								
5	3	3000	2000	2500								
6	4		1000									
7												
8	IRR	R(B2:B5)										

The resulting IRR is 8.21%.

Function Arguments

IRR

Values B2:B5 = {-5000;1000;2000;3000}
Guess = number

= 0.082082635

Returns the internal rate of return for a series of cash flows.

Values is an array or a reference to cells that contain numbers for which you want to calculate the internal rate of return.

Formula result = 8.21%

Help on this function

Figure 25.6 The IRR Function menu

The IRR is calculated by a trial and error process starting with a guess rate. After a number of iterations, Excel finds the rate which makes the NPV equal to zero.

An example using the IRR function

On the *IRR* sheet of the Chapter 25 Excel file, you will find a number of projects. See Figure 25.5. It is clear that Project 4 will yield a negative IRR. Future cash flows are lower than the

	A	B	C	D	E	F
1	Time	Project 1	Project 2	Project 3	Project 4	
2	0	-5000	-5000	-5000	-3000	
3	1	1000	4000	2500	1000	
4	2	2000	3000	0	500	
5	3	3000	2000	2500	500	
6	4		1000		500	
7						
8	IRR	8.21%	42.06%	0.00%	-19.89%	
9						
10		=IRR(B2:B5)				
11						

Figure 25.7 Calculated IRRs

initial investment. Unlike the Excel NPV function, the Excel IRR will include the initial investment (the negative cash flow of time 1) as part of the function.

As you can see in Figure 25.6, I calculated the IRR for Project 1 and included the initial cash flow of time 0. The resulting IRR is 8.21 percent. I did not enter a value in the Guess cell. Excel uses the default value of 10 percent for Guess if you do not include it.

In Figure 25.7, I have the rest of the IRR calculations for the other projects. As expected, Project 4 yields a negative IRR.

Based on the IRR—you should be choosing Project 2 with the highest IRR.

REVIEW QUESTIONS

You will find these examples in the Excel Chapter 25 file:

1. You are to invest $6,000 today and receive $3,000 in year 1, $2,000 two years from now, and $3,000 three years from now. Using a discount rate of 10%, what is the net present value of this investment?
2. Using a discount rate of 10%, calculate the NPV of the following investment:

Time	0	1	2	3	4	5
Cash Flow	−$3,000	−$5,000	$3,000	$3,000	$3,000	$3,000

3. An author signs a contract with a publisher. He has one of three choices. His first option is to receive an immediate lump sum of $300,000. His second choice is to receive $160,000 both at the end of year one and at the end of year two. The third option is to receive $400,000 three years from now. Which choice is the best one for him using a discount rate of 10%?
4. You are to invest $6,000 today and receive $3,000 in year 1, $2,000 two years from now, and $3,000 three years from now. Using a discount rate of 10%, what is the NPV of the investment? What is the IRR of this investment?
5. Calculate the IRR of the following investment:

Time	0	1	2	3	4	5
Cash Flow	−$3,000	−$5,000	$3,000	$3,000	$3,000	$3,000

6. The first option the author had in review question 1 was to receive $300,000 today. Now compute the IRR of the second and third choices:
   For the **second option**, assume that the "initial investment" was −$300,000 (as the first attentive said: "receive a lump sum of $300,000"). In this option you have three cash flows: a cash flow of −$300,000 at time 0 and two cash flows: $160,000 at time 1 and one cash flow of $160,000 at time 2.

For the **third option**, assume that the "initial investment" was −$300,000 (as the first attentive said: "receive a lump sum of $300,000"). In this option you have two cash flows: a cash flow of −$300,000 at time 0 and one cash flow of $450,000 at time 3. Calculate the IRR of these two options.

ANSWERS

1. $634.11.
2. $1,099.63.
3. The first option is $300,000, the second option has an NPV of $277,685.95, and the third has an NPV of $273,205.38.
4. The NPV is $634.11. The IRR is 15.94%.
5. 15.57%.
6. 4.41% and 7.46%.

CHAPTER 26

Unconventional Financial Functions: XNPV and XIRR

You can use IRR and NPV to calculate internal rate of return and net present values for even interval cash flows. In the examples, you saw in the previous chapters, we used even end-of-year cash flows. The functions can handle similar end-of-month cash flows.

For uneven interval cash flows, use the XNPV and XIRR functions. They are part of the Excel Analysis ToolPak Add-In. If you use the Add-In, you may remember how to activate it. To invoke the Add-In, click on the Office button 🔘 ⇨ Excel Tools ⇨ Add-Ins and activate the Analysis ToolPak.

Let me repeat the process here if you did not read chapter 11, explaining how to activate the Analysis ToolPak Add-In. Follow these steps:

1. Click on the Office 🔘 icon.
2. In the menu click on Excel Options.
3. In the Excel Options menu select Add-Ins on the left.
4. In the Add-Ins menu choose the Analysis ToolPack and click on Go.
5. Choose again the Analysis ToolPack in the small menu.
6. Click on Yes when you are asked to install it.

It will take Excel a few seconds to install the Analysis ToolPak.

See Figure 26.1. All the other Excel Add-Ins can be activated/installed with the same procedure.

Amazingly, very few Excel users know about these two functions. Some "power-users" will even create very complicated functions and macros to achieve this result, when these functions are readily available.

EXCEL XNPV—THE NET PRESENT VALUE FUNCTION FOR UNEVEN INTERVALS

Consider an example where you invest $50,000 on a certain date and the cash flows are as shown in the following table.

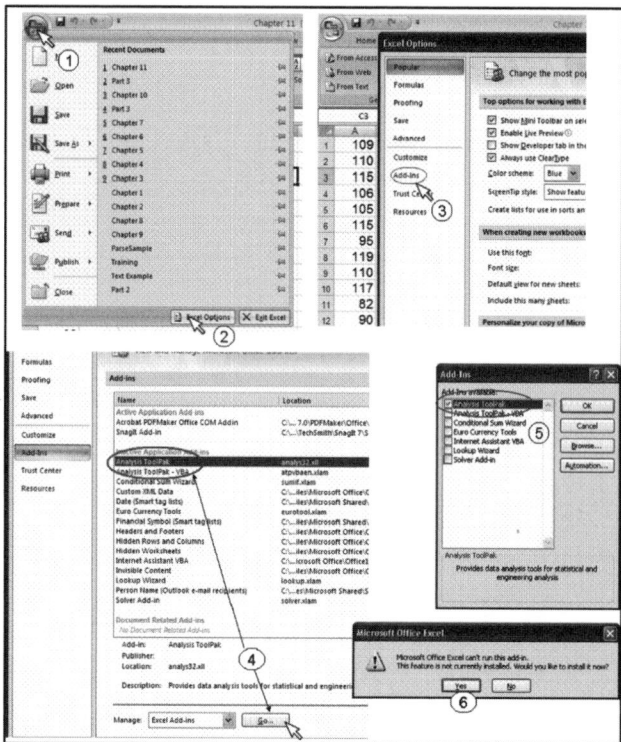

Figure 26.1 To activate the Add-In

January 1, 2009	October 1, 2009	June 15, 2010	October 25, 2010	December 31, 2010	March 1, 2011	June 15, 2012
−$50,000.00	$12,000.00	$6,000.00	$15,000.00	$8,000.00	$7,000.00	$15,000.00

You cannot use the NPV on this uneven interval cash flow case; however, you can use the XNPV function. This time, when you use the XNPV function, you **do** have to include the initial investment cash flow in the function. (The NPV does not allow inclusion of the initial investment, which then needs to be subtracted from the Excel-calculated NPV.)

The syntax of the function is: XNPV (rate, values, dates). In Figure 26.2, you can see that I selected cell E1, previously named Rate, for the Rate on the Function Arguments menu. For the values I selected cells B2:B8 (the cash flow of the project/investment) and for the Date cells A2:A8. The resulting XNPV is $326.37.

The Rate is a number specifying the annual discount (or interest) rate.

The Values are the numbers that specify cash flow values. There must be in your data selection at least one negative value (a payment), as well as one positive value (a receipt).

The first date represents the start of the project. The dates may occur in any order afterward, as long as they are after the start date.

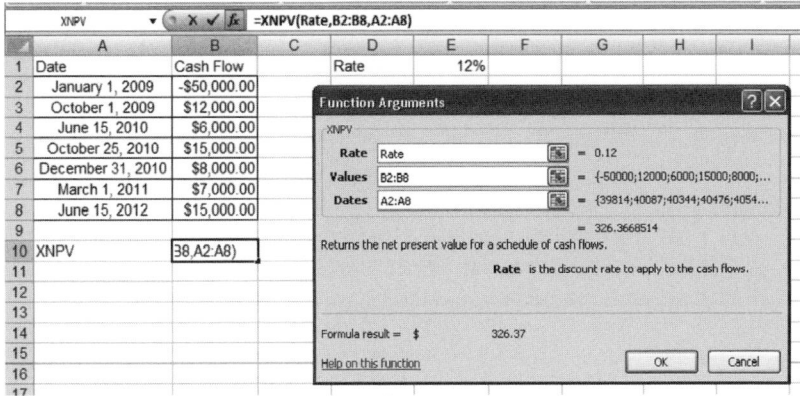

Figure 26.2 The XNPV menu

EXCEL XIRR—THE INTERNAL RATE OF RETURN FUNCTION FOR UNEVEN INTERVALS

Consider again the same example where you invest $50,000 on a certain date and the cash flows are as shown in the following table:

January 1, 2009	October 1, 2009	June 15, 2010	October 25, 2010	December 31, 2010	March 1, 2011	June 15, 2012
−$50,000.00	$12,000.00	$6,000.00	$15,000.00	$8,000.00	$7,000.00	$15,000.00

You cannot use the IRR on this uneven interval cash flow case, but you may use the XIRR function.

The syntax of the function is XIRR (values, dates, guess). In Figure 26.3, you can see that I selected cells B2:B8 for the Values. For the Dates, I selected cells A2:A8. I left the Guess cell empty—Excel uses 0.10 as a default value for that cell. The resulting XIRR is 12.38 percent.

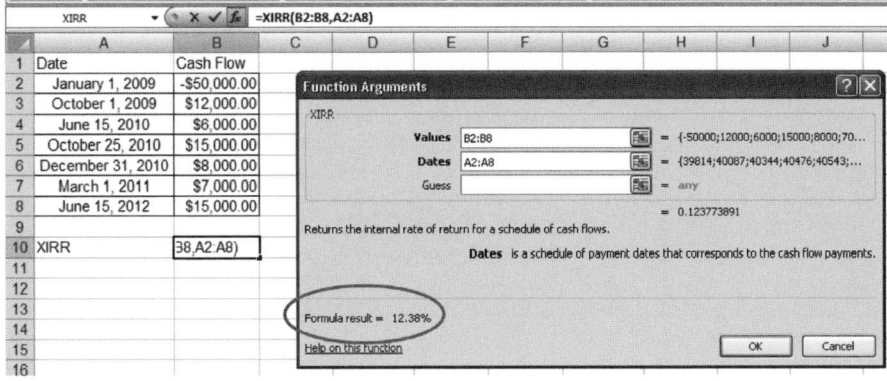

Figure 26.3 The XIRR menu

Here we have to follow again the same definitions and rules that we used for the XNPV: the values are the numbers or number that specify cash flow values. There must be in your data selection at least one negative value (a payment), as well as one positive value (a receipt).

The first date represents the start of the project. The dates may occur in any order afterward, as long as they are after the start date. The guess value is either your guess or 10 percent—the default value.

REVIEW QUESTIONS

You will find these examples in the Excel Chapter 26 file:

1. As part of a 4-year investment scheme, a real-estate company is about to invest $4,000,000 to purchase an apartment building consisting of 40 units. The company's exit strategy is to sell the building in two years.

   As an analyst for the real estate company, you need to determine an accurate Net Present Value of the investment. Based on past experience, the costs for the next four years can be estimated. These are: maintenance costs, labor, advertisement, commission, real estate taxes, and so on. The income cash flows are also known. They are the rental fees. The selling price two years from now from now is estimated to be $4,400,000.

   The problem is that the cash flows are not always received or paid in monthly intervals. Some corporate customers may pay once every quarter, and maintenance costs and taxes are also deducted at dates that are not necessarily end-of-month dates. You wish to calculate an accurate NPV taking into consideration the different intervals.

   Use the XNPV function to work with the data on the *Review* sheet. The discount rate to be used is 10 percent.

Date	Cash Flow	Date	Cash Flow	Date	Cash Flow	Date	Cash Flow
5-May-10	-4,000,000	5-Dec-10	24,000	5-Jun-11	26,000	5-Jan-12	17,000
5-Jun-10	24,000	5-Jan-11	2,350	5-Jul-11	26,000	20-Jan-12	62,000
5-Jul-10	24,000	20-Jan-11	58,000	5-Aug-11	8,900	5-Feb-12	26,000
5-Aug-10	8,400	5-Feb-11	24,000	5-Sep-11	26,000	5-Mar-12	26,000
5-Sep-10	24,000	5-Mar-11	24,000	20-Sep-11	62,000	5-Apr-12	13,000
20-Sep-10	58,000	5-Apr-11	8,400	5-Oct-11	26,000	5-May-12	62,000
5-Oct-10	13,200	5-May-11	24,000	5-Nov-11	26,000	20-May-12	4,400,000
5-Nov-10	24,000	20-May-11	59,000	5-Dec-11	22,000		

2. Use the XIRR to figure out the internal rate of return on the above investment.

ANSWERS

1. $367,159.28.
2. 15.274 percent.

CHAPTER 27

Frequently Used Financial Functions

There are a few Excel financial functions that look and feel alike. After you understand and master one of these functions, you can navigate and utilize all of them with relative ease. All these financial functions deal with a stream of equal periodical payments called annuities. Annuities could include loans, mortgages, or retirement funds; where you receive or pay a series of equal cash payments for a specific number of periods at equal intervals. An annuity is essentially a level stream of cash flows for a fixed period of time.

These functions include, PMT, IPMT, PPMT, FV, RATE, NPER, and PV.

I can start with an example that you will be familiar with if you read some of the previous chapters. This example analyzed the payment of a car loan. Consider the example I used before again: You are purchasing a car for $22,000. You are required to give $4,000 as a down payment. The annual interest rate is 8.00 percent and the loan period is three years. Assume end-of-period monthly payments. The following is the model created for this loan, see Figure 27.1. We named the cells in column B by the designations in the cells of column A. You will find the example on the sheet named *Car loan* in the Chapter 27 workbook.

What is of interest to us in this example is the PMT, the Payment function in cell B7. Once you understand all the features of this function, you will be able to apply your know-how to the range of functions previously mentioned. See Figure 27.2 for the Functions Arguments menu associated with the PMT function.

This function calculates the payment for a loan based on constant payments and a constant interest rate, as defined within the dialog box. The Excel syntax of the function is:

PMT (rate, nper, pv, fv, type)

Where:

> **rate** is the interest rate per period. In this example, the loan is at an 8 percent annual interest rate and since the payments are on a monthly basis, the interest rate per month is 8%/12, or 0.67 percent. You could enter 8%/12, or Rate/12, 0.67%, or 0.0067, in the field for the **rate**.
>
> **nper** is the total number of payment periods in a loan or annuity. In this example, the loan reimbursement is through monthly payments, therefore your loan has 3*12 or Years*12 periods. You could also enter 36 into the formula for **nper**.
>
> **pv** is the present value of the loan. It is also referred to as the principal. You should always enter it as a negative value in the Excel formula. This amount in this example is −$18,000.

	Payment	▼	fx	=PMT(Rate/12,Years*12,-Loan)				Payment	▼	fx	=PMT(Rate/12,Years*12,-Loan)

	A	B	C	D	E
1	Item	Car			
2	Price	$ 22,000.00			
3	Down Payment	$ 4,000.00			
4	Loan	$ 18,000.00			
5	Rate	8.00%			
6	Years	3			
7	Payment	$564.05			
8	Total Payments	$ 20,305.96			
9	Total Interest	$ 2,305.96			

	A	B
1	Item	Car
2	Price	22000
3	Down Payment	4000
4	Loan	=Price-Down_Payment
5	Rate	0.08
6	Years	3
7	Payment	=PMT(Rate/12,Years*12,-Loan)
8	Total Payments	=Payment*12*Years
9	Total Interest	=Total_Payments-Loan

Figure 27.1   The car loan model

fv is defined as " . . . the future value, or a cash balance you want to attain after the last payment is made." This is what we call a balloon payment, it is a large, lump sum payment made at the end of a long-term balloon loan. Balloon payments are most commonly found in mortgages, but could also be attached to auto and personal loans as well. If the FV field is not filled, it is assumed to be 0 (zero)—meaning that the future value of the loan after the last payment is made will be 0. If the FV is not 0, make sure that you add a – (minus) sign in front of the number value. For example: **PMT** (0.5%, 48, −20000, −**5000**).

type indicates when payments are due and is either the number 0 or 1. When type is omitted, it is assumed to be 0, which means that the payments are made at the end of the period. When the type is 1, it is assumed that the payments are due at the beginning of the period, as is the case in some mortgage situations.

Similar Excel Functions

PV—Present Value   Present Value is the total amount that a series of future payments or cash flows is worth today, given a specified rate of return. If you are offered an investment that will pay you $500 per month for the next 10 years, and if you could earn a rate of 8 percent

Figure 27.2   The Payment Function menu

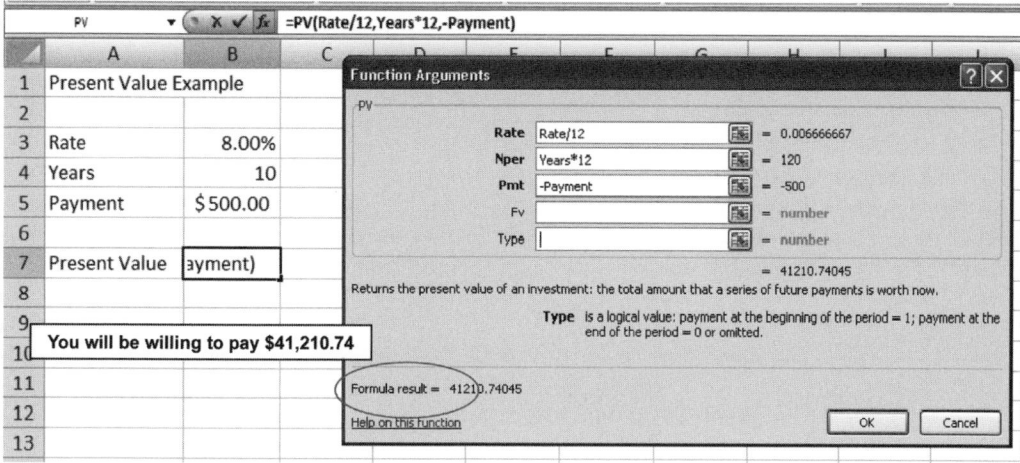

Figure 27.3   The Present Value (PV) Function

per year on similar investments (you may want to call in opportunity cost), how much should you be willing to pay for this annuity? This is an example of when you will be using the PV function. As you can see in Figure 27.3, the present value of the investment is $41,210.74. This is the amount you should be willing to pay today to secure the future return at the specified rate.

FV—Future Value   Future Value is the value of an investment based on periodic, constant payments, and a constant interest rate. Suppose that you will be paying $500 every month, for 10 years, at a rate of 8 percent, and then receiving a lump sum back immediately after paying the last payment. How much would you have to get in the future? This is an example of when you will be using the FV function. As you can see in Figure 27.4 you will have to pay $91,473.02.

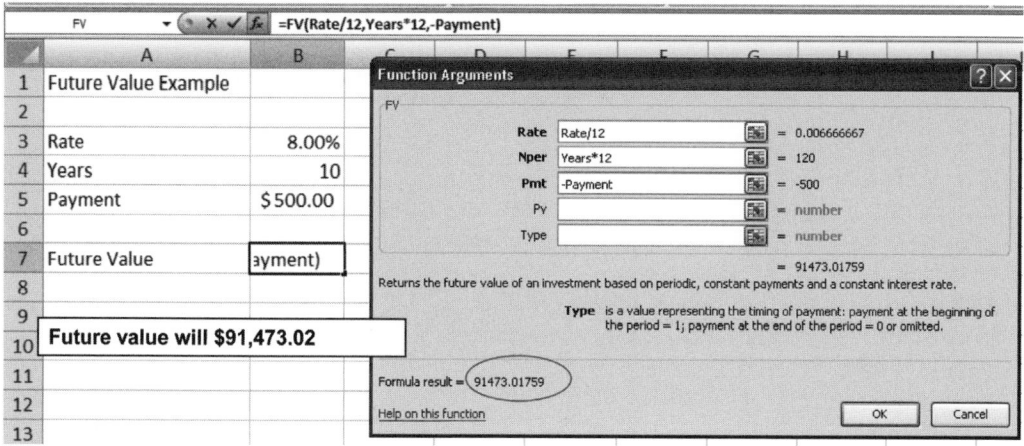

Figure 27.4   The Future Value (FV) Function

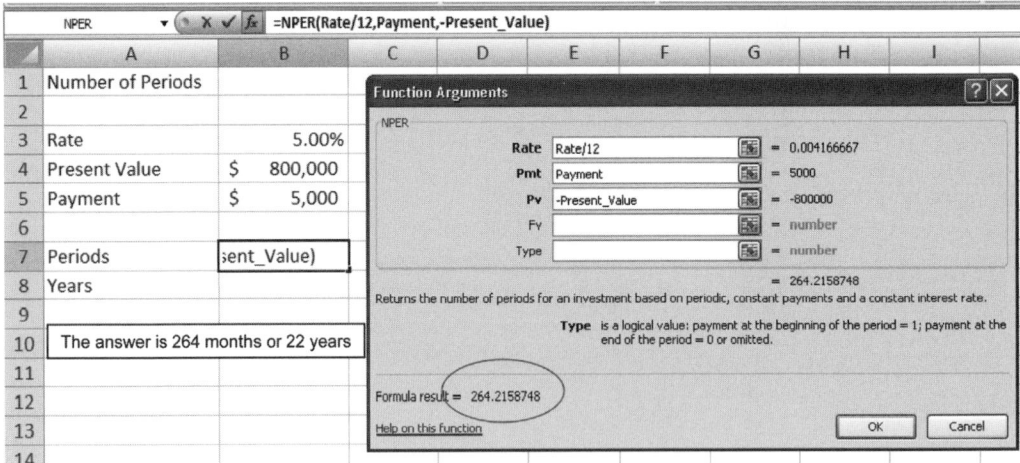

Figure 27.5 The NPER—Number of Periods function

NPER—Number of Periods Consider, for example, that you are about to retire. You have a sum of $800,000 available in your savings (the amount that you will be drawing on for the rest of your life). If you expect to earn 5 percent per year on average (the discount rate) and withdraw $5,000 per month, how long will it take to burn through your savings (in other words, how long can you afford to live)? The answer, as you can see in Figure 27.5 is 264 months or 22 years.

RATE In this last example, assume that you invest $30,000 (say, in a piece of equipment), and that this investment will generate $500 net income per month over the next seven years. If you purchase this piece of equipment or make any other such investment, what is your compounded average annual rate of return? The answer, as shown in Figure 27.6, is 0.84 percent per month or 10.13 percent per year.

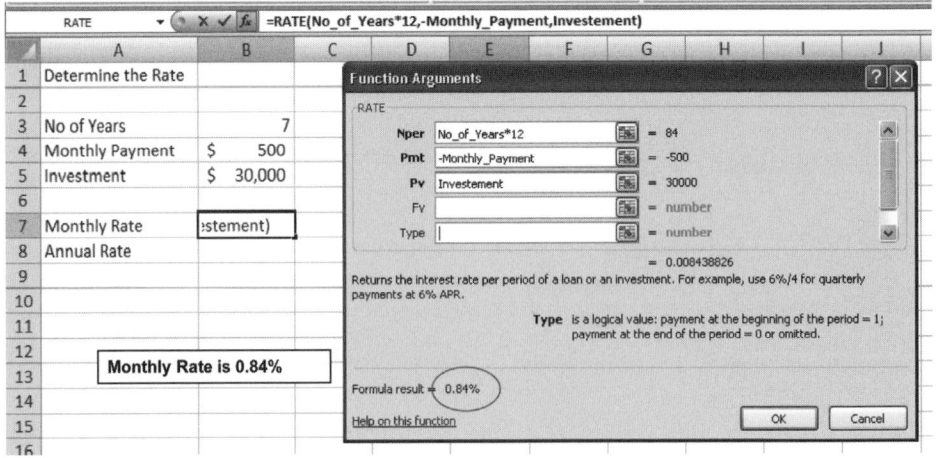

Figure 27.6 The Rate Function menu

As you can see, the "family" of annuity functions look and feel the same for all functions. In the next chapter, you will practice using these and similar functions in an amortization table.

REVIEW QUESTIONS

1. What would be the monthly payments on a six-year loan of $50,000, with an interest rate of 6 percent?
2. A student needs $1,000 a month for college for the next four years. If the interest rate is 5.2 percent, how much money do his parents have to put away in the bank today to be able to handle this annuity?
3. If you are going to retire in 15 years and you are putting away $1,200 a month with an interest rate of 5 percent, how much money will you have in the bank?
4. You took a loan of $15,000 with an interest rate of 7 percent and you are paying $500 a month. How many months will it take you to pay off the loan?
5. You got a loan of $15,000 and you are paying it off in three years—36 monthly payments of $450 each. What interest rate is the bank charging you?

ANSWERS

1. Use the PMT function. $828.64.
2. Use the PV function. $43,252.59.
3. Use the FV function. $320,746.73.
4. Use the NPER function. 33.07 months or 2.67 years.
5. Use the Rate function. A monthly rate of 0.42 percent or 5.06 percent per year.

CHAPTER 28

Amortization Tables

Amortization is a common concept used in finance and accounting. It is defined as being the steady decrease of a loan/liability by installments or loan repayments. By using an amortization table, you are calculating the reduction of the balance of a loan over time.

It is possible to download a number of amortization table programs or ready-made Excel spreadsheets from the Internet; however, creating one by yourself will allow you to master some of your Excel financial skills. This chapter will incorporate some of these functions in addition to the PMT (Payment), which was covered in the previous chapter. You will learn to apply the additional PPMT, IPMT, CUMIPMT, and CUMPRINC Excel functions.

Amortization Example

Consider a home loan/mortgage of $600,000 to be paid off in monthly installments over a period of 25 years, applying an interest rate of 6.00 percent. You have to create a loan amortization table for the 300 monthly payments (25 years × 12 months/year). In addition, you may want to calculate the cumulative interest for certain years, since in some countries—such as the US—it is possible to deduct this amount from your annual income when doing a tax return declaration.

Figure 28.1 shows the example described. I calculated the monthly payment using the PMT function as covered in the previous chapter. Since excellent comprehension of the PMT function is important before moving on to applying the other financial functions, a brief review is in order.

In general, the PMT function is used to calculate the payment for a loan based on constant payments and a constant (fixed) interest rate. The Excel syntax of the function is:

$$PMT\ (\textbf{rate, nper, pv, fv, type})$$

Where:

> **rate** is the interest rate per period and is expressed as a percentage. In this example, the loan is made at a 6 percent annual interest rate, and paid back in monthly installments. The interest rate per month is 0.5 percent (6/12).
>
> **nper** is the total number of payment periods for a loan or annuity. In this example, since the payments are made on a monthly basis, the loan has 12*25, or 300 monthly payment periods.

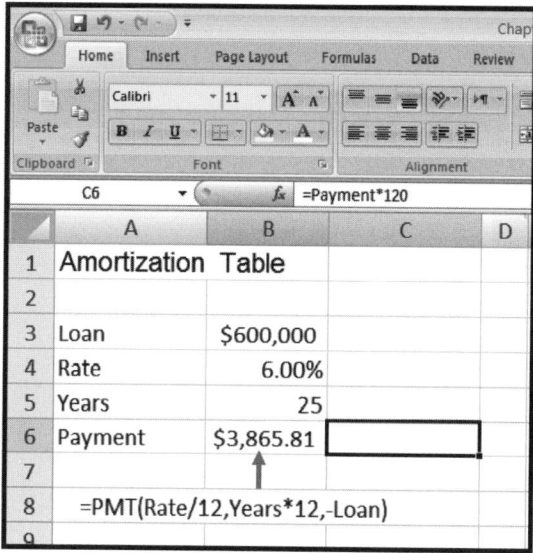

Figure 28.1 The monthly payment of the loan—using the Payment function to calculate the monthly mortgage payment

pv is the present value of the loan; in this case, $600,000.

fv is defined as " . . . the future value, or a cash balance due after the last payment is made." This is what we call a balloon payment, it is a lump sum payment made at the end of a long-term balloon loan. We do not use it here.

type indicates when payments are due and is either the number 0 or 1. When type is omitted, it is assumed to be 0, which means that the payments are made at the end of the period. When the type is 1, it is assumed that the payments are due at the beginning of the period, as is the case in some mortgage situations.

The Amortization Table

The amortization table will have a number of components. The table headers will be Month, Payment Date, Principal, Interest, and Balance. You need to set up the table for the various calculations as shown in Figure 28.2.

Since the table will be set up to calculate the complete duration of the loan, it will need to show 300 months. You have to enter the values 1 to 300 on the left side of the table (the first column). To enter automatically without effort the values 1 to 300, follow this procedure:

- Type the number 1 in the first cell E2 and hit Enter.
- Reselect the E2 cell and under the Home ribbon, use Fill ⇨ Series.
- In the Fill Series menu, select Columns, Linear, and then type 300 for the stop value. See Figure 28.3.

	A	B	C	D	E	F	G	H	I
1	Amortization Table				Month	Payment Date	Principal	Interest	Balance
2					1				
3	Loan	$600,000							
4	Rate	6.00%							
5	Years	25							
6	Payment	$3,865.81							
7									
8	=PMT(Rate/12,Years*12,-Loan)								

Figure 28.2   Preparing the amortization table

This just created the desired outcome. The result is shown in Figure 28.4. The series of numbers from 1 to 300 was filled in in column E.

The next step is to enter the payment dates. If, for example, the first payment of the mortgage is on March 9, 2009, all future payments will be on the ninth of every month for the following 300 months. Excel has a nice AutoFill feature that can do that for you.

- Type the date March 9, 2009, in cell F2.
- Double-click on the drag handle (the lower right corner of the cell when the pointer becomes a crosshair). It will result in a sequence of daily dates, March 9, March 10, and so on. Figure 28.5 shows the result. This is the default setting and is not the desired result in this case.

Since you want the dates to be every ninth day of the month, click on the small AutoFill menu that appeared at the lower right of the selection and select Fill Months in the local

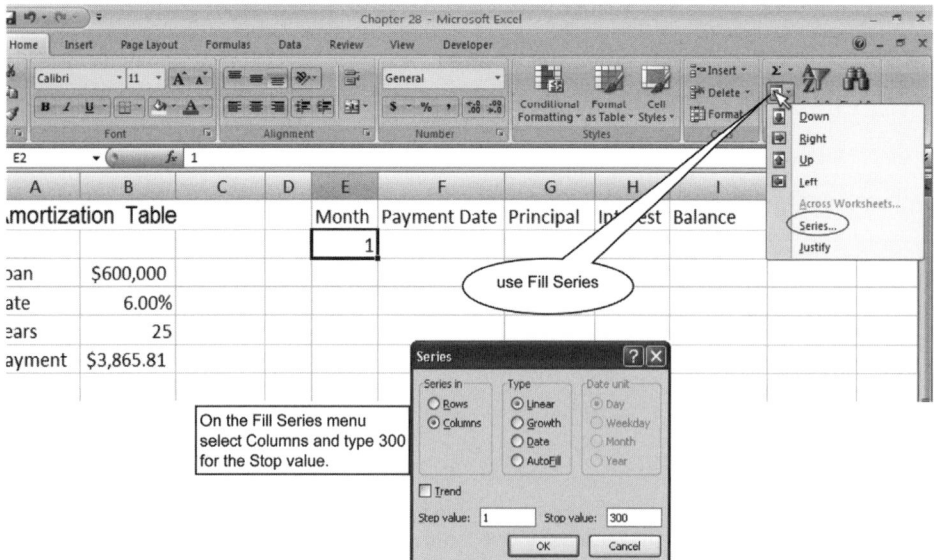

Figure 28.3   Using the Fill Series menu

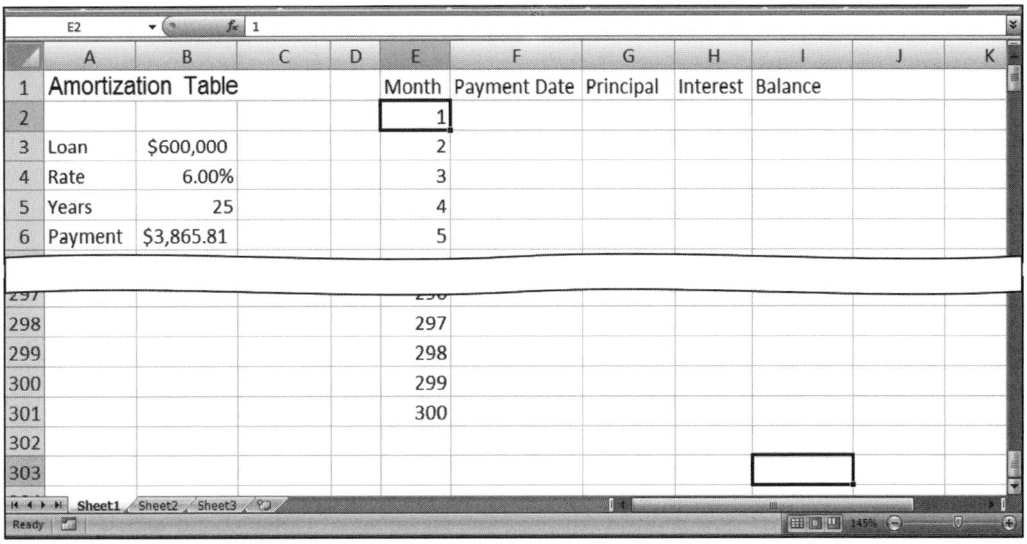

Figure 28.4 Column E has the values from 1 to 300

menu. See Figure 28.6 for the procedure and Figure 28.7 for the results. The payment dates will appear as every ninth day of the 300 months in the table. You are now ready to calculate the actual entries in the amortization table.

To fill the table, you have to calculate the Principal, the Interest, and the remaining Balance for each one of the 300 months or periods. The **Principal** is the part of the monthly

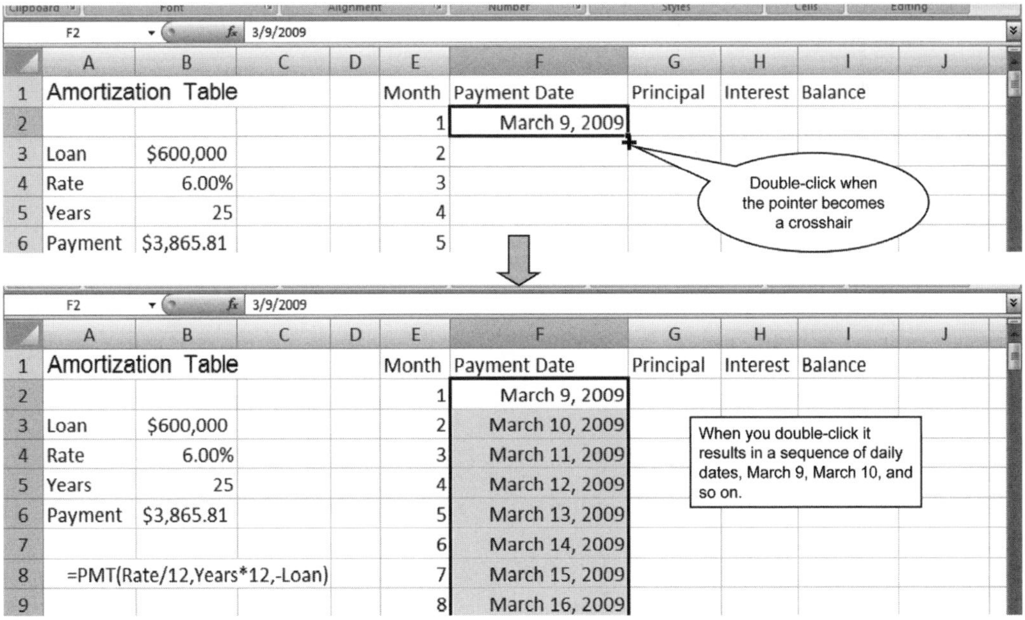

Figure 28.5 Preparing the payment dates

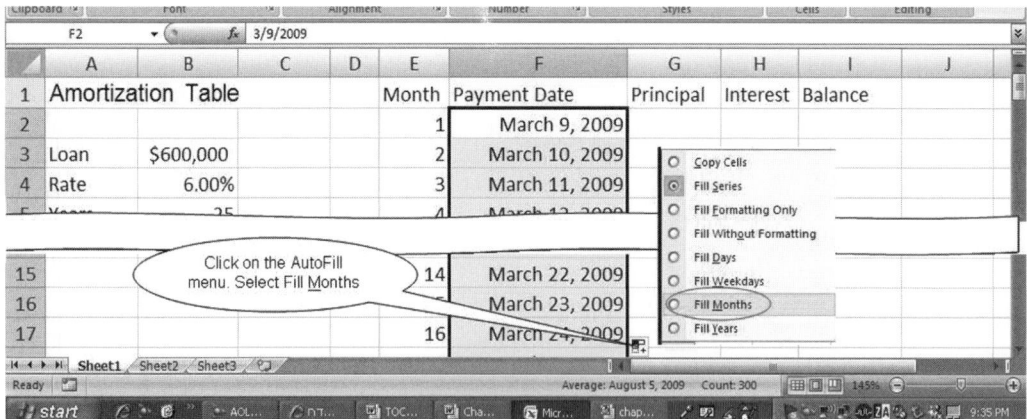

Figure 28.6   Using the AutoFill menu for monthly dates

payment that is actually repaying back the loan. The Principal is subtracted from the **Balance** every month to create the next month's Balance. The **Interest** is monthly interest (0.5 percent) on the Balance of the loan for the current month. Adding the monthly Interest and the monthly Principal will equal the payment amount for a single month. This is how it is calculated:

Principal—PPMT Function   The PPMT function will calculate the monthly principal repayment for each of the 300 months. Principal reimbursements are very low at the beginning of the loan, since the interest on the remaining principal balance is high. The principal repayment portion will be much higher toward the end of the loan since the interest amounts will be smaller on a lower remaining principal balance.

This is how to calculate the PPMT. It has all the components of the PMT, the Payments function that we calculated above, with one additional input, the period numbers:

	A	B	C	D	E	F	G	H	I	J
1	Amortization	Table			Month	Payment Date	Principal	Interest	Balance	
2					1	March 9, 2009				
3	Loan	$600,000			2	April 9, 2009				
4	Rate	6.00%			3	May 9, 2009				
5	Years	25			4	June 9, 2009				
6	Payment	$3,865.81			5	July 9, 2009				
7					6	August 9, 2009				
297					296	October 9, 2033				
298					297	November 9, 2033				
299					298	December 9, 2033				
300					299	January 9, 2034				
301					300	February 9, 2034				

Figure 28.7   The completed list of monthly dates

PPMT (rate, per, nper, pv, fv, type)

Where:

rate is the interest rate per period.

per specifies the period and must be in the range 1 to **nper.**

nper is the total number of payment periods in an annuity.

pv is the present value—the total amount that a series of future payments is worth now.

fv is the future value, or the cash balance you want to attain after the last payment is made. If **fv** is omitted, it is assumed to be 0 (zero), that is, the future value of the loan after the last payment would be 0.

type is the number 0 or 1 and indicates whether payments are due at the start (1) or at the end (0) of each period.

In Figure 28.8 you can see the Function Arguments menu for PPMT. Note that the **type** field is not visible on the menu. Use the scroll bar on the right side of the menu to make it visible.

The monthly Principal part in this example for the first period—month 1 is only $865.81 of the $3,865.81 monthly payment. As was just pointed out, and is also a well-known fact, the principal repayment portion is very low at the beginning of the loan and the interest portion—as you will calculate in the next step—is high.

Double-click on the drag handle of the just calculated PPMT result in cell G2 and Excel will AutoFill the series until the end of the defined periods. Note again the big differences in the principal amounts from the first to the last months' amounts. See Figure 28.9.

Interest—IPMT Function   The IPMT function will calculate the monthly interest for each of the 300 months. Interest amounts vary monthly as they are calculated on the remaining

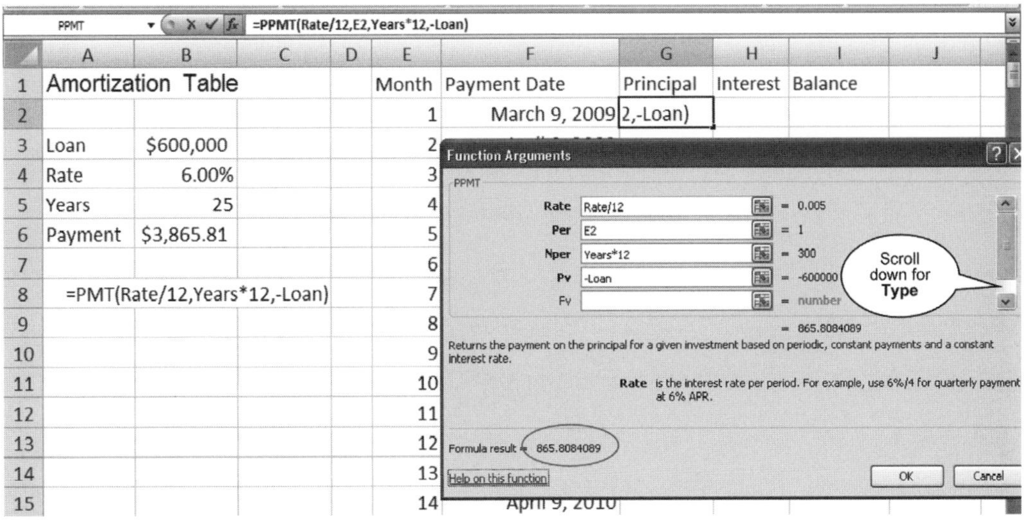

Figure 28.8   The Principal Function menu

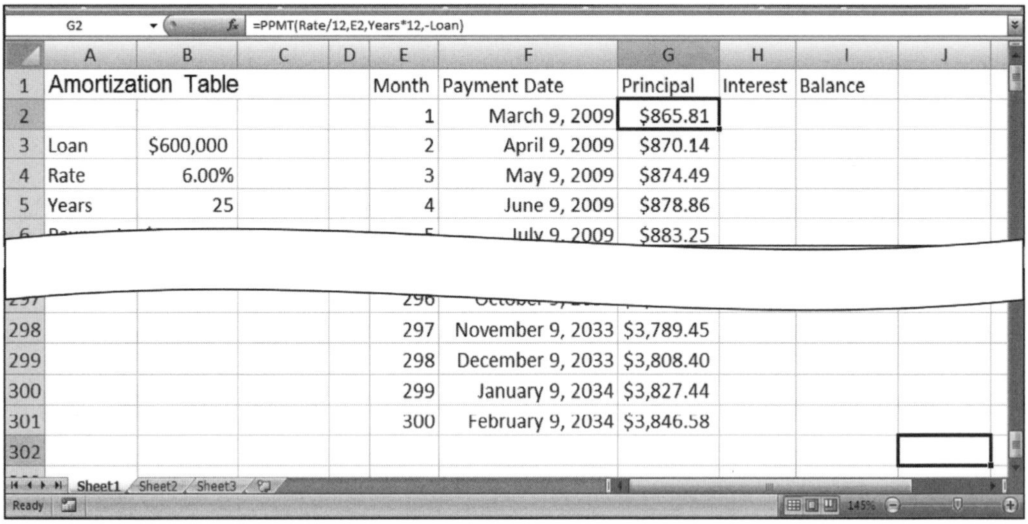

G2 =PPMT(Rate/12,E2,Years*12,-Loan)

	A	B	C	D	E	F	G	H	I	J
1	Amortization Table				Month	Payment Date	Principal	Interest	Balance	
2					1	March 9, 2009	$865.81			
3	Loan	$600,000			2	April 9, 2009	$870.14			
4	Rate	6.00%			3	May 9, 2009	$874.49			
5	Years	25			4	June 9, 2009	$878.86			
6					5	July 9, 2009	$883.25			
298					297	November 9, 2033	$3,789.45			
299					298	December 9, 2033	$3,808.40			
300					299	January 9, 2034	$3,827.44			
301					300	February 9, 2034	$3,846.58			
302										

Sheet1 / Sheet2 / Sheet3

Figure 28.9 The principal calculated for all months

balance of the principal portion. The interest portion is very high at the beginning of the loan and gradually decreases, getting low toward the end. The IPMT has all the components of the PMT, the payments function, with an additional input, the period numbers. It is the similar to the PPMT:

> **IPMT (rate, per, nper, pv, fv, type)**

Follow the same procedure used for the PPMT to create the IPMT, in the Interest column. Figure 28.10 shows the calculated results after applying the IPMT function. Note again that the interest amounts decrease over time. Note that the annual Rate is 6.00 percent and that the monthly rate is 0.5 percent (6.00%/12). If you calculate 0.5 percent of the $600,000, the initial loan, it will be $3,000.00. This is exactly the monthly interest of Month 1, as calculated by the IPMT function.

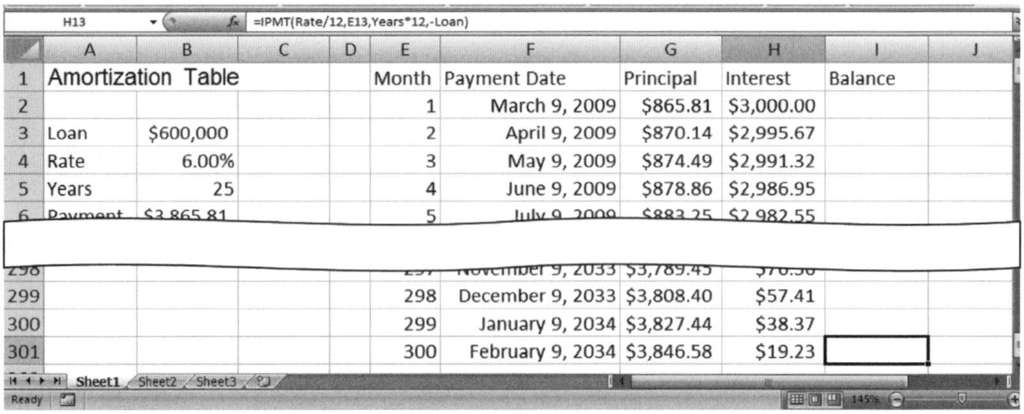

H13 =IPMT(Rate/12,E13,Years*12,-Loan)

	A	B	C	D	E	F	G	H	I	J
1	Amortization Table				Month	Payment Date	Principal	Interest	Balance	
2					1	March 9, 2009	$865.81	$3,000.00		
3	Loan	$600,000			2	April 9, 2009	$870.14	$2,995.67		
4	Rate	6.00%			3	May 9, 2009	$874.49	$2,991.32		
5	Years	25			4	June 9, 2009	$878.86	$2,986.95		
6	Payment	$3,865.81			5	July 9, 2009	$883.25	$2,982.55		
298					297	November 9, 2033	$3,789.45	$76.36		
299					298	December 9, 2033	$3,808.40	$57.41		
300					299	January 9, 2034	$3,827.44	$38.37		
301					300	February 9, 2034	$3,846.58	$19.23		

Sheet1 / Sheet2 / Sheet3

Figure 28.10 The interest calculated for all months

Calculating the Balance is simple. For the first month only, subtract the Principal payment from the original loan. For all the other months, subtract the monthly Principal payment from the previous month's Balance.

The calculations and the results are shown are shown in Figure 28.11. For Month 1, subtract in cell I2 the principal of month 1 from the original loan of cell B3, named Loan. For month 2, in cell I3 subtract the principal of month 2 from the balance of month 1, located in cell I2 (=I2 – G3). The rest of the calculations for the Balance are the same. Just double-click the drag handle at the lower right corner of cell I3 and the formula will be carried down for all the cells.

The amortization table reflects what was said before. The Principal repayment portion is low in the beginning and the Interest portion is high. The Balance diminishes over time.

CUMIPMT and CUMPRINC Two more Excel functions are part of the loan amortization functions family: CUMIPMT and CUMPRINC. The CUMIPMT function calculates the cumulative interest between two specific periods, or—in other words—over a given length of time. CUMPRINC calculates the cumulative principal between two specific periods. The former is important when a person can deduct the interest paid for income tax purposes.

Example: Your accountant might ask you for the amount of interest that was paid on the loan from January 1, 2010, through December 31, 2010. You can use the CUMIPMT function for the 11th through the 22nd months/periods. The answer is $35,163.28.

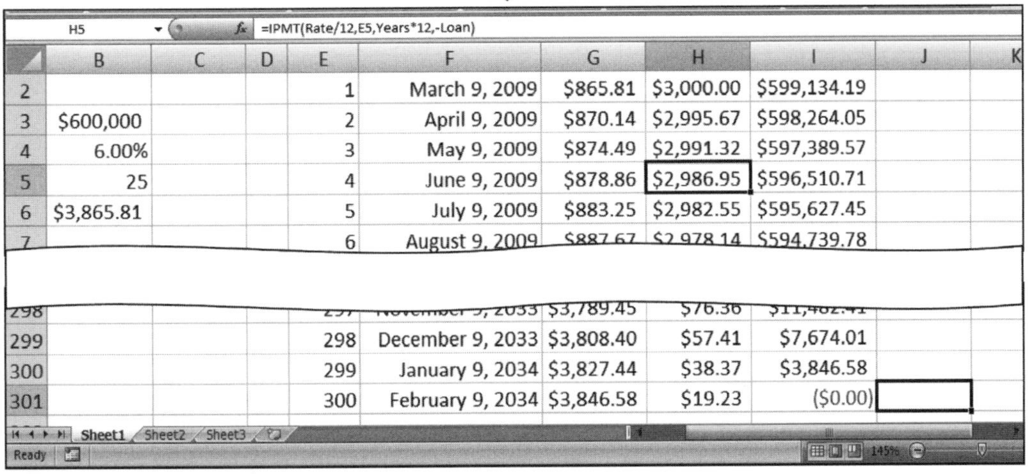

Figure 28.11 Loan balances

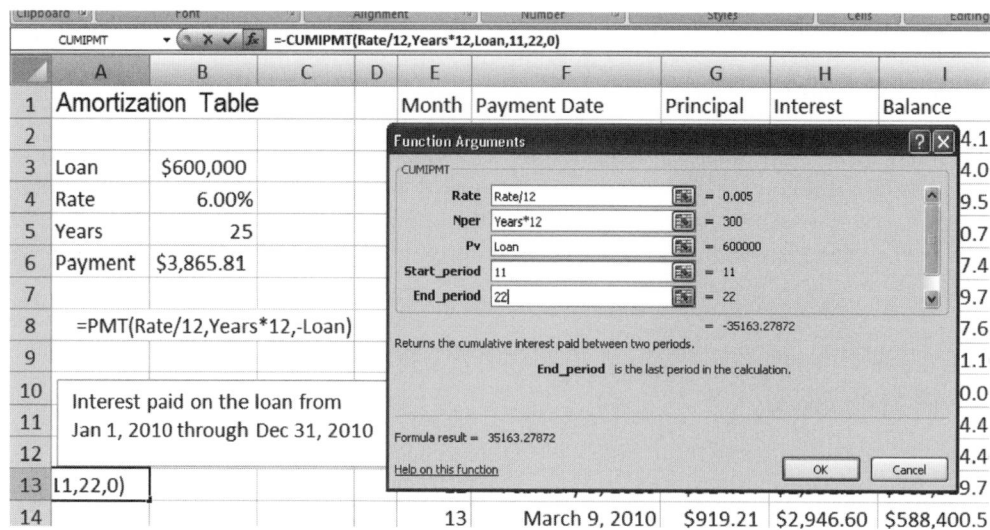

Figure 28.12 Cumulative Interest Payment function

Two notable differences from the previous functions:

- You **do** need to enter a 0 or a 1 for the **Type**. Previously it was 0 by default.
- You cannot enter a – (minus) sign in front of the PV as we did before. The – sign has to be in front of the function:
- [=−CUMIPMT(Rate/12,Years∗12,Loan,11,22,0)]

Figure 28.12 shows the CUMIPMT Function Arguments menu. Use the scroll bar to make the Type field accessible for filling.

The CUMPRINC, cumulative principal, has the same structure:

$$\text{CUMPRINC (rate, nper, pv, start\_period, end\_period, type)}$$

For example, say you wanted to calculate the principal portion paid over the first 10 years of the loan, in order to figure out the balance left to pay.

Use Excel's CUMPRINC function and the result will be:

=−**CUMPRINC(Rate/12,Years∗12,Loan,1,120,0)** resulting in $141,888.12. The balance of the loan after 120 payments (or 10 years) is still $458,111.88. Amazing; you paid 120 installments of $3,865.81 totaling $463,897.01 on a $600,000.00 loan and your balance is still over 75% of the originally borrowed amount.

REVIEW QUESTIONS

You will find these examples in the Excel Chapter 28 file:

1. Create new names and calculate the loan payment for the example in the Chapter 28 file's *Review* sheet. The loan amount is $300,000, the interest rate is 7.12 percent, and the number of years is 10.

2. Create an amortization table for the loan beginning on February 15, 2010. The table should have 120 months.

3. Using the CUMIPMT function, calculate the interest paid for the year 2012.

4. Using the CUMPRINC function, calculate the principal paid for the first five years of the loan. What would be the balance of the loan after five years?

ANSWERS

1. Creating the names.

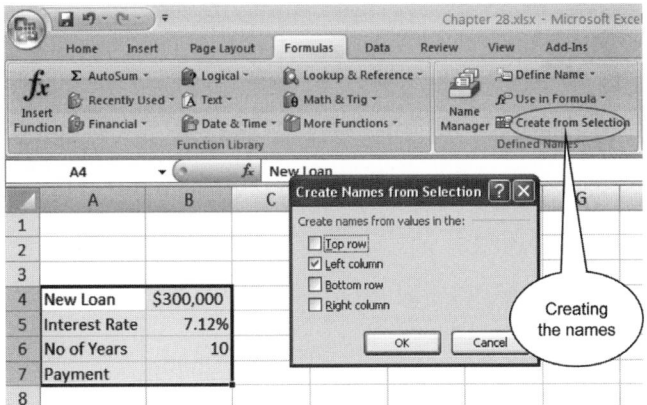

2.

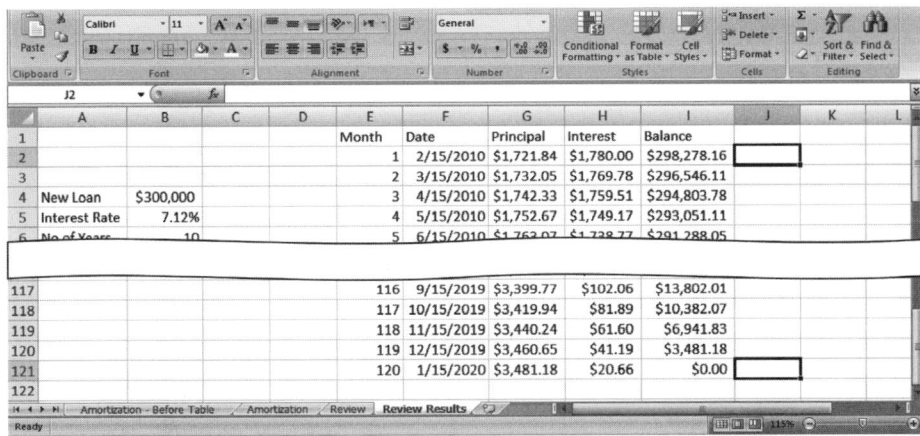

3. The year 2012 is period 24–35.
   = −CUMIPMT(Interest_Rate/12,No_of_Years*12,New_Loan,24,35,0) The value is: $17,560.38.

4. $17,560.38 = −CUMPRINC(Interest_Rate/12,No_of_Years*12,New_Loan,1,60,0)
   The principal paid: $123,654.92. The balance $176,345.08.

CHAPTER 29

Accounting Depreciation Functions

Wikipedia defines depreciation as, "Depreciation is a term used in accounting, economics and finance to spread the cost of an asset over the span of several years." Excel has a number of these functions as part of its financial functions. All these function have similar features: initial cost, salvage value, and the numbers of years. This chapter will cover only two functions: the Straight Line Depreciation, SLD, and the Sum of the Years Digits, SYD. The first function is a simple depreciation method and the second one is an accelerated one.

SLD STRAIGHT LINE DEPRECIATION

This function assumes the same, or a uniform, depreciation rate for all of the years of the economic life of the asset. For example if the initial value of the asset is $60,000 and the salvage value five years later is $10,000, then the annual depreciation would be $10,000 [(60,000-10,000)/5]. The following is the syntax of the Straight Line Depreciation function:

SLN (cost, salvage, life)

Cost is the initial cost of the asset.
Salvage is the value at the end of the depreciation period or the economic life of the asset.
Life is the number of periods over which the asset is depreciated.
The function is shown in Figure 29.1. The depreciation is $10,000 per year for the lifetime of the asset.

SYD SUM OF THE YEARS DIGITS

Sum of the Years Digits is different. This is an accelerated depreciation function. The depreciation rate is different from year to year. The syntax of this function is:

SYD (cost, salvage, life, per)

Cost is the initial cost of the asset.
Salvage is the value at the end of the economic life of the asset.
Life is the number of periods over which the asset is depreciated.
Per is the year number. It is different for every year.
In this example the initial value of the asset is $55,000, the salvage value is $10,000, and the number of years, or the lifetime of the asset, is five. Figure 29.2 illustrates the function and Figure 29.3 shows the results for each of the different years.

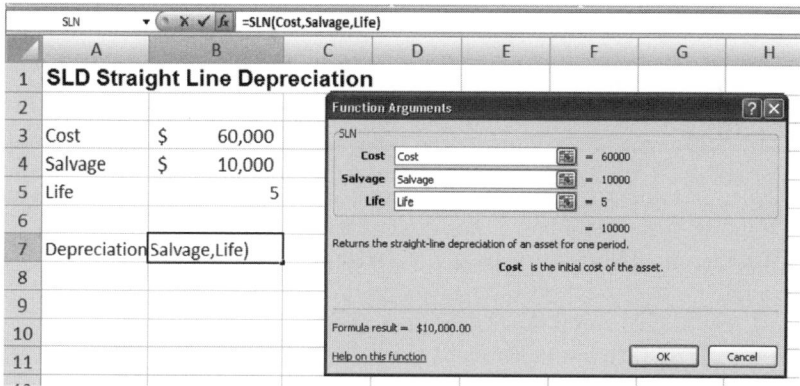

Figure 29.1 Straight Line Depreciation

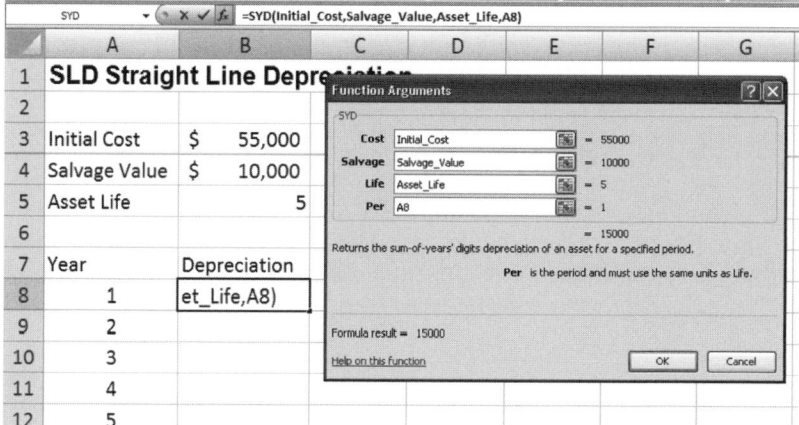

Figure 29.2 Straight Line Depreciation

	A	B	C	D	E	F	G	H
1	**SLD Straight Line Depreciation**							
2								
3	Initial Cost	$ 55,000						
4	Salvage Value	$ 10,000						
5	Asset Life	5						
6								
7	Year	Depreciation						
8	1	$15,000	=SYD(Initial_Cost,Salvage_Value,Asset_Life,A8)					
9	2	$12,000	=SYD(Initial_Cost,Salvage_Value,Asset_Life,A9)					
10	3	$9,000	=SYD(Initial_Cost,Salvage_Value,Asset_Life,A10)					
11	4	$6,000	=SYD(Initial_Cost,Salvage_Value,Asset_Life,A11)					
12	5	$3,000	=SYD(Initial_Cost,Salvage_Value,Asset_Life,A12)					

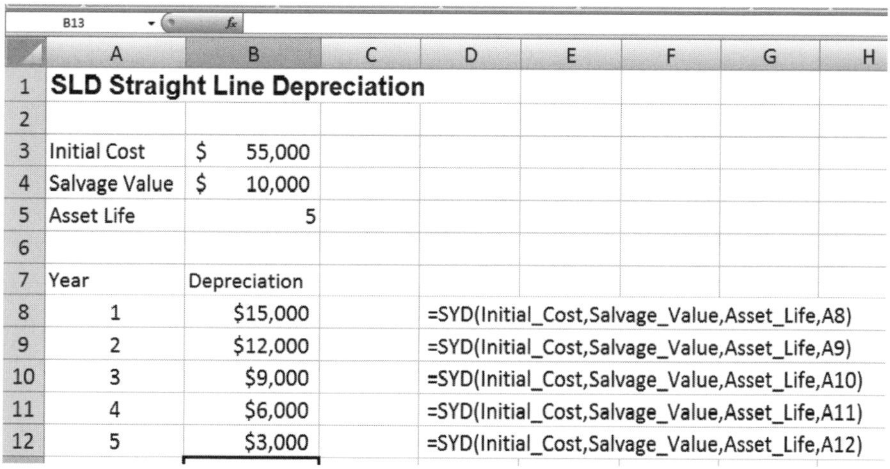

Figure 29.3 Results and formulas for the SLD—Straight Line Depreciation

Notice the accelerated depreciation: higher rates in the first years and lower toward the end.

REVIEW QUESTIONS

It is interesting to note that different assets have different "economic lives" or guidelines for depreciable life. Land, for example, is not depreciable. Buildings have different life spans of 20-60 years. Certain machinery could be depreciated in five years and computers in four years.

1. The initial cost of the asset is $200,000. Its salvage value is $30,000.
   - Calculate the SYD function for five years.
   - Calculate it for seven years.
2. The initial cost of the asset is $30,000. Its salvage value is $3,000.
   - Calculate the SLD for six years.
   - Calculate it again for 10 years.

ANSWERS

1. $34,000 for five years and $24,285.71 for seven years.
2.

6 years

Year	Depreciation
1	$7,714.29
2	$6,428.57
3	$5,142.86
4	$3,857.14
5	$2,571.43
6	$1,285.71

10 years

Year	Depreciation
1	$4,909.09
2	$4,418.18
3	$3,927.27
4	$3,436.36
5	$2,945.45
6	$2,454.55
7	$1,963.64
8	$1,472.73
9	$981.82
10	$490.91

Eight

Using the Solver Add-In

Solver is an Excel Add-in. In very simple terms, it is a software tool for "solving" mathematical systems of equations for optimizations. This part of the book does not attempt to teach the mathematical aspect of using the solver. It will show you how to use the solver for three different applications. The first case is when you want to use the Goal Seek, but you want to have more than one changing cell or decision variable. The second case will demonstrate how to use it for a linear optimization problem and the last case is for a non-linear optimization problem.

CHAPTER 30

Beyond the Goal Seek—More Than One Changing Cell? Use the Solver

The Solver Add-in is generally used in Excel for optimizations. The Solver for optimizations will be covered in the next chapter. However, the Solver can be put to good use for multiple-variable, hypothetical scenario evaluation.

As you saw in chapter 13, the Goal Seek was used to find/seek a single decision variable or a "changing cell" when you needed to evaluate the effect on the outcome of a varying parameter. The Goal Seek is limited to a single changing cell.

What if you need to change more than one input variable? The Goal Seek is not sufficient. We can use the Solver. The Solver can work with up to 200 changing cells.

This is a review of the example we had in chapter 13.

Example—Break Even Point

In Figure 30.1 you can see a budget that projects loses of $140,000.

The objective here is to have this project at least break-even. In other words, what do you have to change to eliminate the $140,000 negative gap and change it to 0? The tool to

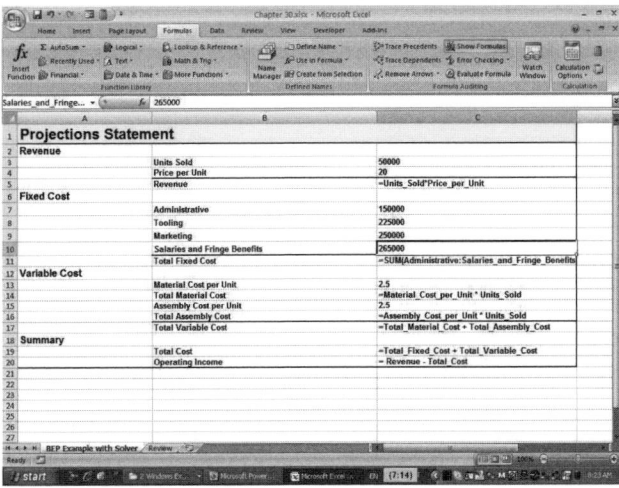

Figure 30.1 The break event point example

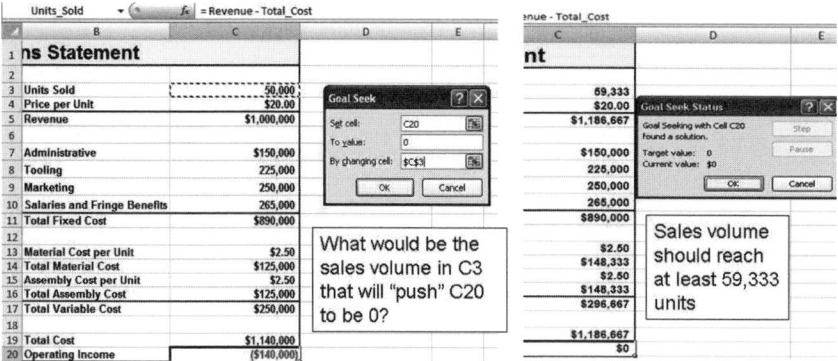

Figure 30.2 The Goal Seek for a BEP with Units Sold

use is the Goal Seek. You can use the Goal Seek and check the results of changing a few of the inputs, one at a time: either the Sales Volume, Price per Unit, or any one of the other inputs. Again only one input at a time.

To repeat the example, start with the number of units sold. How many units do you have to sell in order to break even? If you use the Goal Seek tool, you will find out that the sales volume must reach at least 59,333 units in order to break even. See Figure 30.2.

You can try the Goal Seek for the other input variables. I tried Goal Seek for the Price per Unit in Figure 30.3 and the reduction of the marketing budget in Figure 30.4. In each case only one input variable was changed at a time.

What if you wanted to use more than one input variable at a time in the changing cell? For example, finding out how varying both the unit price and the number of units sold would influence the outcome. The Goal Seek has the limit of one changing cell and cannot do it. The alternative is to use the Solver.

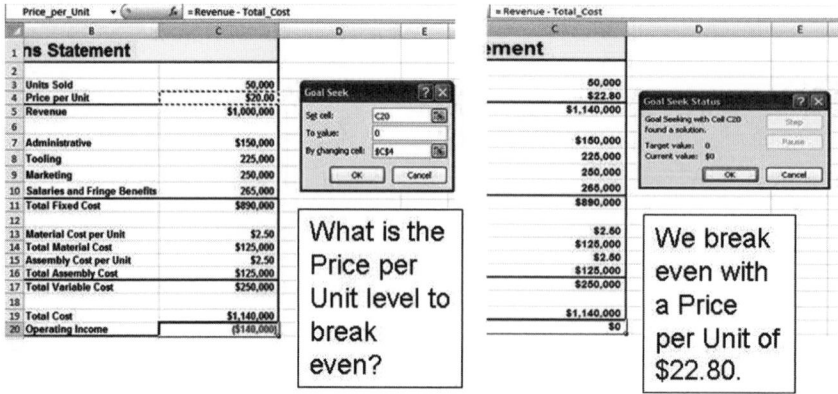

Figure 30.3 BEP with Price

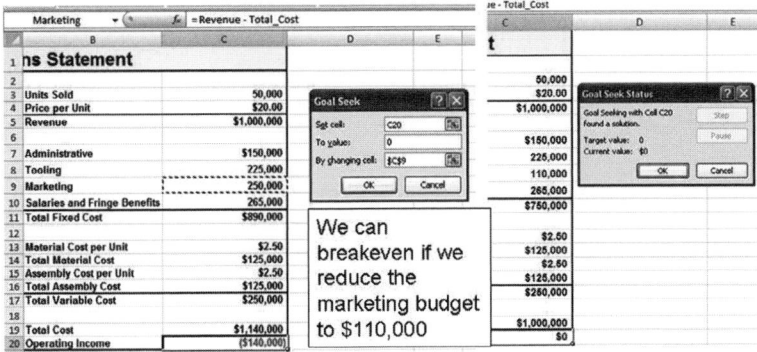

Figure 30.4 BEP with marketing budget reduced

Using the Solver

To activate the Solver do the following:

- Click on the Office® icon.
- In the resulting menu, click on Excel Options.
- Select Add-Ins.
- Choose Solver Add-in and click on Go. See Figure 30.5.
- Check the Solver Add-in box in the Add-ins window. See Figure 30.6.

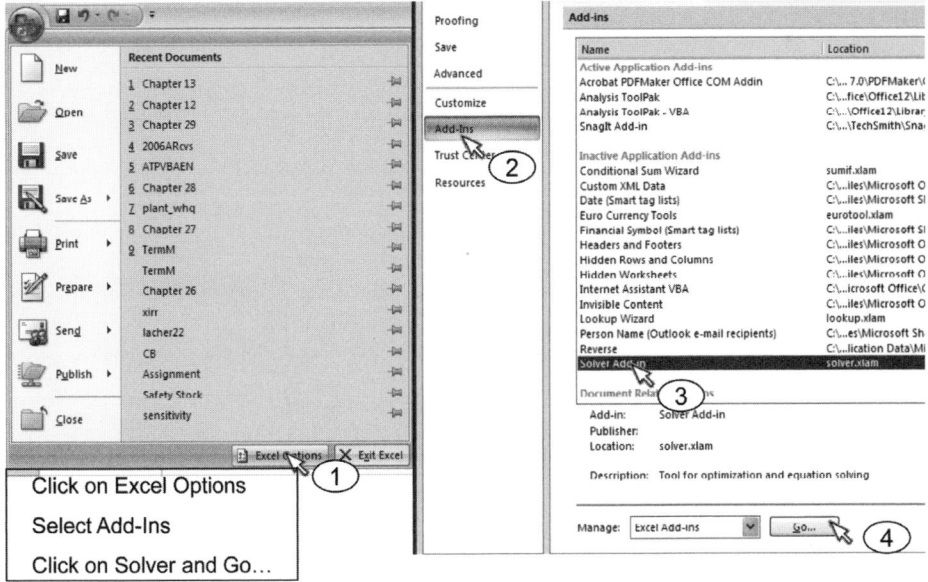

Figure 30.5 Adding the Excel Solver Add-in

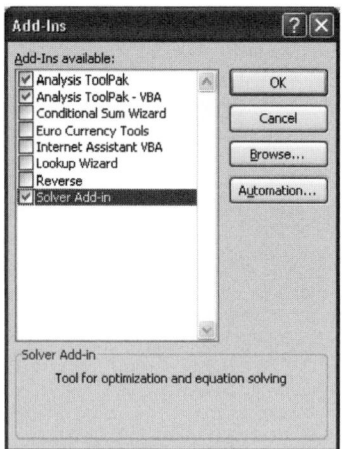

Figure 30.6 The Add-Ins menu

The Solver is now installed and can be used. You will find it either under the Data ribbon or in other instances under the Add-ins ribbon.

Go over the problem again—using the above data, the goal is to breakeven. You want to figure out how many units you need to sell, as well as their selling price to attain your goal. Also, your marketing department is convinced that the highest price the market can bear is $21.00, an increase of 5 percent above the current price. What should you do?

Using the Solver you can apply the following procedure:

- Click on the target cell C20, where the current value is –$140,000.
- Activate/click the Solver icon under the Data ribbon.
- Select Value of 0 (the default is Max). In other words you want your Operating Income to be at least 0.
- In the Cell: By Changing Cells select cell C3 (Units Sold).
- Type, (comma).
- Select cell C4 (Price per Unit). Now both C3 and C4 are the changing cells or the decision variables.

See Figure 30.7.

Since the cells C3 and C4 were named before, they will change in the Solver Parameters menu. They will reappear later as **Units Sold** and **Price per Unit**.

Remembering the marketing department's input about market price, you want to add a constraint for the unit price. See the steps in Figure 30.8.

1. Click on Add constraint.
2. Add the constraint C4 < = 21.
3. Click on Solve.

The Solver calulated a solution where the number of units to be sold is 55,625 and the price should be $21.00 in order to break even (C20 = $0).

C3	▾	*fx*	= Revenue - Total_Cost				

Projections Statement table / Solver Parameters dialog:

	A	B	C
1	**Projections Statement**		
2	**Revenue**		
3		Units Sold	50,000
4		Price per Unit	$20.00
5		Revenue	$1,000,000
6	**Fixed Cost**		
7		Administrative	$150,000
8		Tooling	225,000
9		Marketing	250,000
10		Salaries and Fringe Benefits	265,000
11		Total Fixed Cost	$890,000
12	**Variable Cost**		
13		Material Cost per Unit	$2.50
14		Total Material Cost	$125,000
15		Assembly Cost per Unit	$2.50
16		Total Assembly Cost	$125,000
17		Total Variable Cost	$250,000
18	**Summary**		
19		Total Cost	$1,140,000
20		Operating Income	($140,000)

Figure 30.7 The Solver menu

See Figure 30.9.

You can try and add one more constraint. For example, limit the units sold to 54,000 units (imagine a maximum production capacity for instance), and add a new changing cell, say reduce the marketing budget to achieve a breakeven. See Figure 30.10.

The final solution says that in order to break even with these constraints, you have to sell 54,000 units at $21.00 a piece. Additionally, the marketing expense has to be reduced to $224,000.

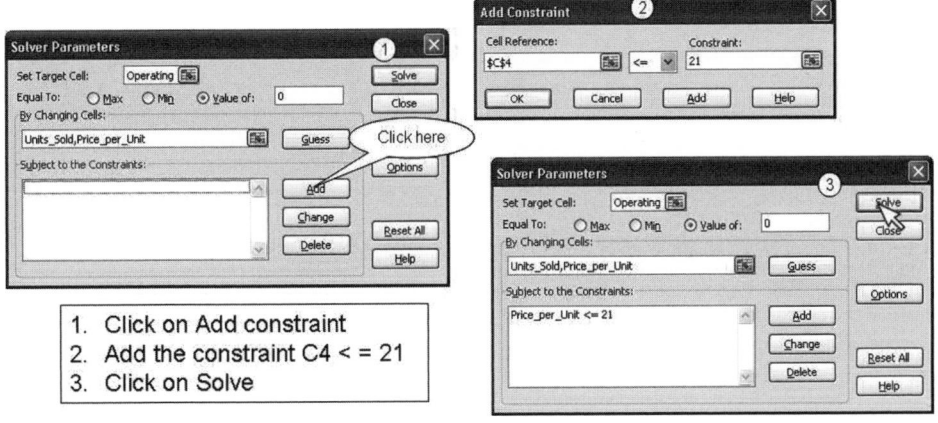

1. Click on Add constraint
2. Add the constraint C4 < = 21
3. Click on Solve

Figure 30.8 Adding constraints

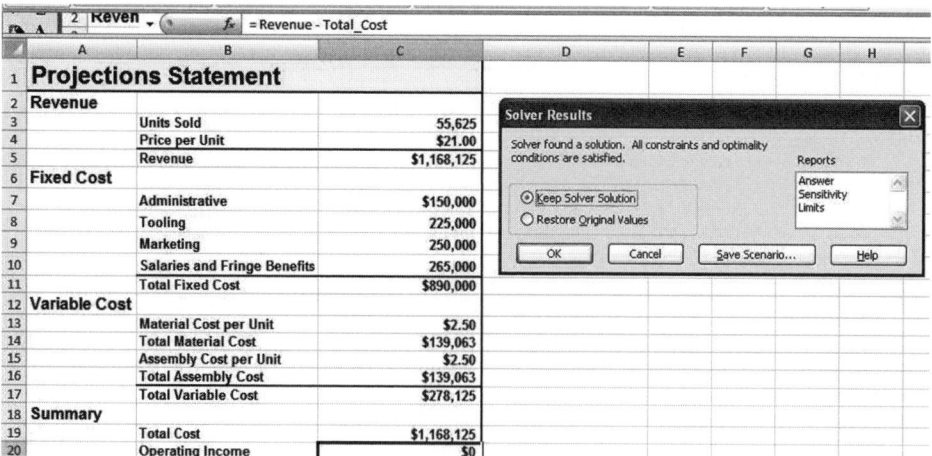

Figure 30.9   Solver results

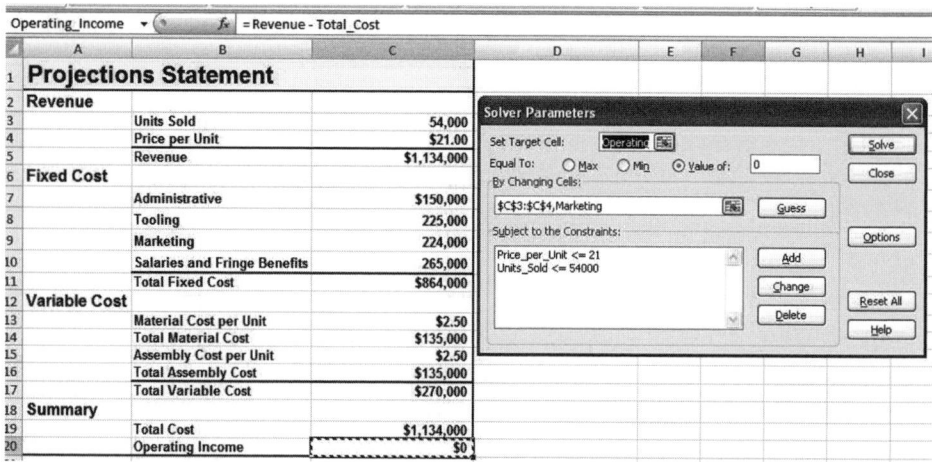

Figure 30.10   Solver results

APPENDIX—USING THE SOLVER IN EXCEL 2003

The only difference in using the Solver Add-in in Excel 2003 or earlier versions is just the way to find and activate it. To find the Add-in, use the Tools menu. The Solver should be visible as you see in Figure 30.11.

If the Solver is not visible when you select the Tool menu in Excel 2003, you will have to activate it. To activate the Solver:

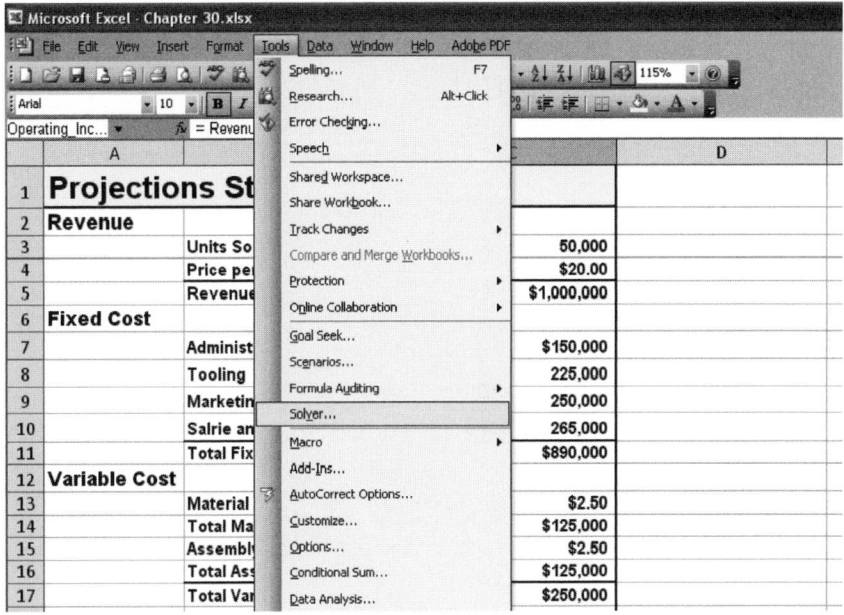

Figure 30.11   Using the Solver in Excel 2003

- Click on the Tools menu.
- Select Add-Ins.
- Check the Solver Add-in box as shown in Figure 30.12.

Once the Solver is activated, you can follow the same procedure described earlier in the chapter.

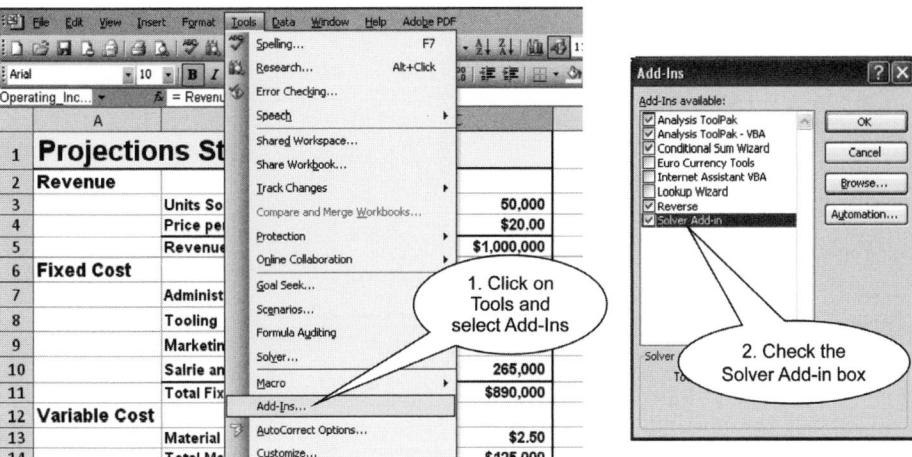

Figure 30.12   Activating the Solver

REVIEW QUESTIONS

You will find these examples in the Excel Chapter 30 file:

1. On the *Review* sheet in the Chapter 30 file, you will find an example that was used before. The example has a net profit of −$4,000, as you can see below. The formulas are shown on the right side of the figure.

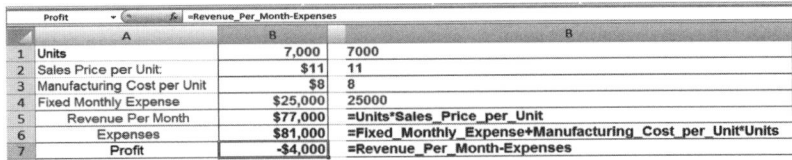

As you want to break even, use the Goal Seek first to find out:

a. What is the selling price that will make this manufacturing proposition break even?
b. At what Unit Cost do you break even?
c. How many units do you have to sell in order to break even?
d. What should the monthly fixed expenses be reduced to in order to break even?

2. Working out all these answers, it becomes obvious that these goals when taken individually cannot be reached. You may have to change two or more of these inputs:

a. If the highest price the product can be sold for is $11.25 (not $11.57), how much would the optimal unit cost and be? Use the Solver to find out.
b. If the maximum price you can charge is $11.15, the unit cost cannot be reduced below $7.80, and monthly expenses can only be reduced by $500, how many units do you have to sell in order to break even?

ANSWERS

1.
   a. $11.57.
   b. $7.43.
   c. 8.33.
   d. $21,000.
2.
   a. $11.25 and $7.68.

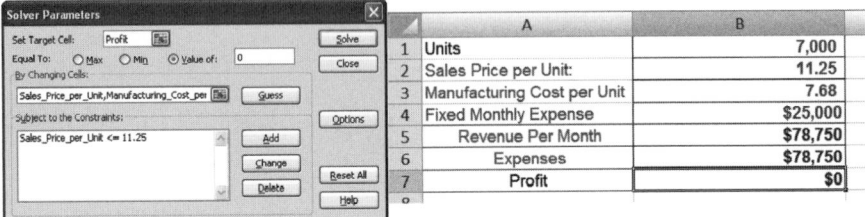

b. 7,425.

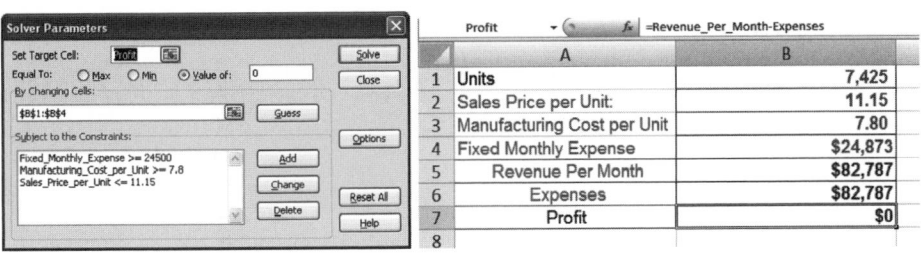

CHAPTER 31

The Solver Add-In—Optimizer

The Solver is an Excel Add-In used for optimizations. For one, it is an optimization tool that helps decision makers maximize profit given limited resources. These resources can be raw materials, time, people, money, or anything else that is known to be limited (scarce resources). The optimal solution can maximize profit, minimize cost, or achieve similar goals.

It could also be an optimization tool that helps the decision maker to minimize cost subject to certain minimum requirements.

There are many books on management science, operations management, and operations research that explain the different uses for the tool. I could list hundreds of topics. In finance: working capital management, capital budgeting, and portfolio optimization. In manufacturing: job shop scheduling and blending. Distribution and networks routing will look for solutions to loading and scheduling constraints, which can also be optimized with the Solver.

This book is about mastering the Excel software; therefore, I am going to explain how to manipulate the Solver in Excel, so that when you want to explore the other techniques, the Excel part will be familiar.

Solver Example

Consider the capital budgeting example in the Chapter 31 file under the sheet named *Solver*. In this example, you have 10 different projects to evaluate as possible investments. Each project has an investment associated with it (the cost). Also, each investment has a different yield, defined as the Net Present Value (NPV, the expected profit.) As in a real-life situation, there are only finite resources, limiting the number of projects you can invest in, the available budget being an unavoidable constraint. Your task is to decide which projects to invest in.

This is the information you have about the capital budget model:

B = the capital available for investment.

C_j = the capital needed for each project.

X_j = the decision variables. They can take either the value of 1 (invest) – or 0 (don't invest).

P_j = the NPV or profit associated with project j.

n= the number of projects.

The general model is formulated as:

$$\text{Maximize}: \text{NPV} = \sum_{j=1}^{n} P_j X_j$$

$$\text{Subject to}: \sum_{j=1}^{n} P_j X_j < B$$

$$X_j : \begin{cases} = 1 \text{ if project j is selected} \\ = 0 \text{ if project j is not selected} \end{cases}$$

Where:

B = the capital available for investment is $7,000 (in $1,000s).

C_j = the capital needed for each project.

Project 1	Project 2	Project 3	Project 4	Project 5	Project 6	Project 7	Project 8	Project 9	Project 10
$628	$352	$1,245	$814	$124	$985	$2,356	$226	$1,650	$714

P_j = the NPV or profit associated with project j.

Project 1	Project 2	Project 3	Project 4	Project 5	Project 6	Project 7	Project 8	Project 9	Project 10
$72	$36	$212	$70	$11	$56	$93	$65	$48	$39

If you wanted to invest in all projects you would need $9,094—more than the $7,000 budget allocated. Your decision variables are in column E. (Remember, they can take either the value of 1 or 0.) The total NPV of your decision will be the multiplication of the NPV of each

F19

	A	B	C	D	E	F	G	H
1		Cost 1,000		NPV 1,000	Invest Yes/No		Investment Constraint	
2	Project 1	$628		$72	0		$628	
3	Project 2	$352		$36	0		$352	
4	Project 3	$1,245		$212	0		$1,245	
5	Project 4	$814		$70	0		$814	
6	Project 5	$124		$11	0		$124	
7	Project 6	$985		$56	0		$985	
8	Project 7	$2,356		$93	0		$2,356	
9	Project 8	$226		$65	0		$226	
10	Project 9	$1,650		$48	0		$1,650	
11	Project 10	$714		$39	0		$714	
12		$9,094		$0			$0	
13							≤	
14							$7,000	
15								
16		=SUMPRODUCT(D2:D11,$E$2:$E$11)				=SUMPRODUCT(G2:G11,$E$2:$E$11)		

Figure 31.1 Capital budgeting example using the Solver

project by the decision variable. Multiplying the NPV by 1 if you choose a project will add its NPV to the total when the decision is to go ahead with the investment. Otherwise, it will be a 0.

The function that multiplies the NPVs by the decision variables is

=SUMPRODUCT(D2:D11,$E$2:$E$11).

The budget/capital constraint is calculated in column G.

=SUMPRODUCT(G2:G11,$E$2:$E$11)

The objective is to find the correct combination of projects that will maximize the total NPV. It is subject to the budget constraints. One more thing: you will have to assign to the decision variables in column E either the value of 0 or 1 (zero or one).

To "optimize" the choice—in other words, to find the optimal solution—you can use Excel Solver. I showed how to activate the Solver in Chapter 30.

The focus of our problem is cell G12. This is the Objective function and you wish to maximize it.

1. Click on cell G12 and select the Solver under the Data ribbon. Select the Max option.
2. In the Solver Parameters menu, select the decision variables in column E (E2:E11) for the By Changing Cells field.
3. Click on Add for the constraints where the total amount of the investment should be <= to the budget.
4. Click one more time on Add and select the Changing Cells of column E on the left part of the menu and select the Bin option—making them binary. In other words, binary means that these cells can take the values of either 0 or 1. See Figure 31.2.

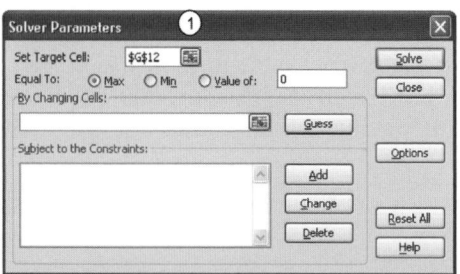

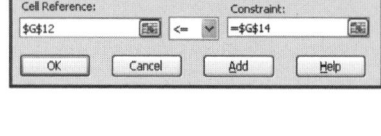

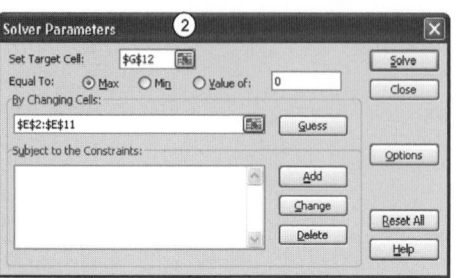

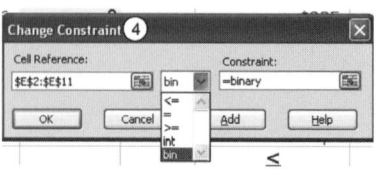

Figure 31.2 The steps to enter data in the Solver

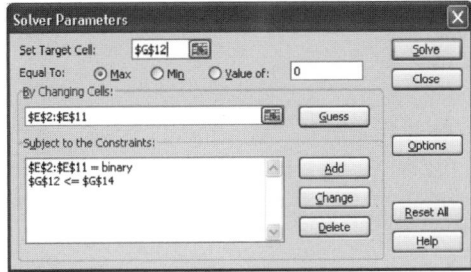

Figure 31.3 The resulting screen

The resulting Solver menu is shown in Figure 31.3. It has the two constraints, the binary constraint and the budget.

Before we run the Solver, we have to click on Options to activate the Solver Options menu and check the Assume Linear Model and Assume Non-Negative boxes. See Figure 31.4.

You can click the OK button and click on Solve. The end result is shown in Figure 31.5.

The Solver chose for you project 3, 6, 7, 9, and 10. You are going to use $6,950 and your NPV will be $448.

In this example the problem was a linear programming problem. There are times when the problem is not linear and the relationship is not a straight line linear relationship. The following example is a case when the relationship is a non-linear one.

Non-Linear Example Using the Solver

A gym operator hired you to figure out the annual membership he should charge in order to maximize his revenue. You were able to figure out that his operating costs are fixed—so you can ignore the negligible variable costs. Following your Economics class, you were able to figure out that his revenue—based on the demand function and the number of memberships he will sell—would be:

$$R = -0.06P^2 + 50P$$

This equation is not a straight line.

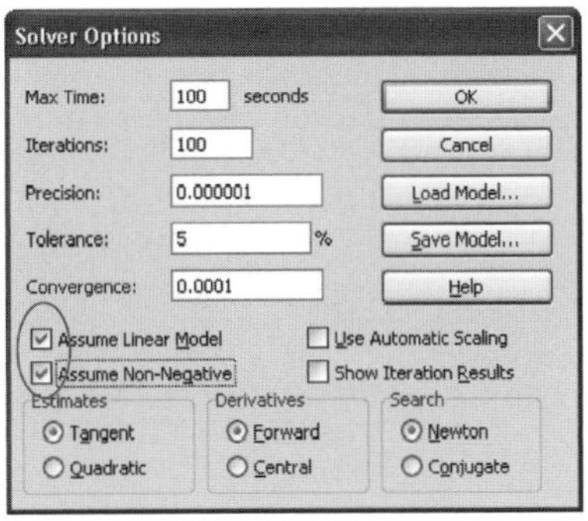

Figure 31.4 Options menu

	G12			*fx*	=SUMPRODUCT(G2:G11,$E$2:$E$11)					
	A	B	C	D	E	F	G	H	I	J
1		Cost 1,000		NPV 1,000	Invest Yes/No		Investment Constraint			
2	Project 1	$628		$72	0		$628			
3	Project 2	$352		$36	0		$352			
4	Project 3	$1,245		$212	1		$1,245			
5	Project 4	$814		$70	0		$814			
6	Project 5	$124		$11	0		$124			
7	Project 6	$985		$56	1		$985			
8	Project 7	$2,356		$93	1		$2,356			
9	Project 8	$226		$65	0		$226			
10	Project 9	$1,650		$48	1		$1,650			
11	Project 10	$714		$39	1		$714			
12		$9,094		$448			$6,950			
13							≤			
14							$7,000			
15										
16		=SUMPRODUCT(D2:D11,$E$2:$E$11)								

Solver Results   [X]

Solver found a solution. All constraints and optimality
conditions are satisfied.

Reports
Answer
Sensitivity
Limits

⦿ Keep Solver Solution
◯ Restore Original Values

[OK]   [Cancel]   [Save Scenario...]   [Help]

Figure 31.5   Solver results

Using the formula in Excel, you were able to calculate the different levels of revenue for different price levels. See Figure 35.6.

You would like to use the Solver to find the price level that will maximize your Revenue. It is already obvious from the graph that the price level will be situated between the $400 to $500 range. Prepare the formula in cell C19 as shown in Figure 35.7 and use the Solver to find the optimal solution.

This time you are dealing with a non-linear problem. See Figure 35.8 for the steps taken to solve the problem.

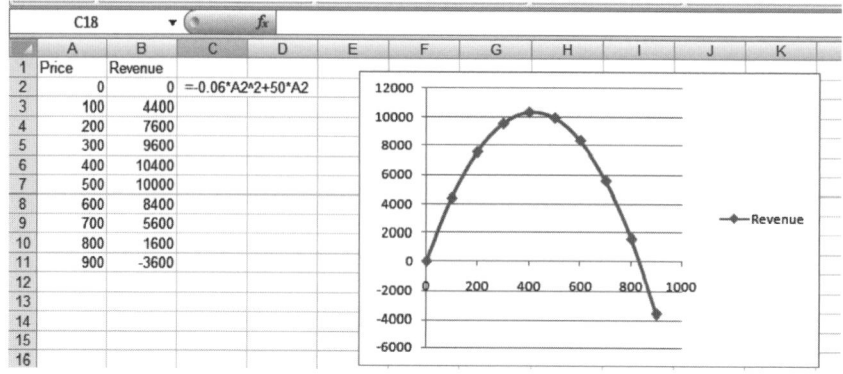

Figure 31.6   Revenue as a function of Price (Non-linear)

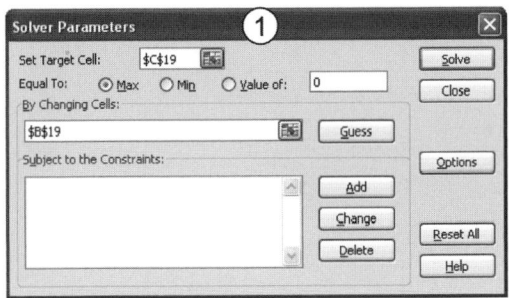

Figure 31.7   The formula R=−0.06P2 + 50P in Excel

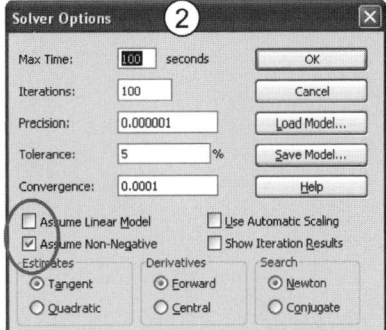

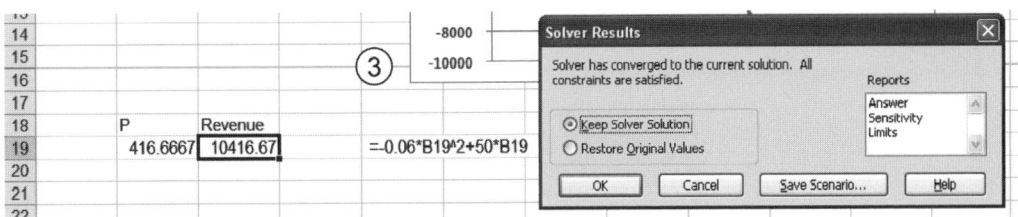

Figure 31.8   The Solver used for non-linear optimization

1. Click on cell C19 and activate the Solver on the Data ribbon. The Target Cell is C19. Select B19 as the Changing Cell.
2. Click on Options and select Assume Non-Negative. Make sure the Assume Linear Model box is unchecked.
3. Click on OK for the options and on the Solve button in the Parameters menu. Solver will provide the results in the spreadsheet.

The results indicate that your best membership price level should be $416.67 and you revenue will be $10,426.67.

APPENDIX—USING THE SOLVER IN EXCEL 2003

Please refer to the Appendix in Chapter 30 for activating the Solver. All the steps described above remain the same.

REVIEW QUESTIONS

You will find these examples in the Excel Chapter 31 file:

1. In the *Review* sheet in the Excel Chapter 31 file, you will find a new capital budget. Use the Solver to find the optimal investment decision.

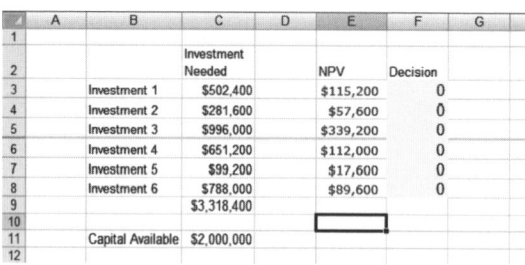

2. A publisher is able to determine the revenue function for his next Economics book as a function of price: $R = -1500P^2 + 150,000P$. Use the Solver to find the optimal price he should charge.

ANSWERS

1.

The solver menus:

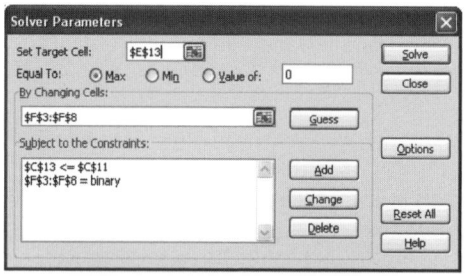

The solution:

		Investment Needed	NPV	Decision	
1					
2					
3	Investment 1	$502,400	$115,200	1	
4	Investment 2	$281,600	$57,600	1	
5	Investment 3	$996,000	$339,200	1	
6	Investment 4	$651,200	$112,000	0	
7	Investment 5	$99,200	$17,600	1	
8	Investment 6	$788,000	$89,600	0	
9		$3,318,400			
10					
11	Capital Available	$2,000,000			
12					
13		$1,879,200	$529,600		
14					

2. The selling price should be $50 and his revenue will be $3,750,000.